To ra do ra !

VOL. 1

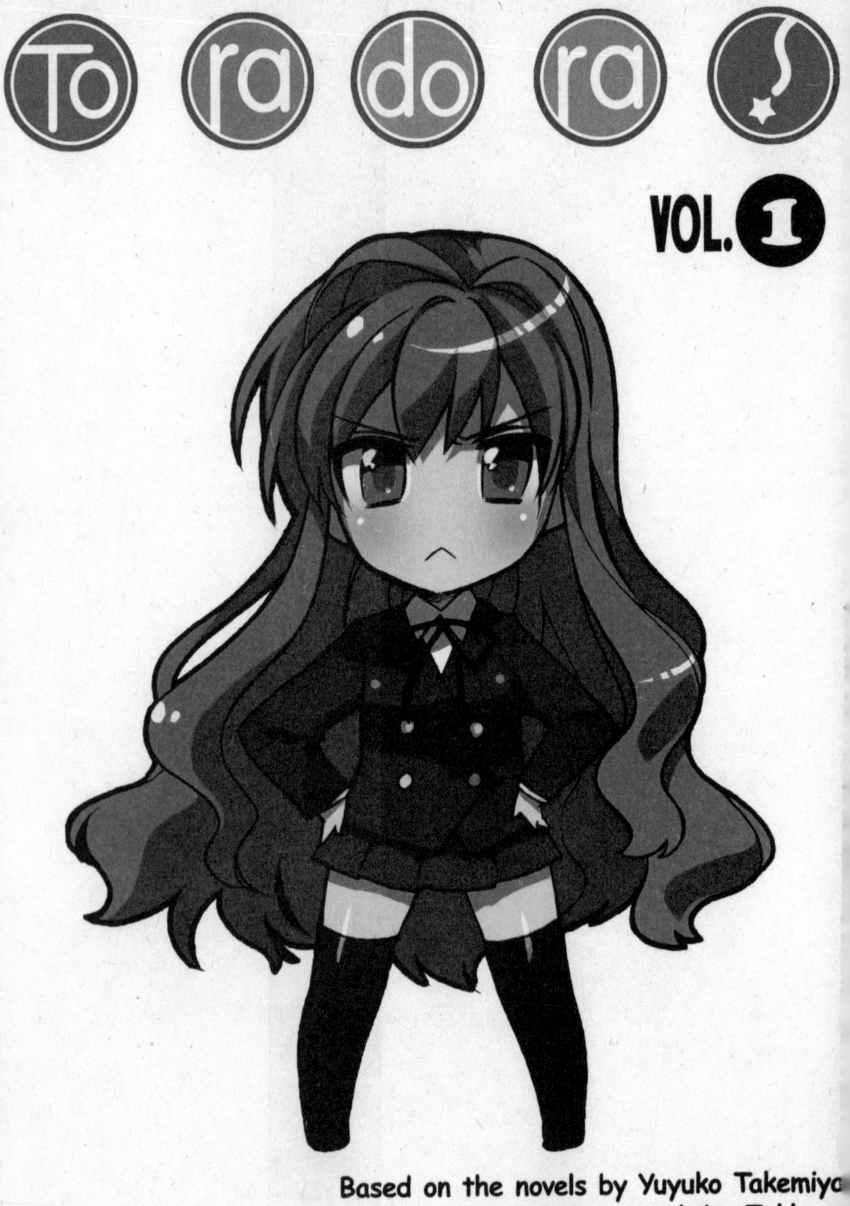

Based on the novels by Yuyuko Takemiya
Manga artwork by Zekkyou
Original character design by Yasu

CONTENTS

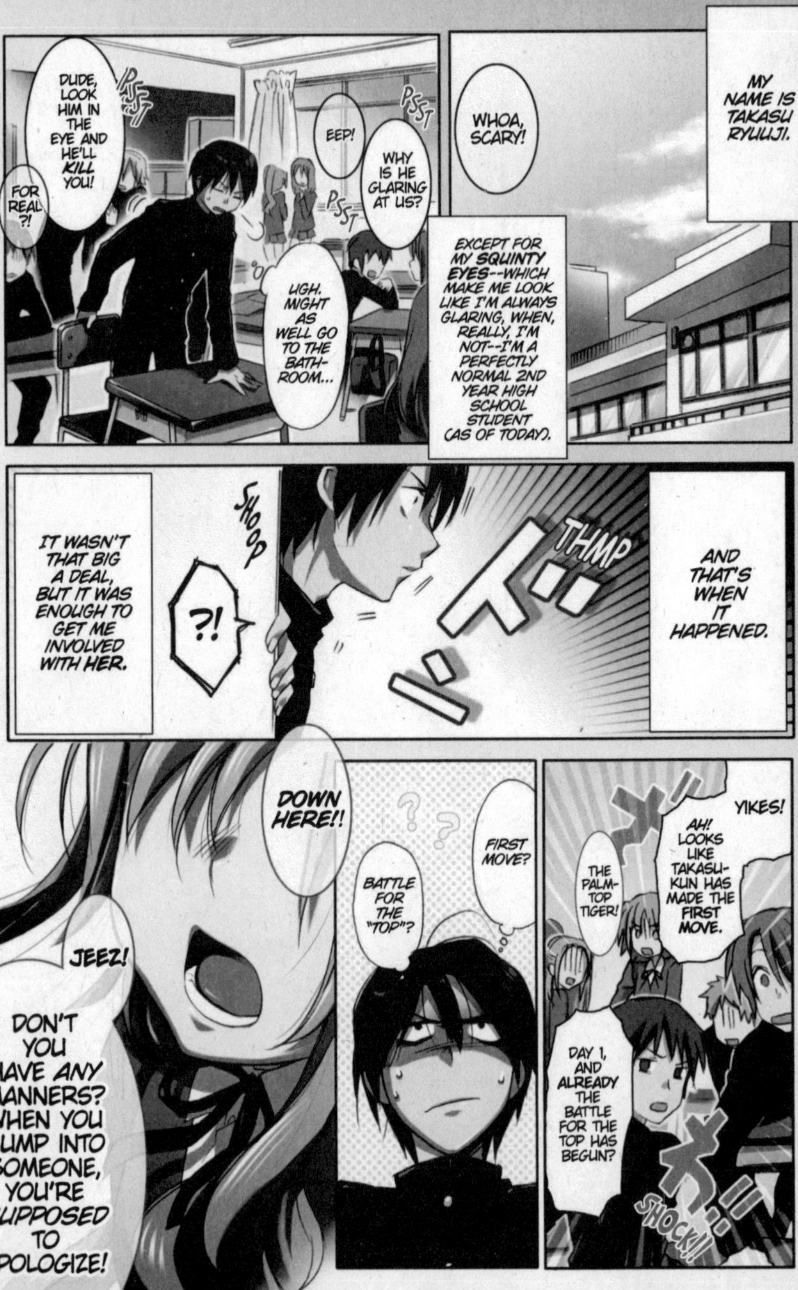
MY NAME IS TAKASU RYUUJI.
WHOA, SCARY!
EXCEPT FOR MY SQUINTY EYES--WHICH MAKE ME LOOK LIKE I'M ALWAYS GLARING, WHEN, REALLY, I'M NOT--I'M A PERFECTLY NORMAL 2ND YEAR HIGH SCHOOL STUDENT (AS OF TODAY).
PSST
WHY IS HE GLARING AT US?
EEP!
PSST
PSST
DUDE, LOOK HIM IN THE EYE AND HE'LL KILL YOU!
FOR REAL?!
UGH. MIGHT AS WELL GO TO THE BATH-ROOM...
AND THAT'S WHEN IT HAPPENED.
THMP
SHOOP
?!
IT WASN'T THAT BIG A DEAL, BUT IT WAS ENOUGH TO GET ME INVOLVED WITH HER.
YIKES!
AH! LOOKS LIKE TAKASU-KUN HAS MADE THE FIRST MOVE.
THE PALM-TOP TIGER!
DAY 1, AND ALREADY THE BATTLE FOR THE TOP HAS BEGUN?
SHOCK!!
FIRST MOVE?
BATTLE FOR THE "TOP"?
DOWN HERE!!
JEEZ!
DON'T YOU HAVE ANY MANNERS? WHEN YOU BUMP INTO SOMEONE, YOU'RE SUPPOSED TO APOLOGIZE!

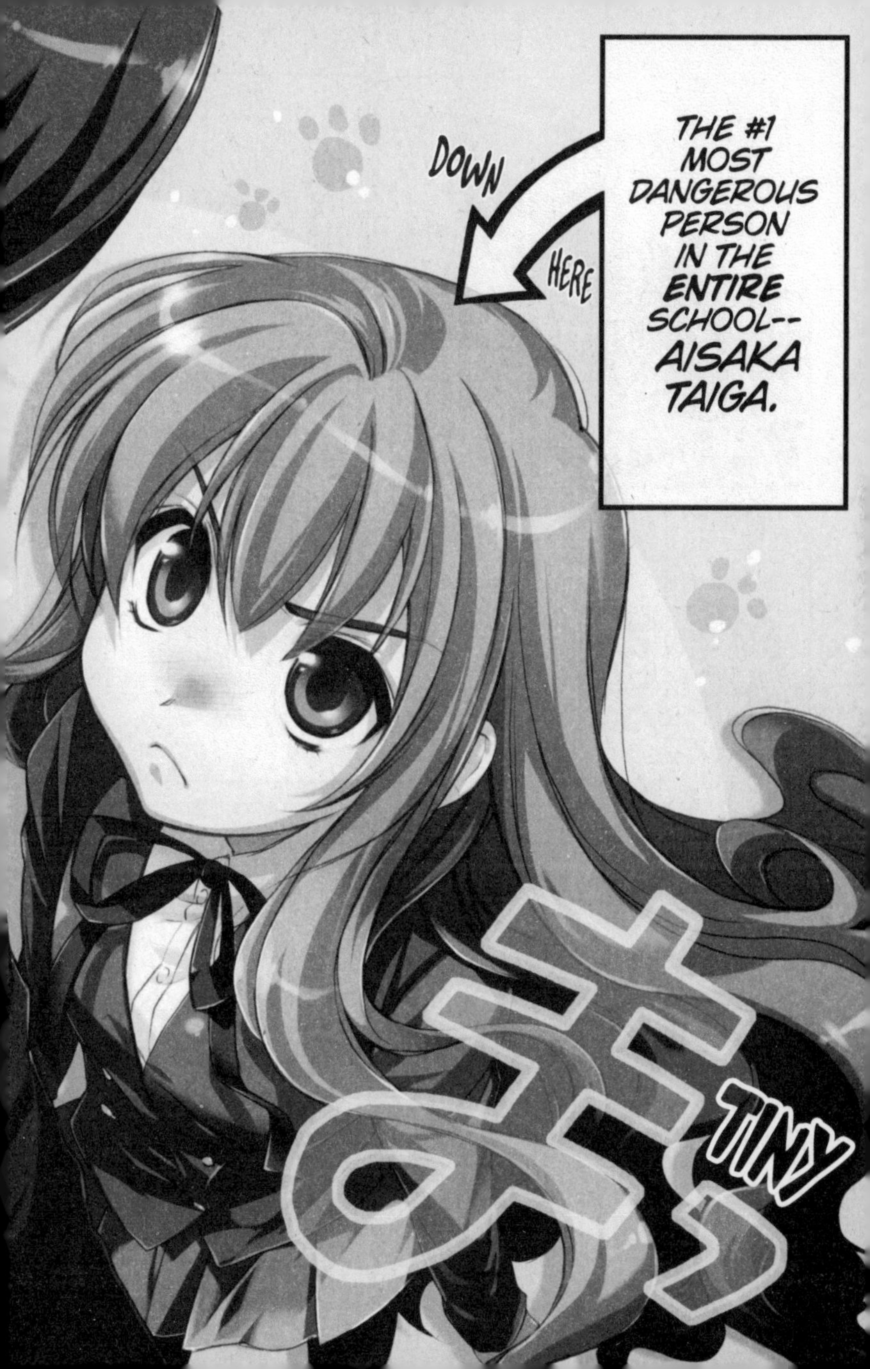
THE #1 MOST DANGEROUS PERSON IN THE ENTIRE SCHOOL--AISAKA TAIGA.
DOWN HERE
TINY

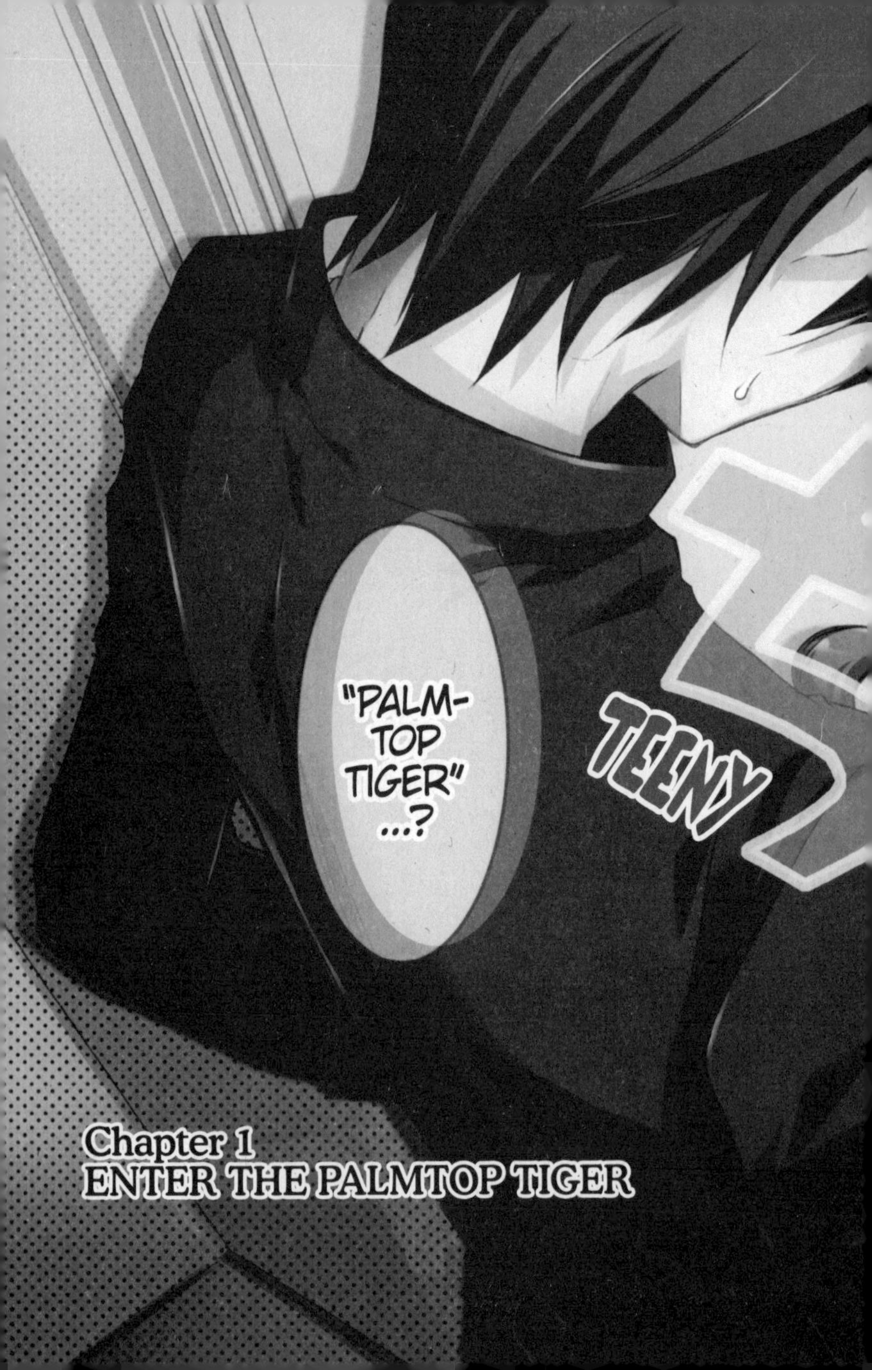
"PALM-TOP TIGER" ...?
TEENY
Chapter 1
ENTER THE PALMTOP TIGER

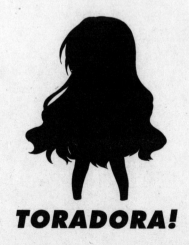

TORADORA!

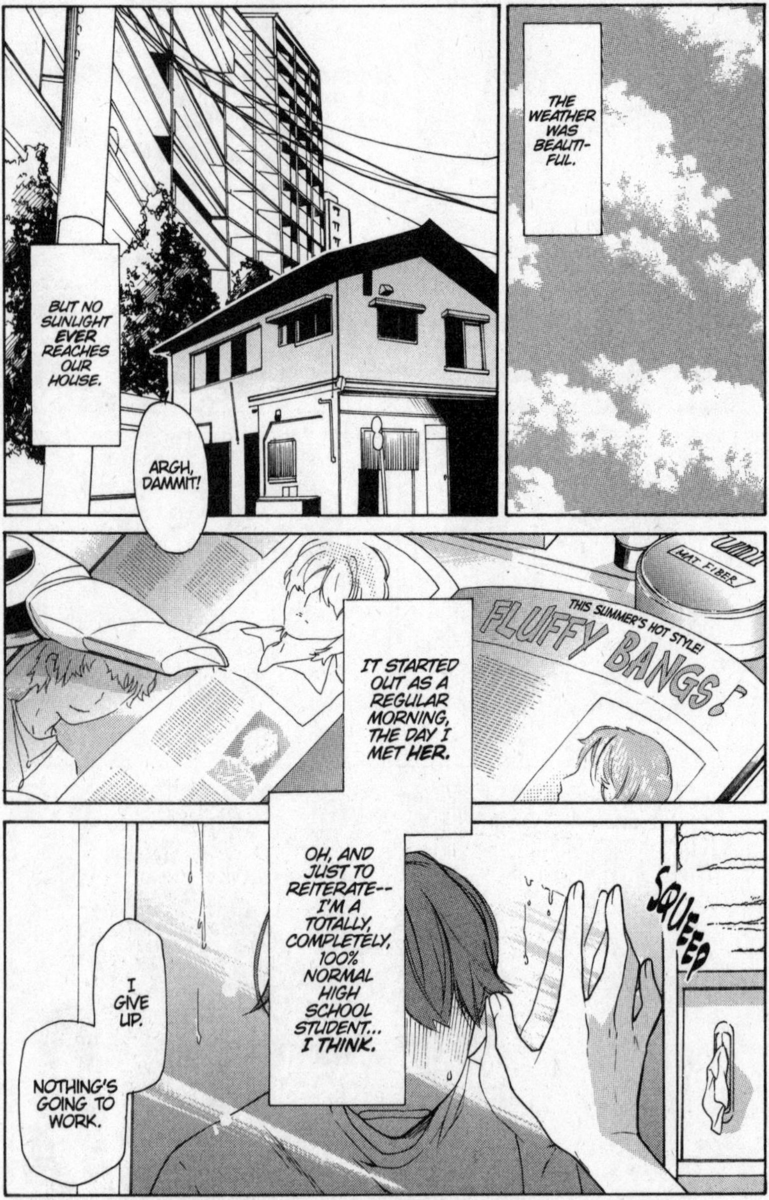
THE WEATHER WAS BEAUTI-FUL.
BUT NO SUNLIGHT EVER REACHES OUR HOUSE.
ARGH, DAMMIT!
MAT FIBER
THIS SUMMER'S HOT STYLE!
FLUFFY BANGS!
IT STARTED OUT AS A REGULAR MORNING, THE DAY I MET HER.
SQUEEP
OH, AND JUST TO REITERATE-- I'M A TOTALLY, COMPLETELY, 100% NORMAL HIGH SCHOOL STUDENT... I THINK.
I GIVE UP.
NOTHING'S GOING TO WORK.

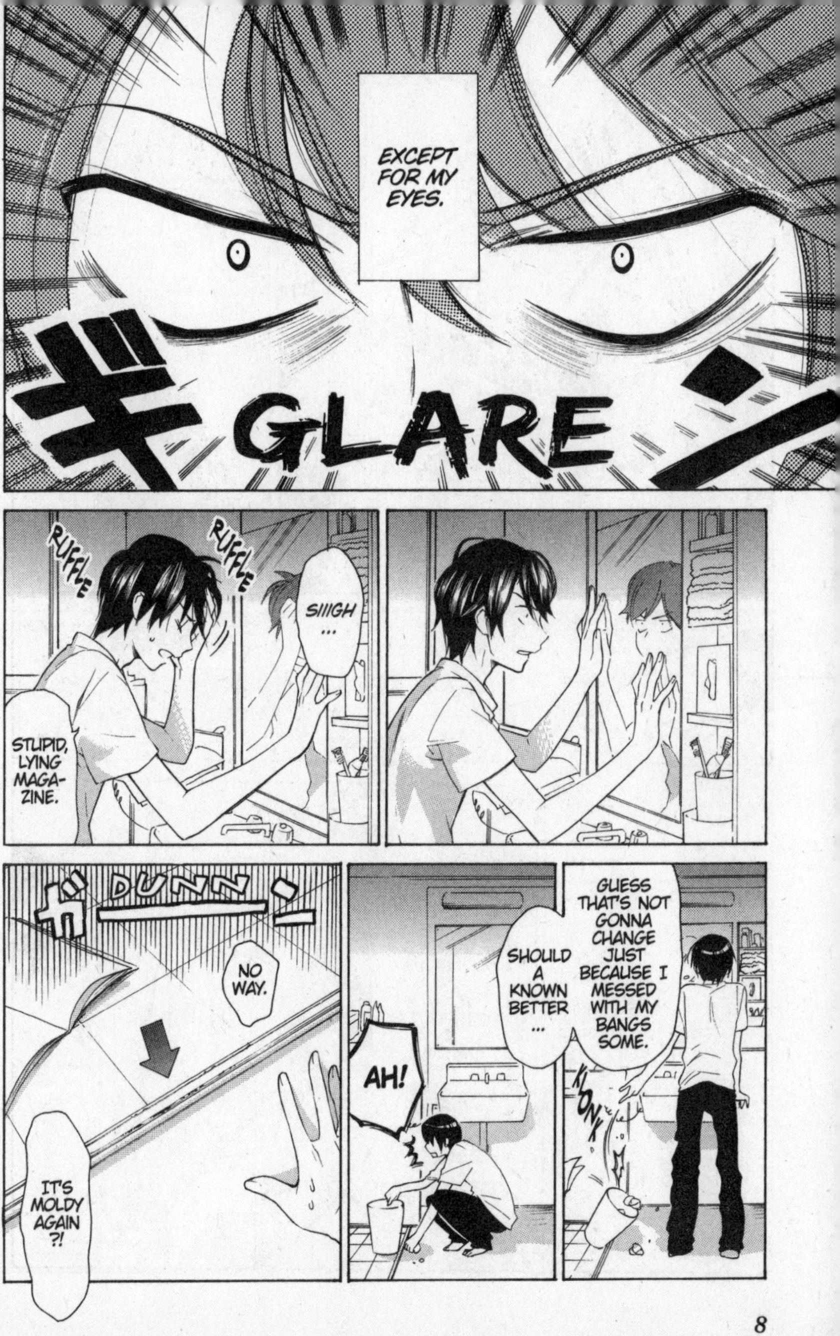
EXCEPT FOR MY EYES.
GLARE
RUFFLE RUFFLE
SIIGH ...
STUPID, LYING MAGA-ZINE.
GUESS THAT'S NOT GONNA CHANGE JUST BECAUSE I MESSED WITH MY BANGS SOME.
SHOULD A KNOWN BETTER ...
KLONK
AH!
DUNN
NO WAY.
IT'S MOLDY AGAIN ?!

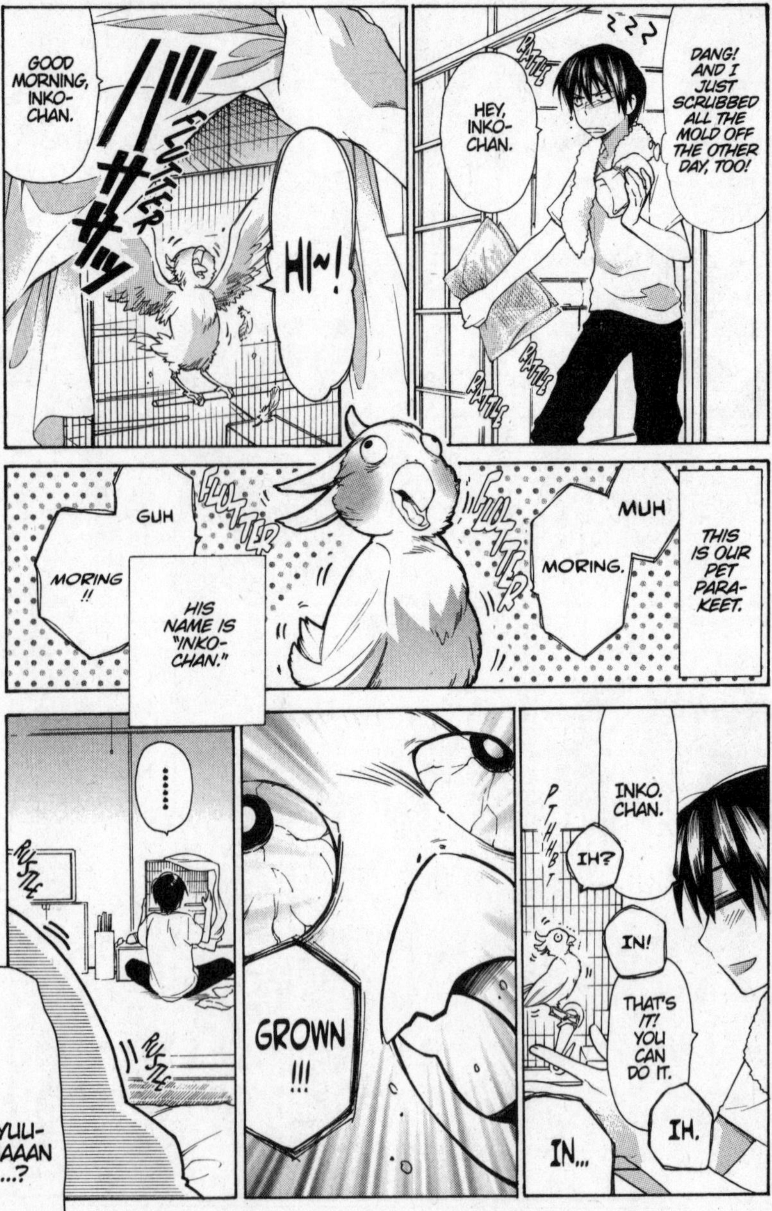
DANG! AND I JUST SCRUBBED ALL THE MOLD OFF THE OTHER DAY, TOO!
RATTLE
HEY, INKO-CHAN.
RATTLE RATTLE
GOOD MORNING, INKO-CHAN.
FLUTTER
HI~!
THIS IS OUR PET PARA-KEET.
MUH MORING.
FLUTTER
FLUTTER
GUH MORING!!
HIS NAME IS "INKO-CHAN."
INKO. CHAN.
PTHHBT
IH?
IN!
THAT'S IT! YOU CAN DO IT.
IH.
IN...
GROWN!!!
......
RUSTLE
RUSTLE
RYUU-CHAAAN...?

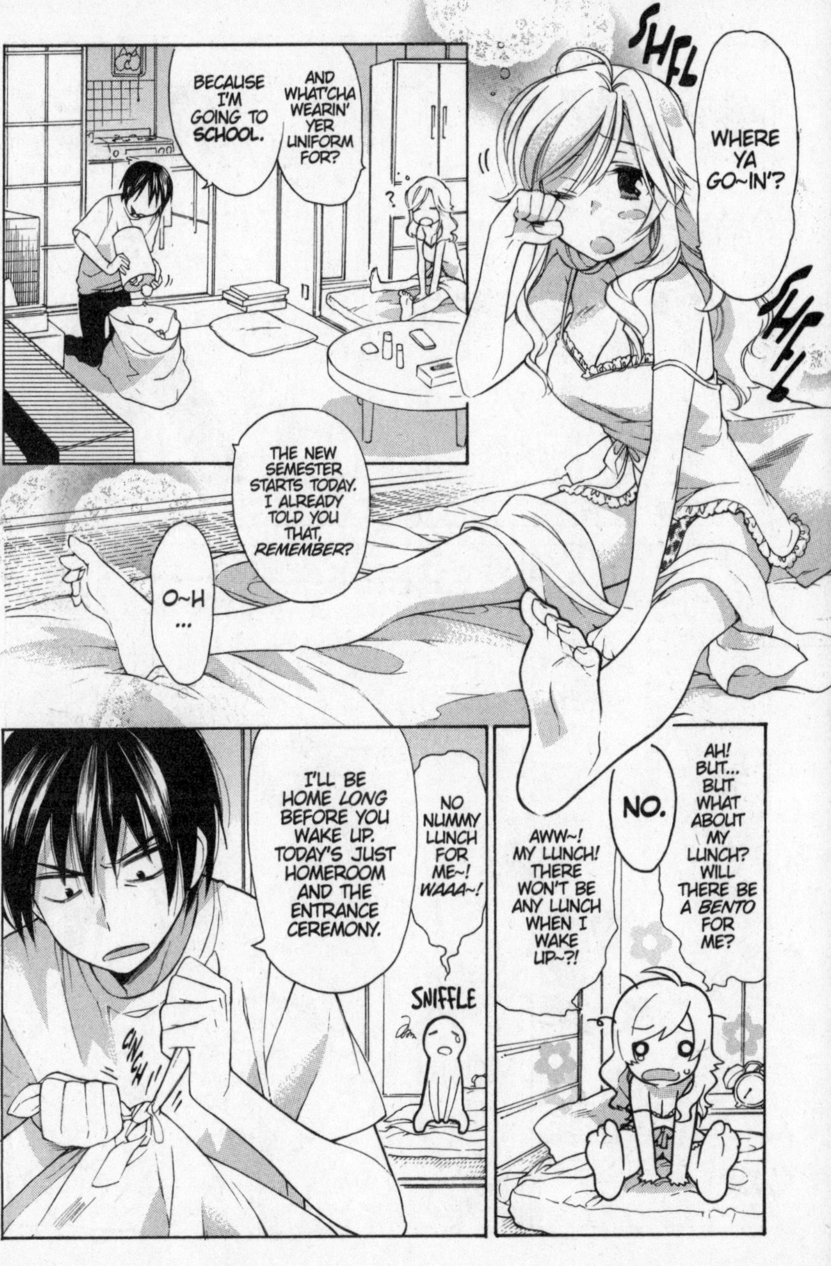
SHFL
WHERE YA GO~IN'?
SHFL
AND WHAT'CHA WEARIN' YER UNIFORM FOR?
BECAUSE I'M GOING TO SCHOOL.
THE NEW SEMESTER STARTS TODAY. I ALREADY TOLD YOU THAT, *REMEMBER?*
O~H ...
AH! BUT... BUT WHAT ABOUT MY LUNCH? WILL THERE BE A *BENTO* FOR ME?
NO.
AWW~! MY LUNCH! THERE WON'T BE ANY LUNCH WHEN I WAKE UP~?!
NO NUMMY LUNCH FOR ME~! *WAAA~!*
SNIFFLE
I'LL BE HOME *LONG* BEFORE YOU WAKE UP. TODAY'S JUST HOMEROOM AND THE ENTRANCE CEREMONY.
CINCH

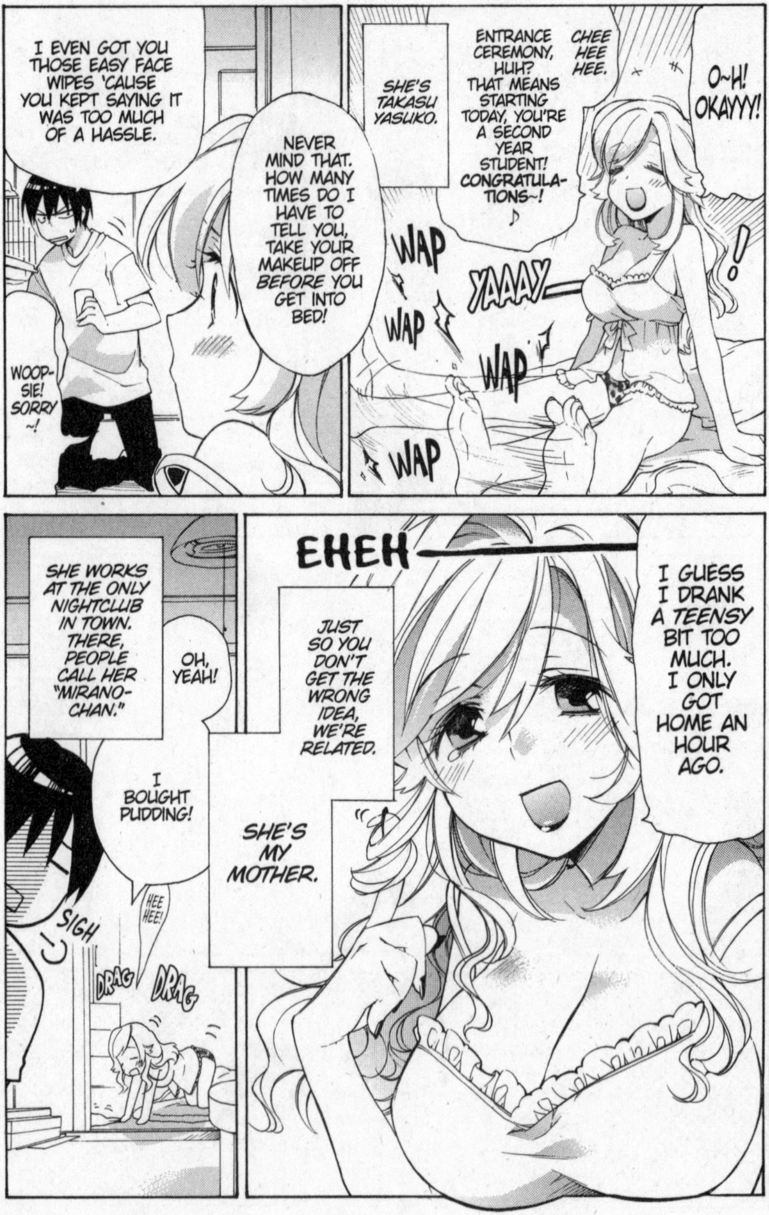
O~H! OKAYYY!
CHEE HEE HEE.
ENTRANCE CEREMONY, HUH? THAT MEANS STARTING TODAY, YOU'RE A SECOND YEAR STUDENT! CONGRATULA-TIONS~! ♪
SHE'S TAKASU YASUKO.
!
YAAAY
WAP
WAP
WAP
WAP
NEVER MIND THAT. HOW MANY TIMES DO I HAVE TO TELL YOU, TAKE YOUR MAKEUP OFF BEFORE YOU GET INTO BED!
I EVEN GOT YOU THOSE EASY FACE WIPES 'CAUSE YOU KEPT SAYING IT WAS TOO MUCH OF A HASSLE.
WOOP-SIE! SORRY ~!
EHEH
I GUESS I DRANK A TEENSY BIT TOO MUCH. I ONLY GOT HOME AN HOUR AGO.
JUST SO YOU DON'T GET THE WRONG IDEA, WE'RE RELATED.
SHE'S MY MOTHER.
SHE WORKS AT THE ONLY NIGHTCLUB IN TOWN. THERE, PEOPLE CALL HER "MIRANO-CHAN."
OH, YEAH!
I BOUGHT PUDDING!
HEE HEE!
SIGH
DRAG
DRAG

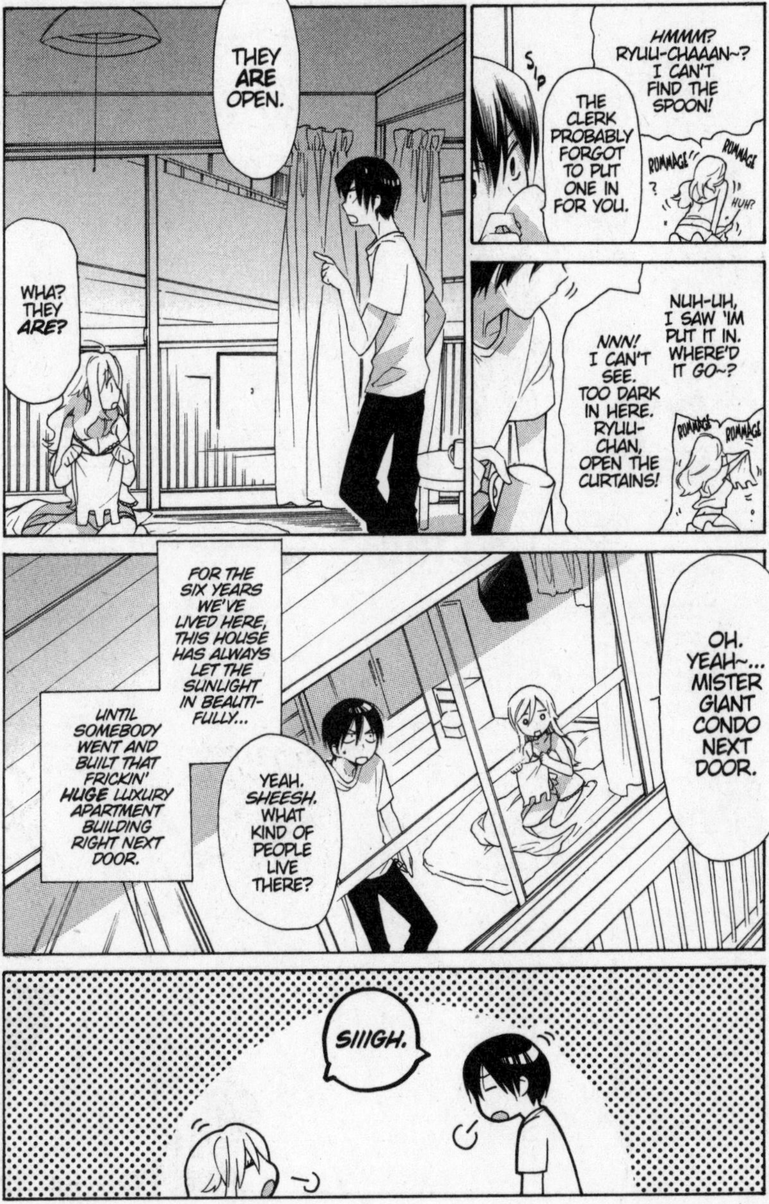
HMMM? RYUU-CHAAAN~? I CAN'T FIND THE SPOON!
SIP
THE CLERK PROBABLY FORGOT TO PUT ONE IN FOR YOU.
RUMMAGE
RUMMAGE
?
HUH?
NUH-UH, I SAW 'IM PUT IT IN. WHERE'D IT GO~?
NNN! I CAN'T SEE. TOO DARK IN HERE. RYUU-CHAN, OPEN THE CURTAINS!
RUMMAGE
RUMMAGE
THEY ARE OPEN.
WHA? THEY ARE?
OH. YEAH~... MISTER GIANT CONDO NEXT DOOR.
FOR THE SIX YEARS WE'VE LIVED HERE, THIS HOUSE HAS ALWAYS LET THE SUNLIGHT IN BEAUTIFULLY...
YEAH. SHEESH. WHAT KIND OF PEOPLE LIVE THERE?
UNTIL SOMEBODY WENT AND BUILT THAT FRICKIN' HUGE LUXURY APARTMENT BUILDING RIGHT NEXT DOOR.
SIIIGH.

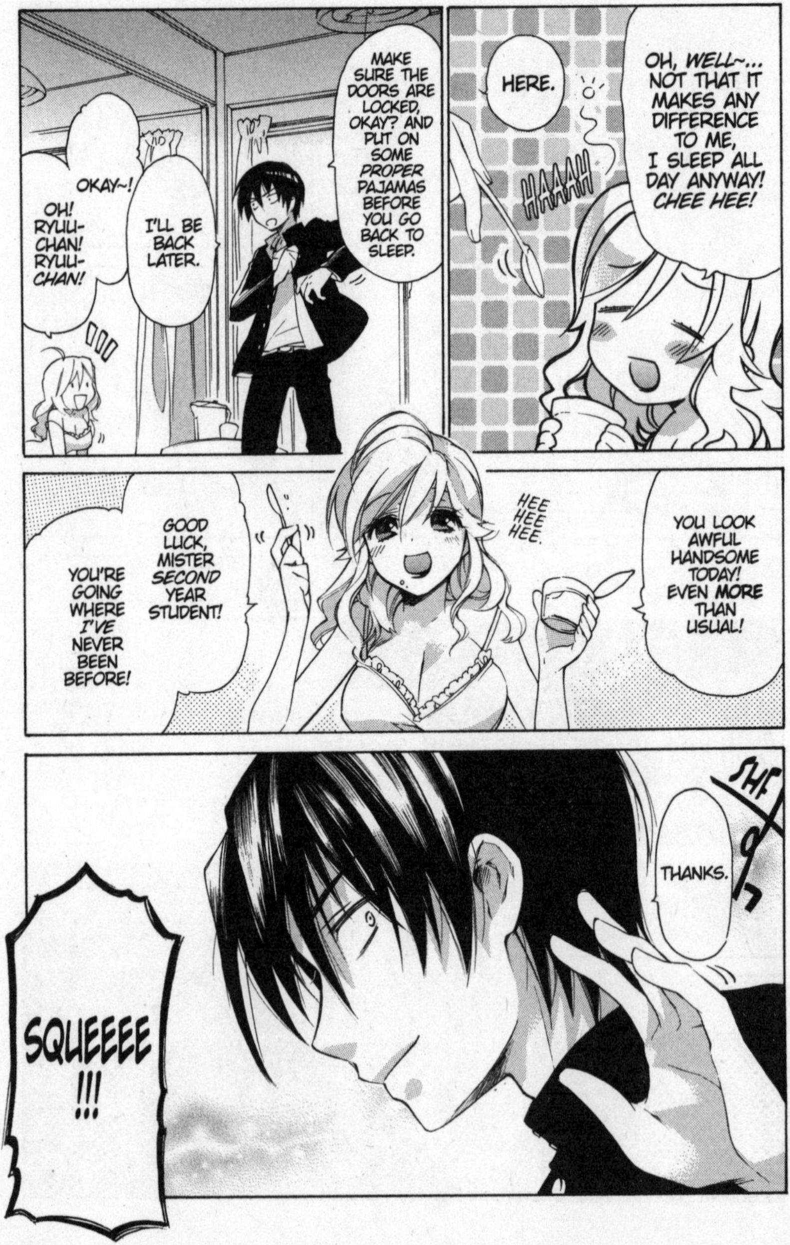
OH, WELL~... NOT THAT IT MAKES ANY DIFFERENCE TO ME, I SLEEP ALL DAY ANYWAY! CHEE HEE!
HERE.
HAAAH
MAKE SURE THE DOORS ARE LOCKED, OKAY? AND PUT ON SOME PROPER PAJAMAS BEFORE YOU GO BACK TO SLEEP.
I'LL BE BACK LATER.
OKAY~!
OH! RYUU-CHAN! RYUU-CHAN!
YOU LOOK AWFUL HANDSOME TODAY! EVEN MORE THAN USUAL!
HEE HEE HEE.
GOOD LUCK, MISTER SECOND YEAR STUDENT!
YOU'RE GOING WHERE I'VE NEVER BEEN BEFORE!
SHF
THANKS.
SQUEEEE !!!

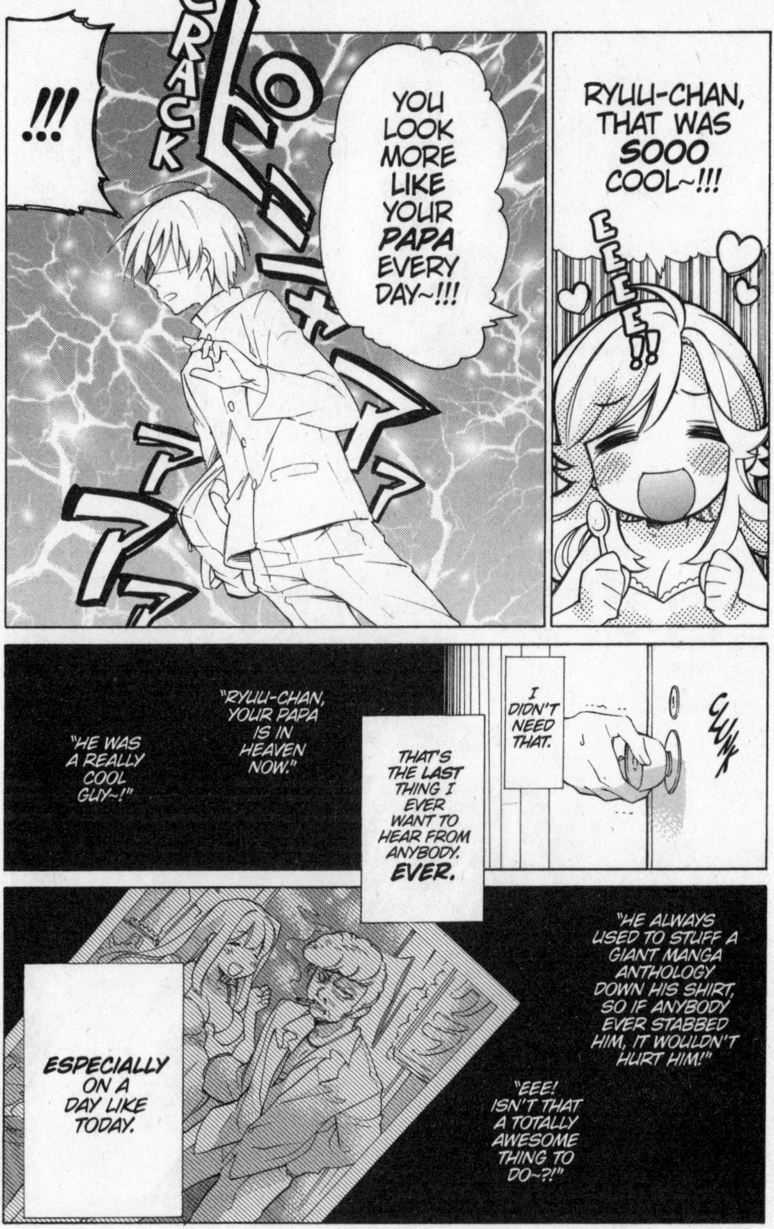
RYUU-CHAN, THAT WAS SOOO COOL~!!!
EEEEE!!
YOU LOOK MORE LIKE YOUR PAPA EVERY DAY~!!!
CRACK
!!!
CLUNK
I DIDN'T NEED THAT.
"RYUU-CHAN, YOUR PAPA IS IN HEAVEN NOW."
"HE WAS A REALLY COOL GUY~!"
THAT'S THE LAST THING I EVER WANT TO HEAR FROM ANYBODY. EVER.
"HE ALWAYS USED TO STUFF A GIANT MANGA ANTHOLOGY DOWN HIS SHIRT, SO IF ANYBODY EVER STABBED HIM, IT WOULDN'T HURT HIM!"
"EEE! ISN'T THAT A TOTALLY AWESOME THING TO DO~?!"
ESPECIALLY ON A DAY LIKE TODAY.

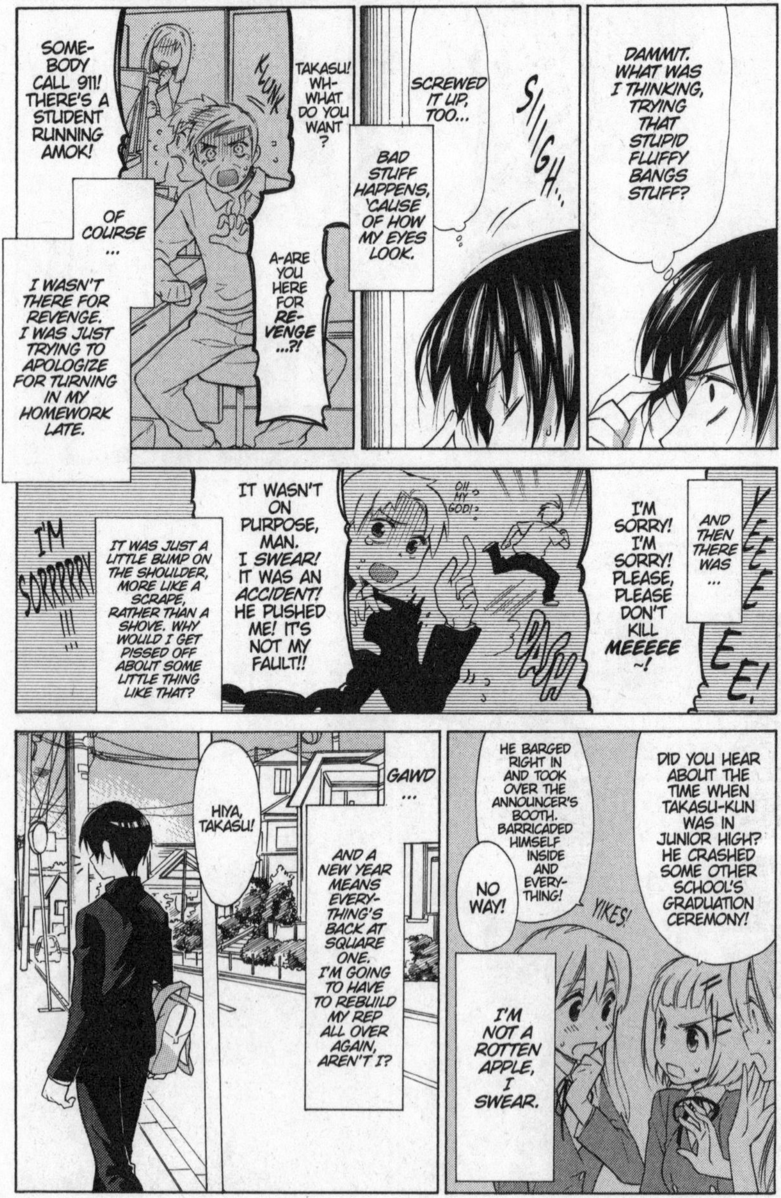
DAMMIT. WHAT WAS I THINKING, TRYING THAT STUPID FLUFFY BANGS STUFF?
SCREWED IT UP, TOO...
SIIGH...
BAD STUFF HAPPENS, 'CAUSE OF HOW MY EYES LOOK.
TAKASU! WH-WHAT DO YOU WANT?
KLUNK
SOME-BODY CALL 911! THERE'S A STUDENT RUNNING AMOK!
A-ARE YOU HERE FOR RE-VENGE ...?!
OF COURSE ...
I WASN'T THERE FOR REVENGE. I WAS JUST TRYING TO APOLOGIZE FOR TURNING IN MY HOMEWORK LATE.
AND THEN THERE WAS ...
YEEEEEE!
I'M SORRY! I'M SORRY! PLEASE, PLEASE DON'T KILL MEEEEE ~!
OH MY GOD!
DASH
IT WASN'T ON PURPOSE, MAN. I SWEAR! IT WAS AN ACCIDENT! HE PUSHED ME! IT'S NOT MY FAULT!!
IT WAS JUST A LITTLE BUMP ON THE SHOULDER, MORE LIKE A SCRAPE, RATHER THAN A SHOVE. WHY WOULD I GET PISSED OFF ABOUT SOME LITTLE THING LIKE THAT?
I'M SORRRRRY!!!
DID YOU HEAR ABOUT THE TIME WHEN TAKASU-KUN WAS IN JUNIOR HIGH? HE CRASHED SOME OTHER SCHOOL'S GRADUATION CEREMONY!
HE BARGED RIGHT IN AND TOOK OVER THE ANNOUNCER'S BOOTH. BARRICADED HIMSELF INSIDE AND EVERY-THING!
NO WAY!
YIKES!
I'M NOT A ROTTEN APPLE, I SWEAR.
GAWD ...
HIYA, TAKASU!
AND A NEW YEAR MEANS EVERY-THING'S BACK AT SQUARE ONE. I'M GOING TO HAVE TO REBUILD MY REP ALL OVER AGAIN, AREN'T I?

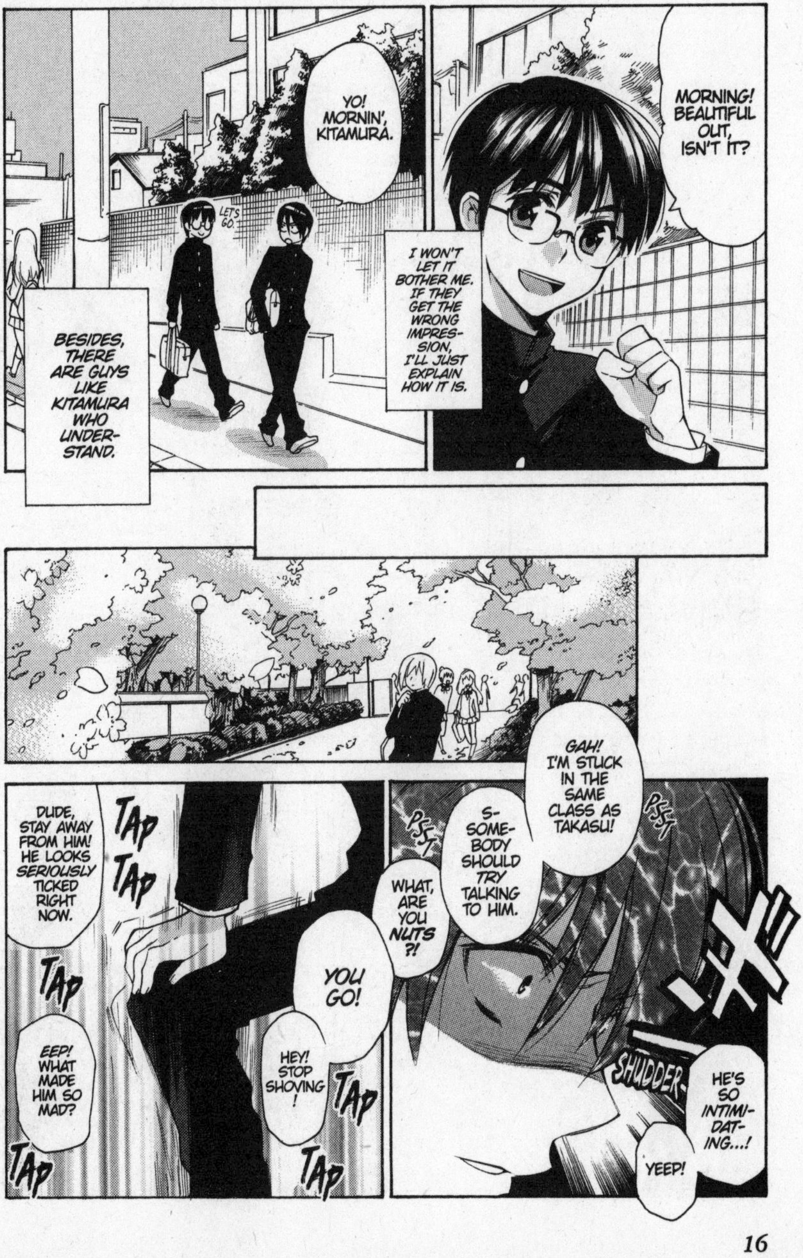
MORNING! BEAUTIFUL OUT, ISN'T IT?
I WON'T LET IT BOTHER ME. IF THEY GET THE WRONG IMPRESSION, I'LL JUST EXPLAIN HOW IT IS.
YO! MORNIN', KITAMURA.
LET'S GO.
BESIDES, THERE ARE GUYS LIKE KITAMURA WHO UNDERSTAND.
PSST
GAH! I'M STUCK IN THE SAME CLASS AS TAKASU!
PSST
S-SOMEBODY SHOULD TRY TALKING TO HIM.
WHAT, ARE YOU NUTS?!
YOU GO!
HEY! STOP SHOVING!
SHUDDER-
HE'S SO INTIMIDATING...!
YEEP!
TAP
TAP
DUDE, STAY AWAY FROM HIM! HE LOOKS SERIOUSLY TICKED RIGHT NOW.
TAP
EEP! WHAT MADE HIM SO MAD?
TAP
TAP
TAP

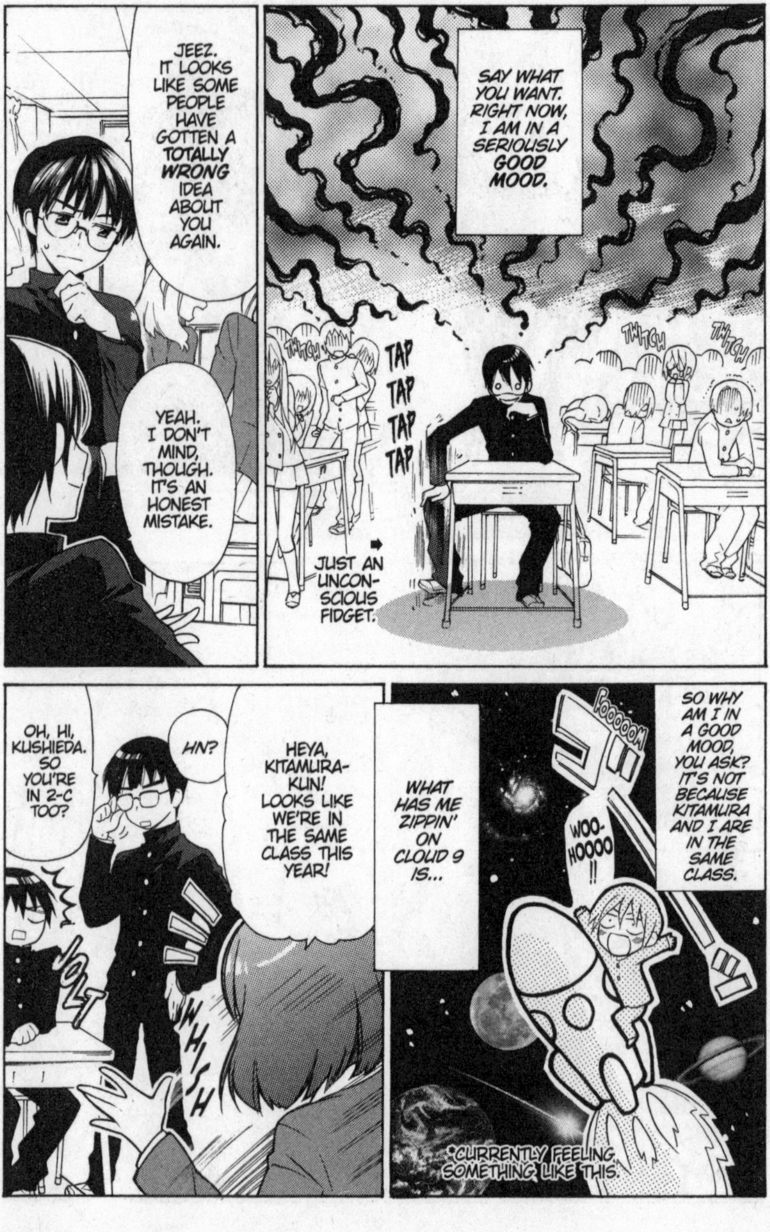
SAY WHAT YOU WANT. RIGHT NOW, I AM IN A SERIOUSLY GOOD MOOD.
TWITCH
TWITCH
TAP TAP TAP TAP
TWITCH
JUST AN UNCONSCIOUS FIDGET.
JEEZ. IT LOOKS LIKE SOME PEOPLE HAVE GOTTEN A TOTALLY WRONG IDEA ABOUT YOU AGAIN.
YEAH. I DON'T MIND, THOUGH. IT'S AN HONEST MISTAKE.
SO WHY AM I IN A GOOD MOOD, YOU ASK? IT'S NOT BECAUSE KITAMURA AND I ARE IN THE SAME CLASS.
FOOOOOM
WOO-HOOOO!!
WHAT HAS ME ZIPPIN' ON CLOUD 9 IS...
*CURRENTLY FEELING SOMETHING LIKE THIS.
HEYA, KITAMURA-KUN! LOOKS LIKE WE'RE IN THE SAME CLASS THIS YEAR!
HN?
OH, HI, KUSHIEDA. SO YOU'RE IN 2-C TOO?
WHISH
JOLT

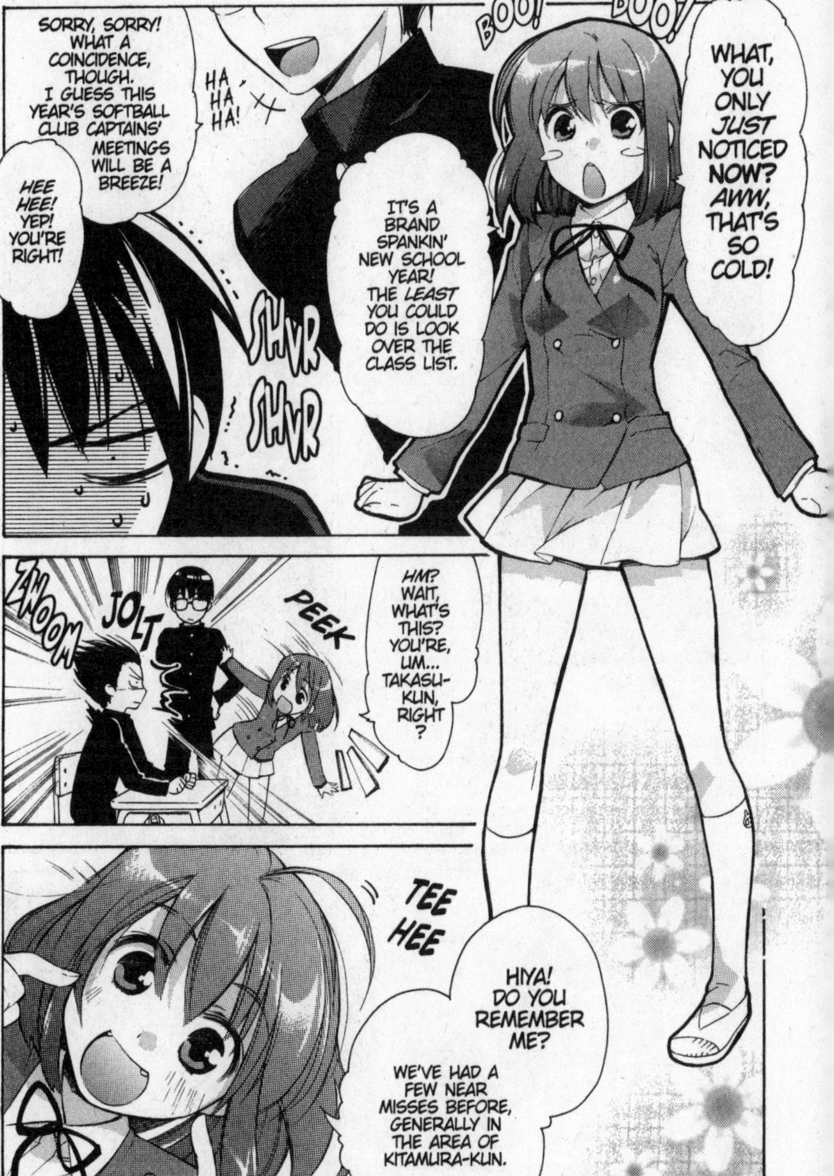
BOO! BOO!
WHAT, YOU ONLY JUST NOTICED NOW? AWW, THAT'S SO COLD!
IT'S A BRAND SPANKIN' NEW SCHOOL YEAR! THE LEAST YOU COULD DO IS LOOK OVER THE CLASS LIST.
SHVR SHVR
SORRY, SORRY! WHAT A COINCIDENCE, THOUGH. I GUESS THIS YEAR'S SOFTBALL CLUB CAPTAINS' MEETINGS WILL BE A BREEZE!
HA HA HA!
HEE HEE! YEP! YOU'RE RIGHT!
HM? WAIT, WHAT'S THIS? YOU'RE, UM... TAKASU-KUN, RIGHT?
PEEK
JOLT
ZAWOOM
TEE HEE
HIYA! DO YOU REMEMBER ME?
WE'VE HAD A FEW NEAR MISSES BEFORE, GENERALLY IN THE AREA OF KITAMURA-KUN.

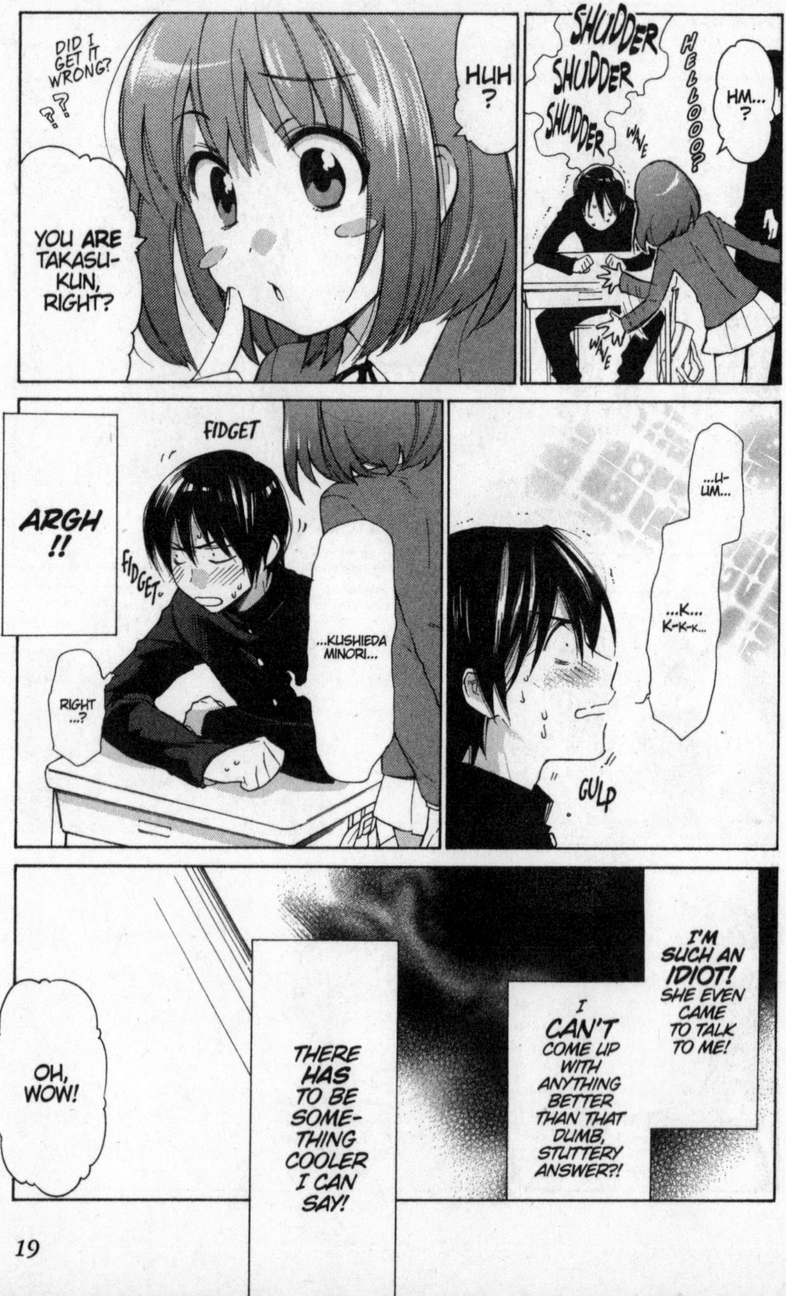
SHUDDER
SHUDDER
SHUDDER
HELLOOOO?
HM...?
WAVE
WAVE
HUH?
DID I GET IT WRONG?
??
YOU ARE TAKASU-KUN, RIGHT?
...U-UM...
...K... K-K-K...
GULP
FIDGET
ARGH!!
FIDGET
...KUSHIEDA MINORI...
RIGHT...?
I'M SUCH AN IDIOT! SHE EVEN CAME TO TALK TO ME!
I CAN'T COME UP WITH ANYTHING BETTER THAN THAT DUMB, STUTTERY ANSWER?!
THERE HAS TO BE SOMETHING COOLER I CAN SAY!
OH, WOW!

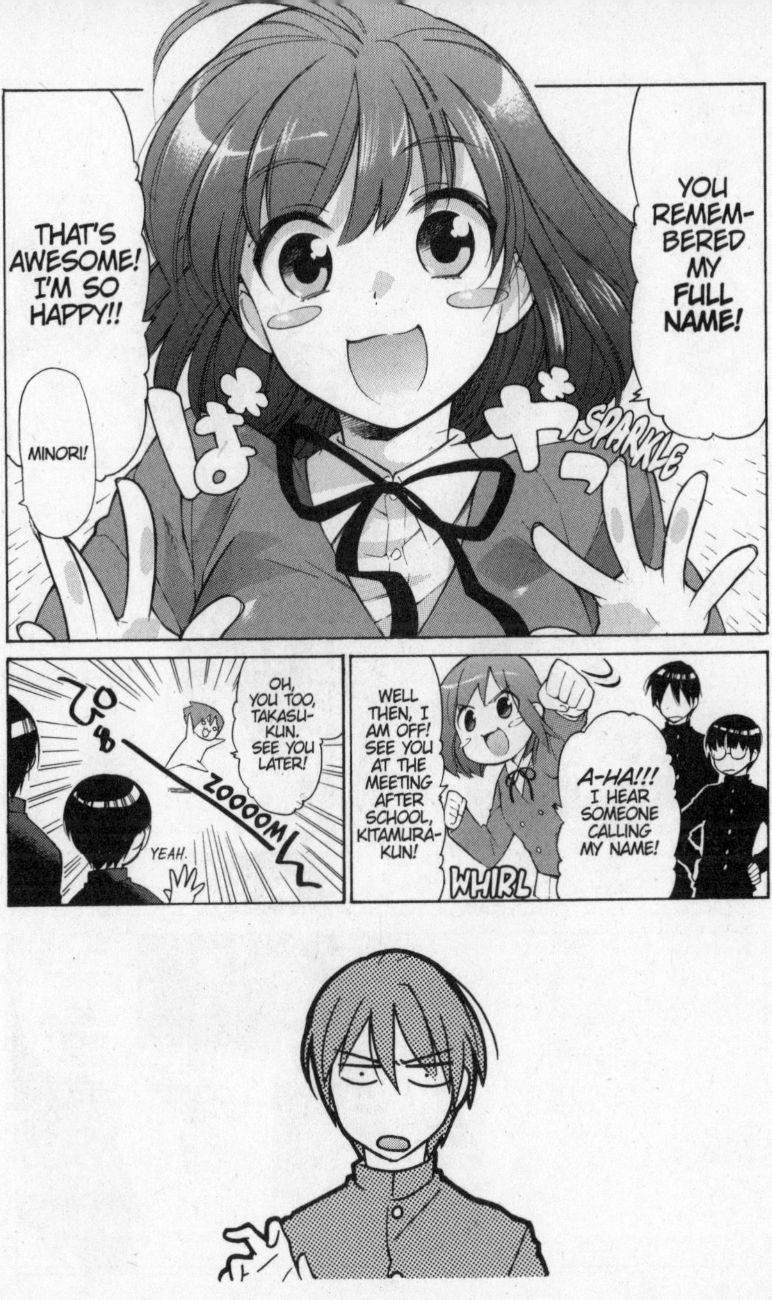
YOU REMEMBERED MY FULL NAME!
SPARKLE
THAT'S AWESOME! I'M SO HAPPY!!
MINORI!
A-HA!!! I HEAR SOMEONE CALLING MY NAME!
WELL THEN, I AM OFF! SEE YOU AT THE MEETING AFTER SCHOOL, KITAMURA-KUN!
WHIRL
OH, YOU TOO, TAKASU-KUN. SEE YOU LATER!
ZOOOOM
YEAH.

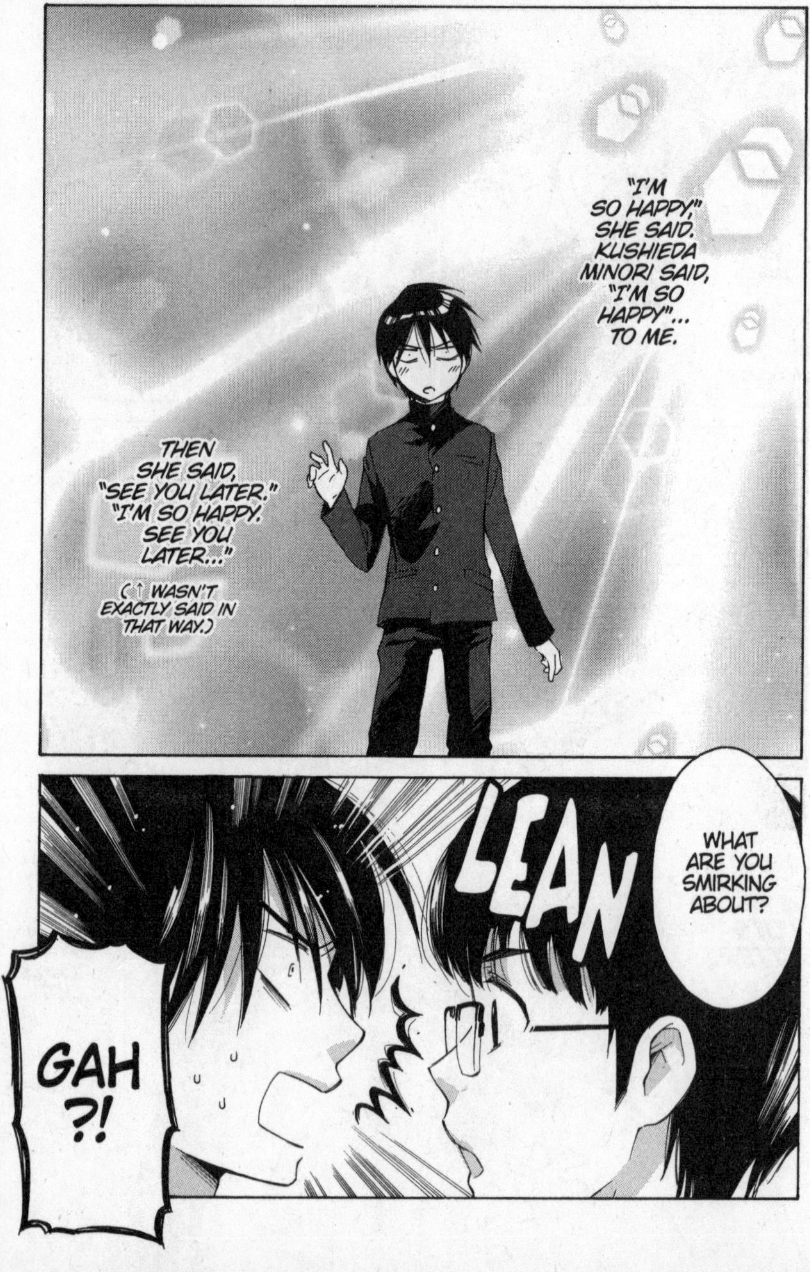
"I'M SO HAPPY," SHE SAID. KUSHIEDA MINORI SAID, "I'M SO HAPPY"... TO ME.
THEN SHE SAID, "SEE YOU LATER." "I'M SO HAPPY. SEE YOU LATER..."
(↑ WASN'T EXACTLY SAID IN THAT WAY.)
WHAT ARE YOU SMIRKING ABOUT?
LEAN
GAH ?!

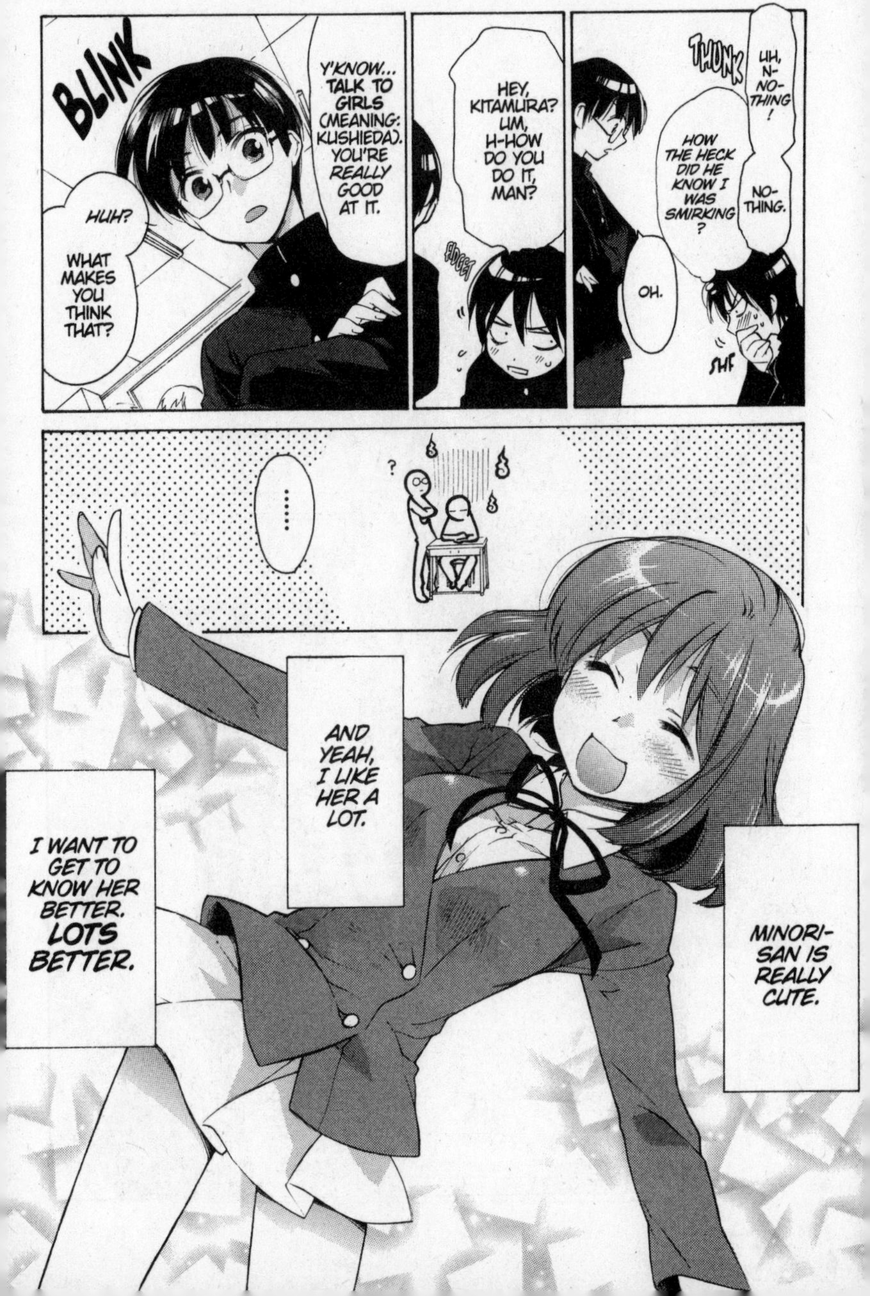
UH, N-NO-THING!
THUNK
HOW THE HECK DID HE KNOW I WAS SMIRKING?
NO-THING.
OH.
SHF
HEY, KITAMURA? UM, H-HOW DO YOU DO IT, MAN?
FIDGET
Y'KNOW... TALK TO GIRLS (MEANING: KUSHIEDA). YOU'RE REALLY GOOD AT IT.
BLINK
HUH?
WHAT MAKES YOU THINK THAT?
......
?
MINORI-SAN IS REALLY CUTE.
AND YEAH, I LIKE HER A LOT.
I WANT TO GET TO KNOW HER BETTER. LOTS BETTER.

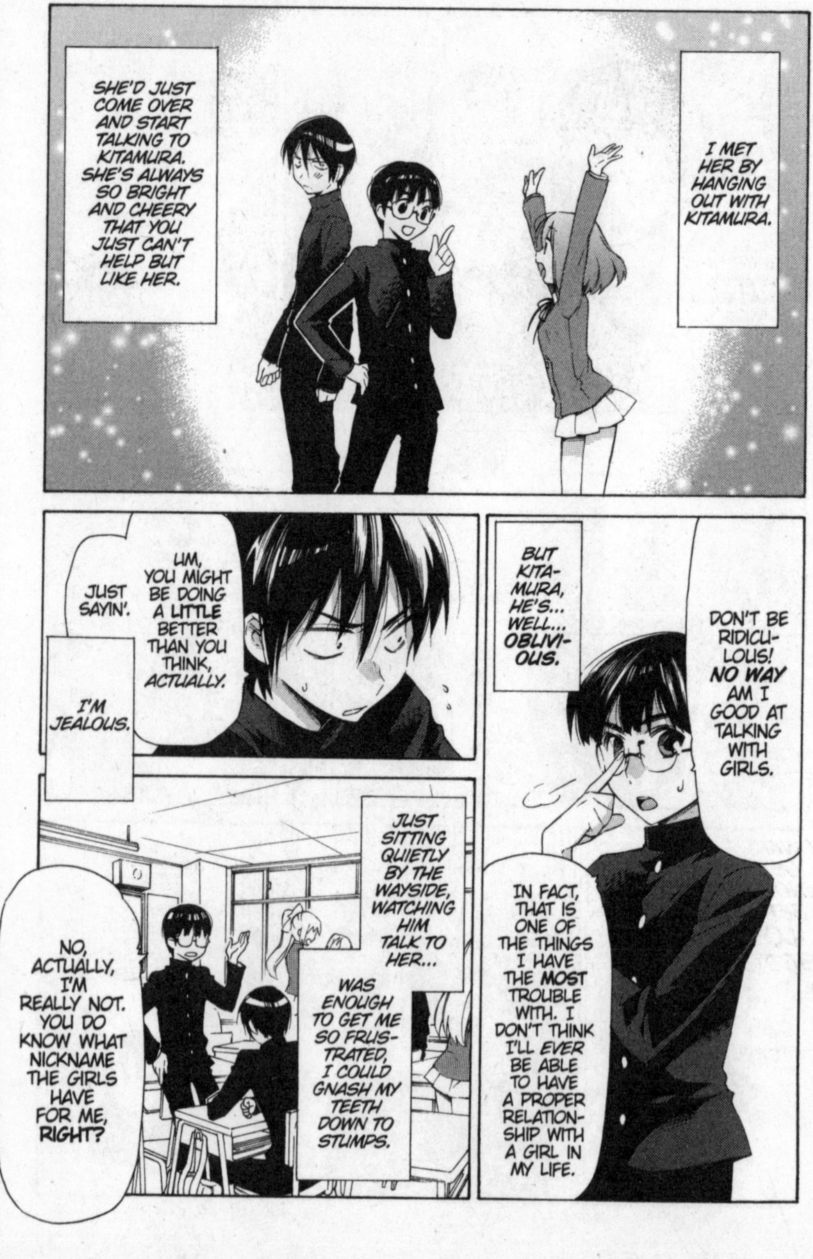
I MET HER BY HANGING OUT WITH KITAMURA.
SHE'D JUST COME OVER AND START TALKING TO KITAMURA. SHE'S ALWAYS SO BRIGHT AND CHEERY THAT YOU JUST CAN'T HELP BUT LIKE HER.
DON'T BE RIDICULOUS! NO WAY AM I GOOD AT TALKING WITH GIRLS.
BUT KITA-MURA, HE'S... WELL... OBLIVI-OUS.
IN FACT, THAT IS ONE OF THE THINGS I HAVE THE MOST TROUBLE WITH. I DON'T THINK I'LL EVER BE ABLE TO HAVE A PROPER RELATION-SHIP WITH A GIRL IN MY LIFE.
UM, YOU MIGHT BE DOING A LITTLE BETTER THAN YOU THINK, ACTUALLY.
JUST SAYIN'.
I'M JEALOUS.
JUST SITTING QUIETLY BY THE WAYSIDE, WATCHING HIM TALK TO HER...
WAS ENOUGH TO GET ME SO FRUS-TRATED, I COULD GNASH MY TEETH DOWN TO STUMPS.
NO, ACTUALLY, I'M REALLY NOT. YOU DO KNOW WHAT NICKNAME THE GIRLS HAVE FOR ME, RIGHT?

↓Maruo-kun from *Chibi Maruko-chan.*

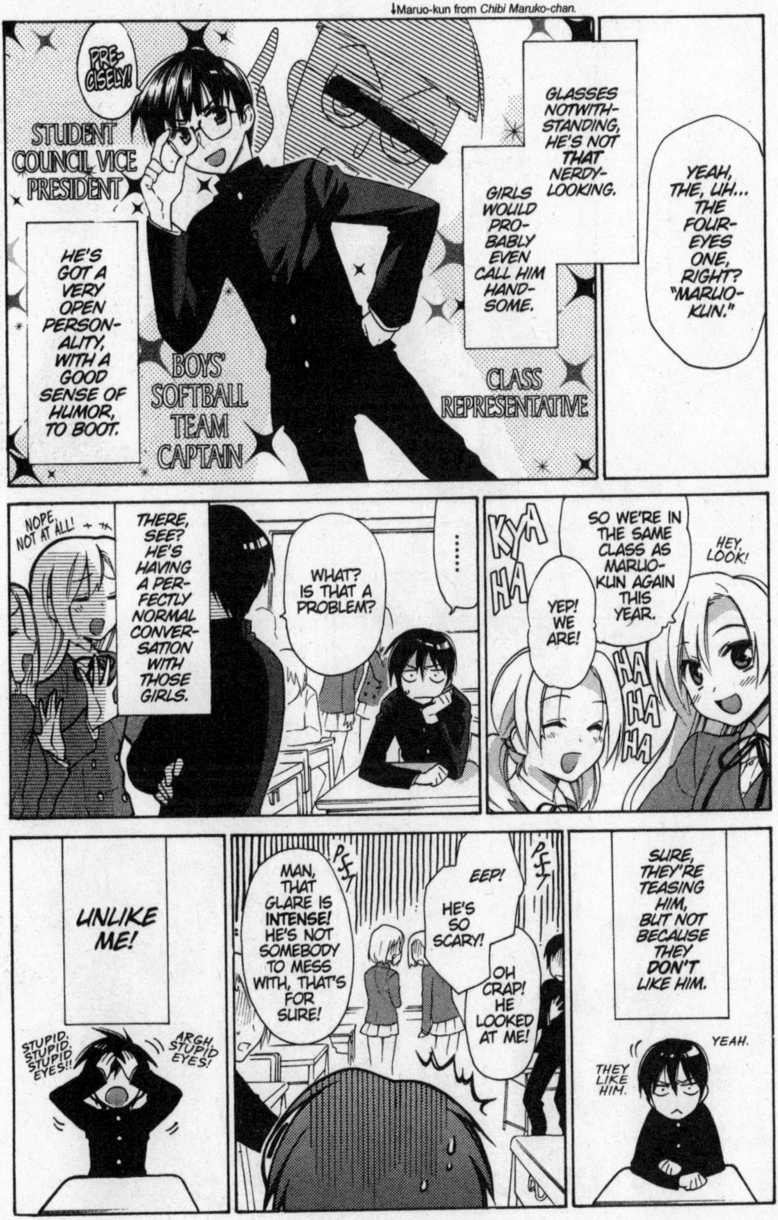
YEAH, THE, UH... THE FOUR-EYES ONE, RIGHT? "MARUO-KUN."
GLASSES NOTWITHSTANDING, HE'S NOT THAT NERDY-LOOKING.
GIRLS WOULD PROBABLY EVEN CALL HIM HANDSOME.
PRE-CISELY!
STUDENT COUNCIL VICE PRESIDENT
CLASS REPRESENTATIVE
BOYS' SOFTBALL TEAM CAPTAIN
HE'S GOT A VERY OPEN PERSONALITY, WITH A GOOD SENSE OF HUMOR, TO BOOT.
HEY, LOOK!
SO WE'RE IN THE SAME CLASS AS MARUO-KUN AGAIN THIS YEAR.
KYA HA HA
YEP! WE ARE!
HA HA HA HA
......
WHAT? IS THAT A PROBLEM?
THERE, SEE? HE'S HAVING A PERFECTLY NORMAL CONVERSATION WITH THOSE GIRLS.
NOPE, NOT AT ALL!
SURE, THEY'RE TEASING HIM, BUT NOT BECAUSE THEY DON'T LIKE HIM.
YEAH.
THEY LIKE HIM.
PSST
EEP!
HE'S SO SCARY!
PSST
MAN, THAT GLARE IS INTENSE! HE'S NOT SOMEBODY TO MESS WITH, THAT'S FOR SURE!
OH CRAP! HE LOOKED AT ME!
UNLIKE ME!
ARGH, STUPID EYES!
STUPID, STUPID, STUPID EYES!!

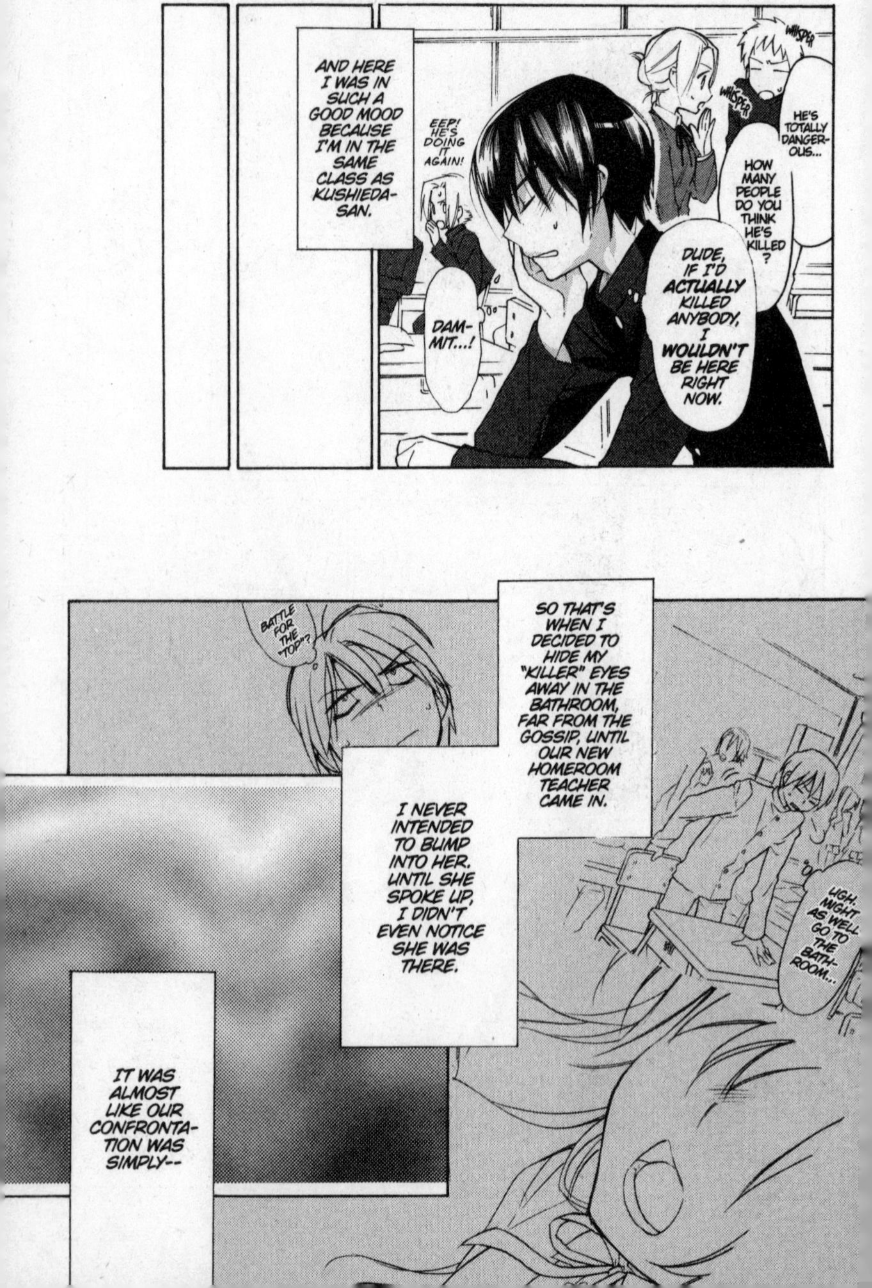
WHISPER
WHISPER
HE'S TOTALLY DANGER-OUS...
HOW MANY PEOPLE DO YOU THINK HE'S KILLED?
AND HERE I WAS IN SUCH A GOOD MOOD BECAUSE I'M IN THE SAME CLASS AS KUSHIEDA-SAN.
EEP! HE'S DOING IT AGAIN!
DUDE, IF I'D ACTUALLY KILLED ANYBODY, I WOULDN'T BE HERE RIGHT NOW.
DAM-MIT...!
SO THAT'S WHEN I DECIDED TO HIDE MY "KILLER" EYES AWAY IN THE BATHROOM, FAR FROM THE GOSSIP, UNTIL OUR NEW HOMEROOM TEACHER CAME IN.
UGH. MIGHT AS WELL GO TO THE BATH-ROOM...
BATTLE FOR THE TOP"?
I NEVER INTENDED TO BUMP INTO HER. UNTIL SHE SPOKE UP, I DIDN'T EVEN NOTICE SHE WAS THERE.
IT WAS ALMOST LIKE OUR CONFRONTA-TION WAS SIMPLY--

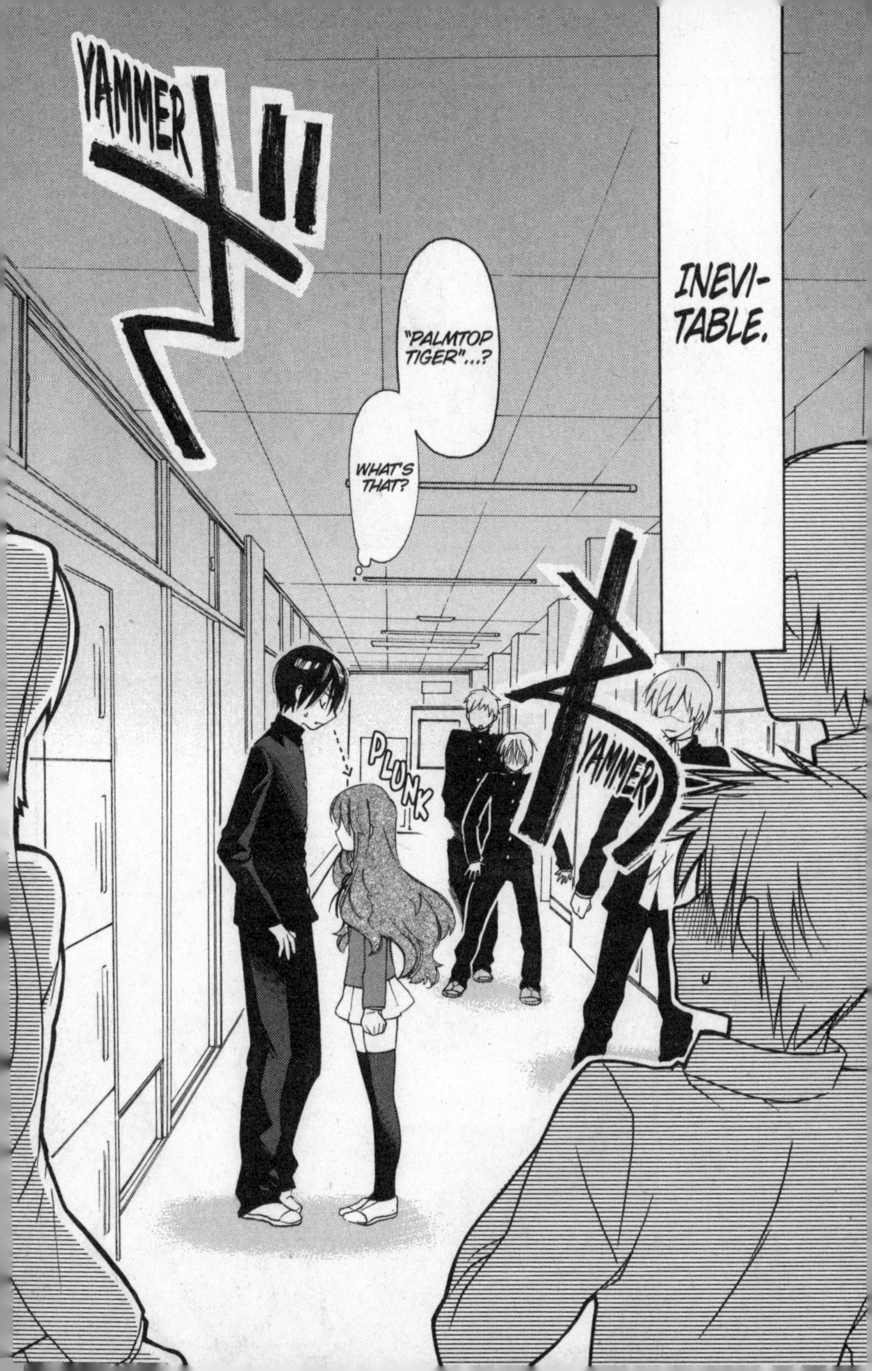
INEVI-
TABLE.
YAMMER
"PALMTOP TIGER"...?
WHAT'S THAT?
YAMMER
PLUNK

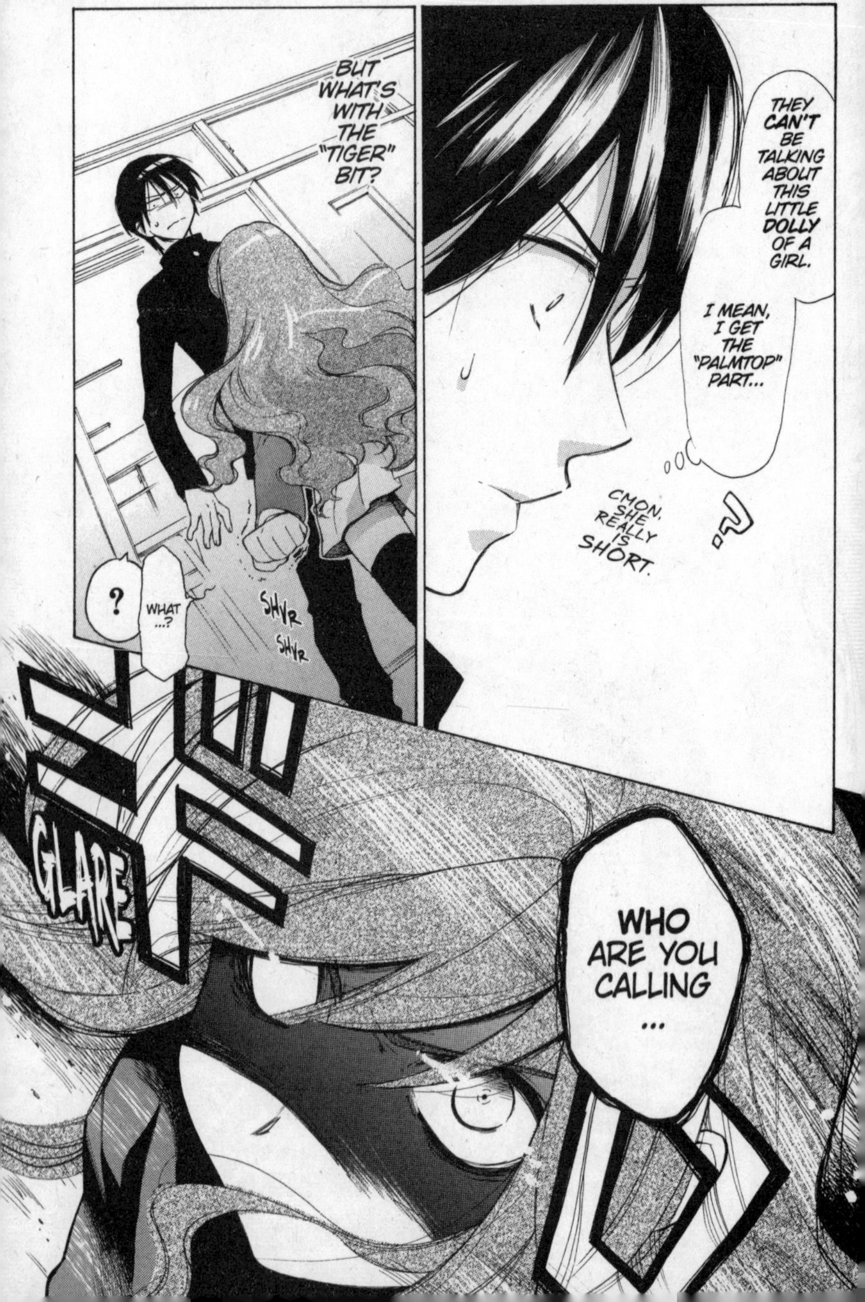
THEY CAN'T BE TALKING ABOUT THIS LITTLE DOLLY OF A GIRL.
I MEAN, I GET THE "PALMTOP" PART...
CMON, SHE REALLY IS SHORT.
?
BUT WHAT'S WITH THE "TIGER" BIT?
?
WHAT ...?
SHVR
SHVR
GLARE
WHO ARE YOU CALLING ...

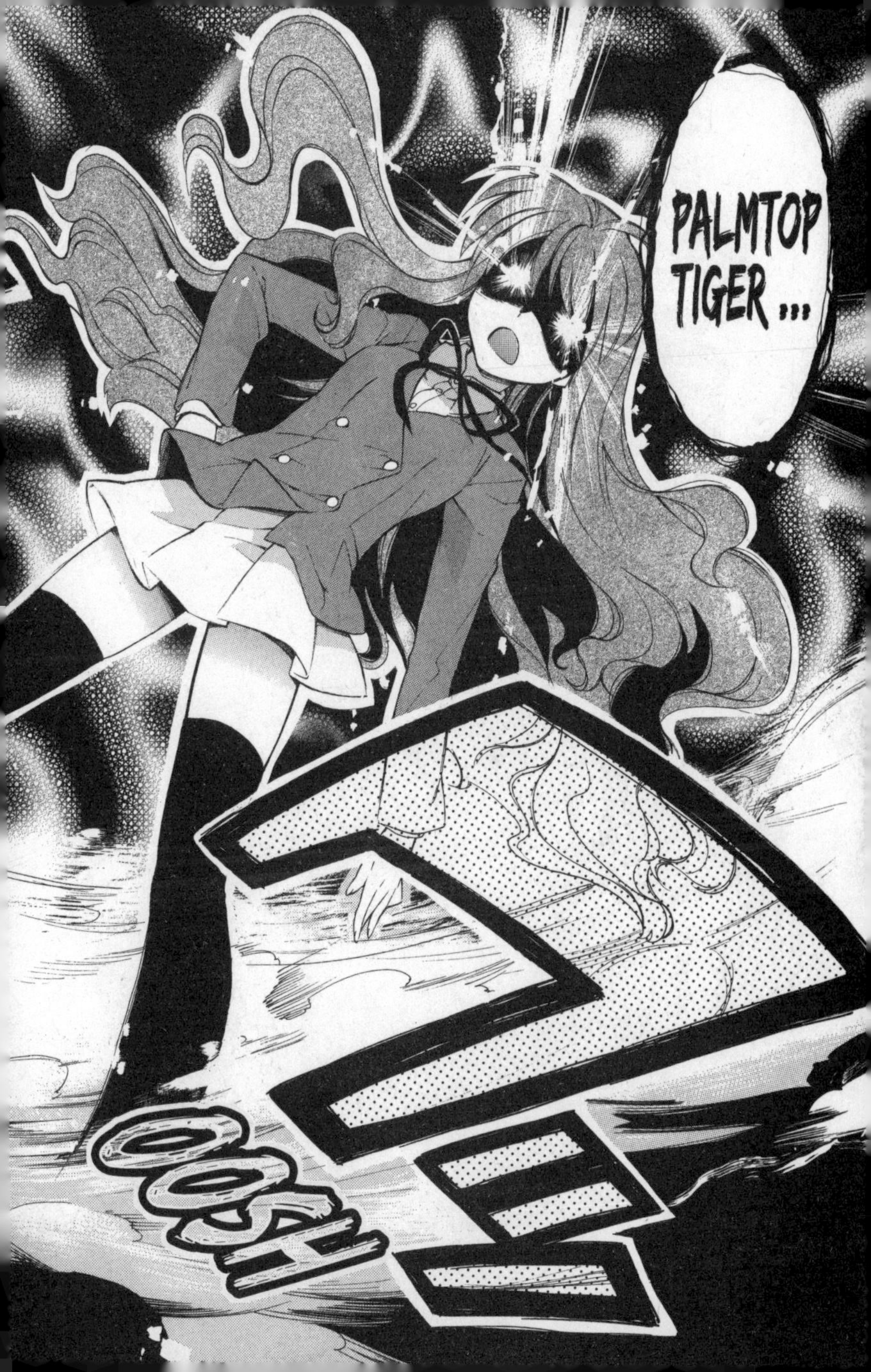
PALMTOP TIGER ...
OOF!!

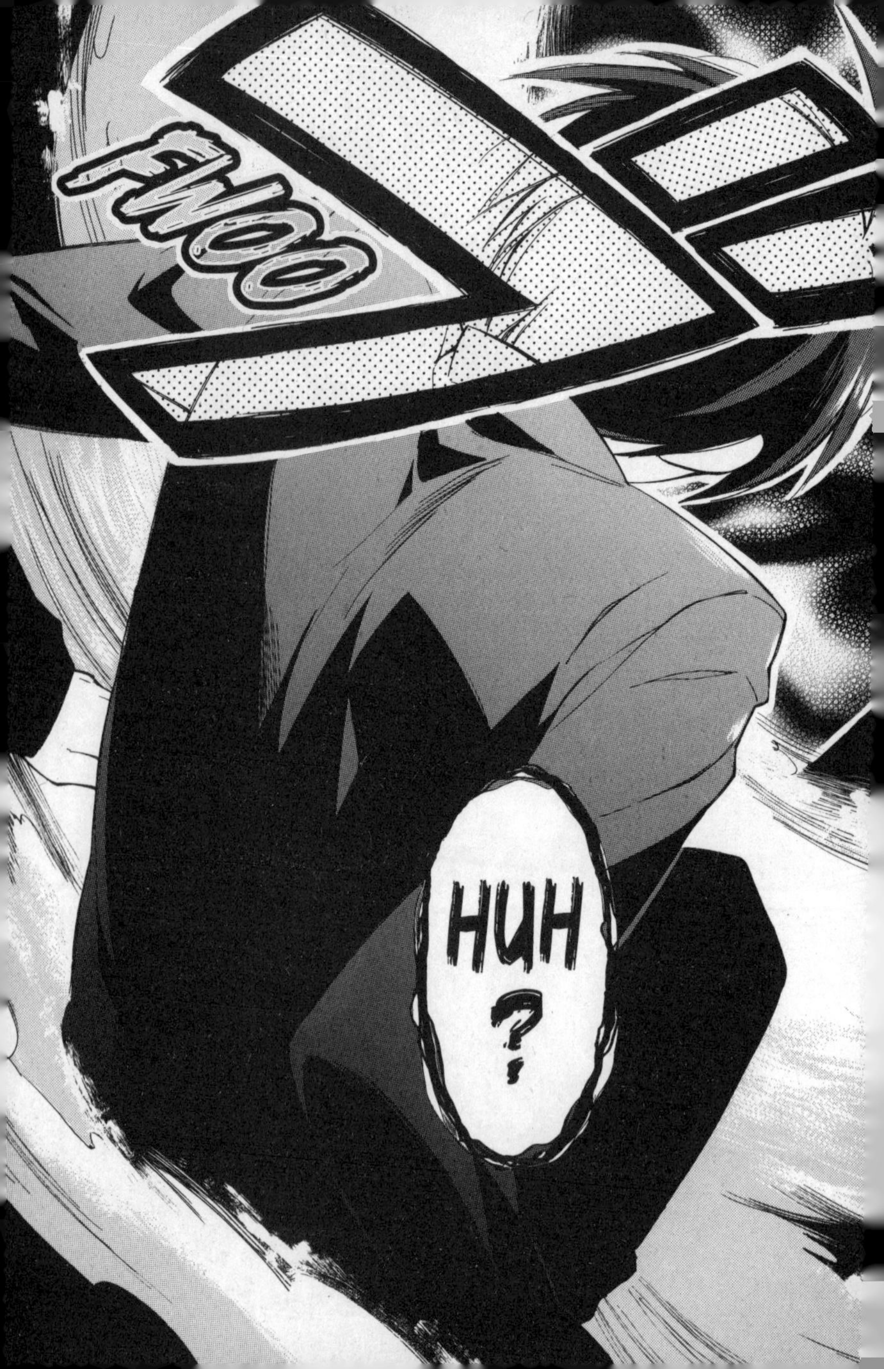
FWOO
HUH ?

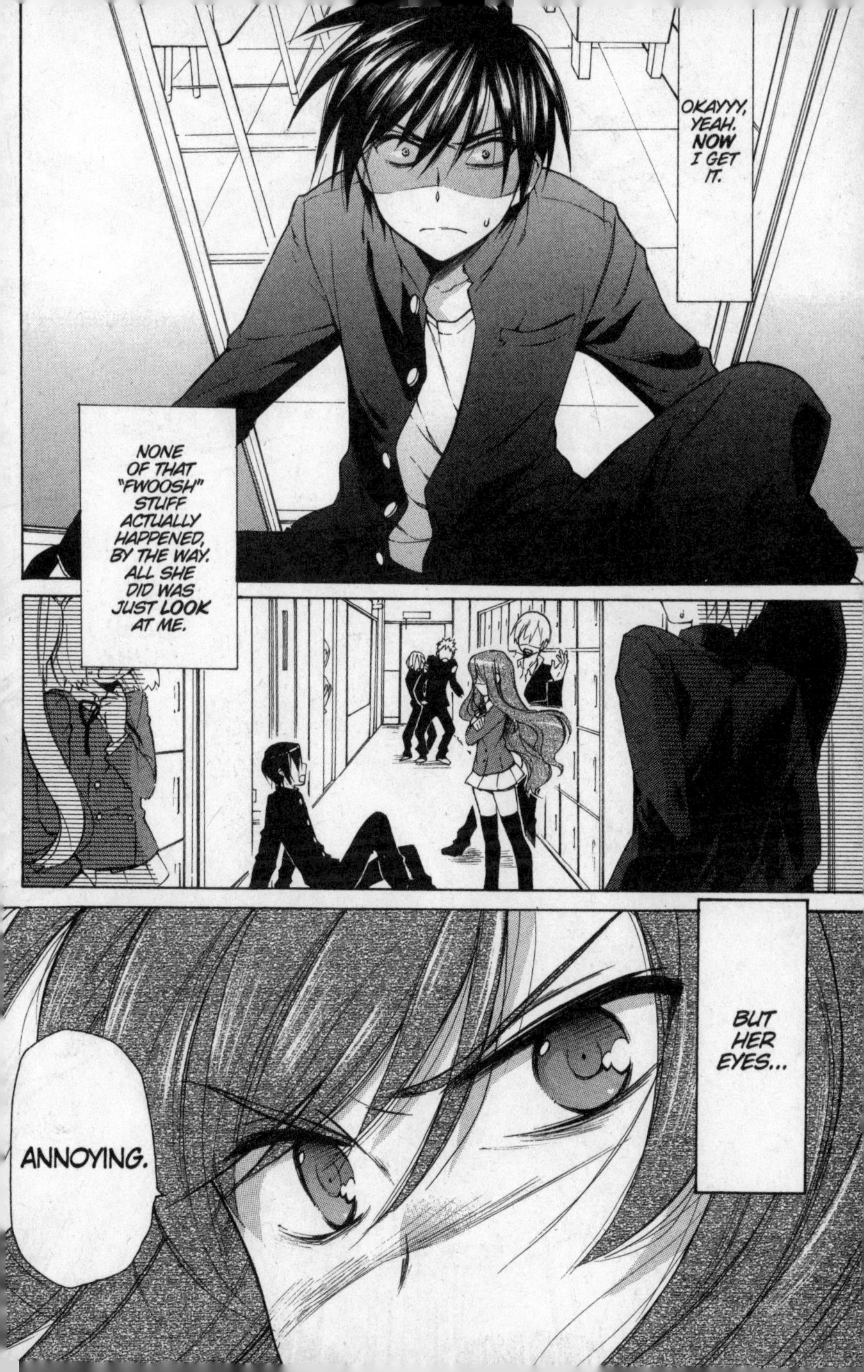
OKAYYY, YEAH. NOW I GET IT.
NONE OF THAT "FWOOSH" STUFF ACTUALLY HAPPENED, BY THE WAY. ALL SHE DID WAS JUST LOOK AT ME.
BUT HER EYES...
ANNOYING.

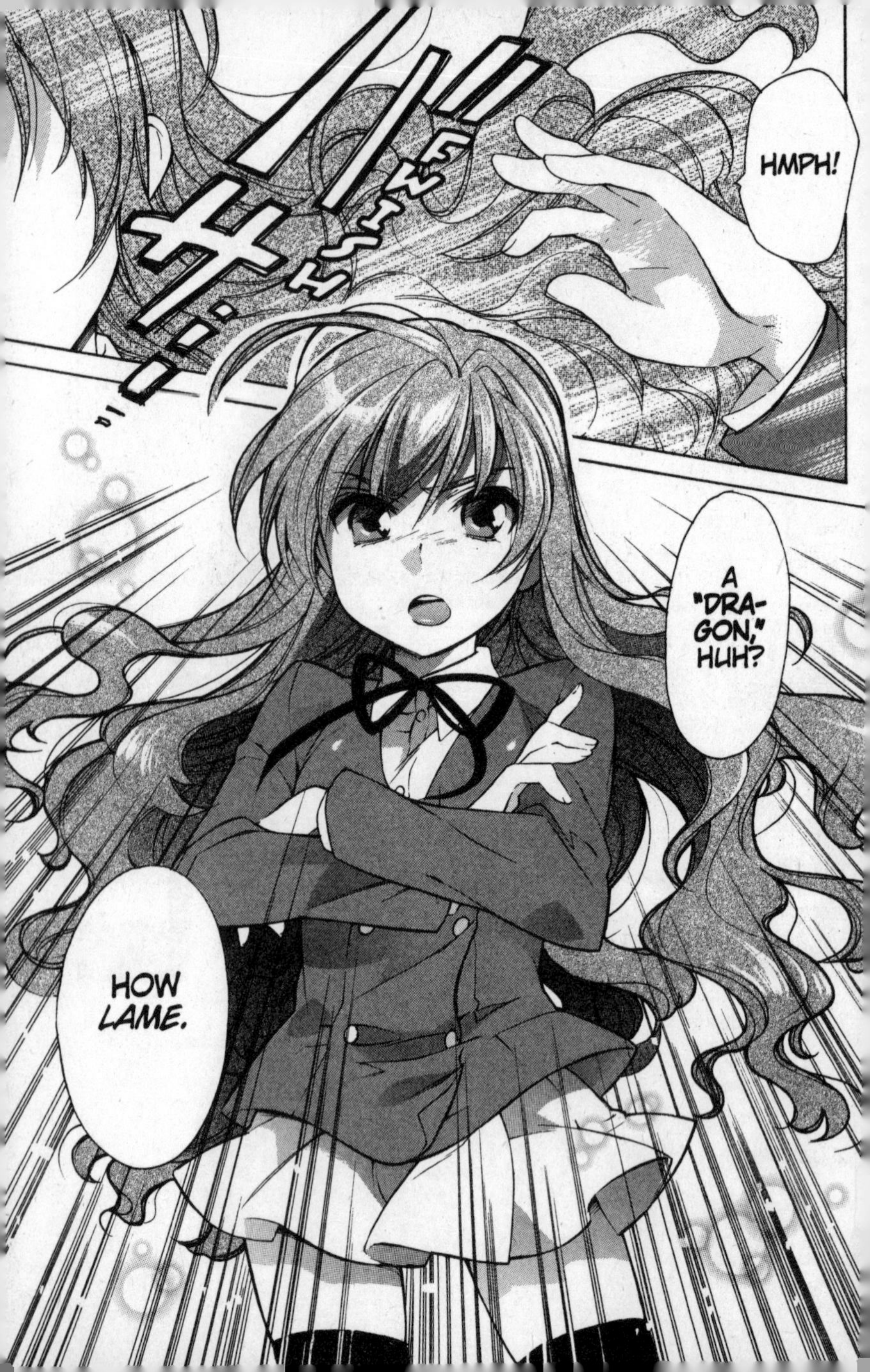
HMPH!
FWISH
A "DRA-GON," HUH?
HOW LAME.

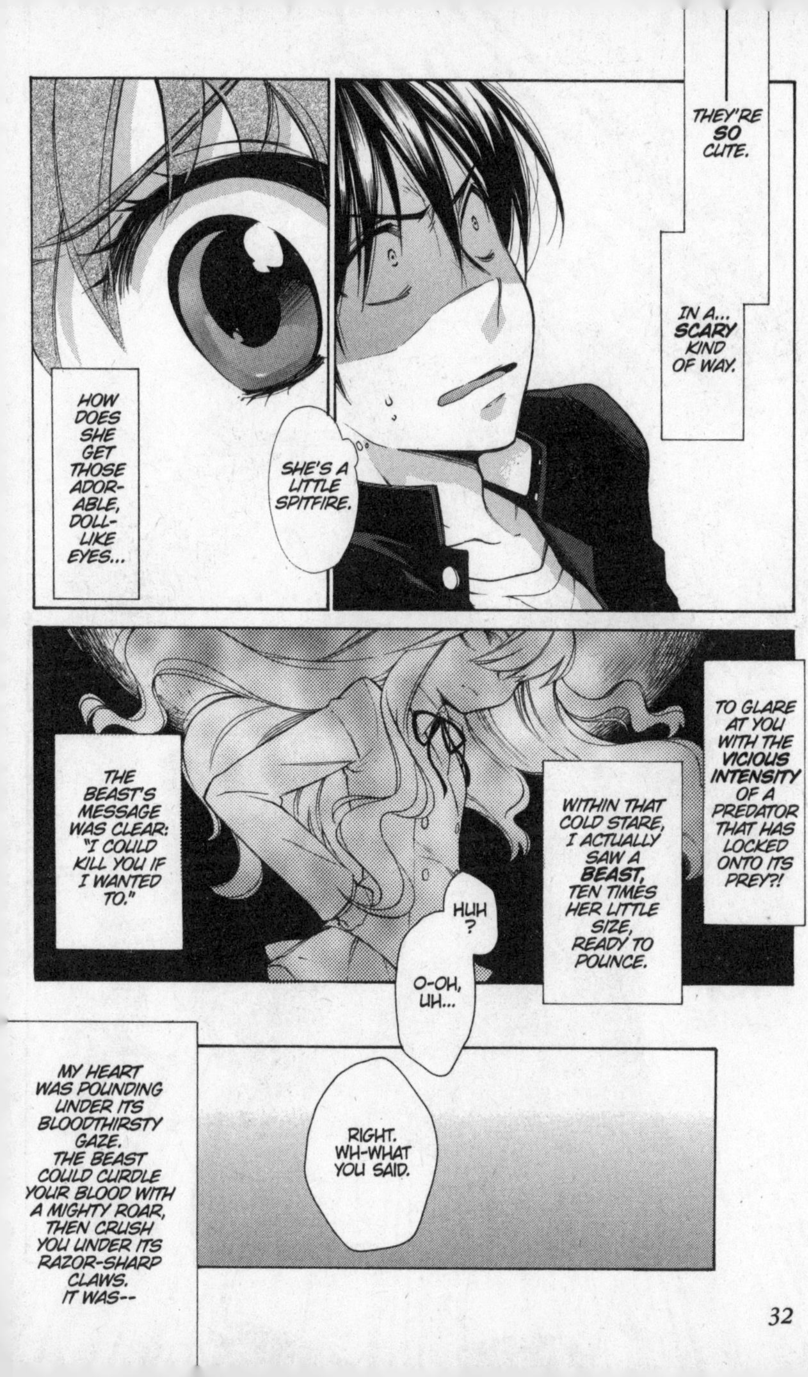
THEY'RE SO CUTE.
IN A... SCARY KIND OF WAY.
SHE'S A LITTLE SPITFIRE.
HOW DOES SHE GET THOSE ADORABLE, DOLL-LIKE EYES...
TO GLARE AT YOU WITH THE VICIOUS INTENSITY OF A PREDATOR THAT HAS LOCKED ONTO ITS PREY?!
WITHIN THAT COLD STARE, I ACTUALLY SAW A BEAST, TEN TIMES HER LITTLE SIZE, READY TO POUNCE.
HUH?
THE BEAST'S MESSAGE WAS CLEAR: "I COULD KILL YOU IF I WANTED TO."
O-OH, UH...
RIGHT. WH-WHAT YOU SAID.
MY HEART WAS POUNDING UNDER ITS BLOODTHIRSTY GAZE. THE BEAST COULD CURDLE YOUR BLOOD WITH A MIGHTY ROAR, THEN CRUSH YOU UNDER ITS RAZOR-SHARP CLAWS. IT WAS--

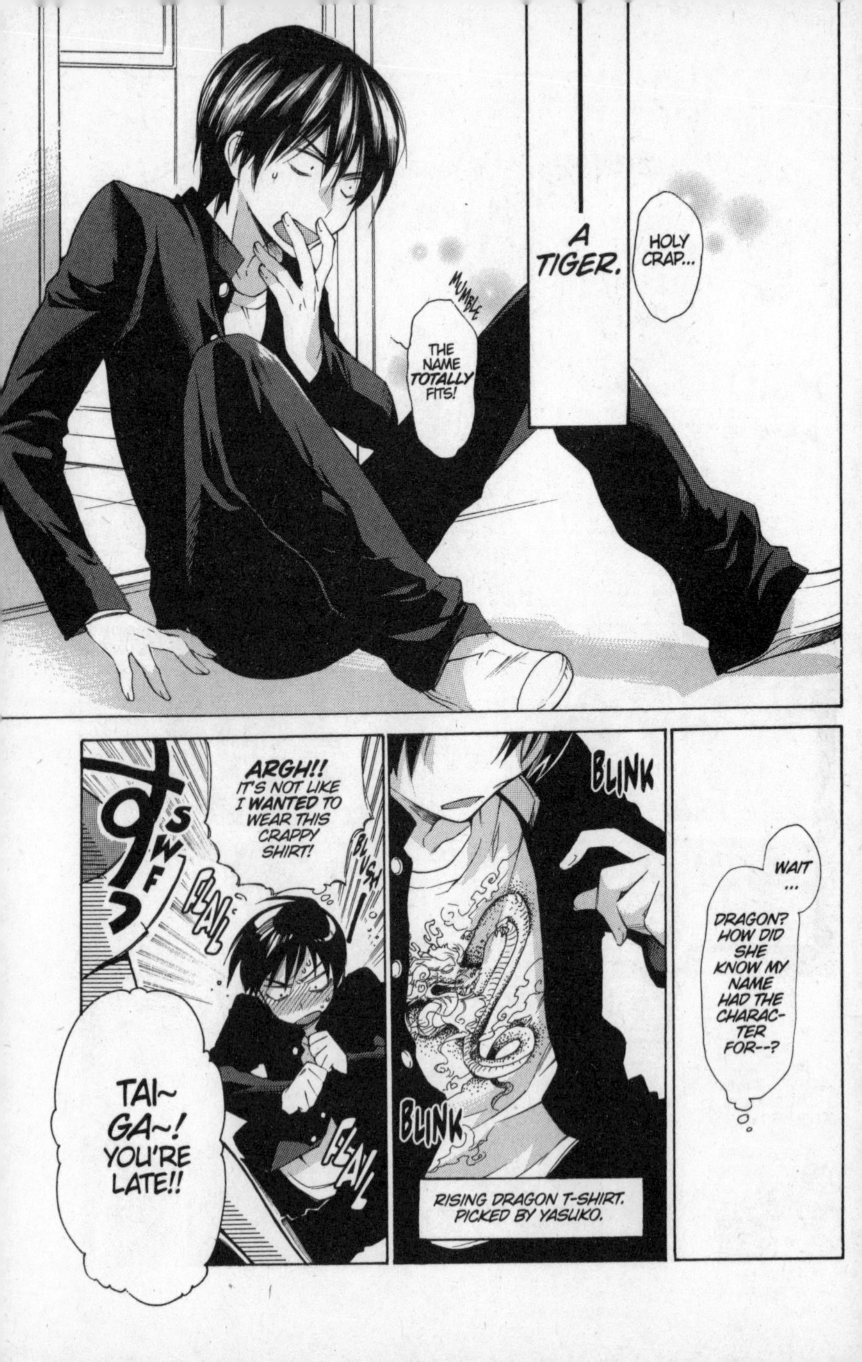
HOLY CRAP...
A TIGER.
MUMBLE
THE NAME TOTALLY FITS!
WAIT ... DRAGON? HOW DID SHE KNOW MY NAME HAD THE CHARACTER FOR--?
BLINK
BLINK
RISING DRAGON T-SHIRT. PICKED BY YASUKO.
ARGH!! IT'S NOT LIKE I WANTED TO WEAR THIS CRAPPY SHIRT!
BLUSH
SWF
FLAIL
FLAIL
TAI~GA~! YOU'RE LATE!!

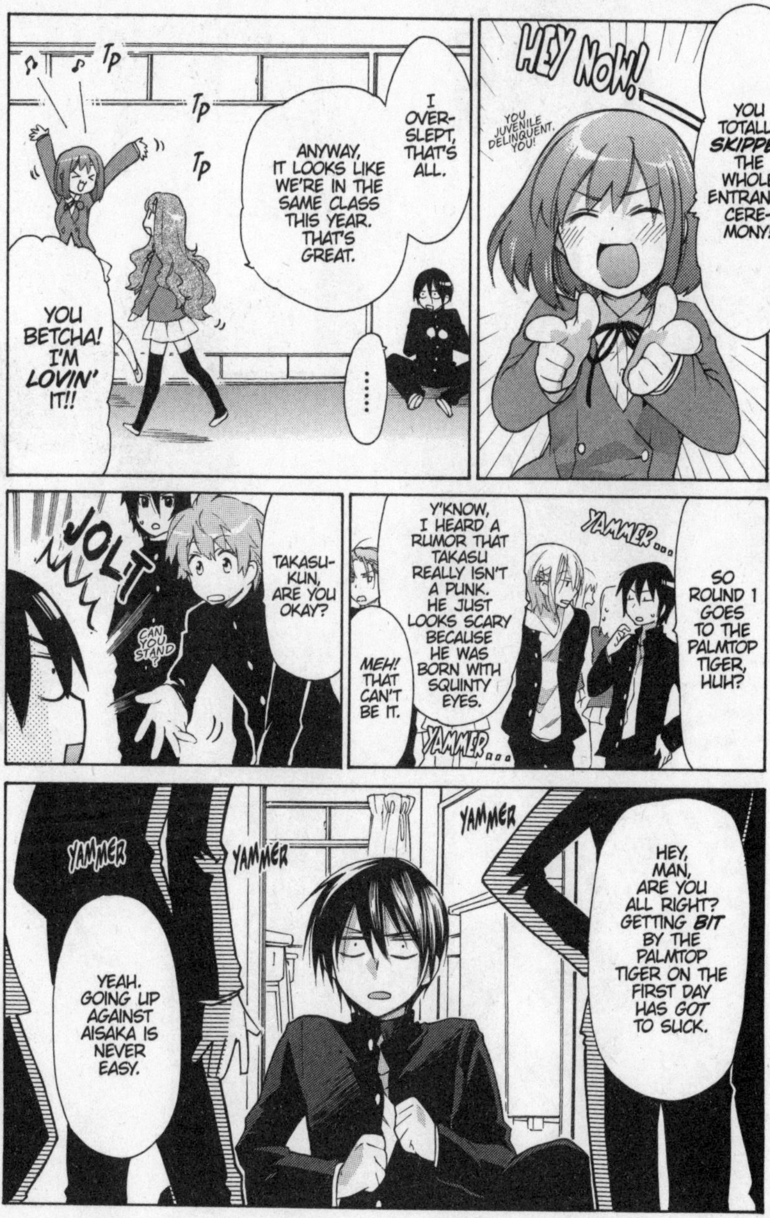
YOU TOTALLY SKIPPED THE WHOLE ENTRANCE CEREMONY!
HEY NOW!
YOU JUVENILE DELINQUENT, YOU!
I OVER-SLEPT, THAT'S ALL.
ANYWAY, IT LOOKS LIKE WE'RE IN THE SAME CLASS THIS YEAR. THAT'S GREAT.
TP
TP
TP
......
YOU BETCHA! I'M LOVIN' IT!!
SO ROUND 1 GOES TO THE PALMTOP TIGER, HUH?
YAMMER...
Y'KNOW, I HEARD A RUMOR THAT TAKASU REALLY ISN'T A PUNK. HE JUST LOOKS SCARY BECAUSE HE WAS BORN WITH SQUINTY EYES.
MEH! THAT CAN'T BE IT.
YAMMER...
TAKASU-KUN, ARE YOU OKAY?
JOLT
CAN YOU STAND?
HEY, MAN, ARE YOU ALL RIGHT? GETTING BIT BY THE PALMTOP TIGER ON THE FIRST DAY HAS GOT TO SUCK.
YAMMER
YAMMER
YAMMER
YEAH. GOING UP AGAINST AISAKA IS NEVER EASY.

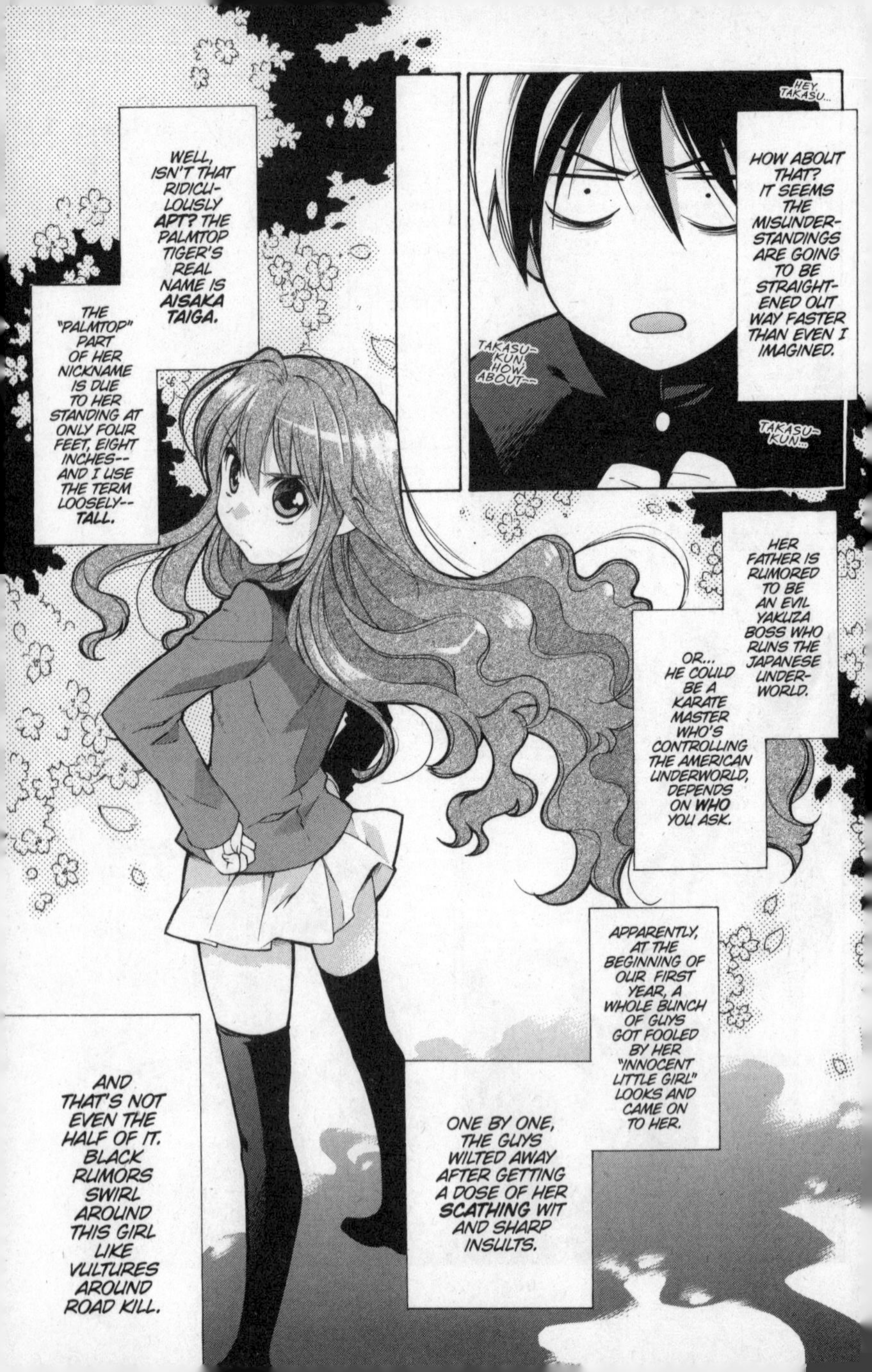
HEY, TAKASU...
HOW ABOUT THAT? IT SEEMS THE MISUNDER-STANDINGS ARE GOING TO BE STRAIGHT-ENED OUT WAY FASTER THAN EVEN I IMAGINED.
TAKASU-KUN, HOW ABOUT--
TAKASU-KUN...
WELL, ISN'T THAT RIDICU-LOUSLY APT? THE PALMTOP TIGER'S REAL NAME IS AISAKA TAIGA.
THE "PALMTOP" PART OF HER NICKNAME IS DUE TO HER STANDING AT ONLY FOUR FEET, EIGHT INCHES-- AND I USE THE TERM LOOSELY-- TALL.
HER FATHER IS RUMORED TO BE AN EVIL YAKUZA BOSS WHO RUNS THE JAPANESE UNDER-WORLD.
OR... HE COULD BE A KARATE MASTER WHO'S CONTROLLING THE AMERICAN UNDERWORLD, DEPENDS ON WHO YOU ASK.
APPARENTLY, AT THE BEGINNING OF OUR FIRST YEAR, A WHOLE BUNCH OF GUYS GOT FOOLED BY HER "INNOCENT LITTLE GIRL" LOOKS AND CAME ON TO HER.
ONE BY ONE, THE GUYS WILTED AWAY AFTER GETTING A DOSE OF HER SCATHING WIT AND SHARP INSULTS.
AND THAT'S NOT EVEN THE HALF OF IT. BLACK RUMORS SWIRL AROUND THIS GIRL LIKE VULTURES AROUND ROAD KILL.

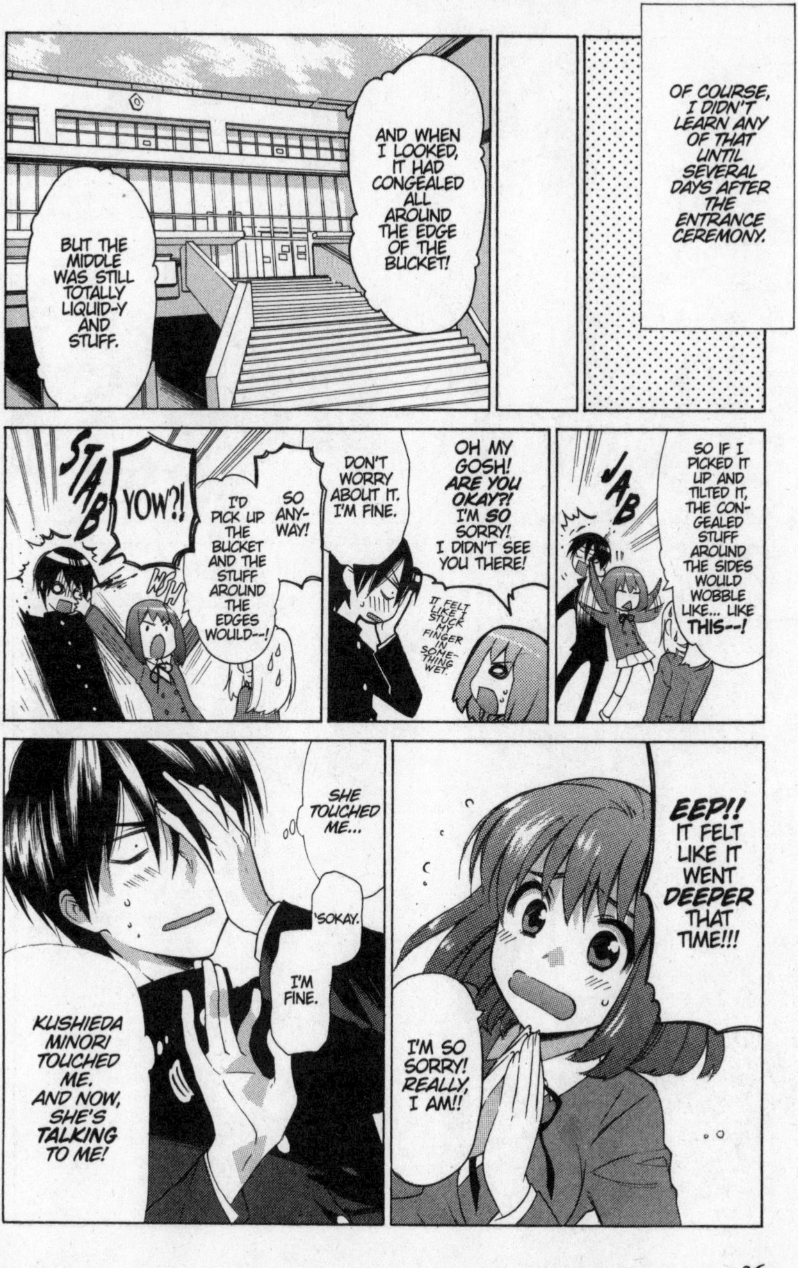
OF COURSE, I DIDN'T LEARN ANY OF THAT UNTIL SEVERAL DAYS AFTER THE ENTRANCE CEREMONY.
AND WHEN I LOOKED, IT HAD CONGEALED ALL AROUND THE EDGE OF THE BUCKET!
BUT THE MIDDLE WAS STILL TOTALLY LIQUID-Y AND STUFF.
SO IF I PICKED IT UP AND TILTED IT, THE CONGEALED STUFF AROUND THE SIDES WOULD WOBBLE LIKE... LIKE THIS--!
JAB
OH MY GOSH! ARE YOU OKAY?! I'M SO SORRY! I DIDN'T SEE YOU THERE!
DON'T WORRY ABOUT IT. I'M FINE.
IT FELT LIKE I STUCK MY FINGER IN SOMETHING WET.
SO ANYWAY!
I'D PICK UP THE BUCKET AND THE STUFF AROUND THE EDGES WOULD--!
YOW?!
STAB
WSH
EEP!! IT FELT LIKE IT WENT DEEPER THAT TIME!!!
I'M SO SORRY! REALLY, I AM!!
SHE TOUCHED ME...
'SOKAY.
I'M FINE.
KUSHIEDA MINORI TOUCHED ME. AND NOW, SHE'S TALKING TO ME!

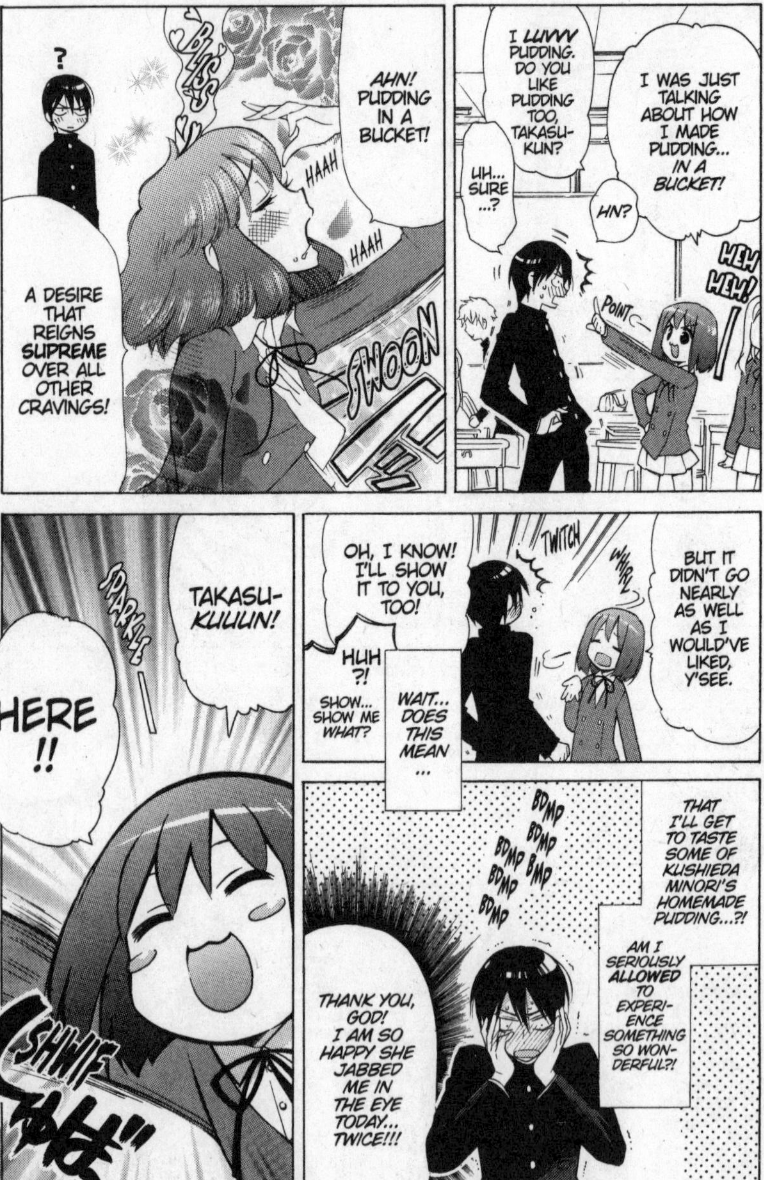
I WAS JUST TALKING ABOUT HOW I MADE PUDDING... IN A BUCKET!
HEH HEH!
POINT
HN?
I LUVVV PUDDING. DO YOU LIKE PUDDING TOO, TAKASU-KUN?
UH... SURE ...?
AHN! PUDDING IN A BUCKET!
BLISS
?
HAAH
HAAH
SWOON
A DESIRE THAT REIGNS SUPREME OVER ALL OTHER CRAVINGS!
BUT IT DIDN'T GO NEARLY AS WELL AS I WOULD'VE LIKED, Y'SEE.
WHIRL
TWITCH
OH, I KNOW! I'LL SHOW IT TO YOU, TOO!
HUH ?!
SHOW... SHOW ME WHAT?
WAIT... DOES THIS MEAN ...
THAT I'LL GET TO TASTE SOME OF KUSHIEDA MINORI'S HOMEMADE PUDDING...?!
AM I SERIOUSLY ALLOWED TO EXPERIENCE SOMETHING SO WONDERFUL?!
BDMP BDMP BDMP BMP BDMP BDMP
THANK YOU, GOD! I AM SO HAPPY SHE JABBED ME IN THE EYE TODAY... TWICE!!!
TAKASU-KUUUN!
SPARKLE
HERE !!
SHWIF

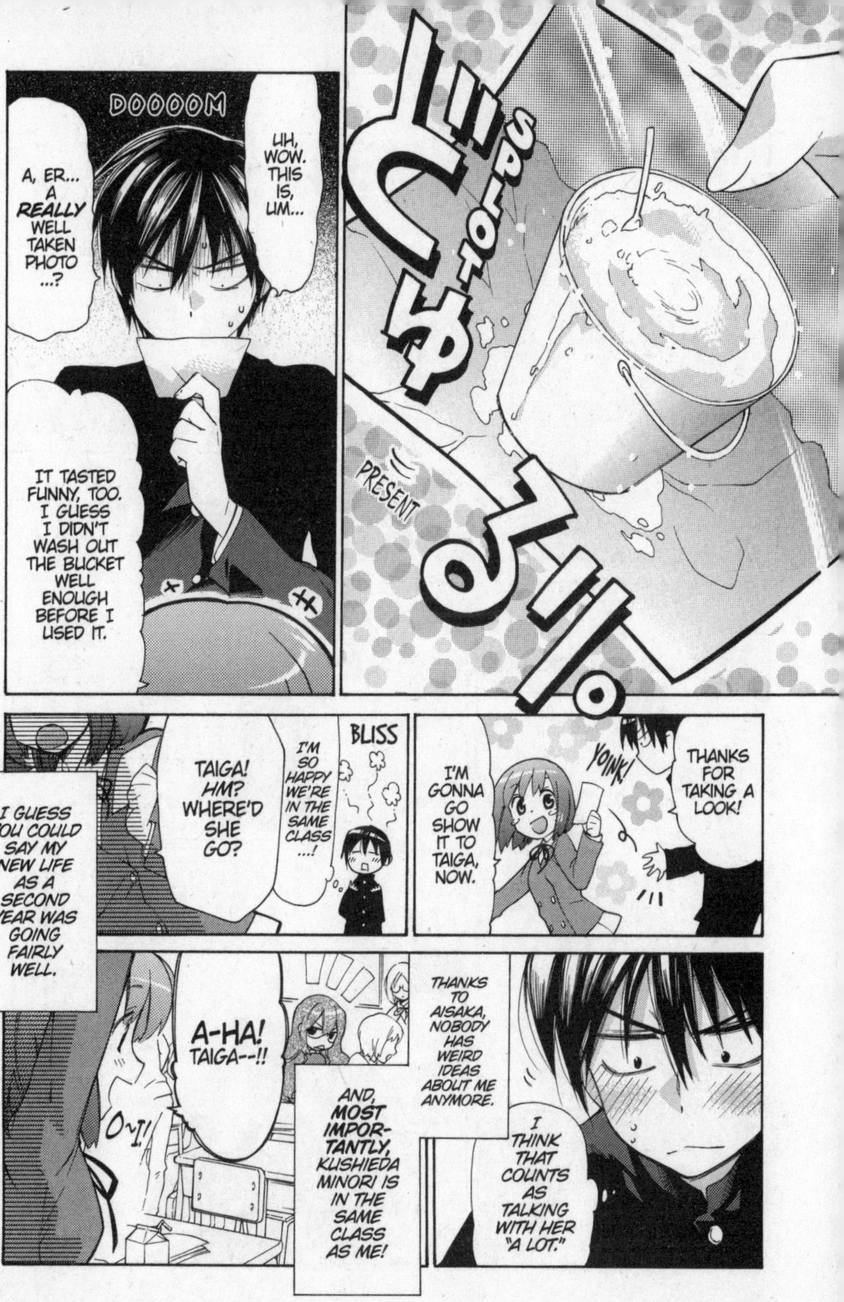
SPLOT
PRESENT
UH, WOW. THIS IS, UM...
DOOOOM
A, ER... A **REALLY** WELL TAKEN PHOTO ...?
IT TASTED FUNNY, TOO. I GUESS I DIDN'T WASH OUT THE BUCKET WELL ENOUGH BEFORE I USED IT.
THANKS FOR TAKING A LOOK!
YOINK!
I'M GONNA GO SHOW IT TO TAIGA, NOW.
BLISS
I'M SO HAPPY WE'RE IN THE SAME CLASS ...!
TAIGA! *HM?* WHERE'D SHE GO?
I GUESS YOU COULD SAY MY NEW LIFE AS A SECOND YEAR WAS GOING FAIRLY WELL.
THANKS TO AISAKA, NOBODY HAS WEIRD IDEAS ABOUT ME ANYMORE.
I THINK THAT COUNTS AS TALKING WITH HER "A LOT."
AND, **MOST IMPORTANTLY**, KUSHIEDA MINORI IS IN THE SAME CLASS AS ME!
A-HA! TAIGA--!!
O~I!

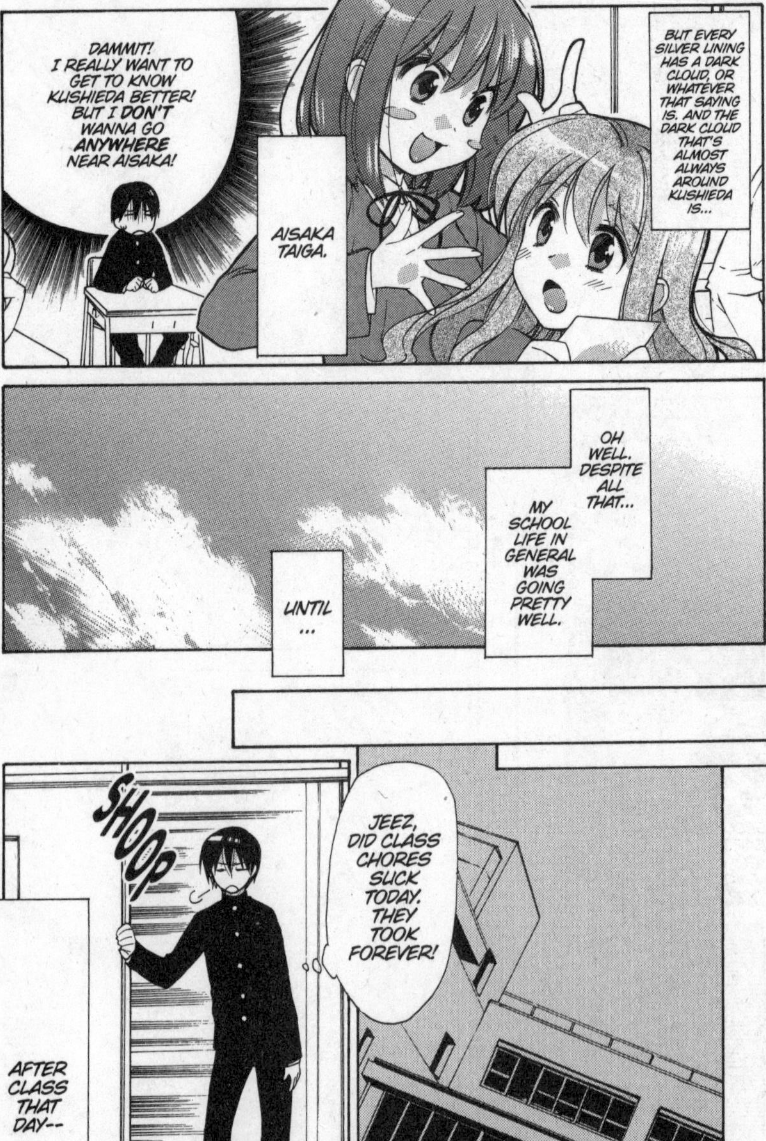
BUT EVERY SILVER LINING HAS A DARK CLOUD, OR WHATEVER THAT SAYING IS. AND THE DARK CLOUD THAT'S ALMOST ALWAYS AROUND KUSHIEDA IS...
AISAKA TAIGA.
DAMMIT! I REALLY WANT TO GET TO KNOW KUSHIEDA BETTER! BUT I DON'T WANNA GO ANYWHERE NEAR AISAKA!
OH WELL. DESPITE ALL THAT...
MY SCHOOL LIFE IN GENERAL WAS GOING PRETTY WELL.
UNTIL ...
JEEZ, DID CLASS CHORES SUCK TODAY. THEY TOOK FOREVER!
SHOOP
AFTER CLASS THAT DAY--

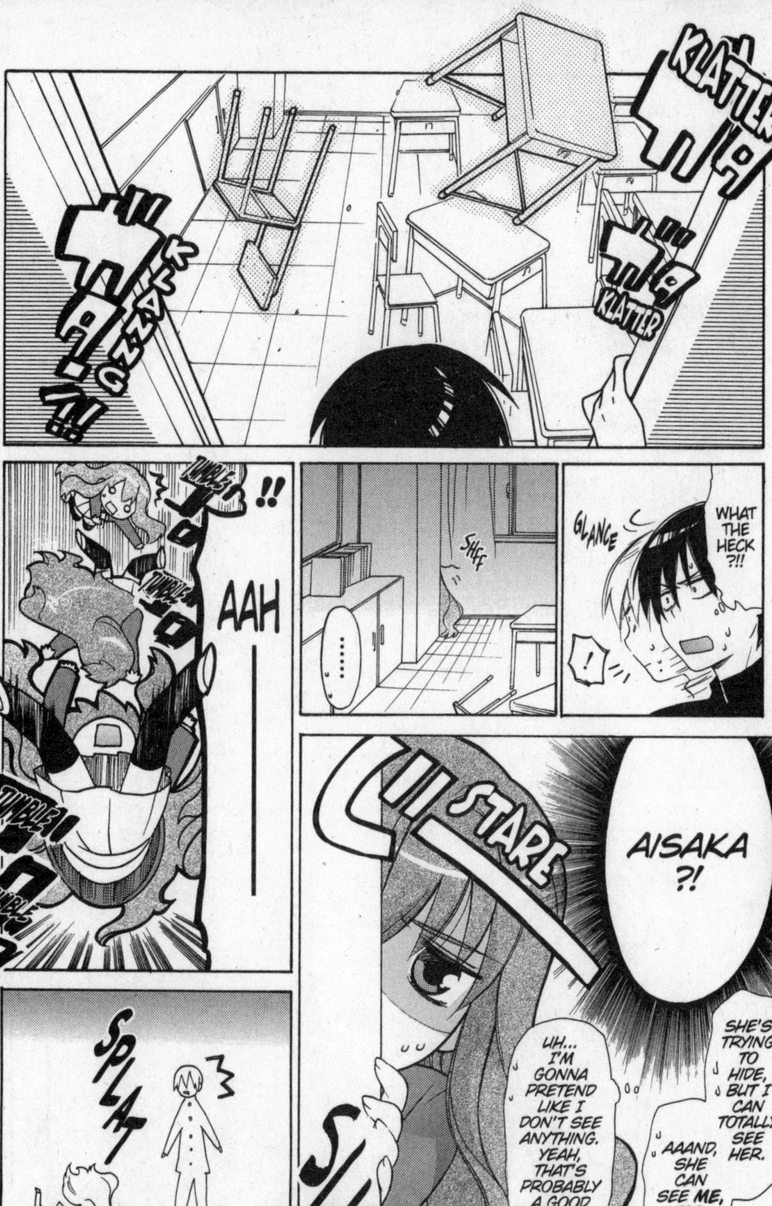
KLATTER
KLATTER
KLANG!!
GLANCE
WHAT THE HECK?!!
!
SHFF
......
TUMBLE
!!
TUMBLE
AAH
TUMBLE
TUMBLE
AISAKA?!
STARE
SHE'S TRYING TO HIDE, BUT I CAN TOTALLY SEE HER.
AAAND, SHE CAN SEE ME, TOO.
UH... I'M GONNA PRETEND LIKE I DON'T SEE ANYTHING. YEAH, THAT'S PROBABLY A GOOD IDEA.
SLIP
SPLAT

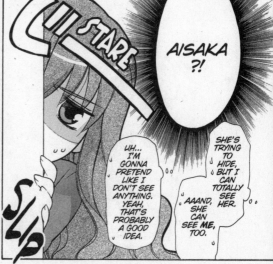

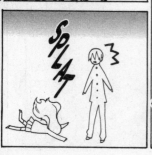

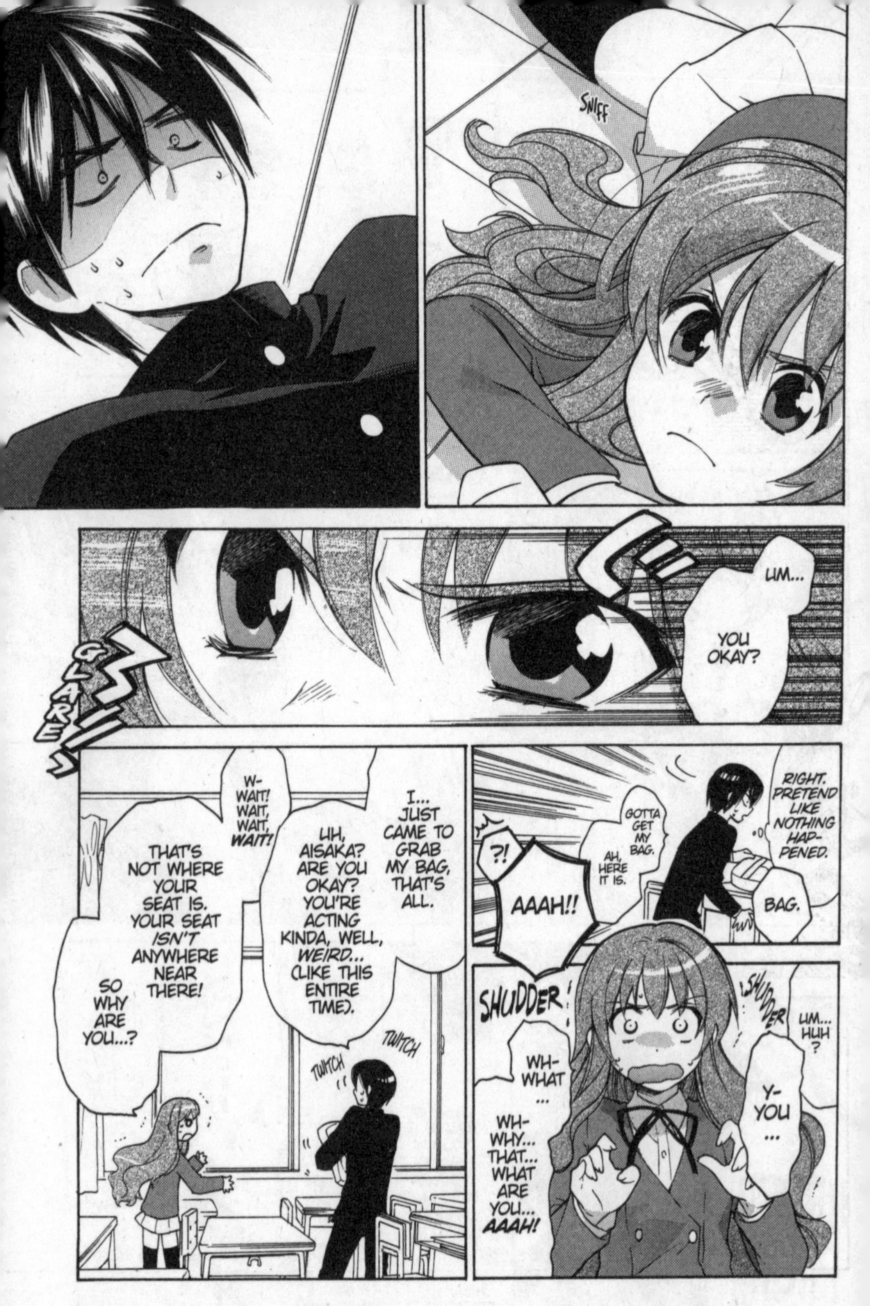
SNIFF
UM...
YOU OKAY?
GLARE!!
RIGHT. PRETEND LIKE NOTHING HAP-PENED.
GOTTA GET MY BAG.
AH, HERE IT IS.
BAG.
?!
AAAH!!
UM... HUH?
SHUDDER
Y-YOU...
WH-WHAT...
WH-WHY... THAT... WHAT ARE YOU... *AAAH!*
SHUDDER
I... JUST CAME TO GRAB MY BAG, THAT'S ALL.
W-WAIT! WAIT, WAIT, *WAIT!*
UH, AISAKA? ARE YOU OKAY? YOU'RE ACTING KINDA, WELL, *WEIRD*... (LIKE THIS ENTIRE TIME).
THAT'S NOT WHERE YOUR SEAT IS. YOUR SEAT *ISN'T* ANYWHERE NEAR THERE!
SO WHY ARE YOU...?
TWITCH
TWITCH

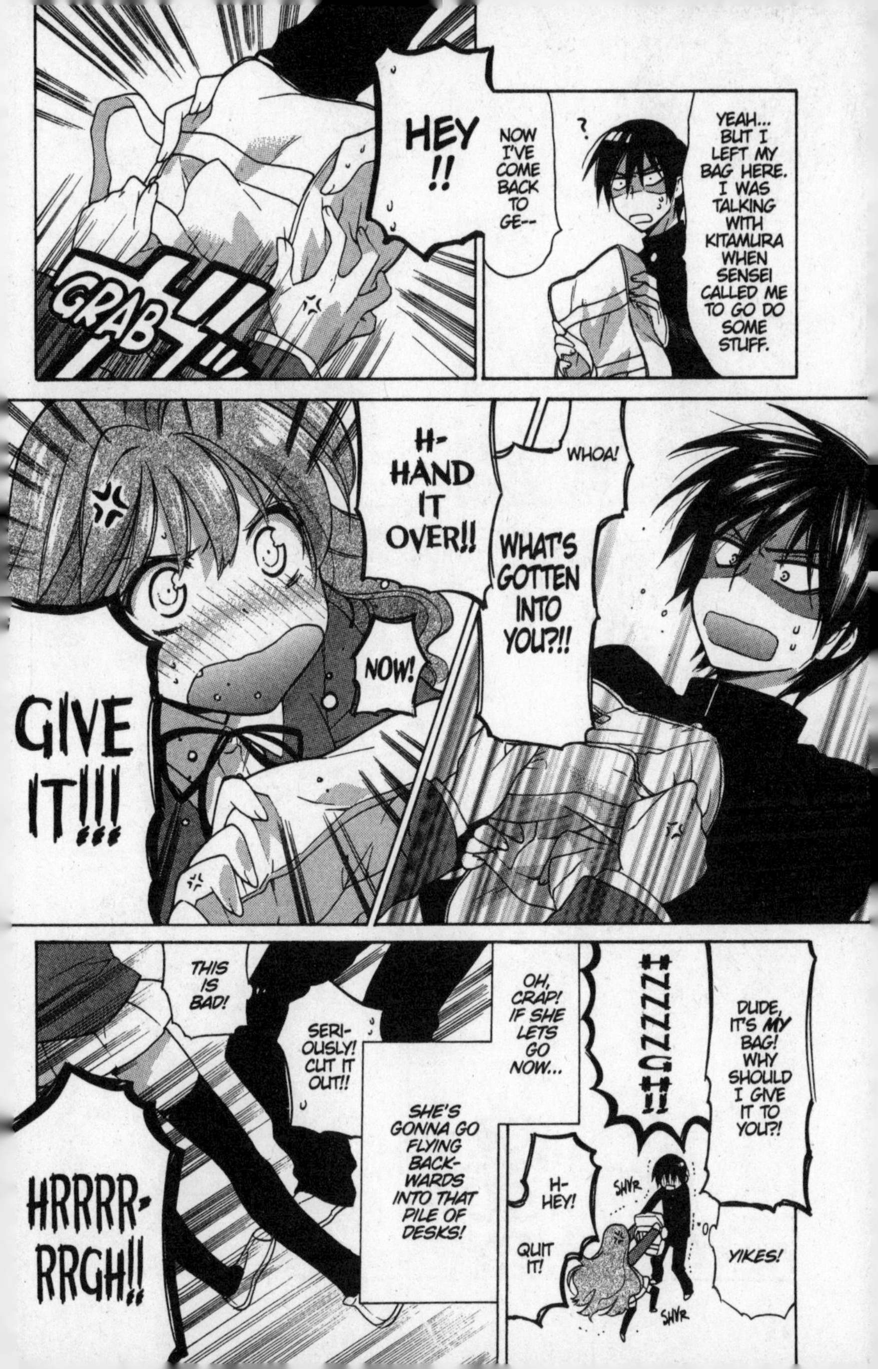
?
YEAH... BUT I LEFT MY BAG HERE. I WAS TALKING WITH KITAMURA WHEN SENSEI CALLED ME TO GO DO SOME STUFF.
NOW I'VE COME BACK TO GE--
HEY!!
GRAB!!
WHOA!
WHAT'S GOTTEN INTO YOU?!!
H-HAND IT OVER!!
NOW!
GIVE IT!!!
DUDE, IT'S MY BAG! WHY SHOULD I GIVE IT TO YOU?!
HNNNNGH!!
OH, CRAP! IF SHE LETS GO NOW...
YIKES!
SHVR
H-HEY!
QUIT IT!
SHVR
SHE'S GONNA GO FLYING BACKWARDS INTO THAT PILE OF DESKS!
SERIOUSLY! CUT IT OUT!!
THIS IS BAD!
HRRRR-RRGH!!

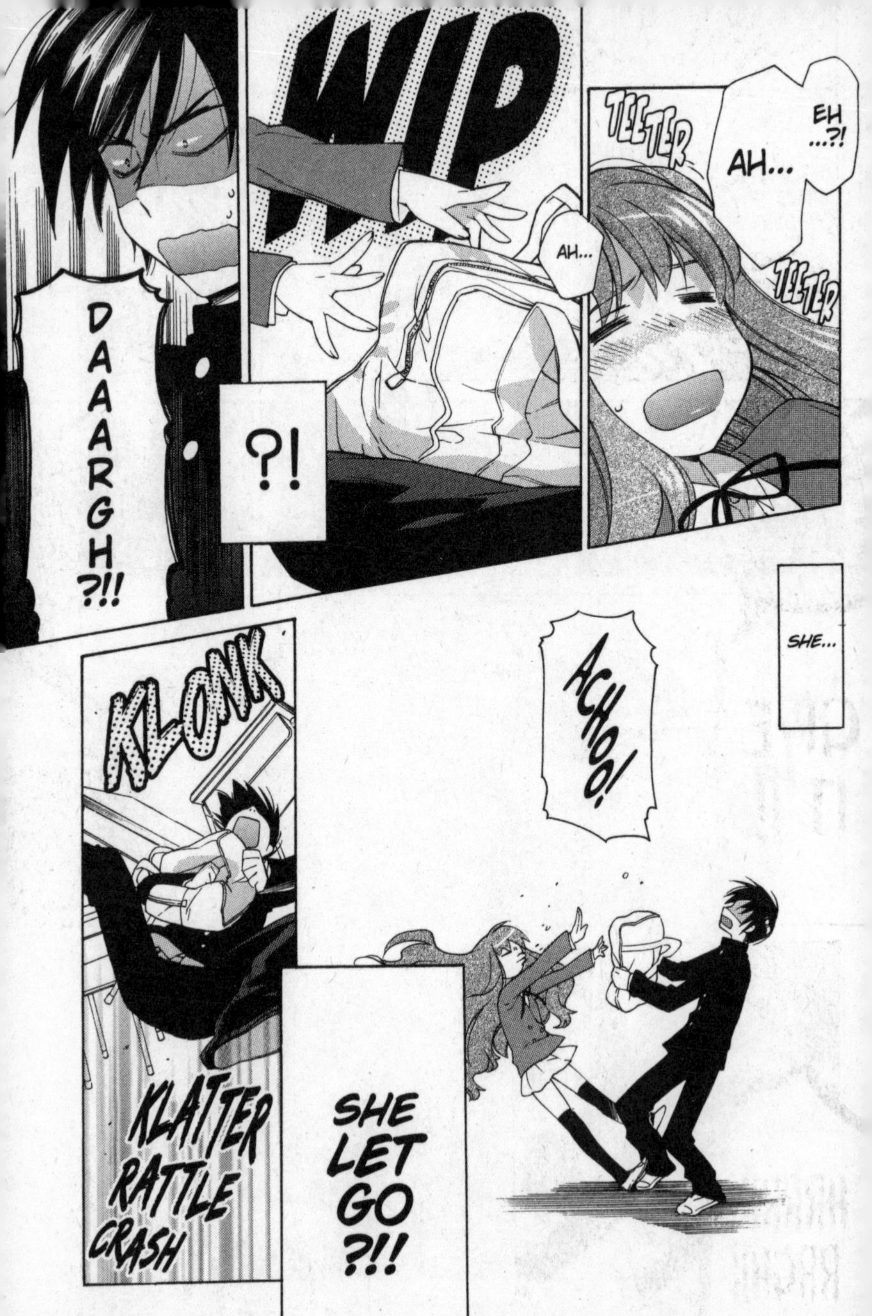
TEETER
EH ...?!
AH...
AH...
TEETER
WIP
?!
DAAAARGH ?!!
SHE...
ACHOO!
SHE LET GO ?!!
KLONK
KLATTER
RATTLE
CRASH

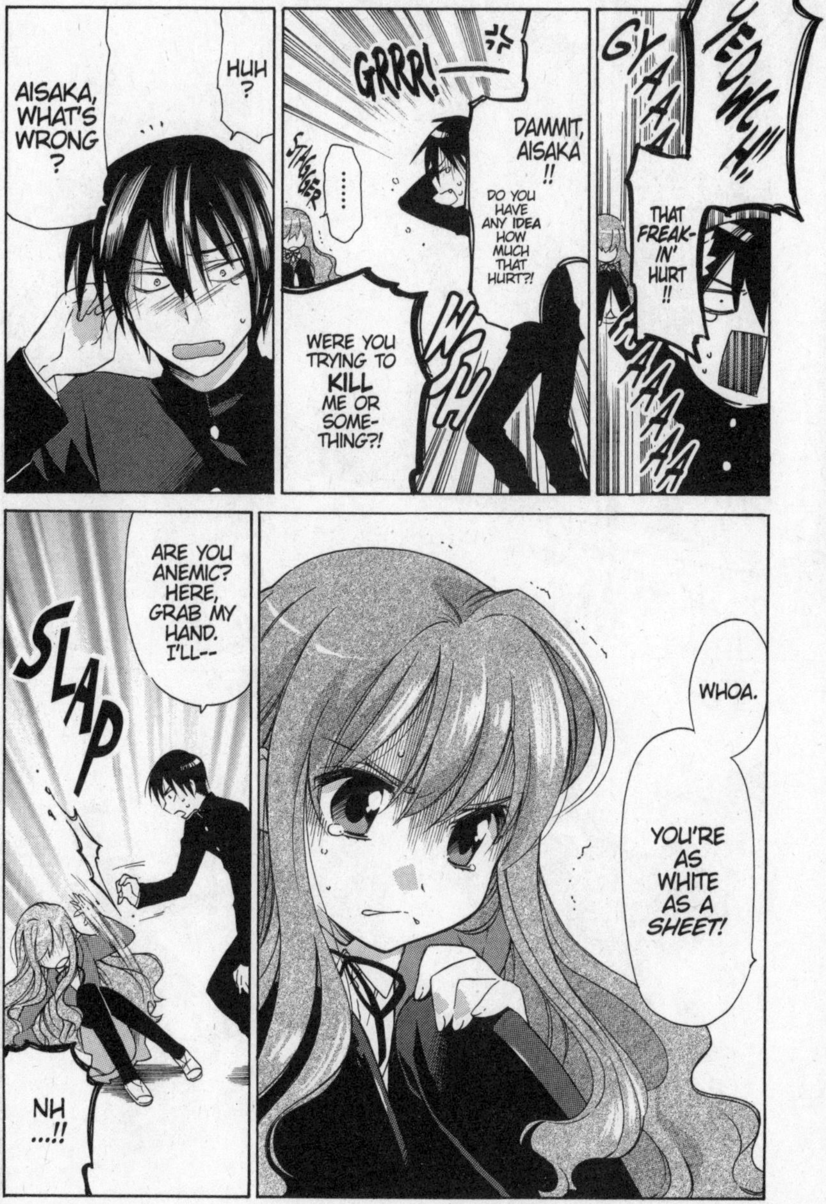
YEOWCH!!
GYAAAA
THAT FREAK-IN' HURT!!
GRRR!
DAMMIT, AISAKA!!
DO YOU HAVE ANY IDEA HOW MUCH THAT HURT?!
STAGGER
......
WERE YOU TRYING TO KILL ME OR SOMETHING?!
HUH?
AISAKA, WHAT'S WRONG?
WHOA.
YOU'RE AS WHITE AS A SHEET!
ARE YOU ANEMIC? HERE, GRAB MY HAND. I'LL--
SLAP
NH...!!

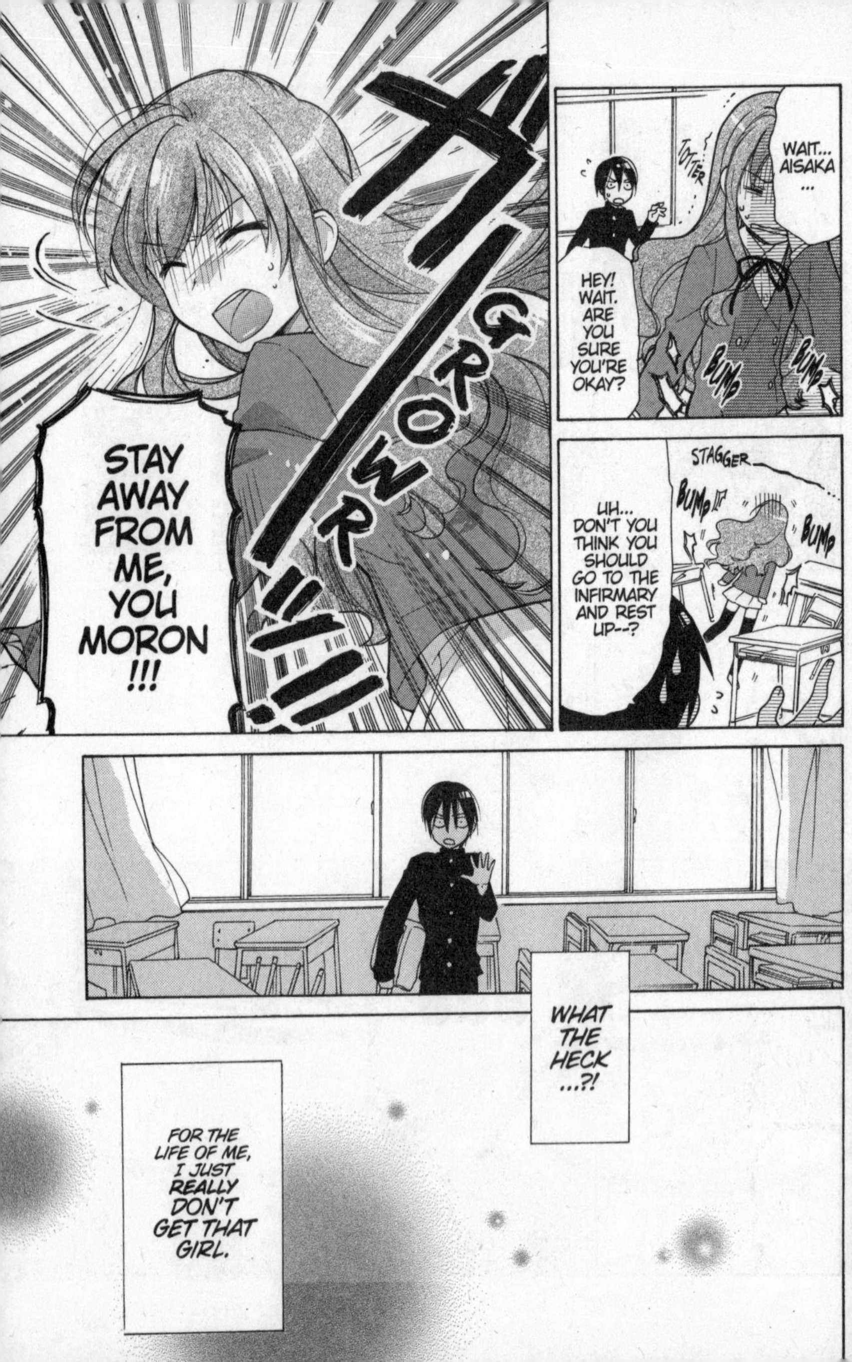
WAIT... AISAKA ...
TOTTER
HEY! WAIT. ARE YOU SURE YOU'RE OKAY?
BUMP
BUMP
STAGGER
BUMP
BUMP
UH... DON'T YOU THINK YOU SHOULD GO TO THE INFIRMARY AND REST UP--?
GROWR!!!
STAY AWAY FROM ME, YOU MORON!!!
WHAT THE HECK ...?!
FOR THE LIFE OF ME, I JUST REALLY DON'T GET THAT GIRL.

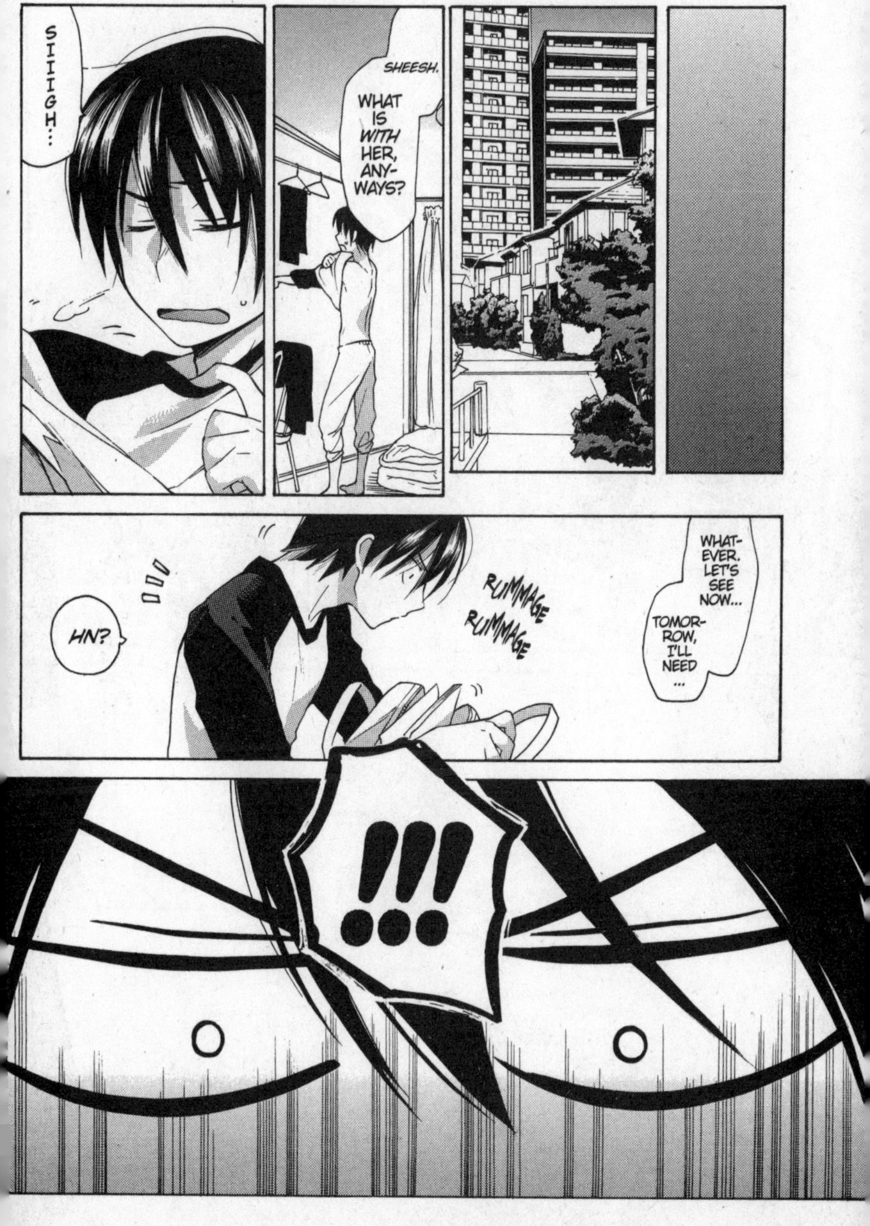
SHEESH.
WHAT IS WITH HER, ANYWAYS?
SIIIGH...
WHATEVER. LET'S SEE NOW...
TOMORROW, I'LL NEED ...
RUMMAGE RUMMAGE
HN?
!!!...

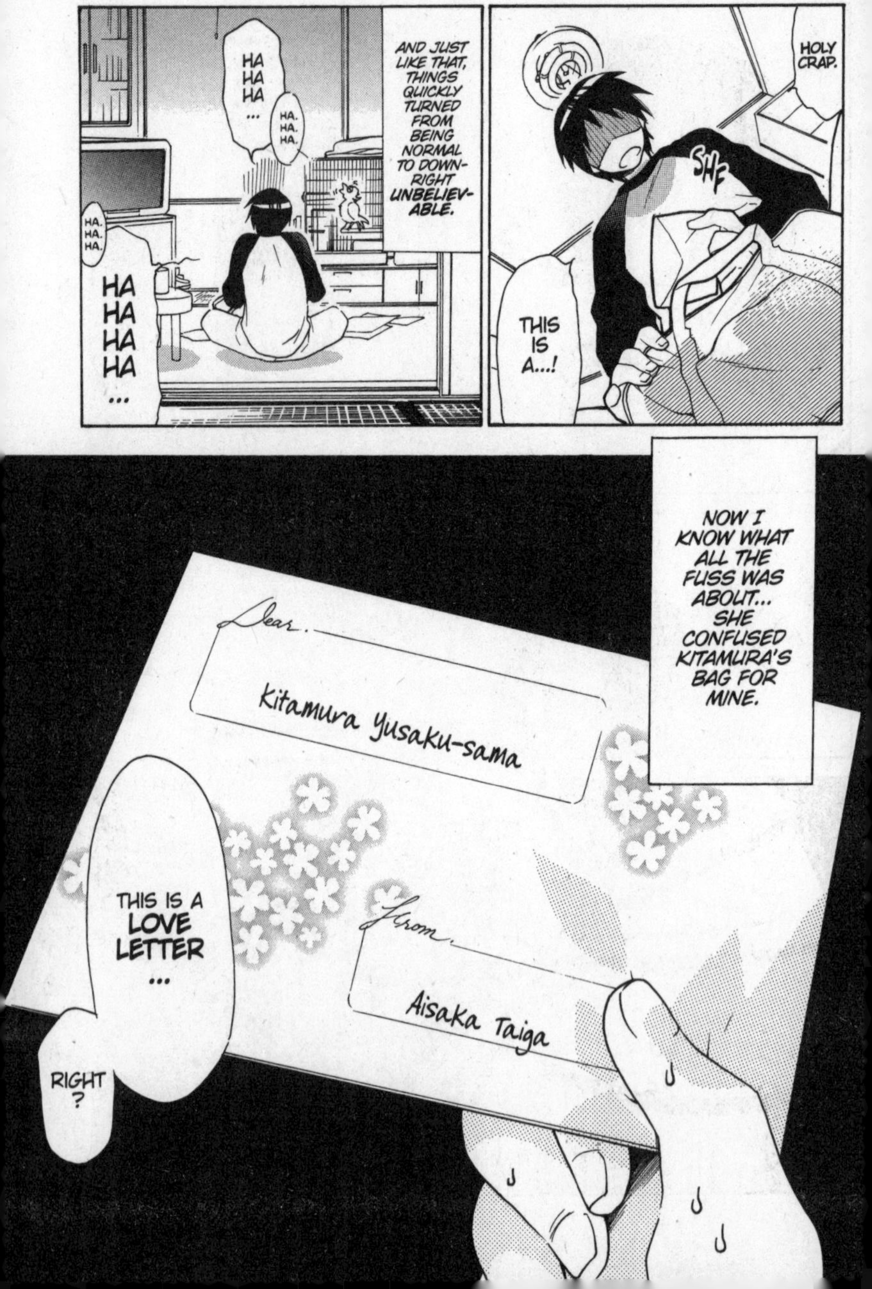
HOLY CRAP.
SHF
THIS IS A...!
AND JUST LIKE THAT, THINGS QUICKLY TURNED FROM BEING NORMAL TO DOWN-RIGHT UNBELIEVABLE.
HA HA HA ...
HA. HA. HA.
HA. HA. HA.
HA HA HA HA ...
NOW I KNOW WHAT ALL THE FUSS WAS ABOUT... SHE CONFUSED KITAMURA'S BAG FOR MINE.
Dear.
Kitamura Yusaku-sama
From.
Aisaka Taiga
THIS IS A LOVE LETTER ...
RIGHT ?

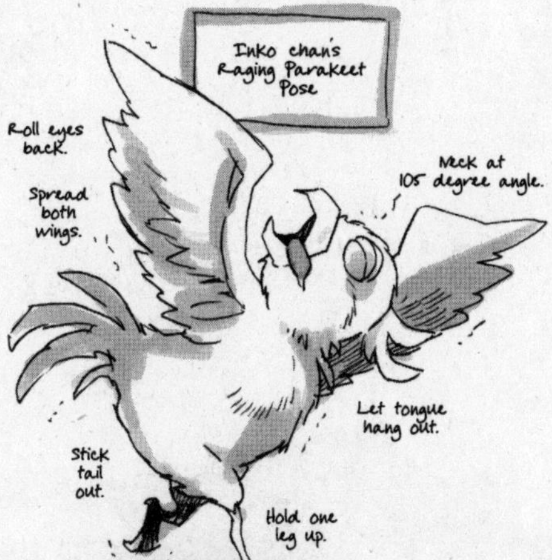
Inko chan's Raging Parakeet Pose
Roll eyes back.
Neck at 105 degree angle.
Spread both wings.
Let tongue hang out.
Stick tail out.
Hold one leg up.

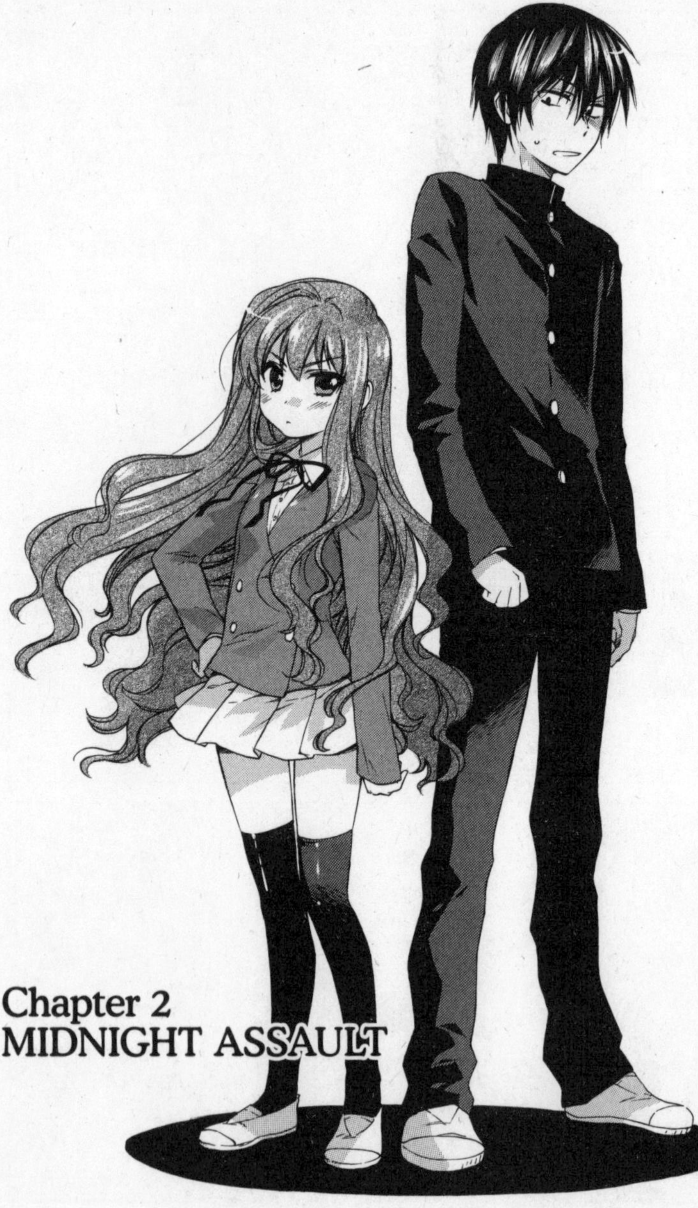

Chapter 2
MIDNIGHT ASSAULT

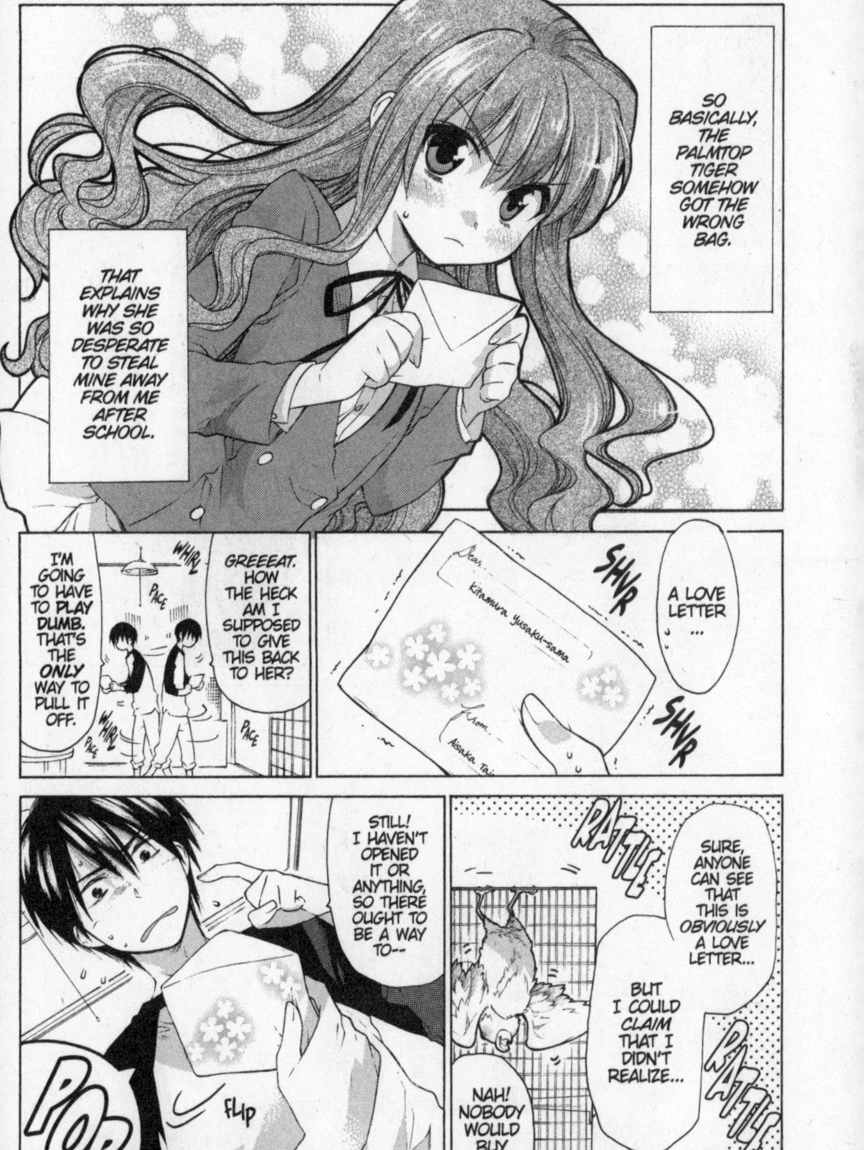
SO BASICALLY, THE PALMTOP TIGER SOMEHOW GOT THE WRONG BAG.
THAT EXPLAINS WHY SHE WAS SO DESPERATE TO STEAL MINE AWAY FROM ME AFTER SCHOOL.
SHVR
A LOVE LETTER ...
SHVR
Dear,
Kitamura Yusaku-sama
From.
Aisaka
GREEEAT. HOW THE HECK AM I SUPPOSED TO GIVE THIS BACK TO HER?
WHIRL
PACE
I'M GOING TO HAVE TO PLAY DUMB. THAT'S THE ONLY WAY TO PULL IT OFF.
WHIRL
PACE
PACE
RATTLE
SURE, ANYONE CAN SEE THAT THIS IS OBVIOUSLY A LOVE LETTER...
BUT I COULD CLAIM THAT I DIDN'T REALIZE...
NAH! NOBODY WOULD BUY THAT.
RATTLE
STILL! I HAVEN'T OPENED IT OR ANYTHING, SO THERE OUGHT TO BE A WAY TO--
FLIP
POP

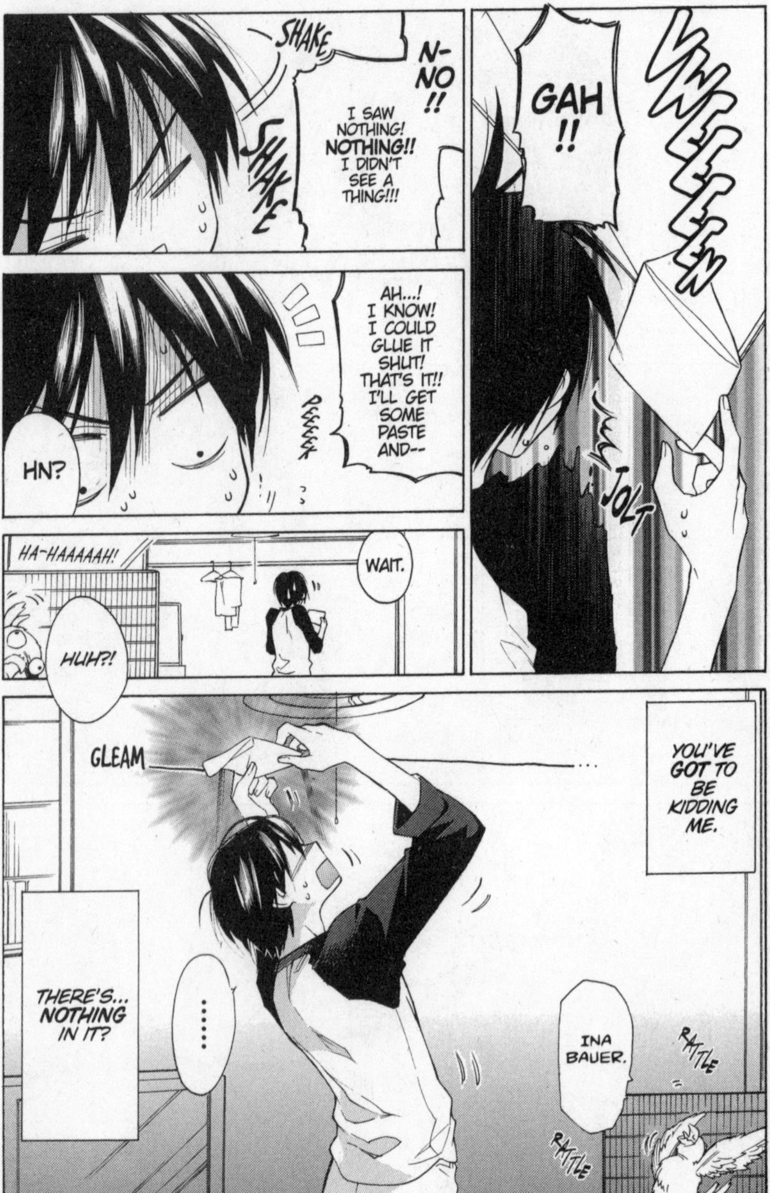
VWEEEEN
GAH!!
JOLT
SHAKE
SHAKE
N-NO!!
I SAW NOTHING! NOTHING!! I DIDN'T SEE A THING!!!
AH...! I KNOW! I COULD GLUE IT SHUT! THAT'S IT!! I'LL GET SOME PASTE AND--
PEEEEK
HN?
WAIT.
HA-HAAAAAH!
HUH?!
YOU'VE GOT TO BE KIDDING ME.
GLEAM
INA BAUER.
RATTLE
RATTLE
......
THERE'S... NOTHING IN IT?

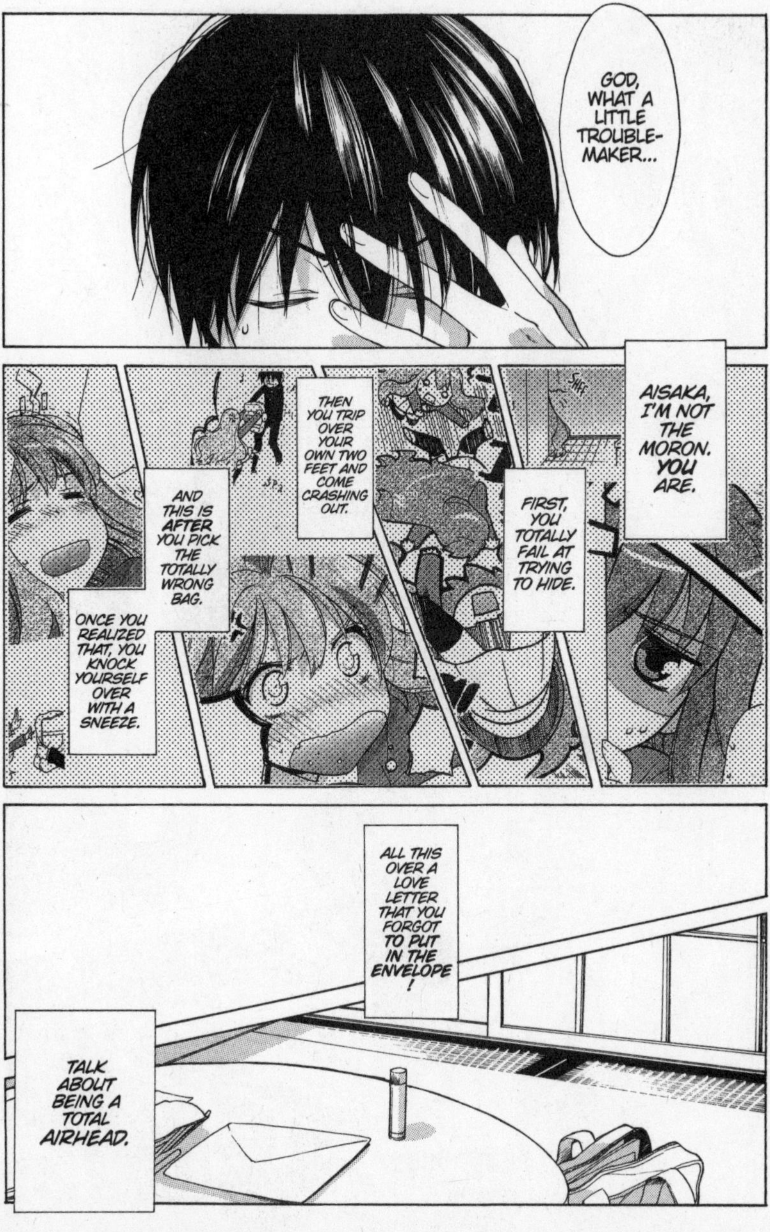
GOD, WHAT A LITTLE TROUBLE-MAKER...
AISAKA, I'M NOT THE MORON. YOU ARE.
FIRST, YOU TOTALLY FAIL AT TRYING TO HIDE.
THEN YOU TRIP OVER YOUR OWN TWO FEET AND COME CRASHING OUT.
AND THIS IS AFTER YOU PICK THE TOTALLY WRONG BAG.
ONCE YOU REALIZED THAT, YOU KNOCK YOURSELF OVER WITH A SNEEZE.
ALL THIS OVER A LOVE LETTER THAT YOU FORGOT TO PUT IN THE ENVELOPE!
TALK ABOUT BEING A TOTAL AIRHEAD.

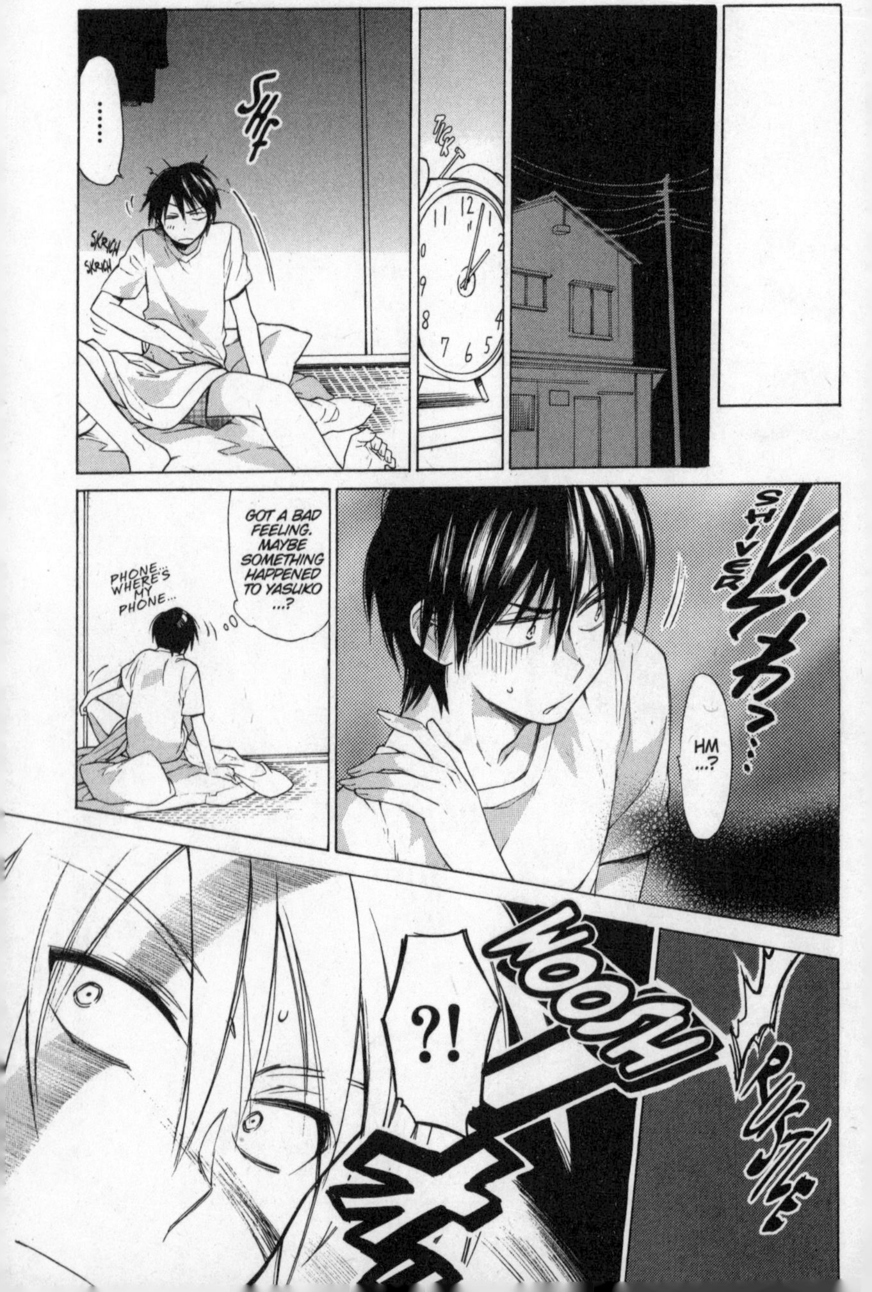
TICK
SHF
......
SKRICH SKRICH
SHIVER
HM ...?
GOT A BAD FEELING. MAYBE SOMETHING HAPPENED TO YASUKO ...?
PHONE... WHERE'S MY PHONE...
RUSTLE
WOOSH
?!

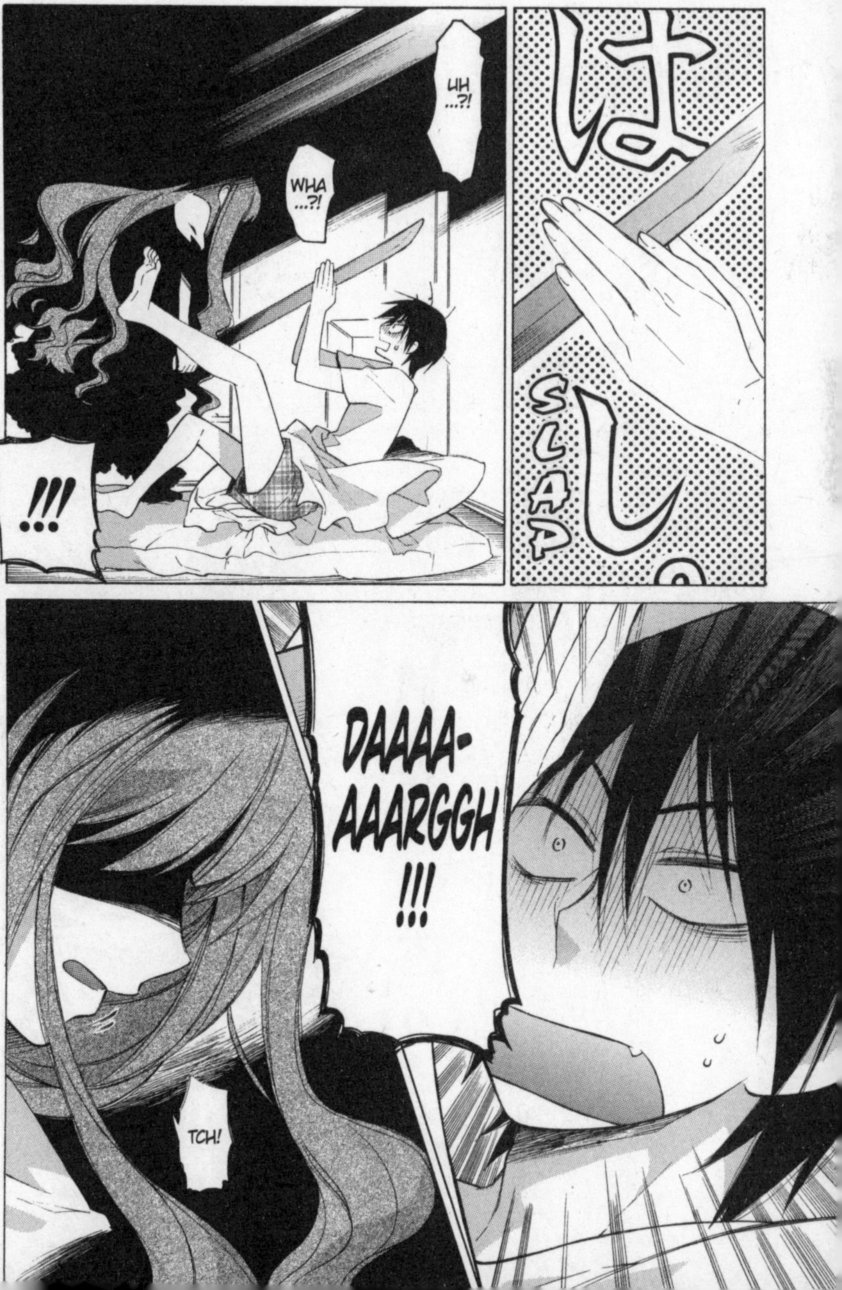
はし
SLAP
UH ...?!
WHA ...?!
!!!
DAAAA-AAARGGH !!!
TCH!

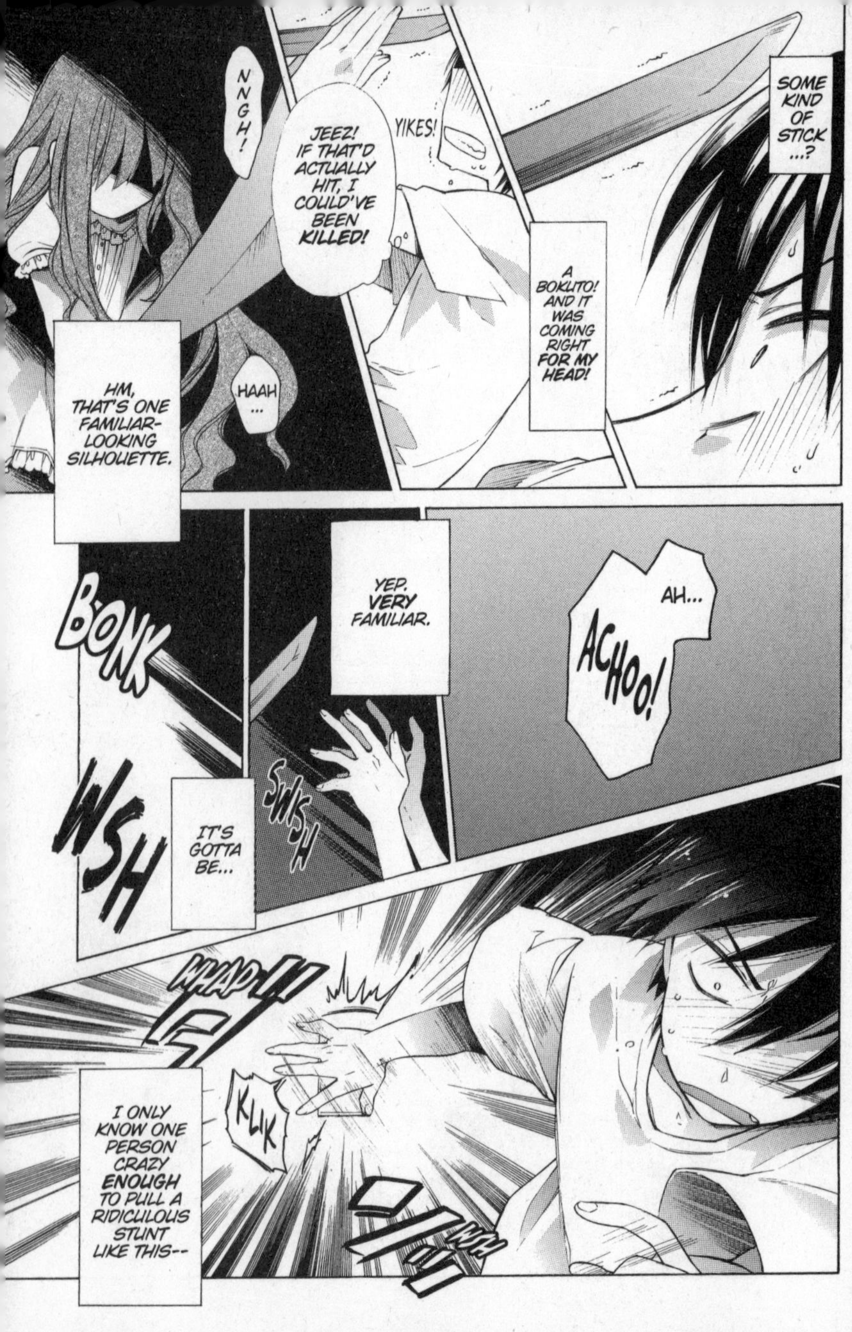
SOME KIND OF STICK ...?
A BOKUTO! AND IT WAS COMING RIGHT FOR MY HEAD!
YIKES!
JEEZ! IF THAT'D ACTUALLY HIT, I COULD'VE BEEN KILLED!
NNGH!
HAAH ...
HM, THAT'S ONE FAMILIAR-LOOKING SILHOUETTE.
AH...
ACHOO!
YEP. VERY FAMILIAR.
SWISH
BONK
WSH
IT'S GOTTA BE...
WHAP
KLIK
WSH
I ONLY KNOW ONE PERSON CRAZY ENOUGH TO PULL A RIDICULOUS STUNT LIKE THIS--

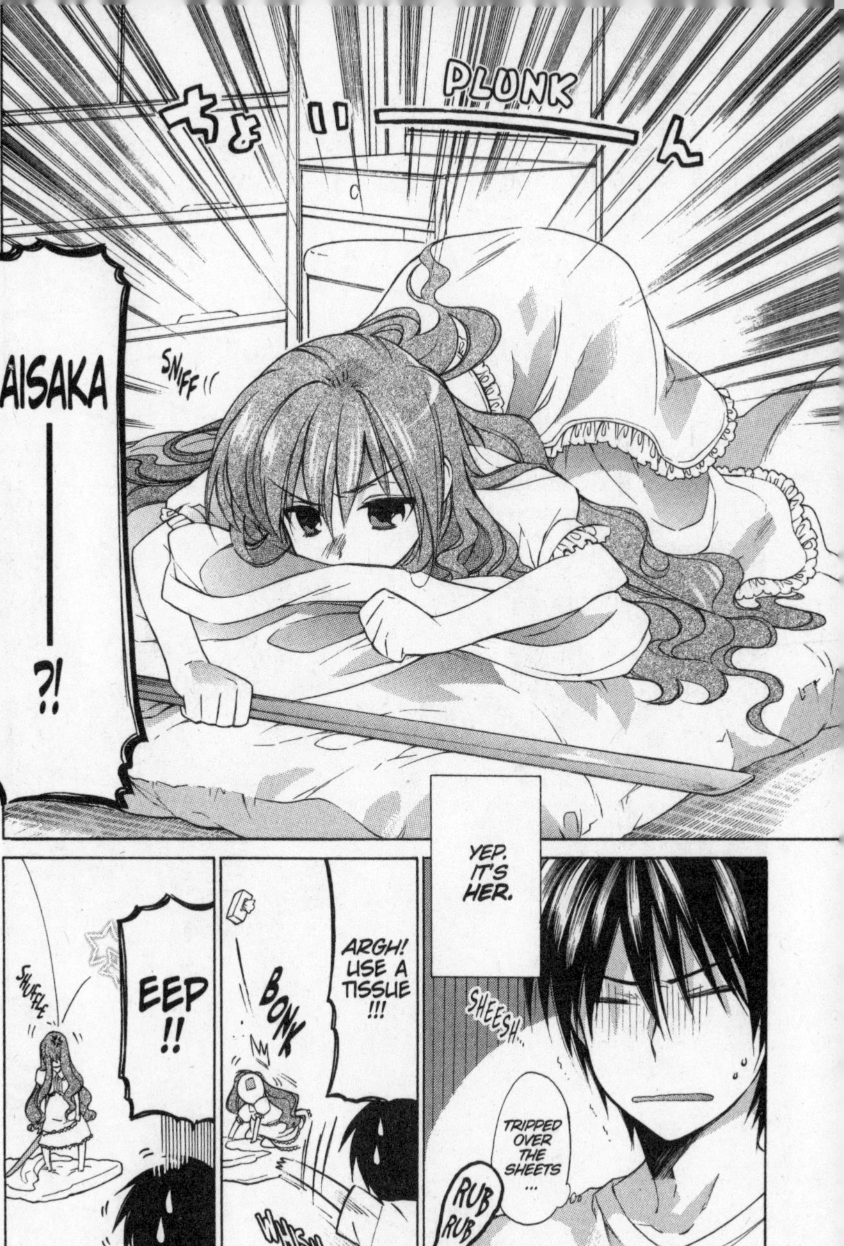
PLUNK
ちょ
ん
SNIFF
AISAKA——?!
YEP. IT'S HER.
SHEESH...
TRIPPED OVER THE SHEETS...
RUB RUB
ARGH! USE A TISSUE!!!
BONK
WHISH
EEP!!
SHUFFLE

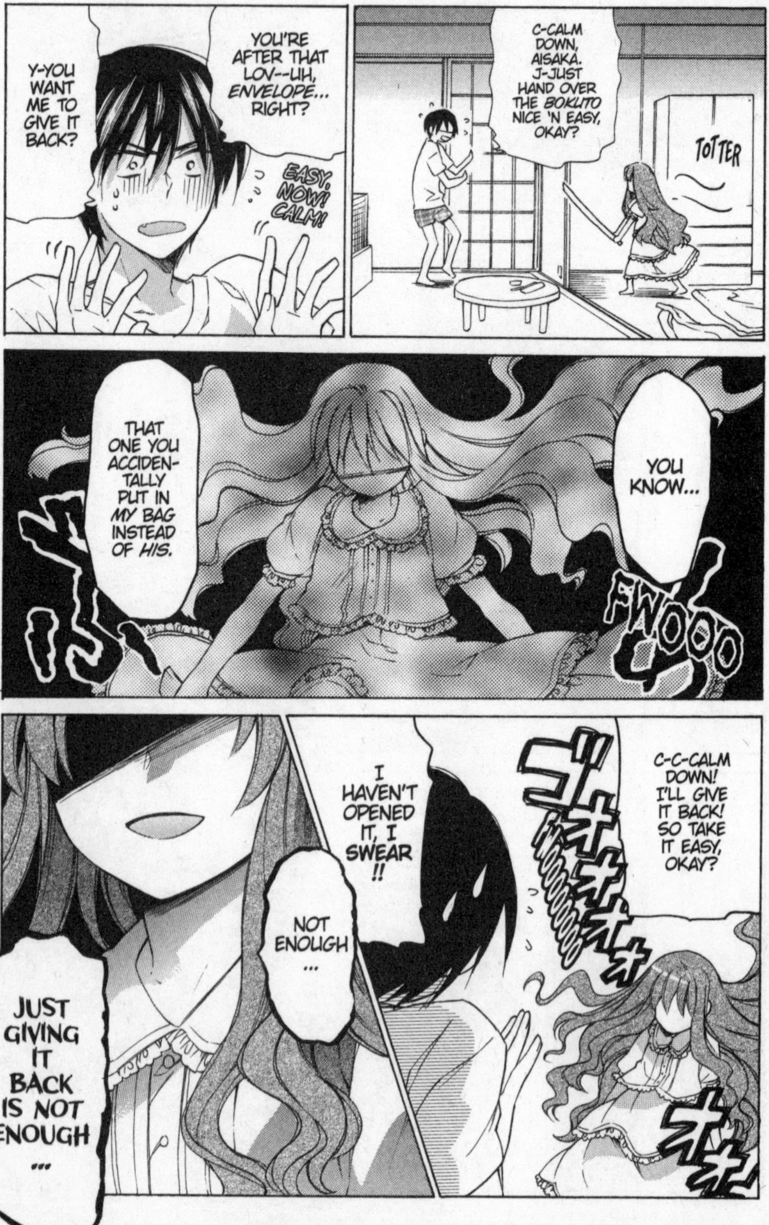
C-CALM DOWN, AISAKA. J-JUST HAND OVER THE *BOKUTO* NICE 'N EASY, OKAY?
TOTTER
YOU'RE AFTER THAT LOV--UH, *ENVELOPE*... RIGHT?
Y-YOU WANT ME TO GIVE IT BACK?
EASY. NOW! CALM!
YOU KNOW...
FWOOO
THAT ONE YOU ACCIDENTALLY PUT IN *MY* BAG INSTEAD OF *HIS*.
C-C-CALM DOWN! I'LL GIVE IT BACK! SO TAKE IT EASY, OKAY?
I HAVEN'T OPENED IT, I SWEAR!!
NOT ENOUGH...
JUST GIVING IT BACK IS NOT ENOUGH...

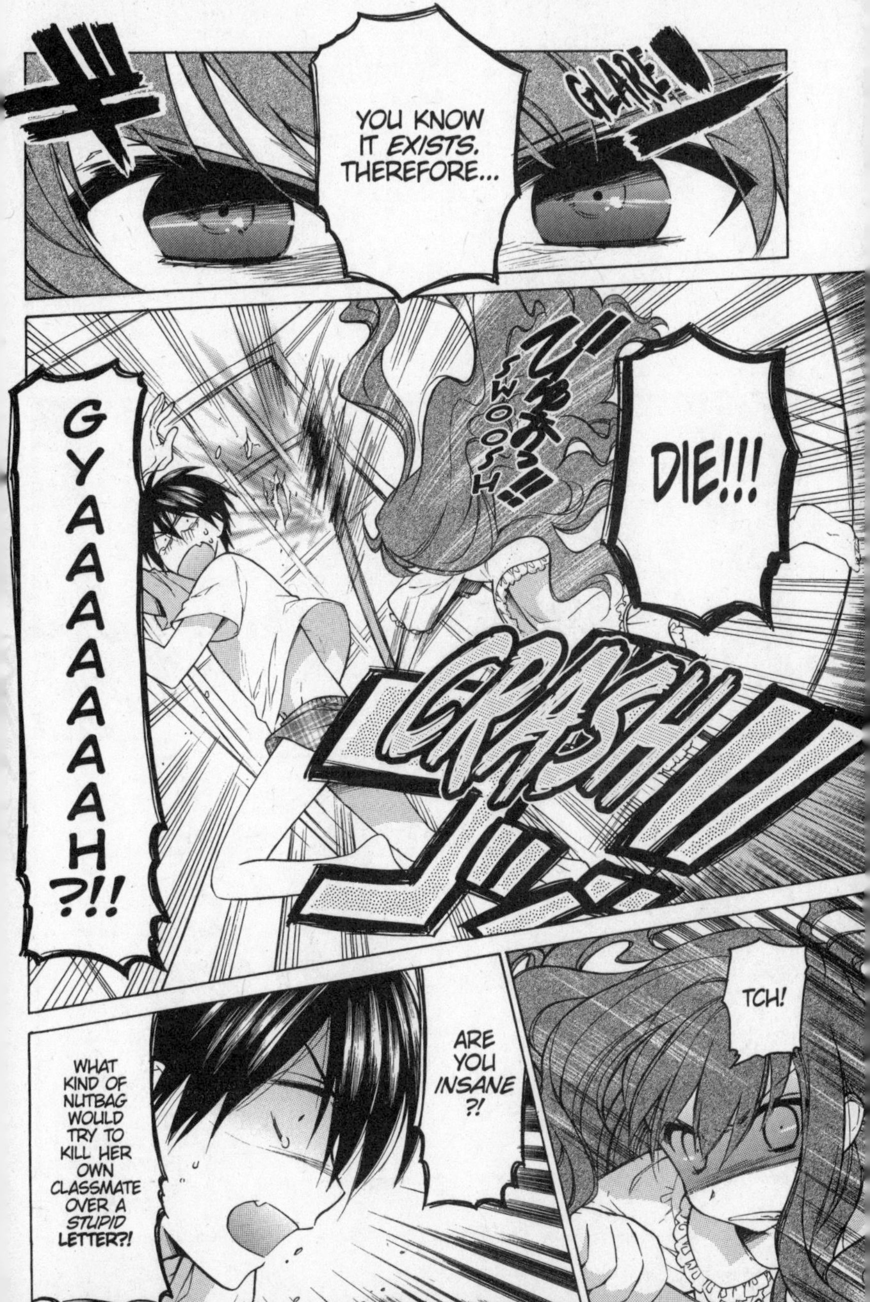
GLARE
YOU KNOW IT *EXISTS*. THEREFORE...
DIE!!!
SWOOSH!!
CRASH!!
GYAAAAAAAH?!!
TCH!
ARE YOU *INSANE*?!
WHAT KIND OF NUTBAG WOULD TRY TO KILL HER OWN CLASSMATE OVER A *STUPID* LETTER?!

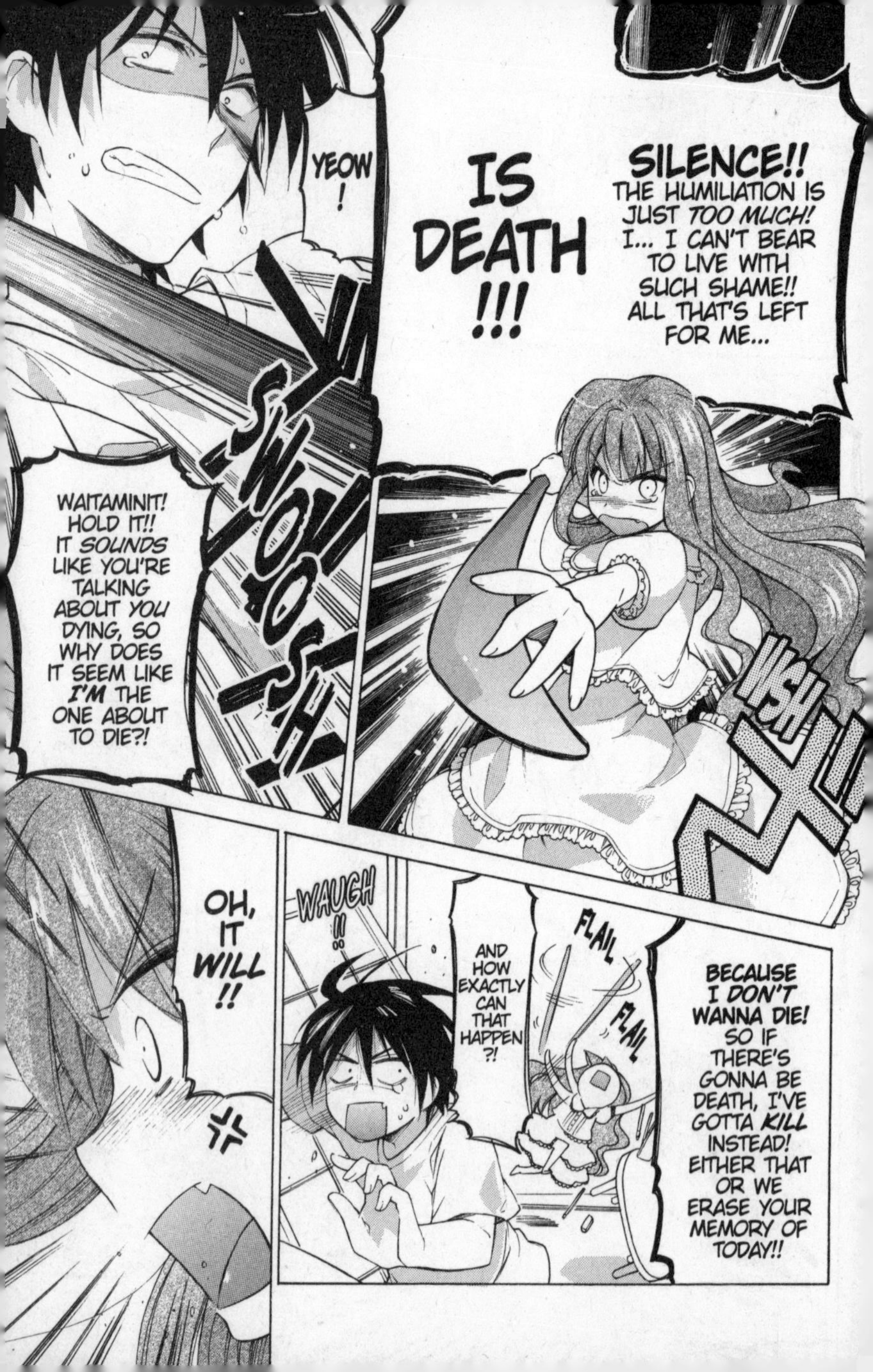
SILENCE!! THE HUMILIATION IS JUST TOO MUCH! I... I CAN'T BEAR TO LIVE WITH SUCH SHAME!! ALL THAT'S LEFT FOR ME...
IS DEATH!!!
SWISH
YEOW!
SWOOSH!
WAITAMINIT! HOLD IT!! IT SOUNDS LIKE YOU'RE TALKING ABOUT YOU DYING, SO WHY DOES IT SEEM LIKE I'M THE ONE ABOUT TO DIE?!
BECAUSE I DON'T WANNA DIE! SO IF THERE'S GONNA BE DEATH, I'VE GOTTA KILL INSTEAD! EITHER THAT OR WE ERASE YOUR MEMORY OF TODAY!!
FLAIL
FLAIL
AND HOW EXACTLY CAN THAT HAPPEN?!
WAUGH!!
OH, IT WILL!!

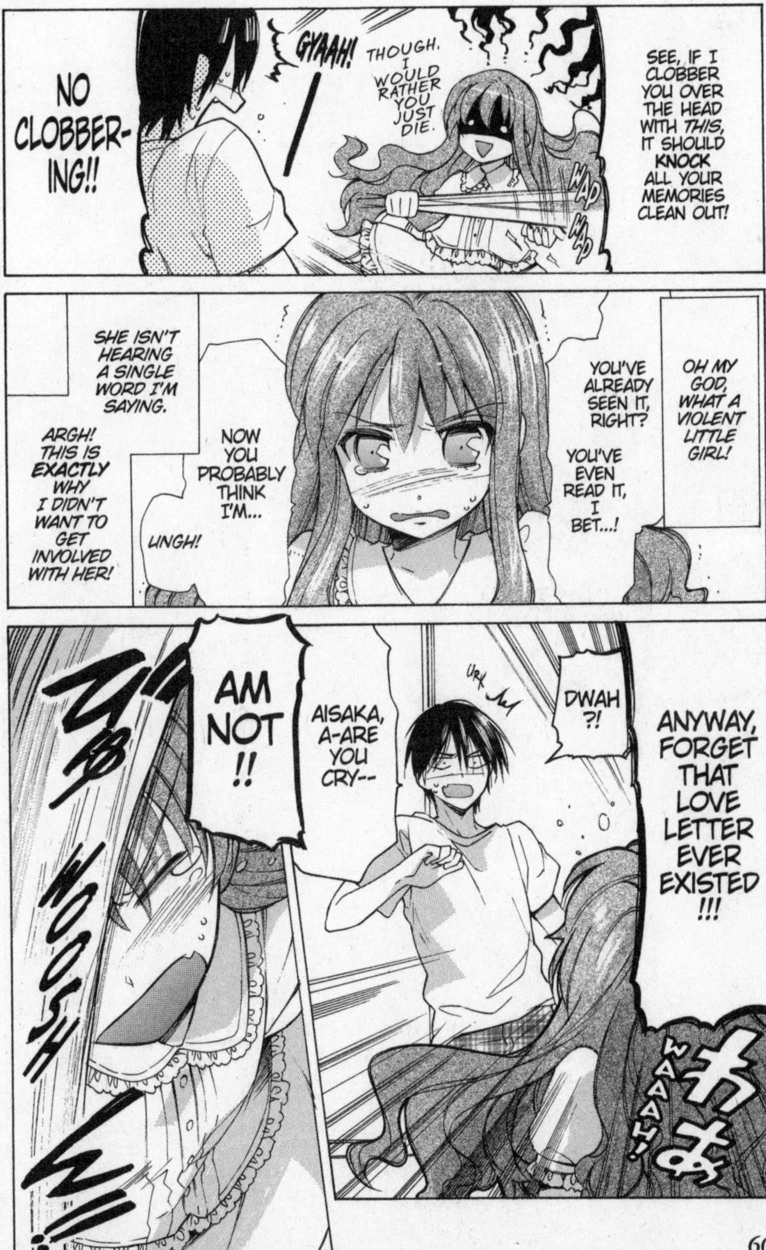
SEE, IF I CLOBBER YOU OVER THE HEAD WITH *THIS*, IT SHOULD **KNOCK** ALL YOUR MEMORIES CLEAN OUT!
THOUGH, I WOULD RATHER YOU JUST DIE.
WAP WAP
GYAAH!
NO CLOBBERING!!
OH MY GOD, WHAT A VIOLENT LITTLE GIRL!
YOU'VE ALREADY SEEN IT, RIGHT?
YOU'VE EVEN READ IT, I BET...!
NOW YOU PROBABLY THINK I'M...
UNGH!
SHE ISN'T HEARING A SINGLE WORD I'M SAYING.
ARGH! THIS IS **EXACTLY** WHY I DIDN'T WANT TO GET INVOLVED WITH HER!
ANYWAY, FORGET THAT LOVE LETTER EVER EXISTED!!!
WAAAAH!
DWAH?!
URK
AISAKA, A-ARE YOU CRY--
AM NOT!!
WOOSH!!

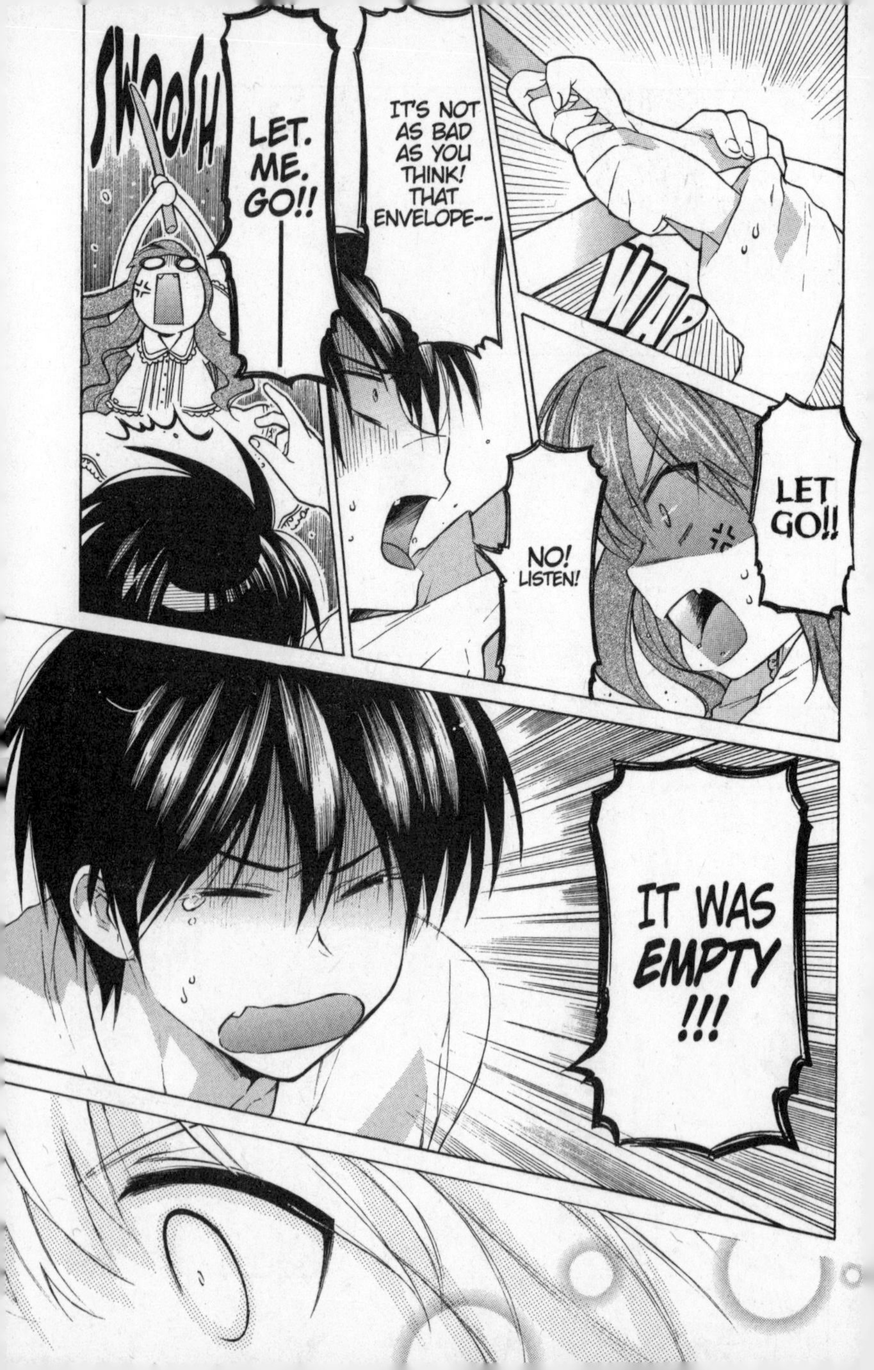
WAP
LET GO!!
IT'S NOT AS BAD AS YOU THINK! THAT ENVELOPE--
NO! LISTEN!
SWOOSH
LET. ME. GO!!
IT WAS EMPTY!!!

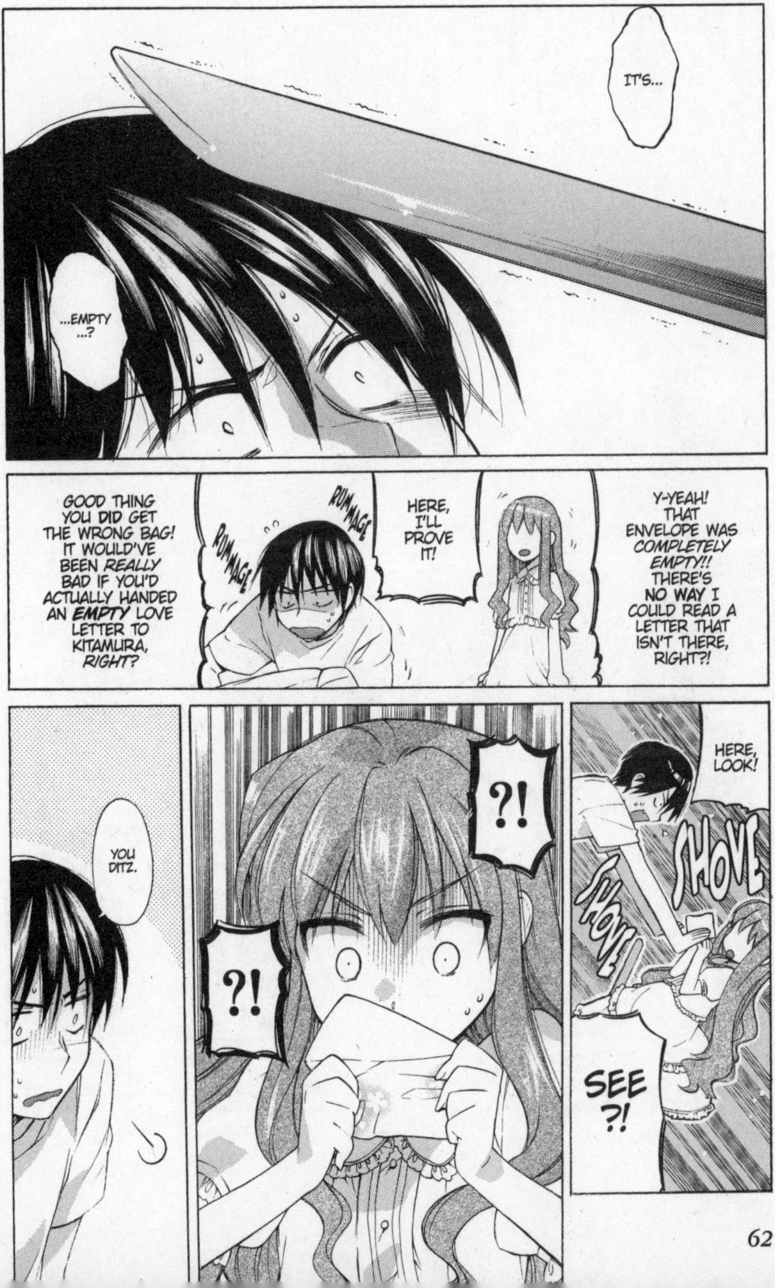
IT'S...
...EMPTY ...?
Y-YEAH! THAT ENVELOPE WAS COMPLETELY EMPTY!! THERE'S NO WAY I COULD READ A LETTER THAT ISN'T THERE, RIGHT?!
HERE, I'LL PROVE IT!
RUMMAGE
RUMMAGE
GOOD THING YOU DID GET THE WRONG BAG! IT WOULD'VE BEEN REALLY BAD IF YOU'D ACTUALLY HANDED AN EMPTY LOVE LETTER TO KITAMURA, RIGHT?
HERE, LOOK!
SHOVE
SHOVE
SEE ?!
?!
?!
YOU DITZ.

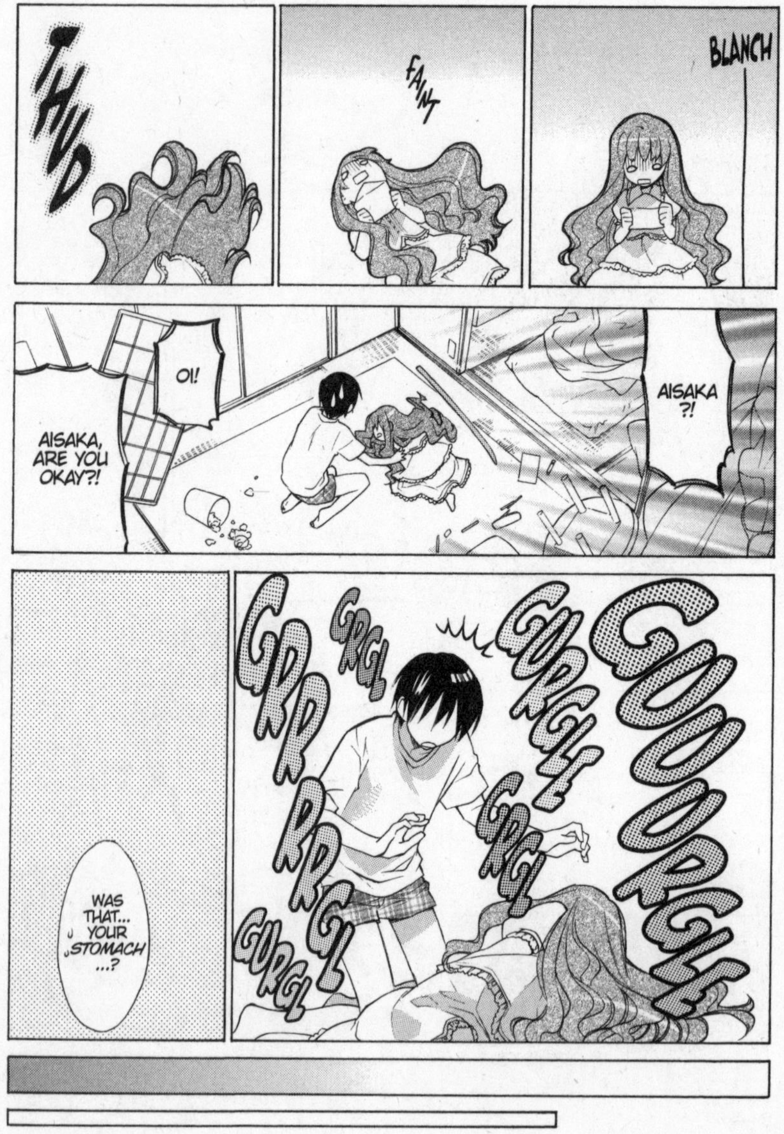
BLANCH
FAINT
THUD
AISAKA ?!
OI!
AISAKA, ARE YOU OKAY?!
GUUURGHL
GURGHL
GRGL
GRGL
GRRRRGL
GURGL
WAS THAT... YOUR STOMACH ...?

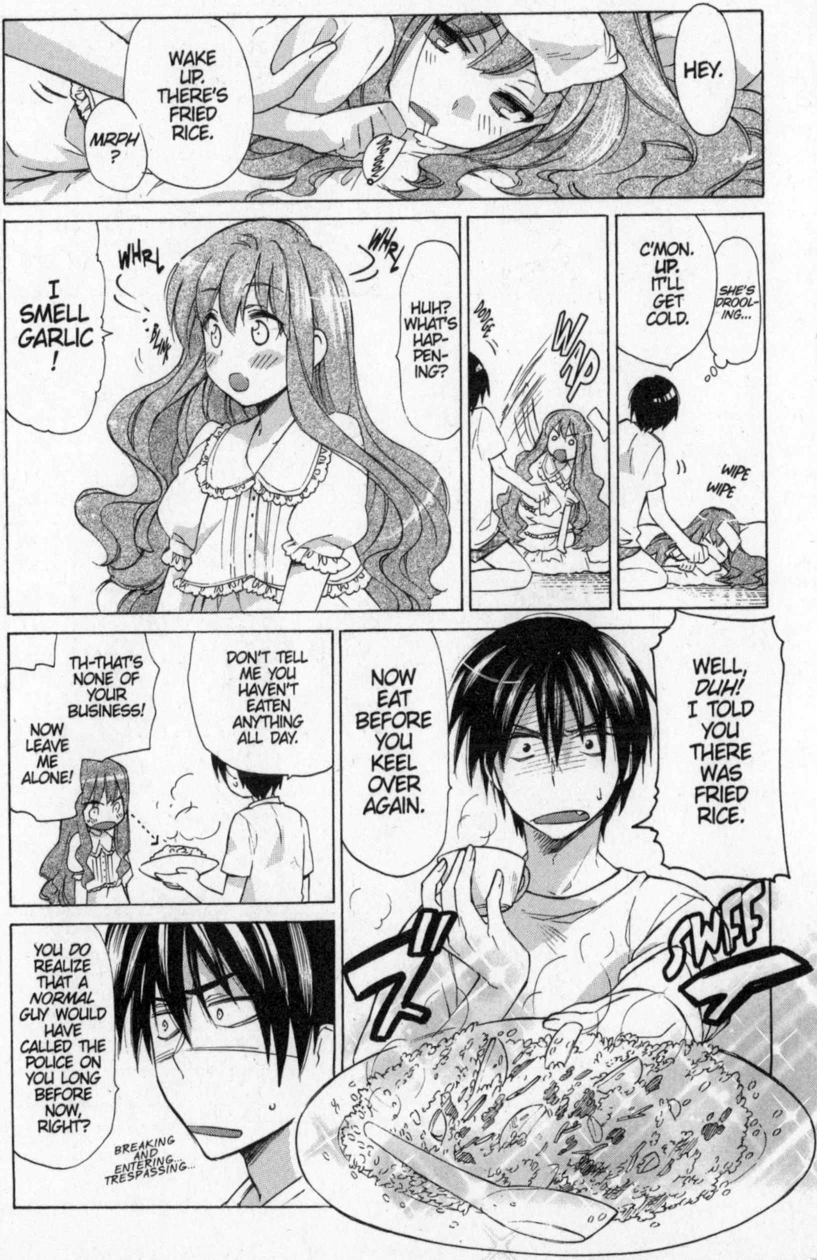
HEY.
WAKE UP. THERE'S FRIED RICE.
MRPH ?
C'MON. UP. IT'LL GET COLD.
SHE'S DROOL-ING...
WIPE WIPE
WAP
DODGE
WHRL
HUH? WHAT'S HAP-PEN-ING?
WHRL
BLINK
I SMELL GARLIC!
WELL, DUH! I TOLD YOU THERE WAS FRIED RICE.
NOW EAT BEFORE YOU KEEL OVER AGAIN.
SWFF
DON'T TELL ME YOU HAVEN'T EATEN ANYTHING ALL DAY.
TH-THAT'S NONE OF YOUR BUSINESS!
NOW LEAVE ME ALONE!
YOU DO REALIZE THAT A NORMAL GUY WOULD HAVE CALLED THE POLICE ON YOU LONG BEFORE NOW, RIGHT?
BREAKING AND ENTERING... TRESPASSING...

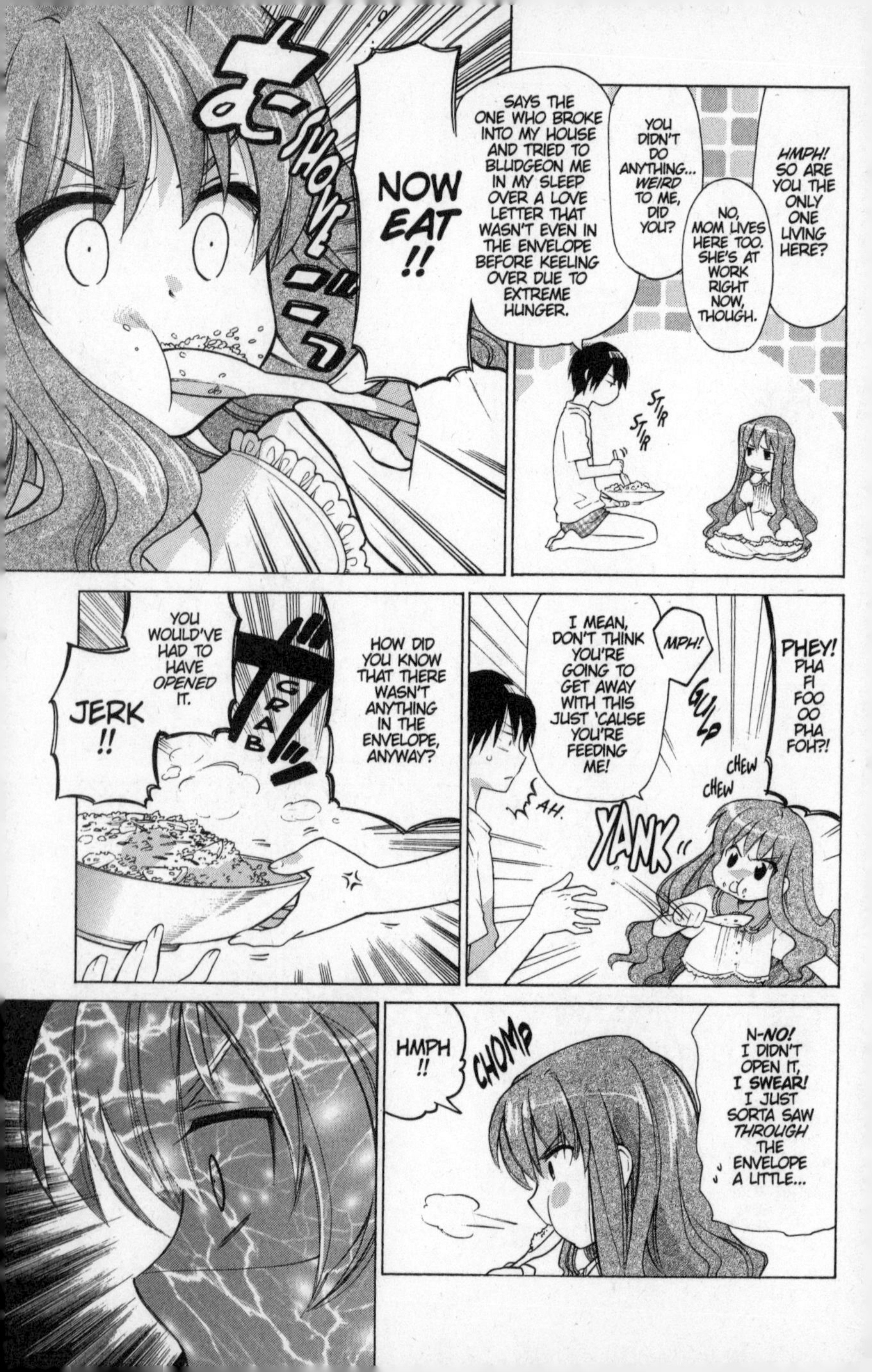
HMPH! SO ARE YOU THE ONLY ONE LIVING HERE?
NO, MOM LIVES HERE TOO. SHE'S AT WORK RIGHT NOW, THOUGH.
YOU DIDN'T DO ANYTHING... WEIRD TO ME, DID YOU?
SAYS THE ONE WHO BROKE INTO MY HOUSE AND TRIED TO BLUDGEON ME IN MY SLEEP OVER A LOVE LETTER THAT WASN'T EVEN IN THE ENVELOPE BEFORE KEELING OVER DUE TO EXTREME HUNGER.
STIR
STIR
NOW EAT!!
SHOVE
PHEY! PHA FI FOO OO PHA FOH?!
MPH!
GULP
CHEW
CHEW
I MEAN, DON'T THINK YOU'RE GOING TO GET AWAY WITH THIS JUST 'CAUSE YOU'RE FEEDING ME!
YANK
AH.
HOW DID YOU KNOW THAT THERE WASN'T ANYTHING IN THE ENVELOPE, ANYWAY?
GRAB
YOU WOULD'VE HAD TO HAVE OPENED IT.
JERK!!
N-NO! I DIDN'T OPEN IT, I SWEAR! I JUST SORTA SAW THROUGH THE ENVELOPE A LITTLE...
CHOMP
HMPH!!

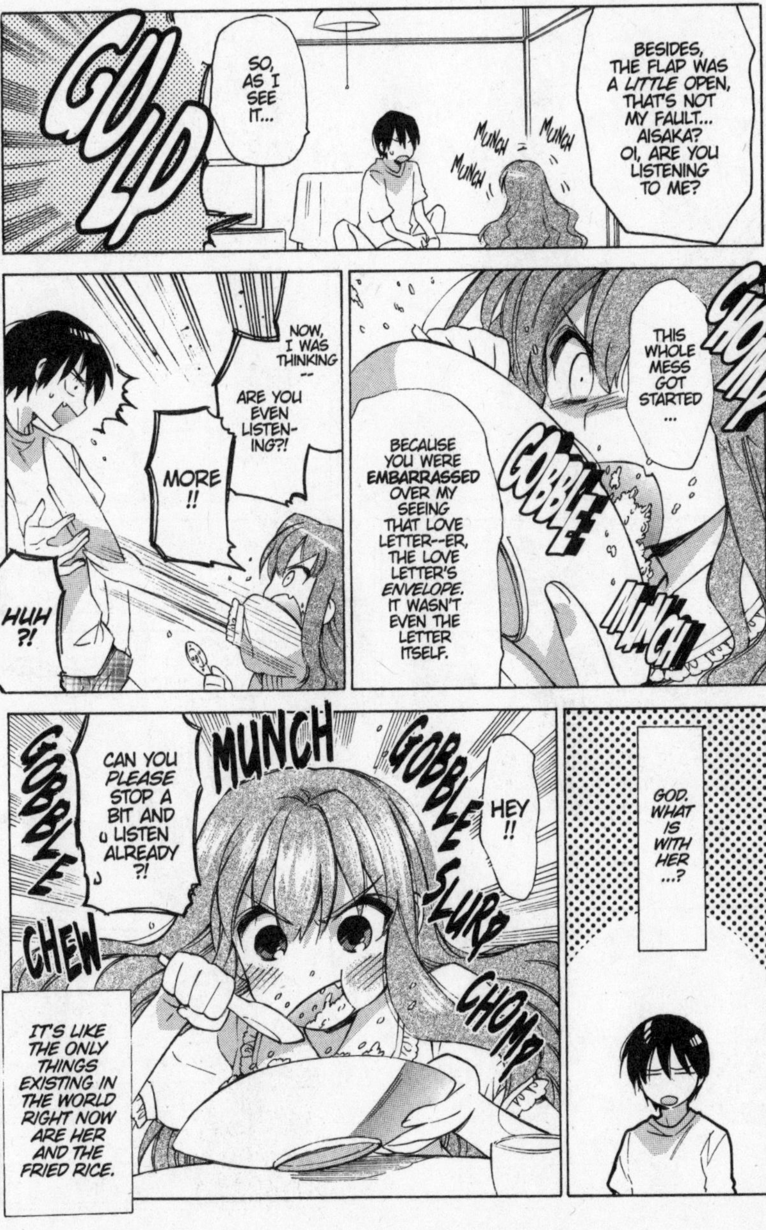
BESIDES, THE FLAP WAS A *LITTLE* OPEN, THAT'S NOT MY FAULT... AISAKA? OI, ARE YOU LISTENING TO ME?
MUNCH MUNCH MUNCH
SO, AS I SEE IT...
GULP
CHOMP
THIS WHOLE MESS GOT STARTED...
GOBBLE
BECAUSE YOU WERE **EMBARRASSED** OVER MY SEEING THAT LOVE LETTER--ER, THE LOVE LETTER'S *ENVELOPE*. IT WASN'T EVEN THE LETTER ITSELF.
MUNCH
NOW, I WAS THINKING --
ARE YOU EVEN LISTENING?!
MORE !!
HUH ?!
GOD. WHAT IS WITH HER ...?
HEY !!
GOBBLE
SLURP
CHOMP
MUNCH
CAN YOU PLEASE STOP A BIT AND LISTEN ALREADY ?!
GOBBLE
CHEW
IT'S LIKE THE ONLY THINGS EXISTING IN THE WORLD RIGHT NOW ARE HER AND THE FRIED RICE.

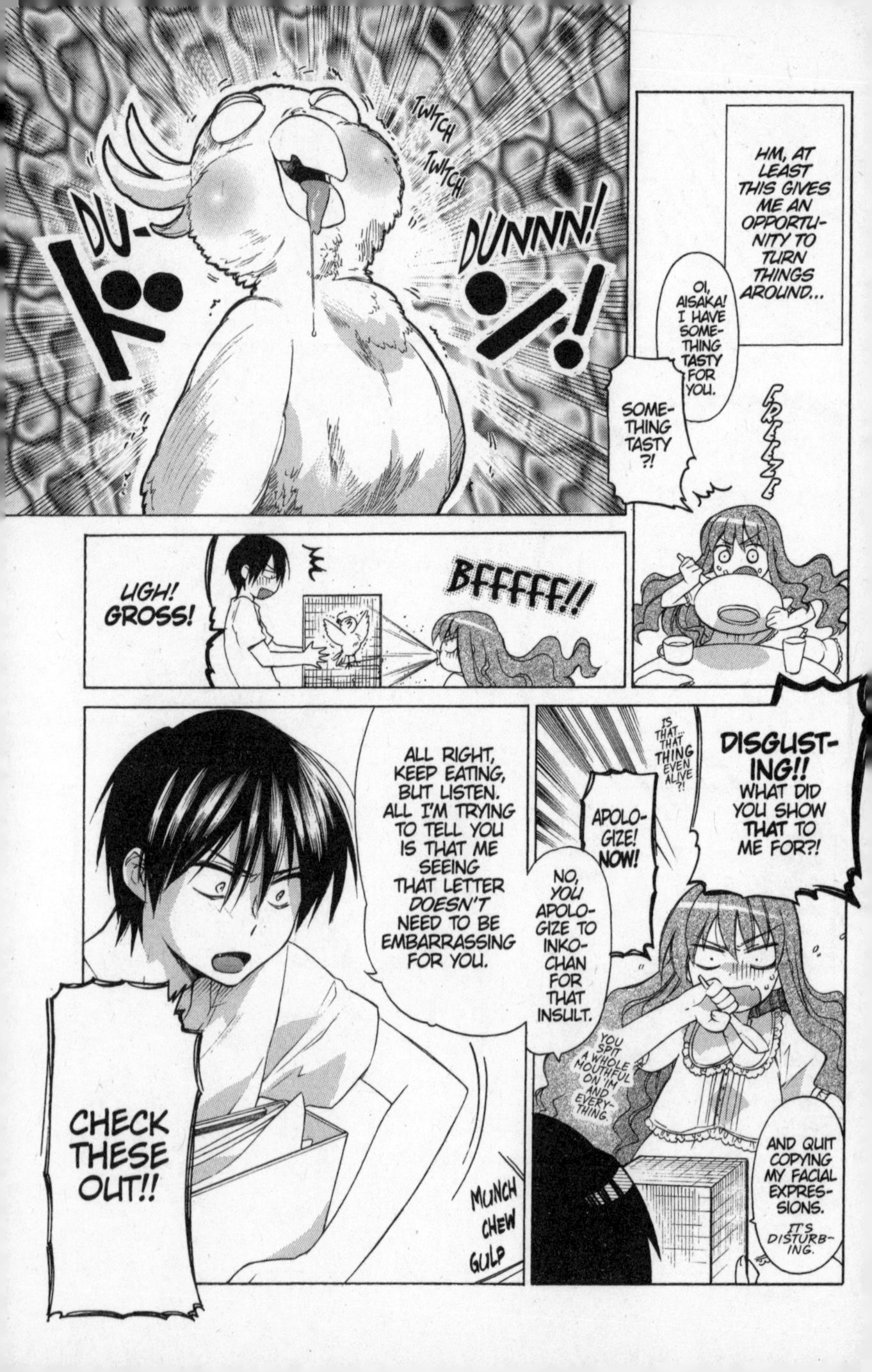
HM, AT LEAST THIS GIVES ME AN OPPORTUNITY TO TURN THINGS AROUND...
OI, AISAKA! I HAVE SOMETHING TASTY FOR YOU.
SOMETHING TASTY?!
TWITCH TWITCH
DU-DUNNN!
UGH! GROSS!
BFFFFF!!
DISGUSTING!! WHAT DID YOU SHOW THAT TO ME FOR?!
IS THAT... THAT THING EVEN ALIVE?!
APOLOGIZE! NOW!
NO, YOU APOLOGIZE TO INKO-CHAN FOR THAT INSULT.
YOU SPIT A WHOLE MOUTHFUL ON 'IM AND EVERYTHING.
AND QUIT COPYING MY FACIAL EXPRESSIONS.
IT'S DISTURBING.
ALL RIGHT, KEEP EATING, BUT LISTEN. ALL I'M TRYING TO TELL YOU IS THAT ME SEEING THAT LETTER *DOESN'T* NEED TO BE EMBARRASSING FOR YOU.
CHECK THESE OUT!!
MUNCH CHEW GULP

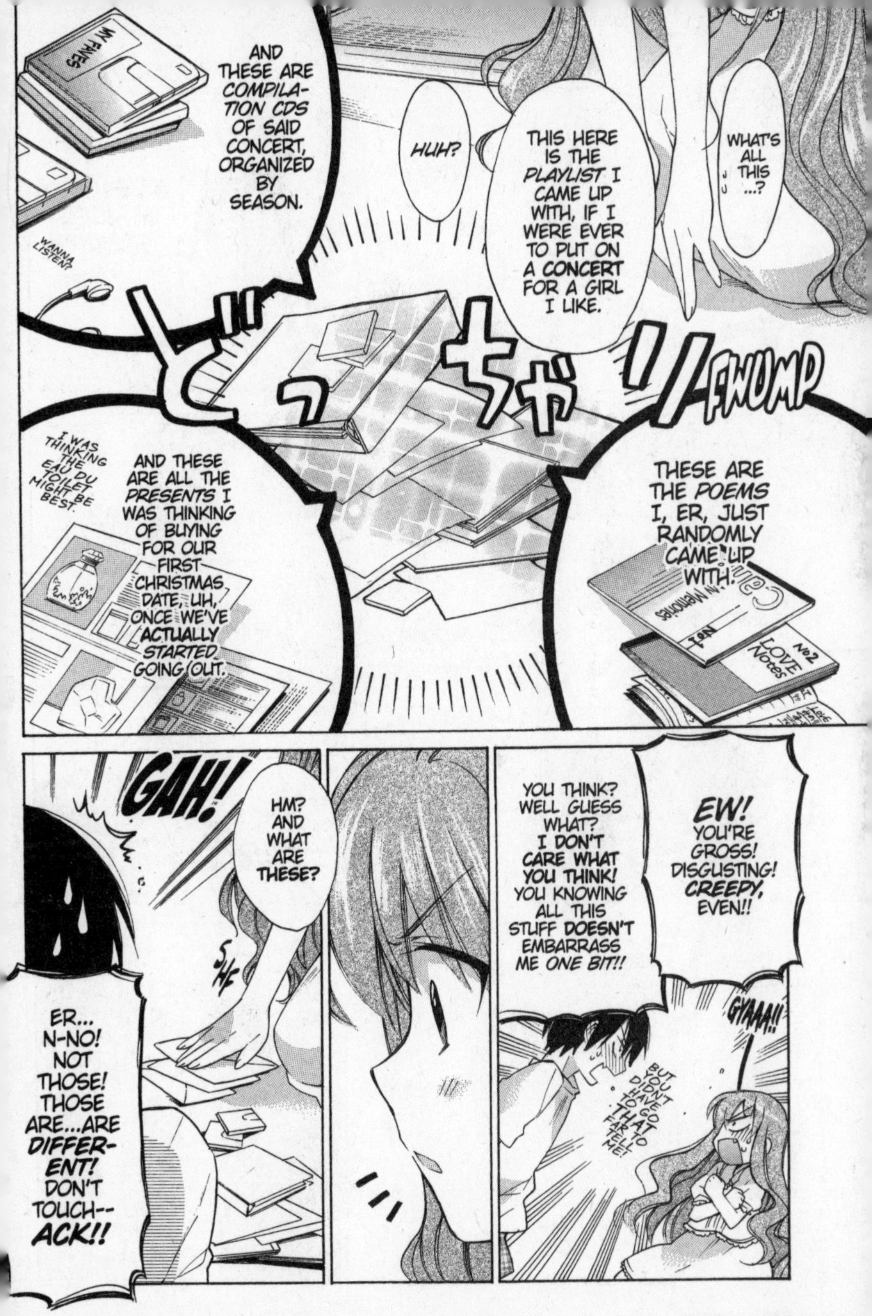
WHAT'S ALL THIS ...?
THIS HERE IS THE PLAYLIST I CAME UP WITH, IF I WERE EVER TO PUT ON A CONCERT FOR A GIRL I LIKE.
HUH?
AND THESE ARE COMPILATION CDS OF SAID CONCERT, ORGANIZED BY SEASON.
MY FAVES
WANNA LISTEN?
FWUMP
THESE ARE THE POEMS I, ER, JUST RANDOMLY CAME UP WITH.
No2 LOVE Notes
AND THESE ARE ALL THE PRESENTS I WAS THINKING OF BUYING FOR OUR FIRST CHRISTMAS DATE, UH, ONCE WE'VE ACTUALLY STARTED GOING OUT.
I WAS THINKING THE EAU DU TOILET MIGHT BE BEST.
EW! YOU'RE GROSS! DISGUSTING! CREEPY, EVEN!!
YOU THINK? WELL GUESS WHAT? I DON'T CARE WHAT YOU THINK! YOU KNOWING ALL THIS STUFF DOESN'T EMBARRASS ME ONE BIT!!
GYAAA!!
BUT YOU DIDN'T HAVE TO GO THAT FAR TO TELL ME!
HM? AND WHAT ARE THESE?
GAH!
SHF
ER... N-NO! NOT THOSE! THOSE ARE...ARE DIFFERENT! DON'T TOUCH--ACK!!

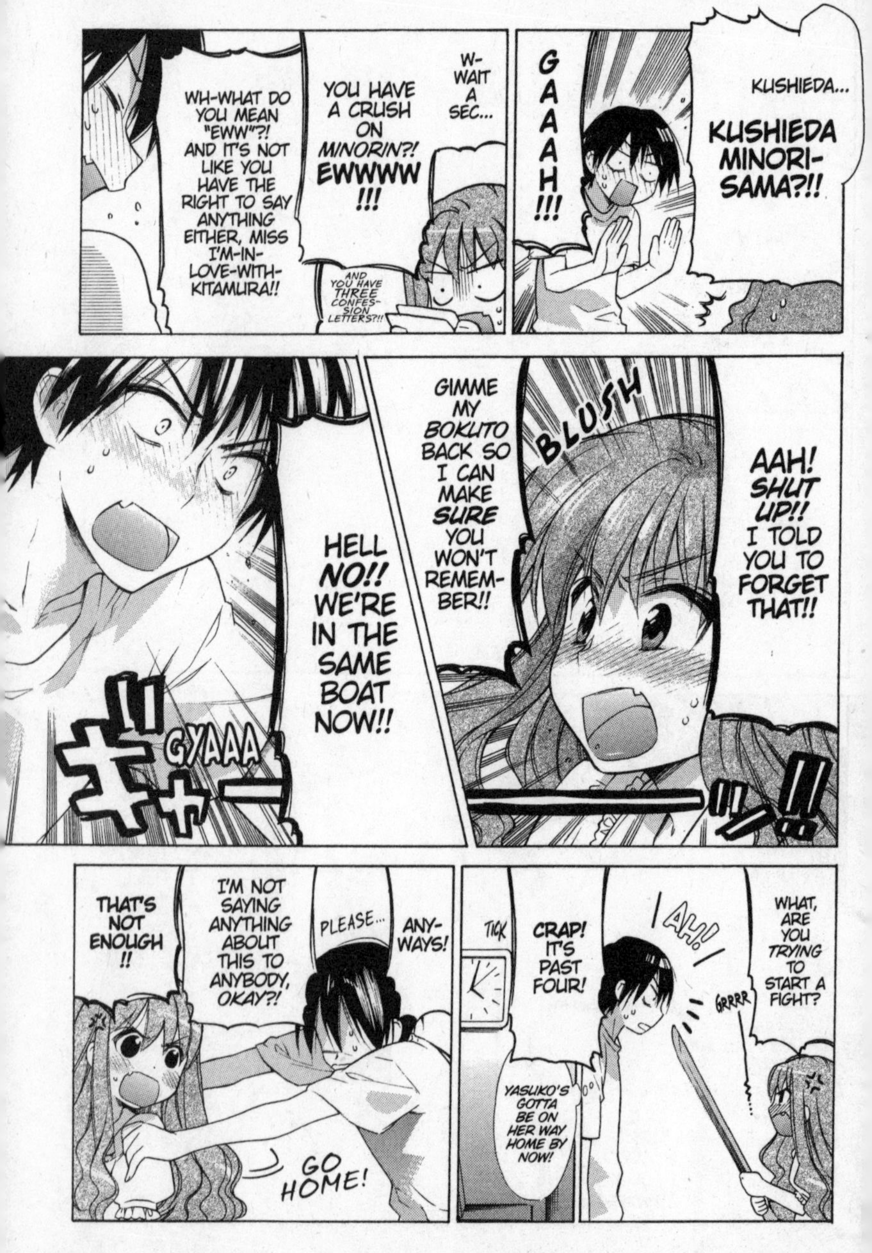
KUSHIEDA...
KUSHIEDA MINORI-SAMA?!!
GAAAAH!!!
W-WAIT A SEC...
YOU HAVE A CRUSH ON MINORIN?! EWWWW!!!
AND YOU HAVE THREE CONFESSION LETTERS?!!
WH-WHAT DO YOU MEAN "EWW"?! AND IT'S NOT LIKE YOU HAVE THE RIGHT TO SAY ANYTHING EITHER, MISS I'M-IN-LOVE-WITH-KITAMURA!!
AAH! SHUT UP!! I TOLD YOU TO FORGET THAT!!
BLUSH
GIMME MY BOKUTO BACK SO I CAN MAKE SURE YOU WON'T REMEMBER!!
HELL NO!! WE'RE IN THE SAME BOAT NOW!!
GYAAA
WHAT, ARE YOU TRYING TO START A FIGHT?
GRRRR
AH!
CRAP! IT'S PAST FOUR!
TICK
YASUKO'S GOTTA BE ON HER WAY HOME BY NOW!
ANY-WAYS!
PLEASE...
I'M NOT SAYING ANYTHING ABOUT THIS TO ANYBODY, OKAY?!
THAT'S NOT ENOUGH!!
GO HOME!

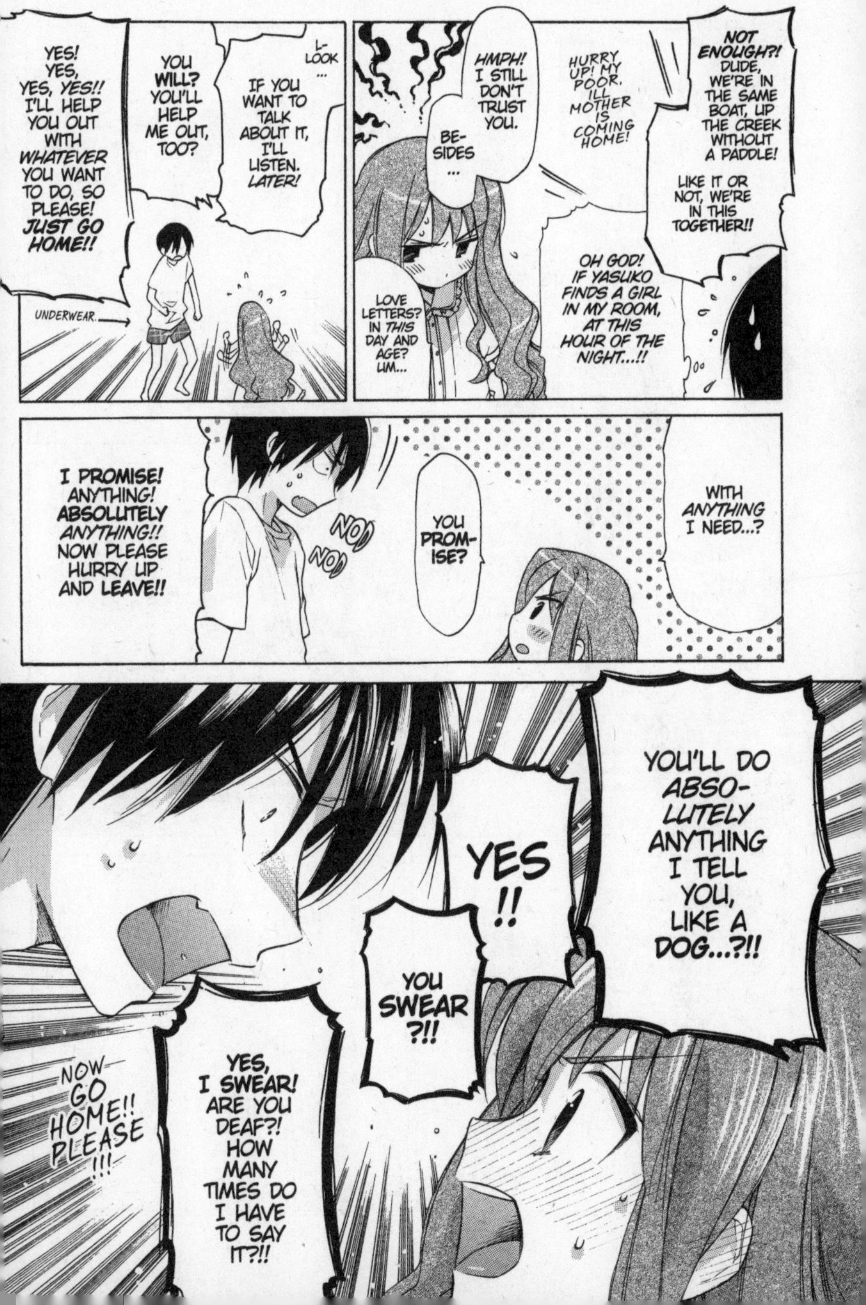
NOT ENOUGH?! DUDE, WE'RE IN THE SAME BOAT, UP THE CREEK WITHOUT A PADDLE!
LIKE IT OR NOT, WE'RE IN THIS TOGETHER!!
HURRY UP! MY POOR, ILL MOTHER IS COMING HOME!
OH GOD! IF YASUKO FINDS A GIRL IN MY ROOM, AT THIS HOUR OF THE NIGHT...!!
HMPH! I STILL DON'T TRUST YOU.
BESIDES...
LOVE LETTERS? IN THIS DAY AND AGE? UM...
L-LOOK...
IF YOU WANT TO TALK ABOUT IT, I'LL LISTEN. LATER!
YOU WILL? YOU'LL HELP ME OUT, TOO?
YES! YES, YES, YES!! I'LL HELP YOU OUT WITH WHATEVER YOU WANT TO DO, SO PLEASE! JUST GO HOME!!
UNDERWEAR.
WITH ANYTHING I NEED...?
YOU PROMISE?
NOD NOD
I PROMISE! ANYTHING! ABSOLUTELY ANYTHING!! NOW PLEASE HURRY UP AND LEAVE!!
YOU'LL DO ABSOLUTELY ANYTHING I TELL YOU, LIKE A DOG...?!!
YES!!
YOU SWEAR?!!
YES, I SWEAR! ARE YOU DEAF?! HOW MANY TIMES DO I HAVE TO SAY IT?!!
NOW GO HOME!! PLEASE!!!

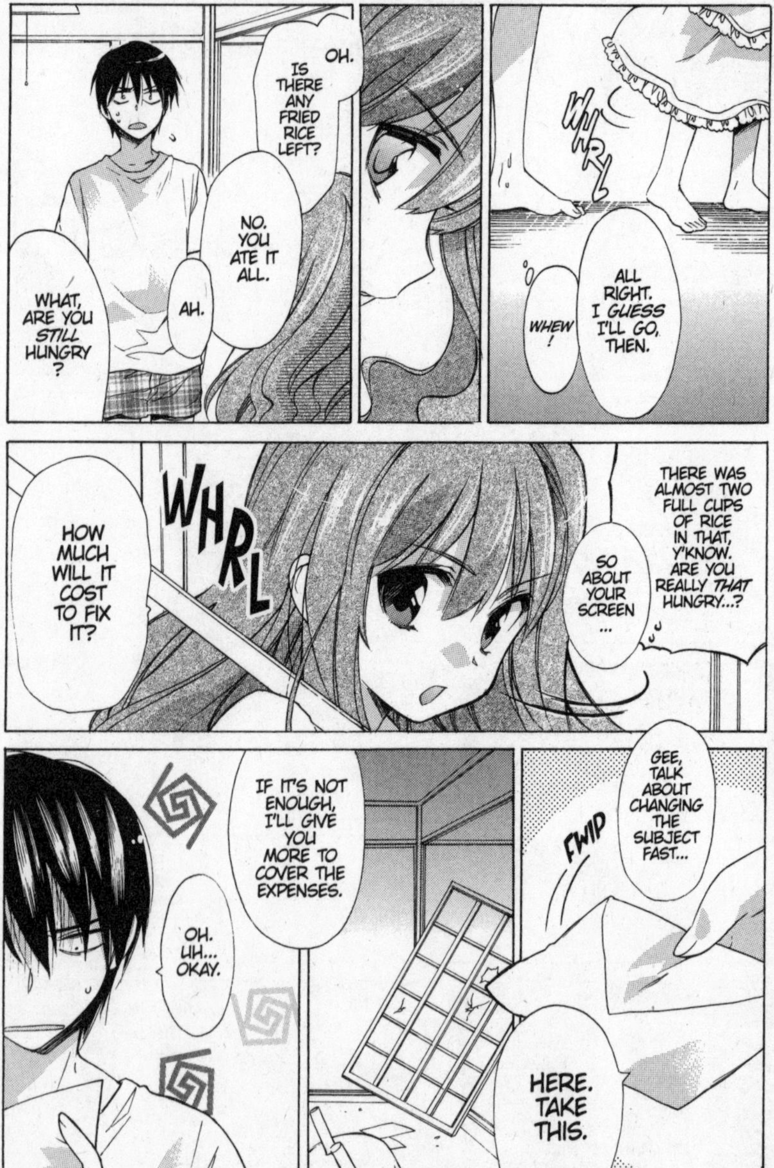

WHRL
ALL RIGHT. I GUESS I'LL GO, THEN.
WHEW!
OH. IS THERE ANY FRIED RICE LEFT?
NO. YOU ATE IT ALL.
AH.
WHAT, ARE YOU STILL HUNGRY?
THERE WAS ALMOST TWO FULL CUPS OF RICE IN THAT, Y'KNOW. ARE YOU REALLY THAT HUNGRY...?
SO ABOUT YOUR SCREEN...
WHRL
HOW MUCH WILL IT COST TO FIX IT?
GEE, TALK ABOUT CHANGING THE SUBJECT FAST...
FWIP
HERE. TAKE THIS.
IF IT'S NOT ENOUGH, I'LL GIVE YOU MORE TO COVER THE EXPENSES.
OH. UH... OKAY.

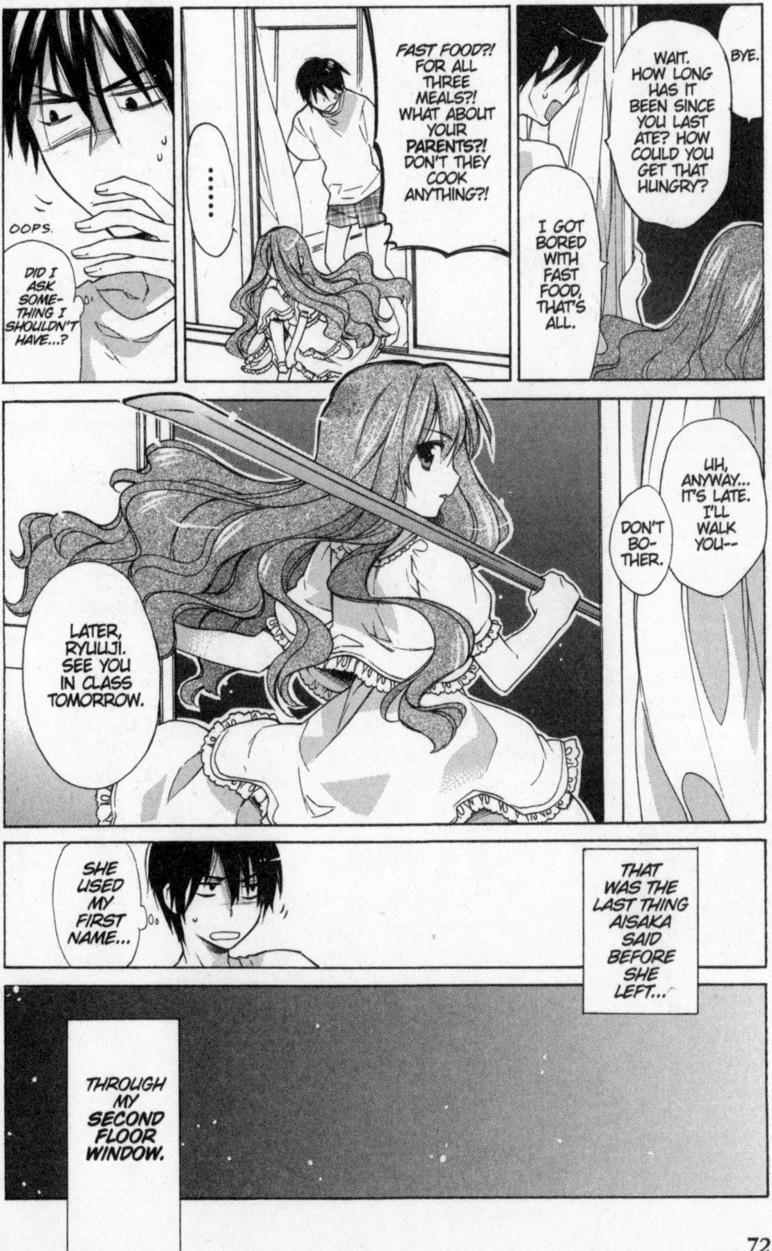
BYE.
WAIT. HOW LONG HAS IT BEEN SINCE YOU LAST ATE? HOW COULD YOU GET THAT HUNGRY?
I GOT BORED WITH FAST FOOD, THAT'S ALL.
FAST FOOD?! FOR ALL THREE MEALS?! WHAT ABOUT YOUR PARENTS?! DON'T THEY COOK ANYTHING?!
......
OOPS.
DID I ASK SOME-THING I SHOULDN'T HAVE...?
UH, ANYWAY... IT'S LATE. I'LL WALK YOU--
DON'T BO-THER.
LATER, RYUUJI. SEE YOU IN CLASS TOMORROW.
THAT WAS THE LAST THING AISAKA SAID BEFORE SHE LEFT...
SHE USED MY FIRST NAME...
THROUGH MY SECOND FLOOR WINDOW.

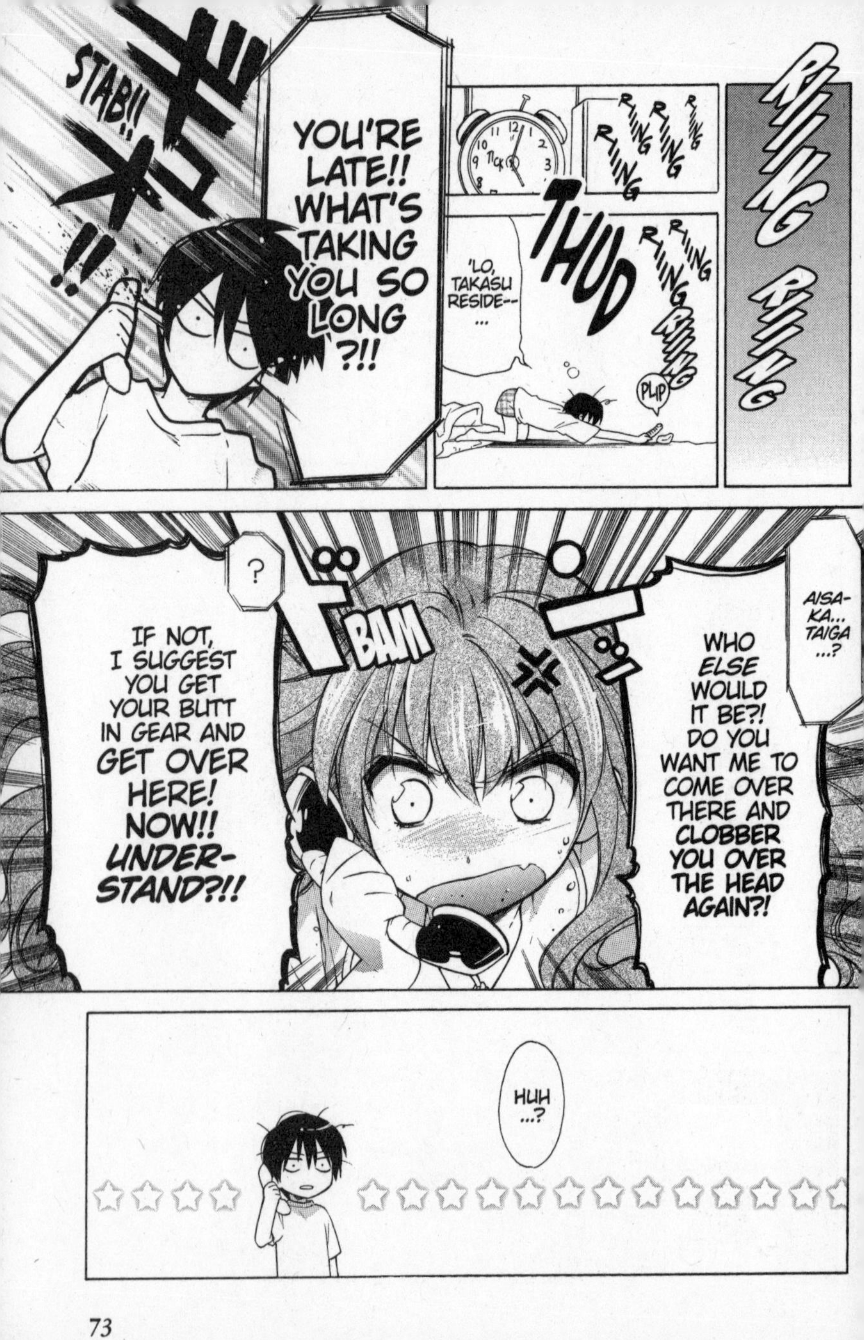
RIIING RIIING RIIING
RING RING RING RING
THUD
RING RIIING RIIING
'LO, TAKASU RESIDE-- ...
PLIP
STAB!!
YOU'RE LATE!! WHAT'S TAKING YOU SO LONG?!!
AISAKA... TAIGA...?
WHO ELSE WOULD IT BE?! DO YOU WANT ME TO COME OVER THERE AND CLOBBER YOU OVER THE HEAD AGAIN?!
BAM
?
IF NOT, I SUGGEST YOU GET YOUR BUTT IN GEAR AND GET OVER HERE! NOW!! UNDER-STAND?!!
HUH...?

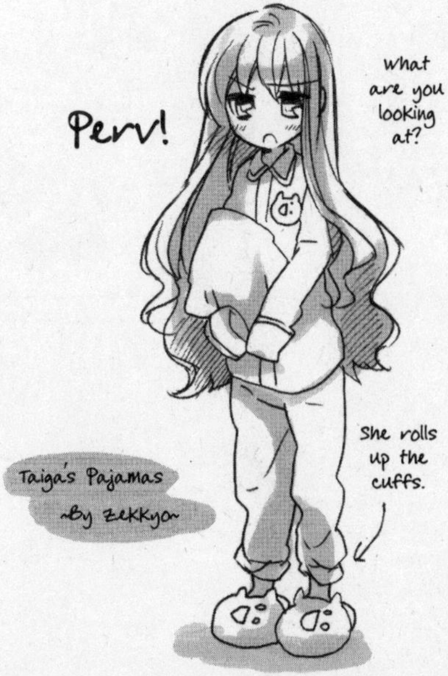
What are you looking at?
Perv!
She rolls up the cuffs.
Taiga's Pajamas
~By Zekkyo~

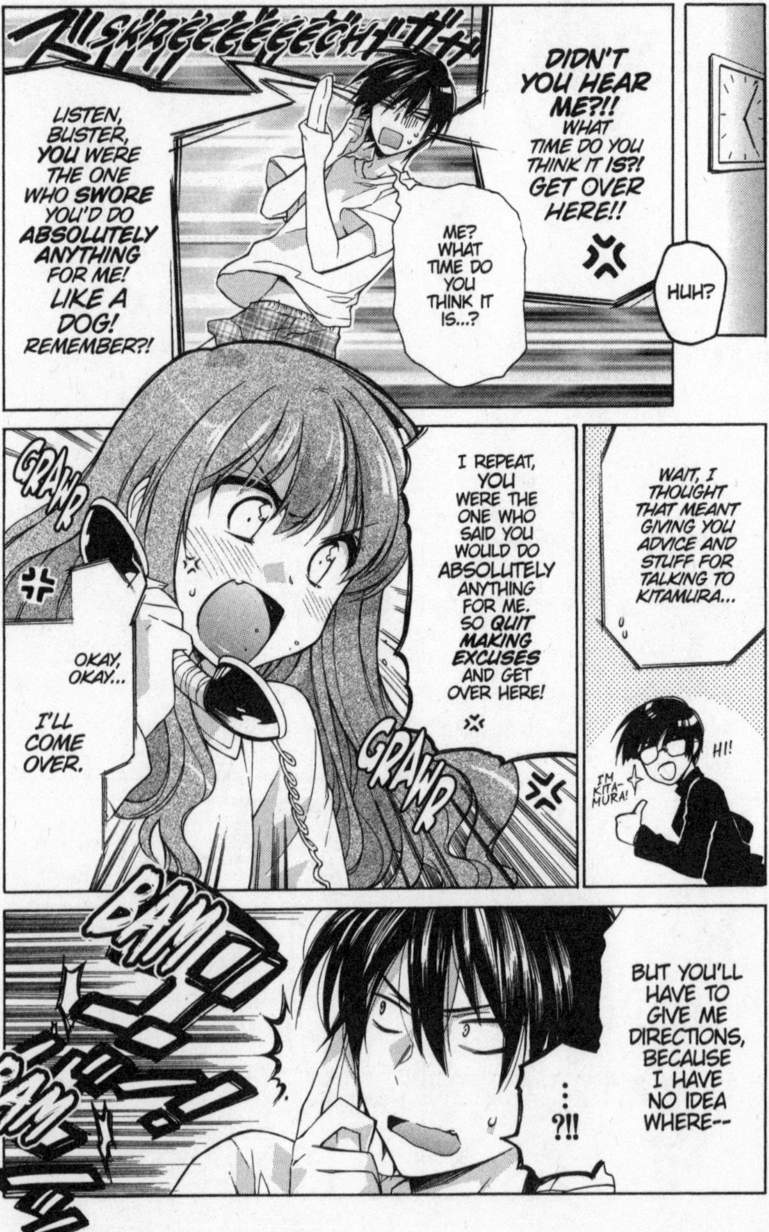
HUH?
SKREEEEEEEEEECH
DIDN'T YOU HEAR ME?!! WHAT TIME DO YOU THINK IT IS?! GET OVER HERE!!
ME? WHAT TIME DO YOU THINK IT IS...?
LISTEN, BUSTER, YOU WERE THE ONE WHO SWORE YOU'D DO ABSOLUTELY ANYTHING FOR ME! LIKE A DOG! REMEMBER?!
WAIT, I THOUGHT THAT MEANT GIVING YOU ADVICE AND STUFF FOR TALKING TO KITAMURA...
HI!
I'M KITA-MURA!
I REPEAT, YOU WERE THE ONE WHO SAID YOU WOULD DO ABSOLUTELY ANYTHING FOR ME. SO QUIT MAKING EXCUSES AND GET OVER HERE!
GRAWR
GRAWR
OKAY, OKAY...
I'LL COME OVER.
BUT YOU'LL HAVE TO GIVE ME DIRECTIONS, BECAUSE I HAVE NO IDEA WHERE--
...?!!

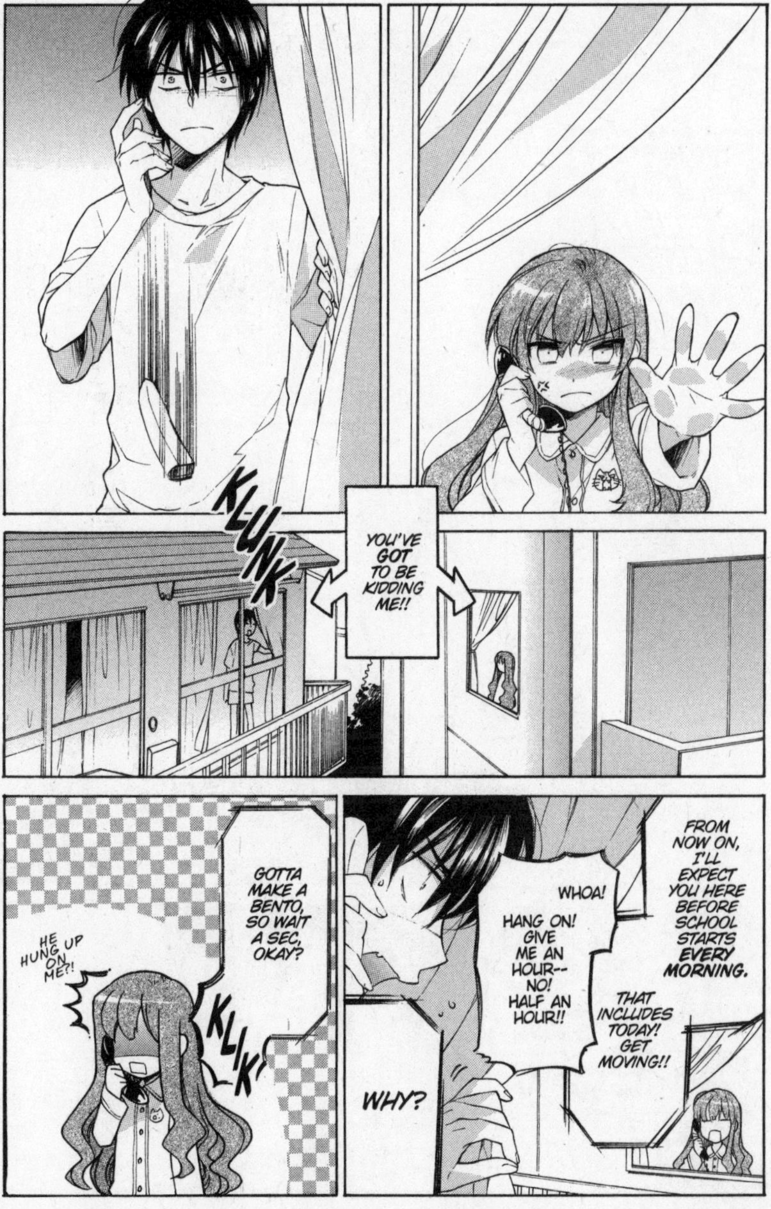
KLUNK
YOU'VE GOT TO BE KIDDING ME!!
FROM NOW ON, I'LL EXPECT YOU HERE BEFORE SCHOOL STARTS EVERY MORNING.
WHOA!
HANG ON! GIVE ME AN HOUR-- NO! HALF AN HOUR!!
THAT INCLUDES TODAY! GET MOVING!!
WHY?
GOTTA MAKE A BENTO, SO WAIT A SEC, OKAY?
KLIK
HE HUNG UP ON ME?!

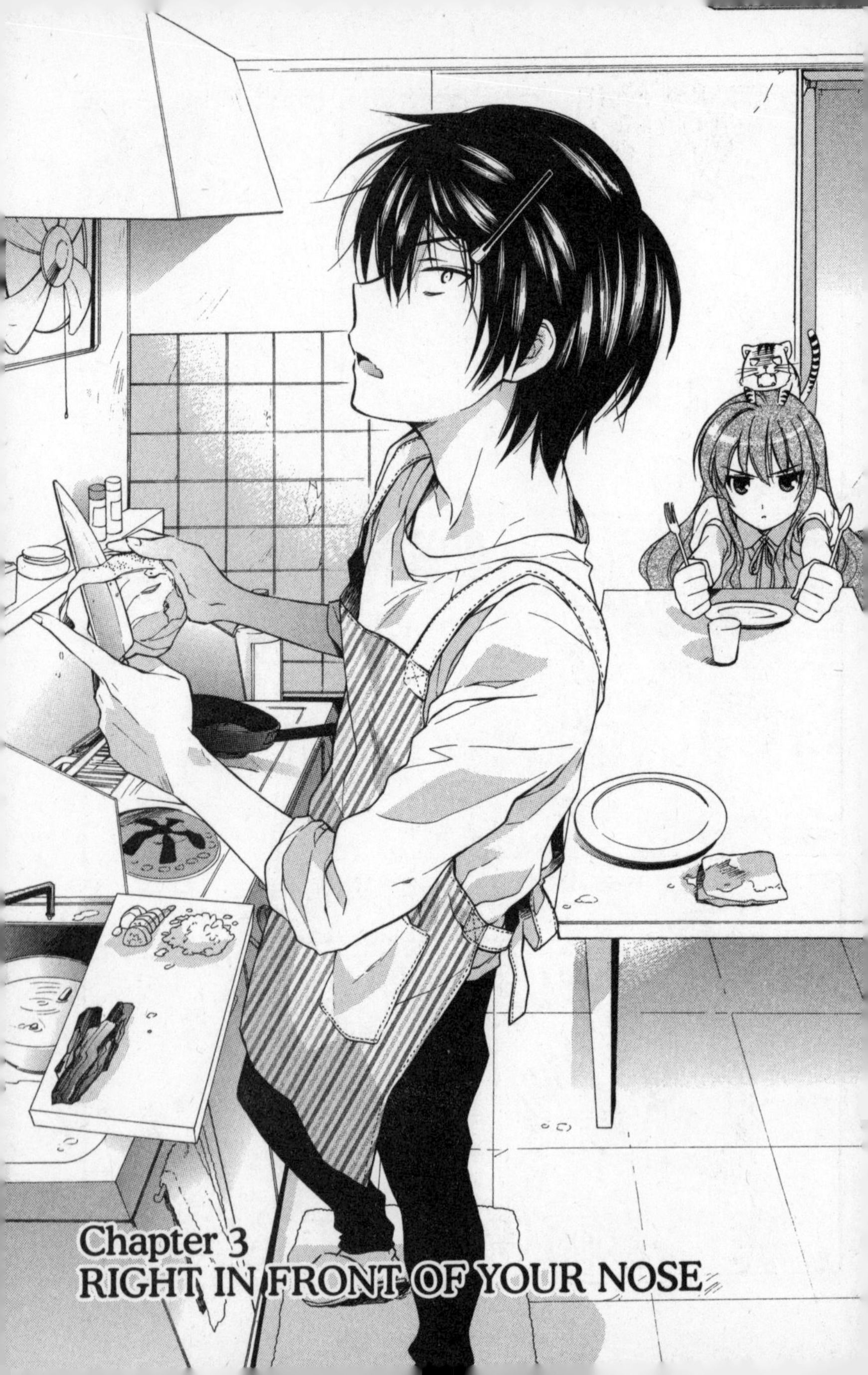
Chapter 3
RIGHT IN FRONT OF YOUR NOSE

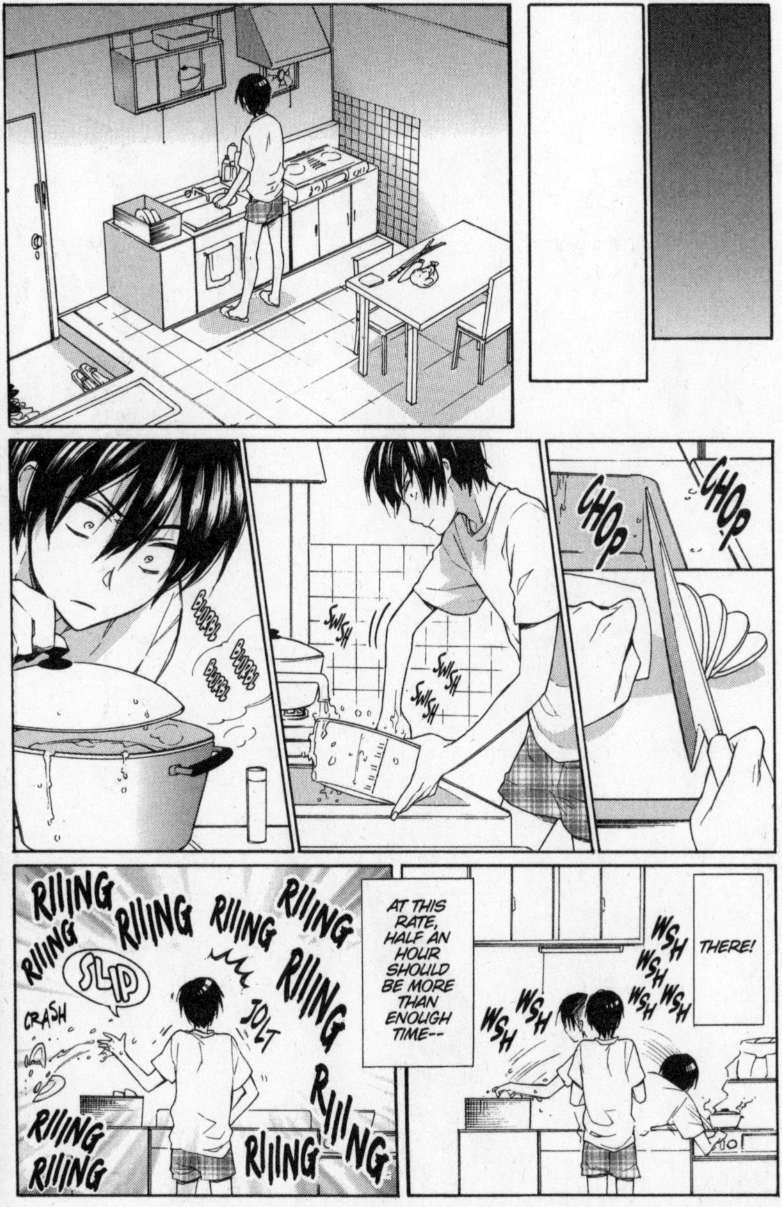
CHOP
CHOP
SWISH
SWISH
SWISH
BUBBL
BUBBL
BUBBL
THERE!
WSH
WSH
WSH
WSH
WSH
WSH
AT THIS RATE, HALF AN HOUR SHOULD BE MORE THAN ENOUGH TIME--
RIIING
RIIING
JOLT
RIIING
RIIING
RIIING
SLIP
RIIING
RIIING
CRASH
RIIING
RIIING
RIIING

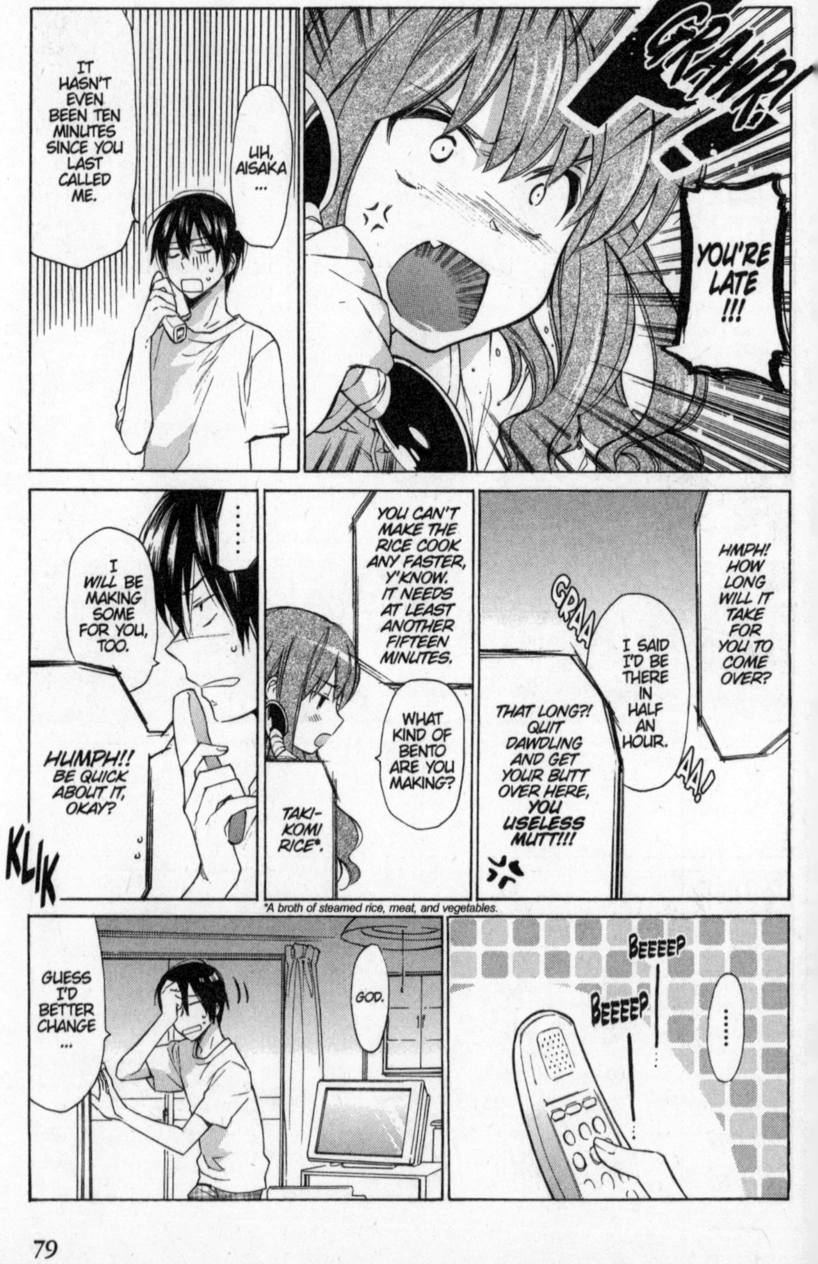
GRAWR!!
YOU'RE LATE!!!
UH, AISAKA...
IT HASN'T EVEN BEEN TEN MINUTES SINCE YOU LAST CALLED ME.
HMPH! HOW LONG WILL IT TAKE FOR YOU TO COME OVER?
I SAID I'D BE THERE IN HALF AN HOUR.
GRAAAA!
THAT LONG?! QUIT DAWDLING AND GET YOUR BUTT OVER HERE, YOU USELESS MUTT!!!
YOU CAN'T MAKE THE RICE COOK ANY FASTER, Y'KNOW. IT NEEDS AT LEAST ANOTHER FIFTEEN MINUTES.
WHAT KIND OF BENTO ARE YOU MAKING?
TAKI-KOMI RICE*.
......
I WILL BE MAKING SOME FOR YOU, TOO.
HUMPH!! BE QUICK ABOUT IT, OKAY?
KLIK
BEEEEP
BEEEEP
......
GOD.
GUESS I'D BETTER CHANGE...

*A broth of steamed rice, meat, and vegetables.

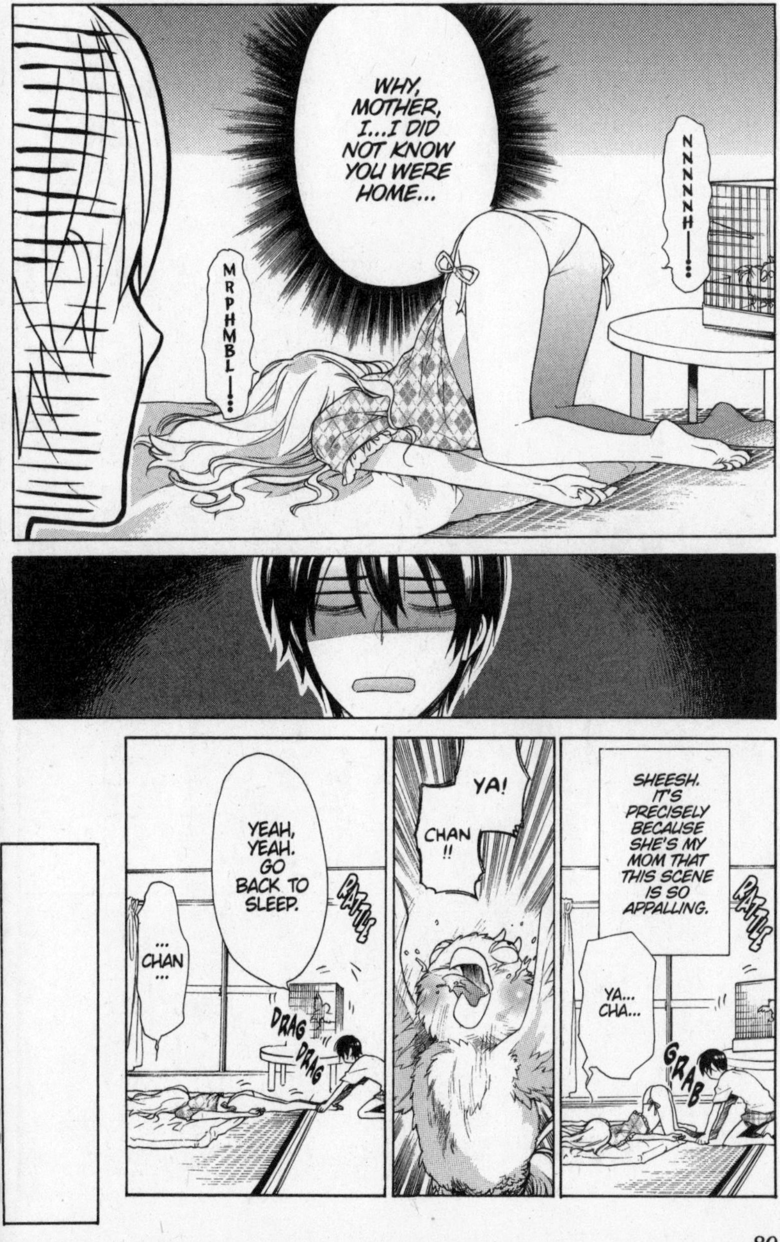
NNNNNH...!
WHY, MOTHER, I...I DID NOT KNOW YOU WERE HOME...
MRPHMBL...!
SHEESH. IT'S PRECISELY BECAUSE SHE'S MY MOM THAT THIS SCENE IS SO APPALLING.
RATTLE
YA... CHA...
GRAB
YA!
CHAN !!
YEAH, YEAH. GO BACK TO SLEEP.
RATTLE
... CHAN ...
DRAG DRAG

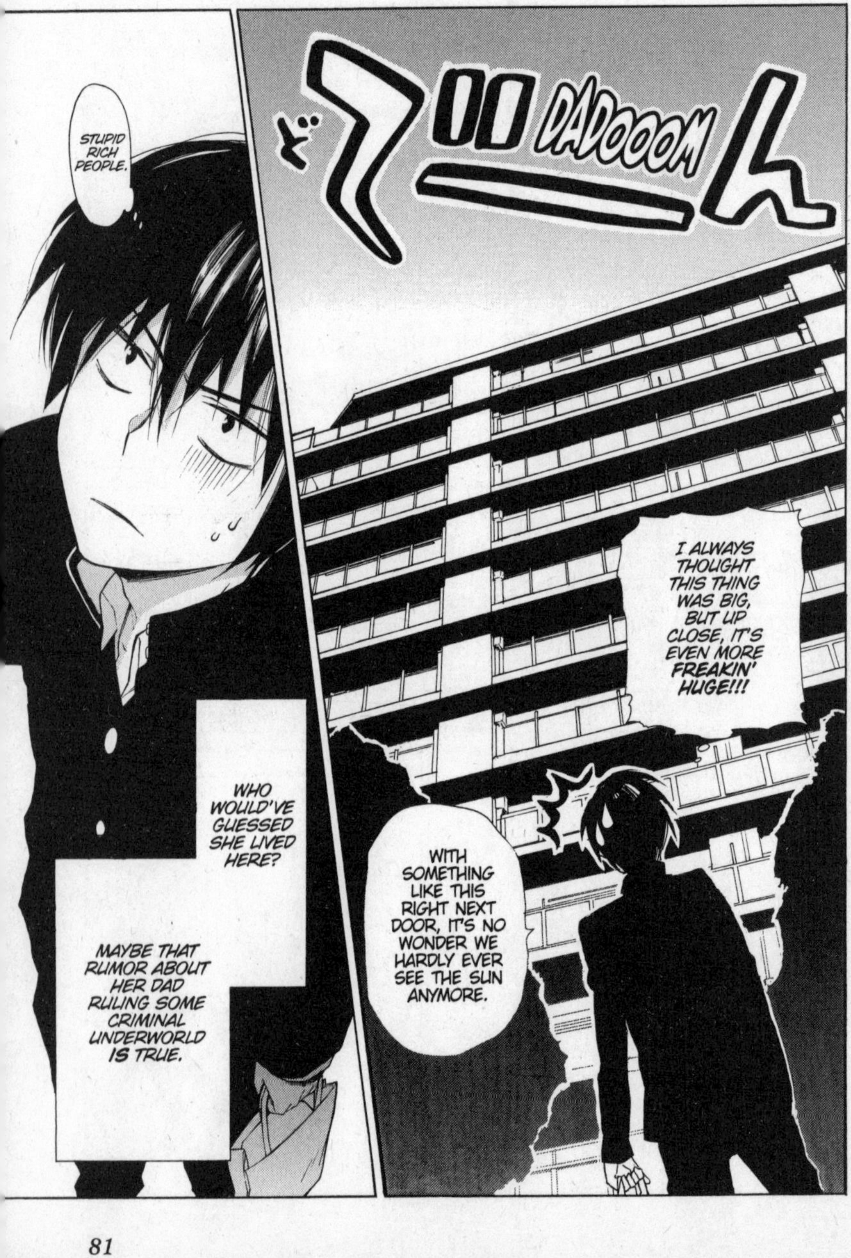
DADOOOM
I ALWAYS THOUGHT THIS THING WAS BIG, BUT UP CLOSE, IT'S EVEN MORE FREAKIN' HUGE!!!
WITH SOMETHING LIKE THIS RIGHT NEXT DOOR, IT'S NO WONDER WE HARDLY EVER SEE THE SUN ANYMORE.
STUPID RICH PEOPLE.
WHO WOULD'VE GUESSED SHE LIVED HERE?
MAYBE THAT RUMOR ABOUT HER DAD RULING SOME CRIMINAL UNDERWORLD IS TRUE.

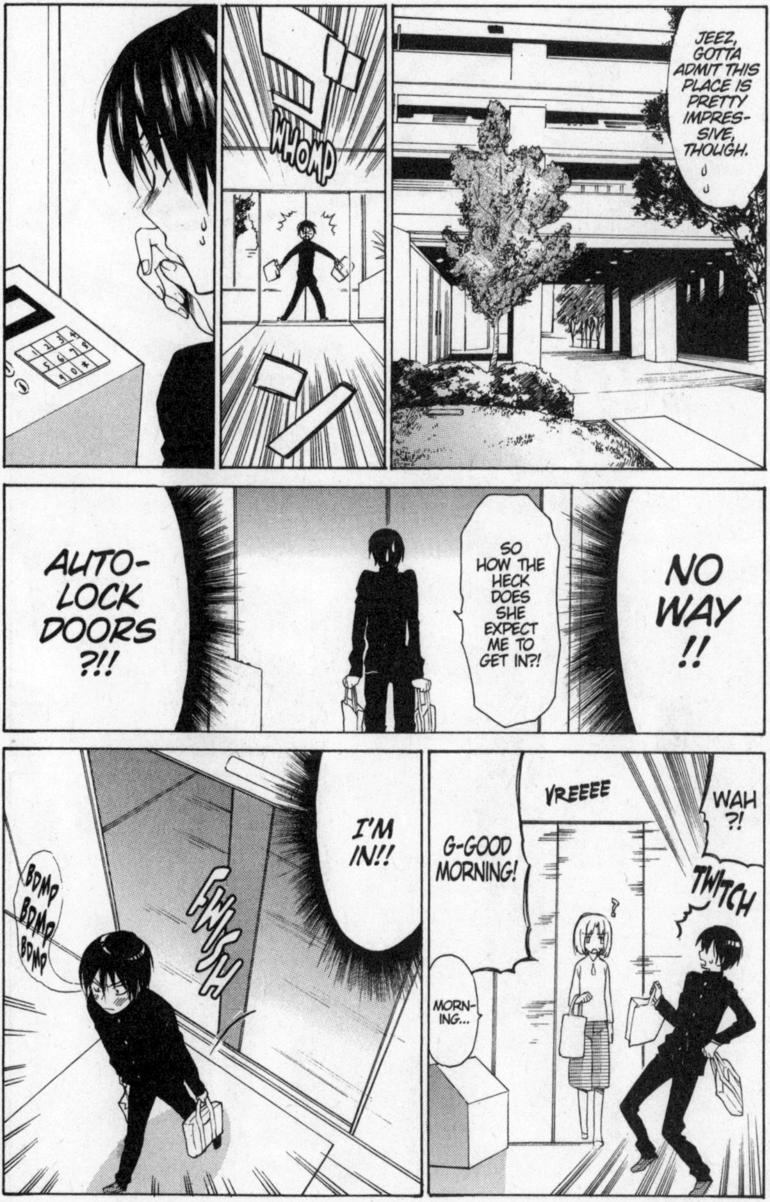
JEEZ, GOTTA ADMIT THIS PLACE IS PRETTY IMPRESSIVE, THOUGH.
WHOMP
NO WAY!!
SO HOW THE HECK DOES SHE EXPECT ME TO GET IN?!
AUTO-LOCK DOORS?!!
WAH?!
TWITCH
VREEEE
G-GOOD MORNING!
MORNING...
I'M IN!!
FWISH
BDMP BDMP BDMP

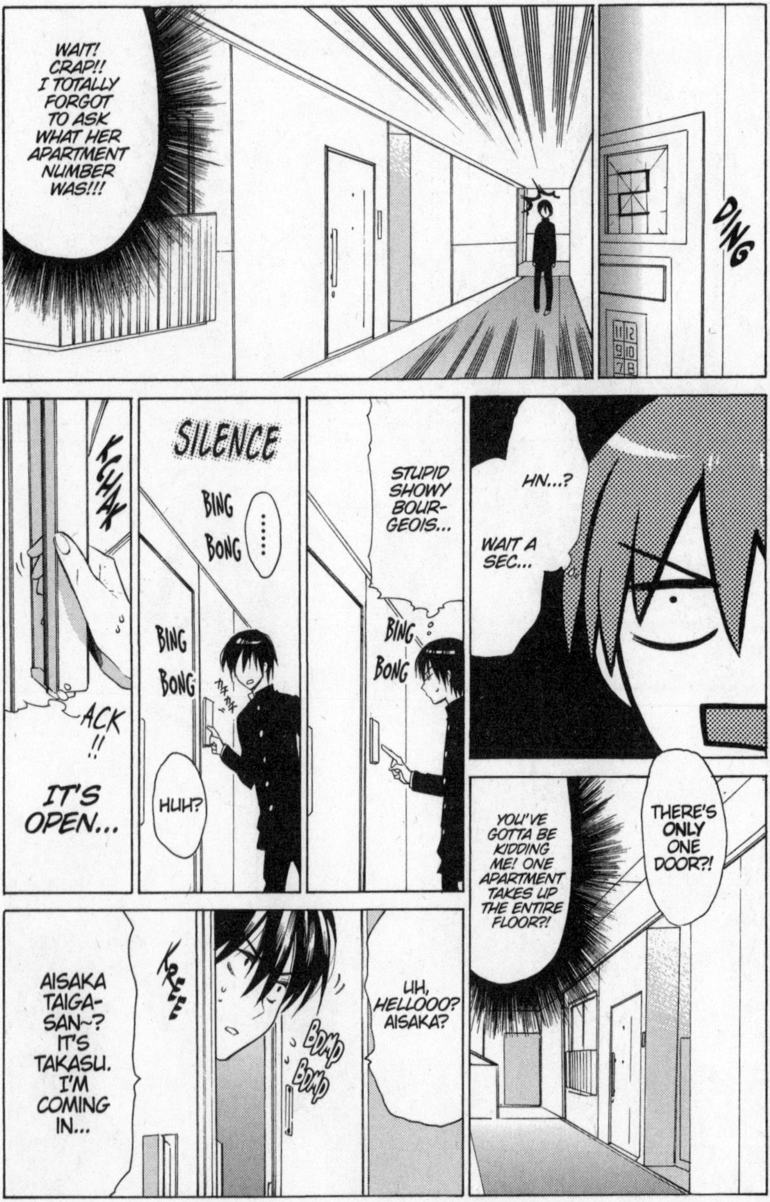
DING
WAIT! CRAP!! I TOTALLY FORGOT TO ASK WHAT HER APARTMENT NUMBER WAS!!!
HN...?
WAIT A SEC...
THERE'S ONLY ONE DOOR?!
YOU'VE GOTTA BE KIDDING ME! ONE APARTMENT TAKES UP THE ENTIRE FLOOR?!
STUPID SHOWY BOURGEOIS...
BING BONG
SILENCE
......
BING BONG
BING BONG
HUH?
KCHAK
ACK!!
IT'S OPEN...
UH, HELLOOO? AISAKA?
BDMP BDMP
KREEE
AISAKA TAIGA-SAN~? IT'S TAKASU. I'M COMING IN...

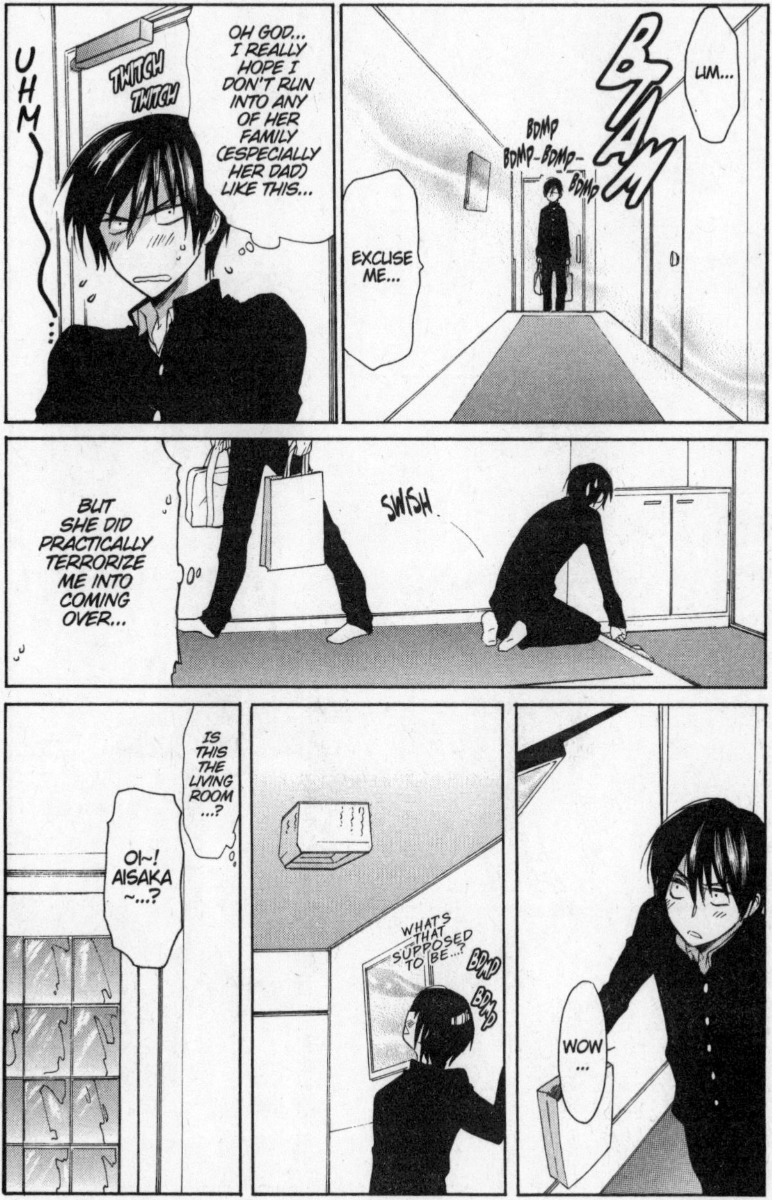
UM...
BAM
BDMP BDMP-BDMP-BDMP
EXCUSE ME...
OH GOD... I REALLY HOPE I DON'T RUN INTO ANY OF HER FAMILY (ESPECIALLY HER DAD) LIKE THIS...
TWITCH TWITCH
UHM...
SWISH
BUT SHE DID PRACTICALLY TERRORIZE ME INTO COMING OVER...
WOW ...
WHAT'S THAT SUPPOSED TO BE...?
BDMP BDMP
IS THIS THE LIVING ROOM ...?
OI~! AISAKA ~...?

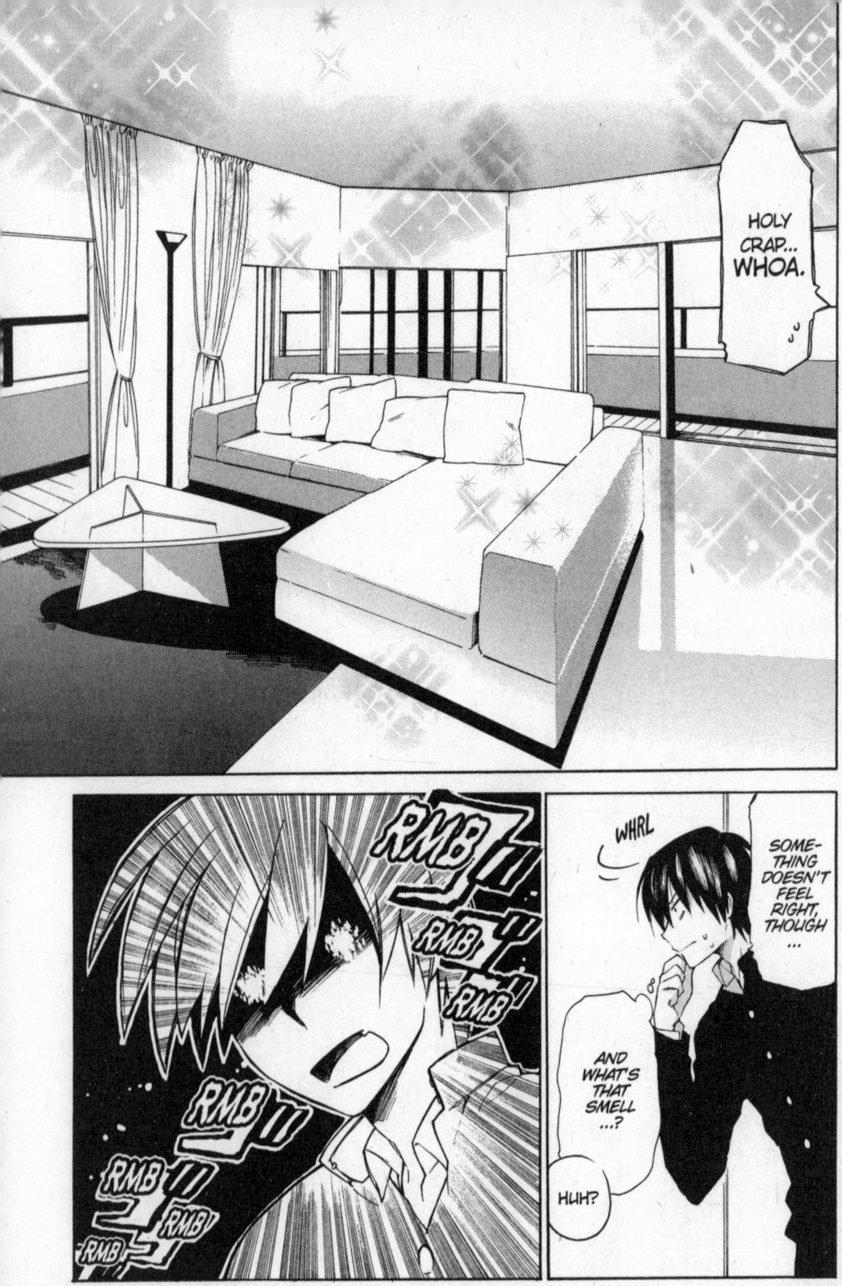
HOLY CRAP... WHOA.
SOMETHING DOESN'T FEEL RIGHT, THOUGH...
WHRL
AND WHAT'S THAT SMELL...?
HUH?
RMB RMB RMB
RMB RMB RMB RMB

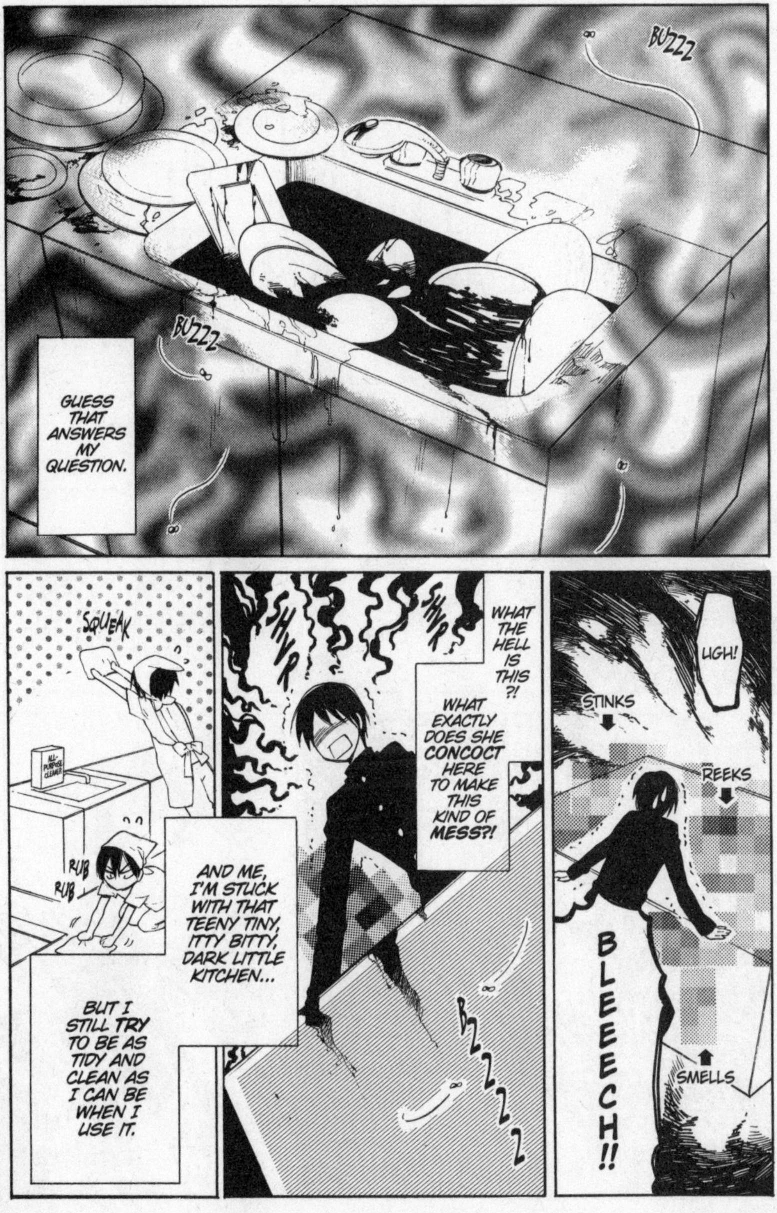
BUZZZ
BUZZZ
GUESS THAT ANSWERS MY QUESTION.
UGH!
STINKS
REEKS
BLEEECH!!
SMELLS
SHVR
SHVR
WHAT THE HELL IS THIS?!
WHAT EXACTLY DOES SHE CONCOCT HERE TO MAKE THIS KIND OF MESS?!
BZZZZZ
SQUEAK
ALL-PURPOSE CLEANER
RUB RUB
AND ME, I'M STUCK WITH THAT TEENY TINY, ITTY BITTY, DARK LITTLE KITCHEN...
BUT I STILL TRY TO BE AS TIDY AND CLEAN AS I CAN BE WHEN I USE IT.

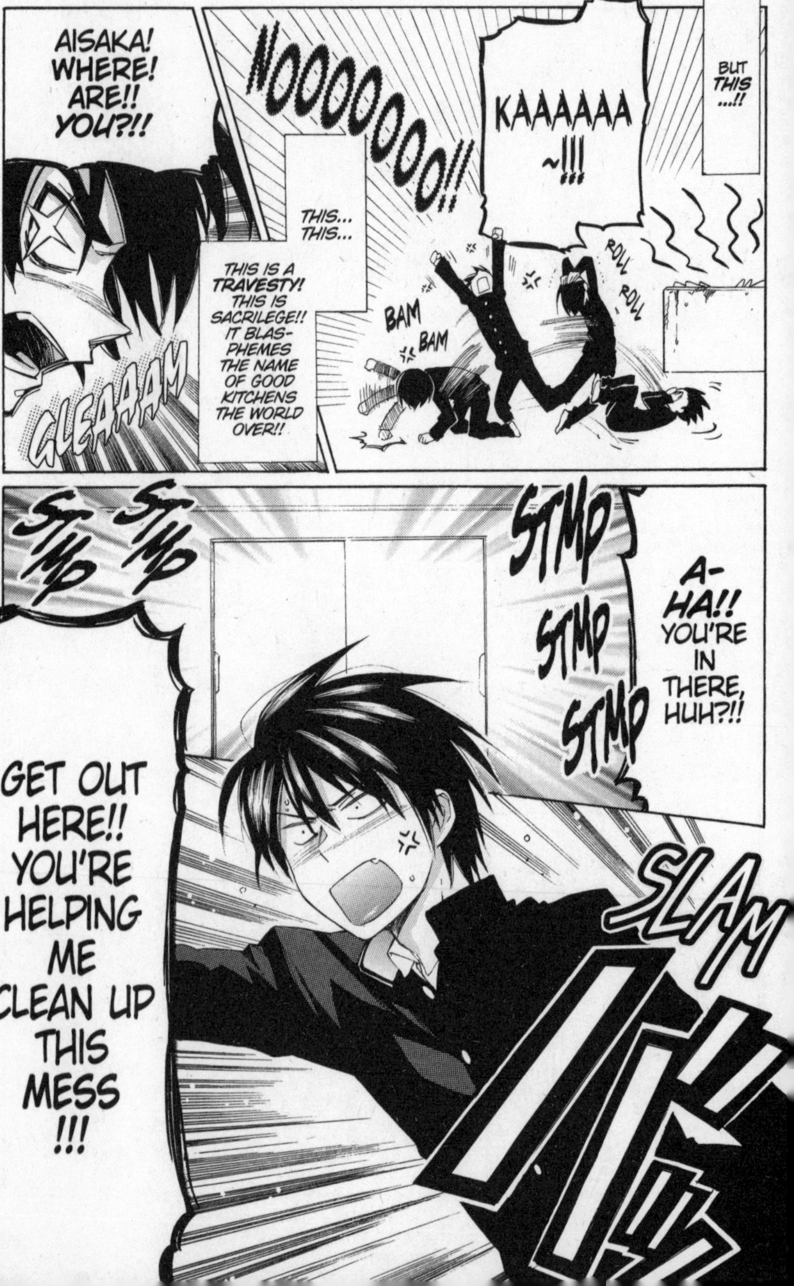
BUT THIS ...!!
KAAAAAA ~!!!
NOOOOOOO!!
THIS... THIS...
THIS IS A TRAVESTY! THIS IS SACRILEGE!! IT BLAS-PHEMES THE NAME OF GOOD KITCHENS THE WORLD OVER!!
ROLL
ROLL
BAM
BAM
AISAKA! WHERE! ARE!! YOU?!!
GLEAAAM
STMP STMP STMP
A-HA!! YOU'RE IN THERE, HUH?!!
STMP STMP
SLAM
GET OUT HERE!! YOU'RE HELPING ME CLEAN UP THIS MESS !!!

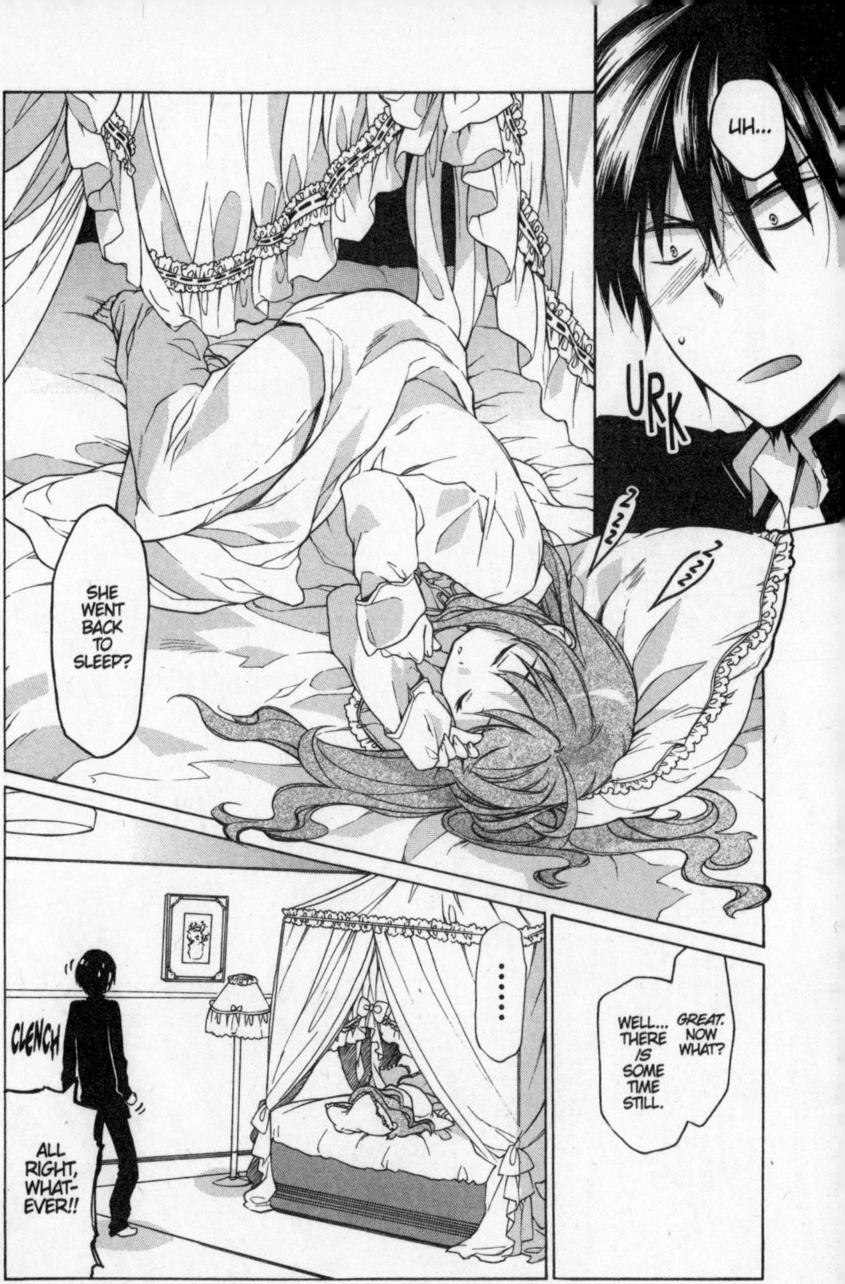
UH...
URK
SHE WENT BACK TO SLEEP?
ZZZ
ZZZ
GREAT. NOW WHAT?
WELL... THERE IS SOME TIME STILL.
......
CLENCH
ALL RIGHT, WHATEVER!!

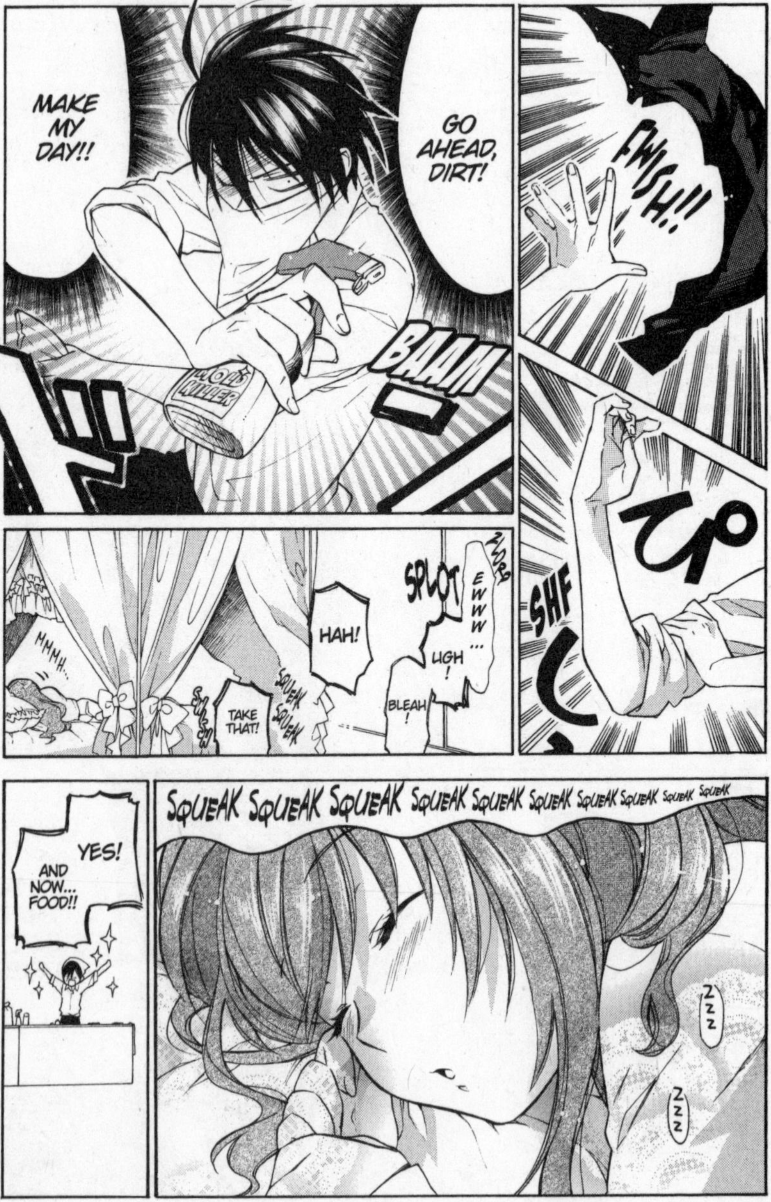
FWISH!!
SHF
GO AHEAD, DIRT!
MAKE MY DAY!!
MOLD KILLER
BAAM
SPLOT
EWWW...
UGH!
BLEAH!
HAH!
TAKE THAT!
SQUEAK SQUEAK
MMMH...
SQUEAK SQUEAK SQUEAK SQUEAK SQUEAK SQUEAK SQUEAK SQUEAK SQUEAK SQUEAK
ZZZ
ZZZ
YES! AND NOW... FOOD!!

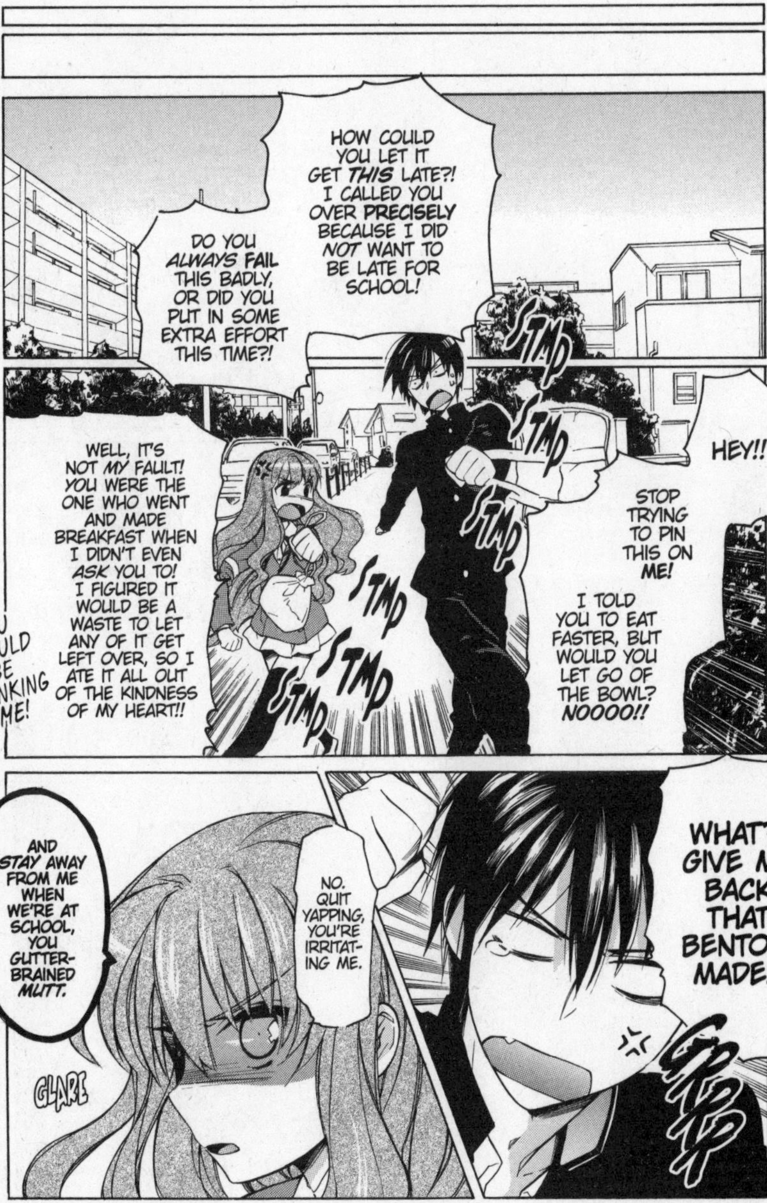
HOW COULD YOU LET IT GET *THIS* LATE?! I CALLED YOU OVER **PRECISELY** BECAUSE I DID *NOT* WANT TO BE LATE FOR SCHOOL!
DO YOU *ALWAYS* **FAIL** THIS BADLY, OR DID YOU PUT IN SOME EXTRA EFFORT THIS TIME?!
HEY!!
STOP TRYING TO PIN THIS ON **ME!**
I TOLD YOU TO EAT FASTER, BUT WOULD YOU LET GO OF THE BOWL? ***NOOOO!!***
STMP STMP STMP STMP STMP STMP
WELL, IT'S NOT *MY* FAULT! *YOU* WERE THE ONE WHO WENT AND MADE BREAKFAST WHEN I DIDN'T EVEN *ASK* YOU TO! I FIGURED IT WOULD BE A WASTE TO LET ANY OF IT GET LEFT OVER, SO I ATE IT ALL OUT OF THE KINDNESS OF MY HEART!!
OU HOULD BE HANKING ME!
WHAT?! GIVE ME BACK THAT BENTO I MADE!!
GRRR
NO. QUIT YAPPING, YOU'RE IRRITATING ME.
AND *STAY AWAY* FROM ME WHEN WE'RE AT SCHOOL, YOU GUTTER-BRAINED *MUTT.*
GLARE

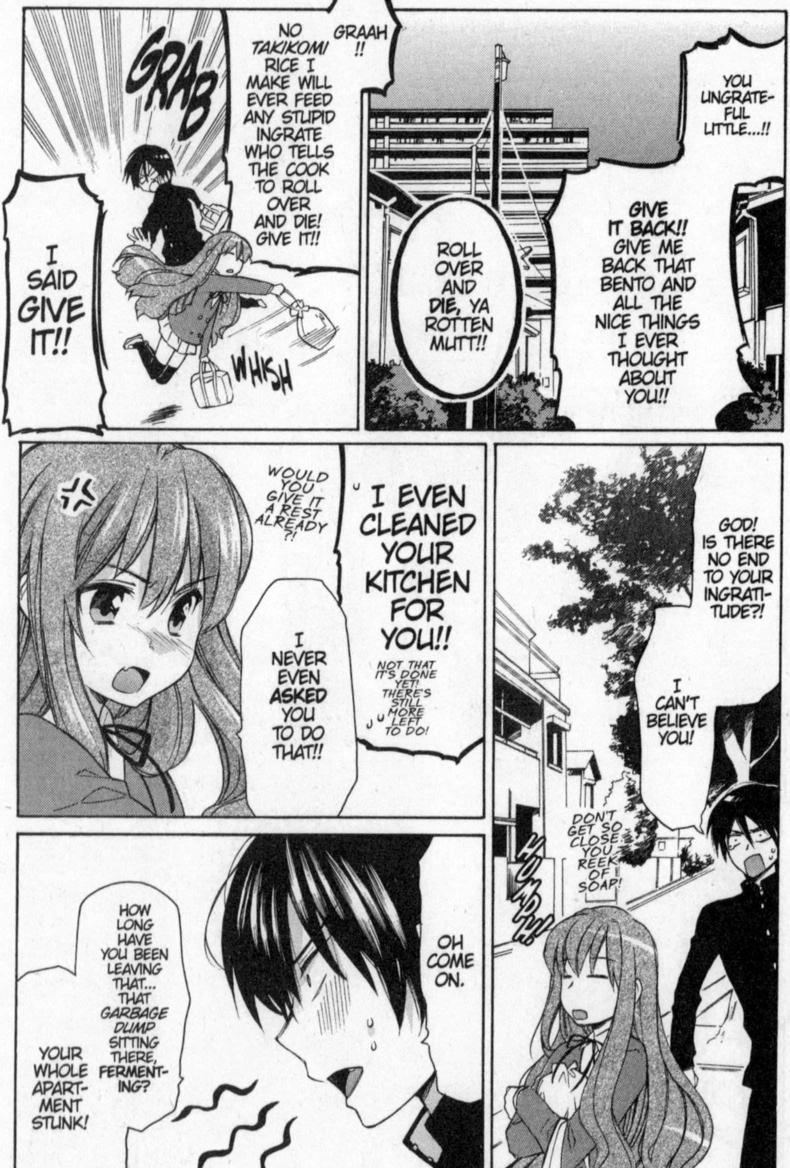
YOU UNGRATEFUL LITTLE...!!
GIVE IT BACK!! GIVE ME BACK THAT BENTO AND ALL THE NICE THINGS I EVER THOUGHT ABOUT YOU!!
ROLL OVER AND DIE, YA ROTTEN MUTT!!
GRAAH!!
NO TAKIKOMI RICE I MAKE WILL EVER FEED ANY STUPID INGRATE WHO TELLS THE COOK TO ROLL OVER AND DIE! GIVE IT!!
GRAB
I SAID GIVE IT!!
WHISH
GOD! IS THERE NO END TO YOUR INGRATITUDE?!
I CAN'T BELIEVE YOU!
DON'T GET SO CLOSE. YOU REEK OF SOAP!
HUMPH!
I EVEN CLEANED YOUR KITCHEN FOR YOU!!
NOT THAT IT'S DONE YET! THERE'S STILL MORE LEFT TO DO!
WOULD YOU GIVE IT A REST ALREADY?!
I NEVER EVEN ASKED YOU TO DO THAT!!
OH COME ON.
HOW LONG HAVE YOU BEEN LEAVING THAT... THAT GARBAGE DUMP SITTING THERE, FERMENTING?
YOUR WHOLE APARTMENT STUNK!

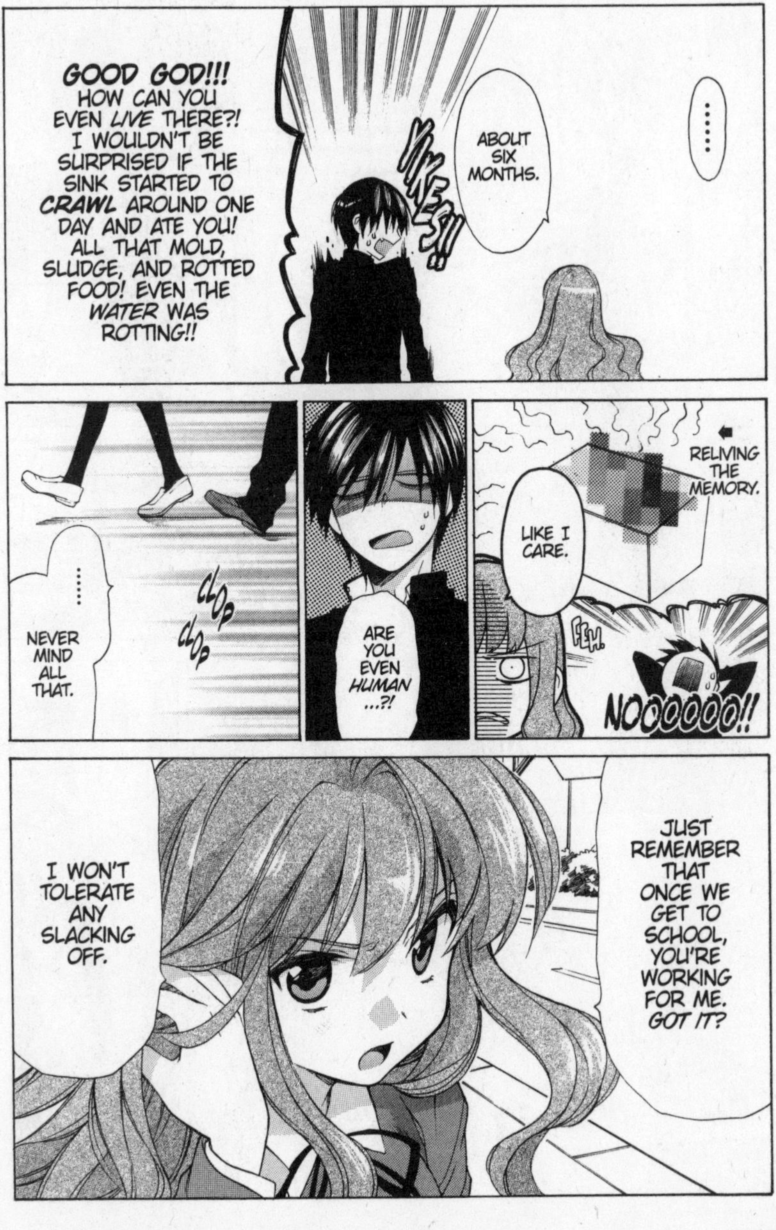
......
ABOUT SIX MONTHS.
YIKES!!
GOOD GOD!!! HOW CAN YOU EVEN LIVE THERE?! I WOULDN'T BE SURPRISED IF THE SINK STARTED TO CRAWL AROUND ONE DAY AND ATE YOU! ALL THAT MOLD, SLUDGE, AND ROTTED FOOD! EVEN THE WATER WAS ROTTING!!
RELIVING THE MEMORY.
LIKE I CARE.
FEH.
NOOOOOOO!!
ARE YOU EVEN HUMAN ...?!
CLOP CLOP
......
NEVER MIND ALL THAT.
JUST REMEMBER THAT ONCE WE GET TO SCHOOL, YOU'RE WORKING FOR ME. GOT IT?
I WON'T TOLERATE ANY SLACKING OFF.

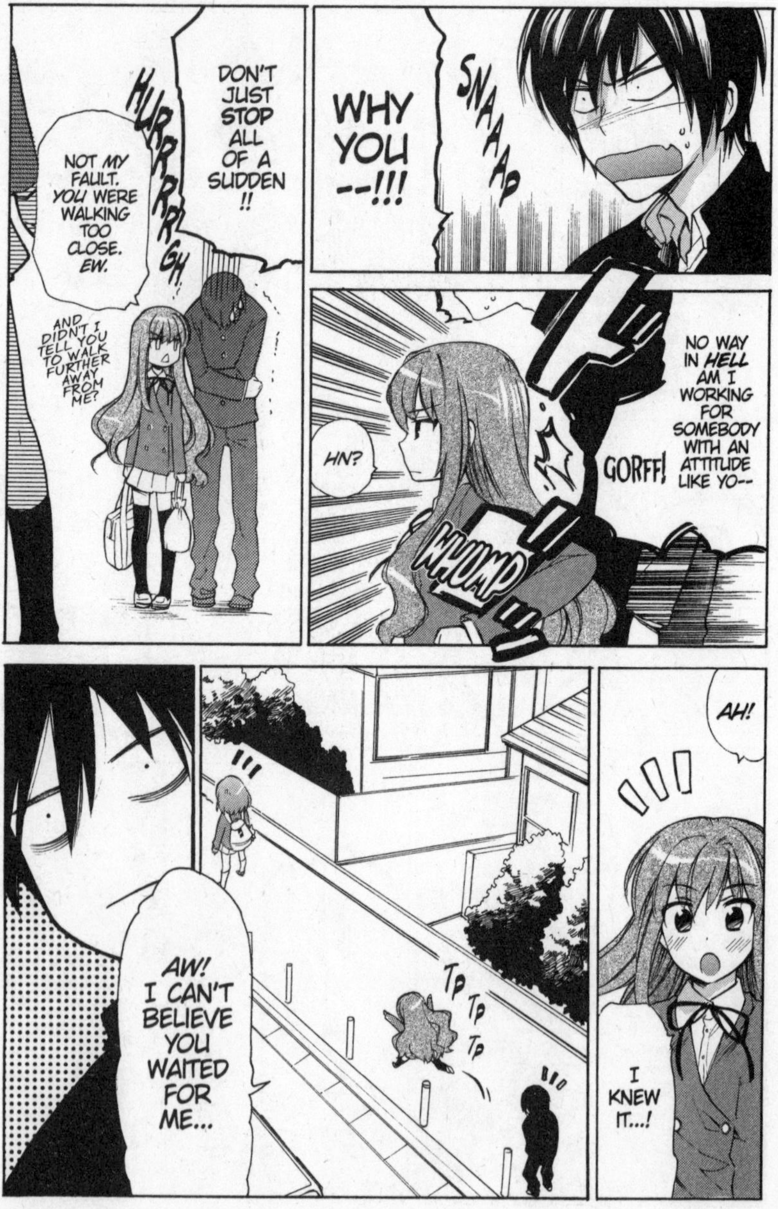
SNAAAAP
WHY YOU --!!!
NO WAY IN HELL AM I WORKING FOR SOMEBODY WITH AN ATTITUDE LIKE YO--
GORFF!
HN?
WHUMP
DON'T JUST STOP ALL OF A SUDDEN !!
HURRRRGH
NOT MY FAULT. YOU WERE WALKING TOO CLOSE. EW.
AND DIDN'T I TELL YOU TO WALK FURTHER AWAY FROM ME?
AH!
I KNEW IT...!
Tp Tp Tp Tp
AW! I CAN'T BELIEVE YOU WAITED FOR ME...

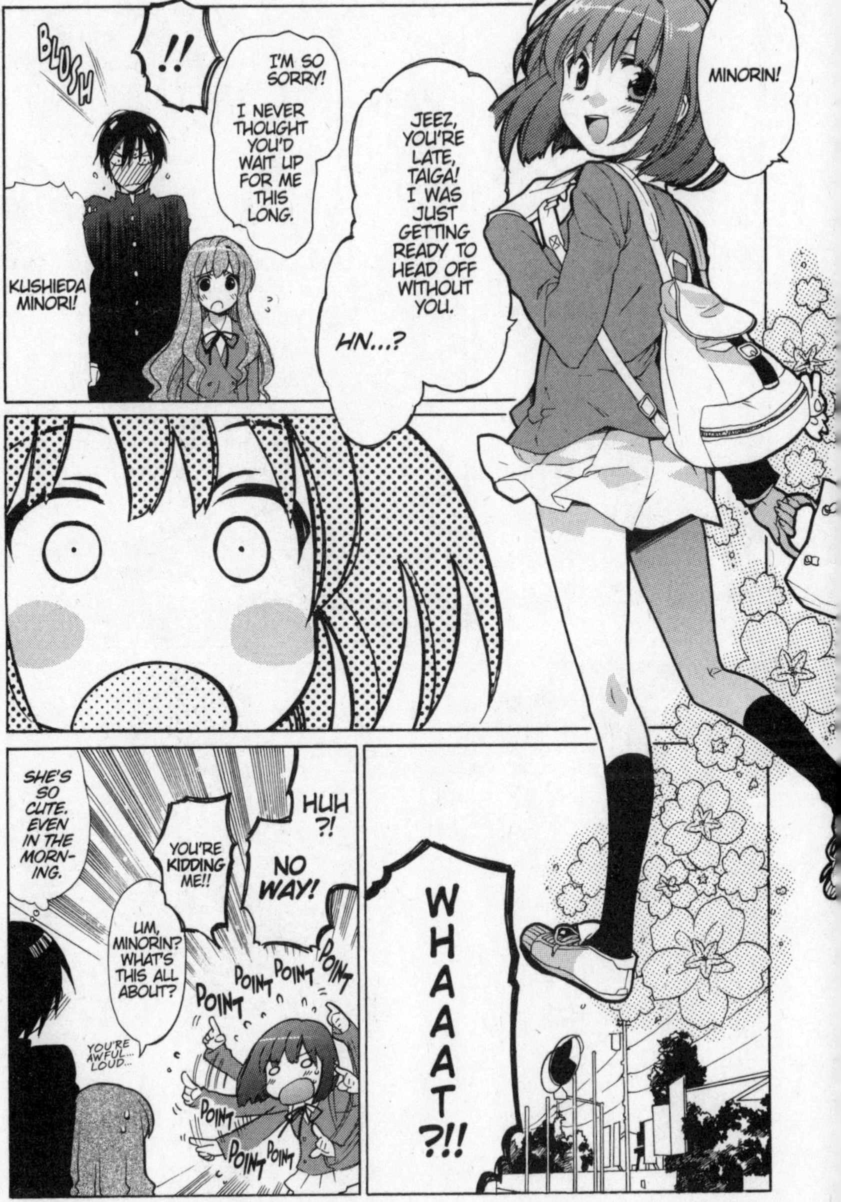
MINORIN!
JEEZ, YOU'RE LATE, TAIGA! I WAS JUST GETTING READY TO HEAD OFF WITHOUT YOU.
HN...?
I'M SO SORRY! I NEVER THOUGHT YOU'D WAIT UP FOR ME THIS LONG.
!!
BLUSH
KUSHIEDA MINORI!
WHAAAT?!!
HUH?! NO WAY!
YOU'RE KIDDING ME!!
POINT POINT POINT POINT POINT POINT
UM, MINORIN? WHAT'S THIS ALL ABOUT?
SHE'S SO CUTE. EVEN IN THE MORN-ING.
YOU'RE AWFUL... LOUD...

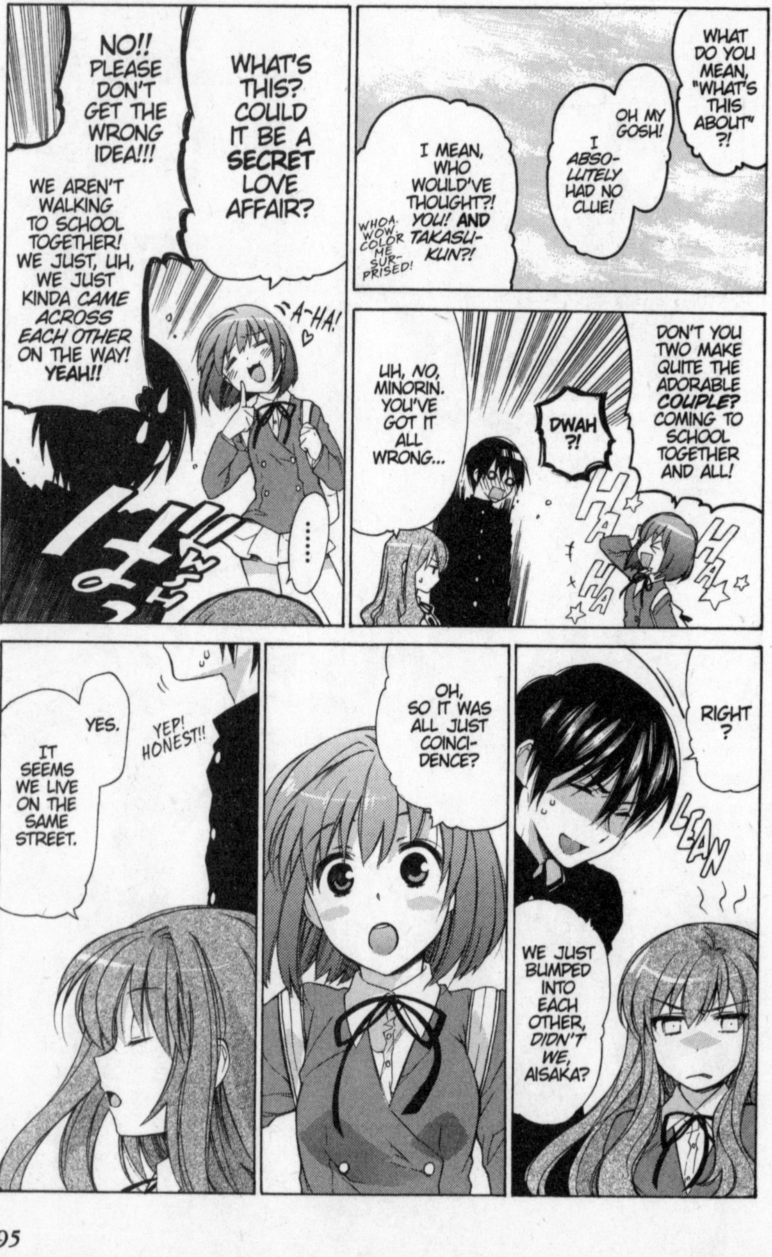
WHAT DO YOU MEAN, "WHAT'S THIS ABOUT"?!
OH MY GOSH!
I ABSOLUTELY HAD NO CLUE!
I MEAN, WHO WOULD'VE THOUGHT?! YOU! AND TAKASU-KUN?!
WHOA. WOW. COLOR ME SURPRISED!
DON'T YOU TWO MAKE QUITE THE ADORABLE COUPLE? COMING TO SCHOOL TOGETHER AND ALL!
DWAH?!
HA HA HA HA HA
UH, NO, MINORIN. YOU'VE GOT IT ALL WRONG...
WHAT'S THIS? COULD IT BE A SECRET LOVE AFFAIR?
A-HA!
NO!! PLEASE DON'T GET THE WRONG IDEA!!!
WE AREN'T WALKING TO SCHOOL TOGETHER! WE JUST, UH, WE JUST KINDA CAME ACROSS EACH OTHER ON THE WAY! YEAH!!
......
RIGHT?
LEAN
WE JUST BUMPED INTO EACH OTHER, DIDN'T WE, AISAKA?
OH, SO IT WAS ALL JUST COINCIDENCE?
YEP! HONEST!!
YES.
IT SEEMS WE LIVE ON THE SAME STREET.

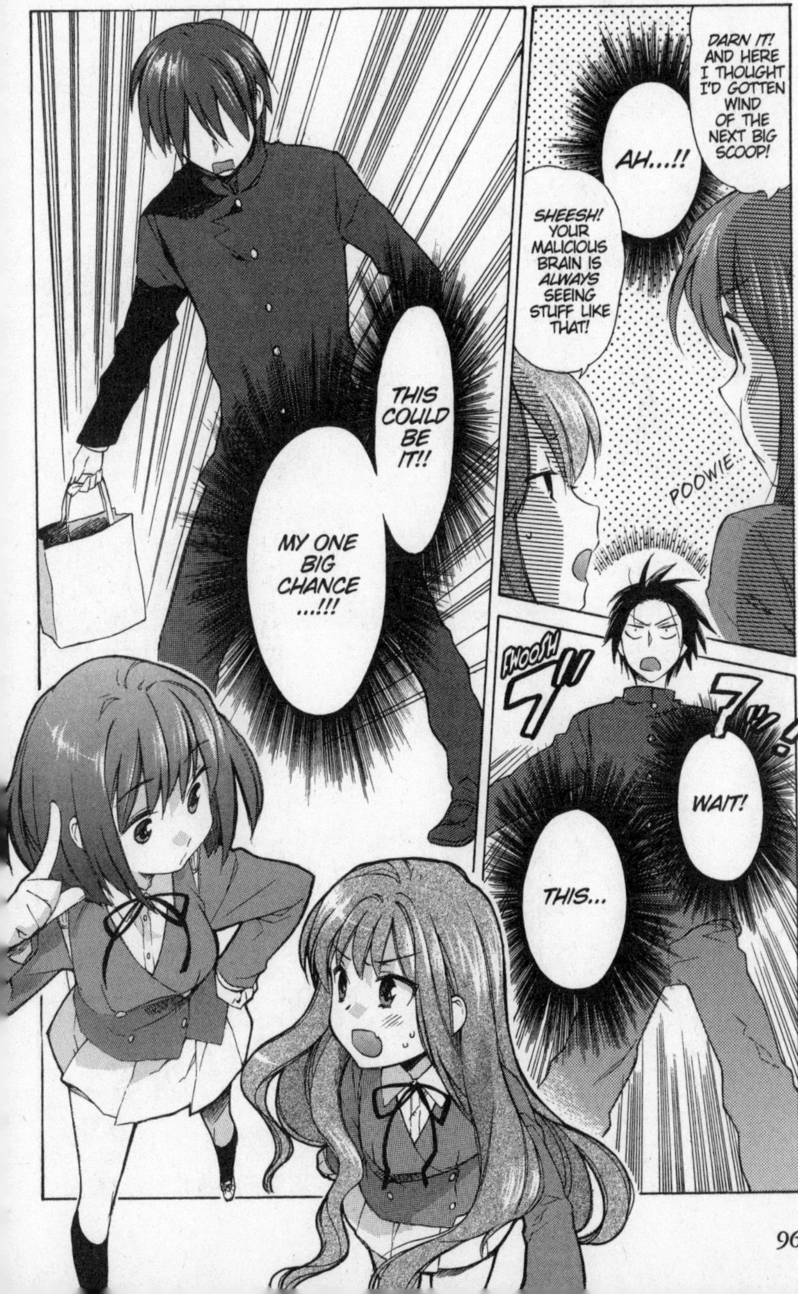
DARN IT! AND HERE I THOUGHT I'D GOTTEN WIND OF THE NEXT BIG SCOOP!
AH...!!
SHEESH! YOUR MALICIOUS BRAIN IS ALWAYS SEEING STUFF LIKE THAT!
POOWIE...
FWOOSH
WAIT!
THIS...
THIS COULD BE IT!!
MY ONE BIG CHANCE ...!!!

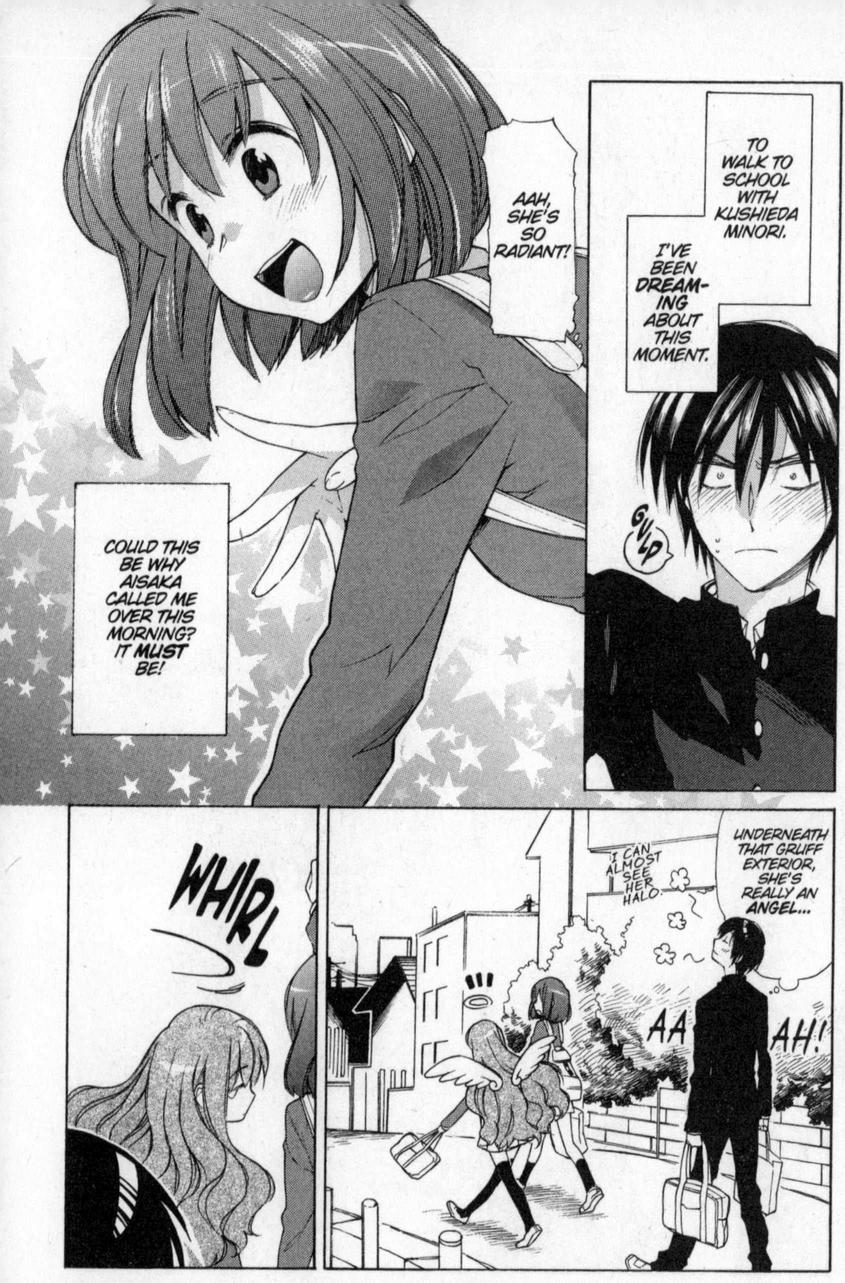
TO WALK TO SCHOOL WITH KUSHIEDA MINORI.
I'VE BEEN DREAMING ABOUT THIS MOMENT.
GULP
AAH, SHE'S SO RADIANT!
COULD THIS BE WHY AISAKA CALLED ME OVER THIS MORNING? IT MUST BE!
UNDERNEATH THAT GRUFF EXTERIOR, SHE'S REALLY AN ANGEL...
I CAN ALMOST SEE HER HALO.
AA AH!
WHIRL

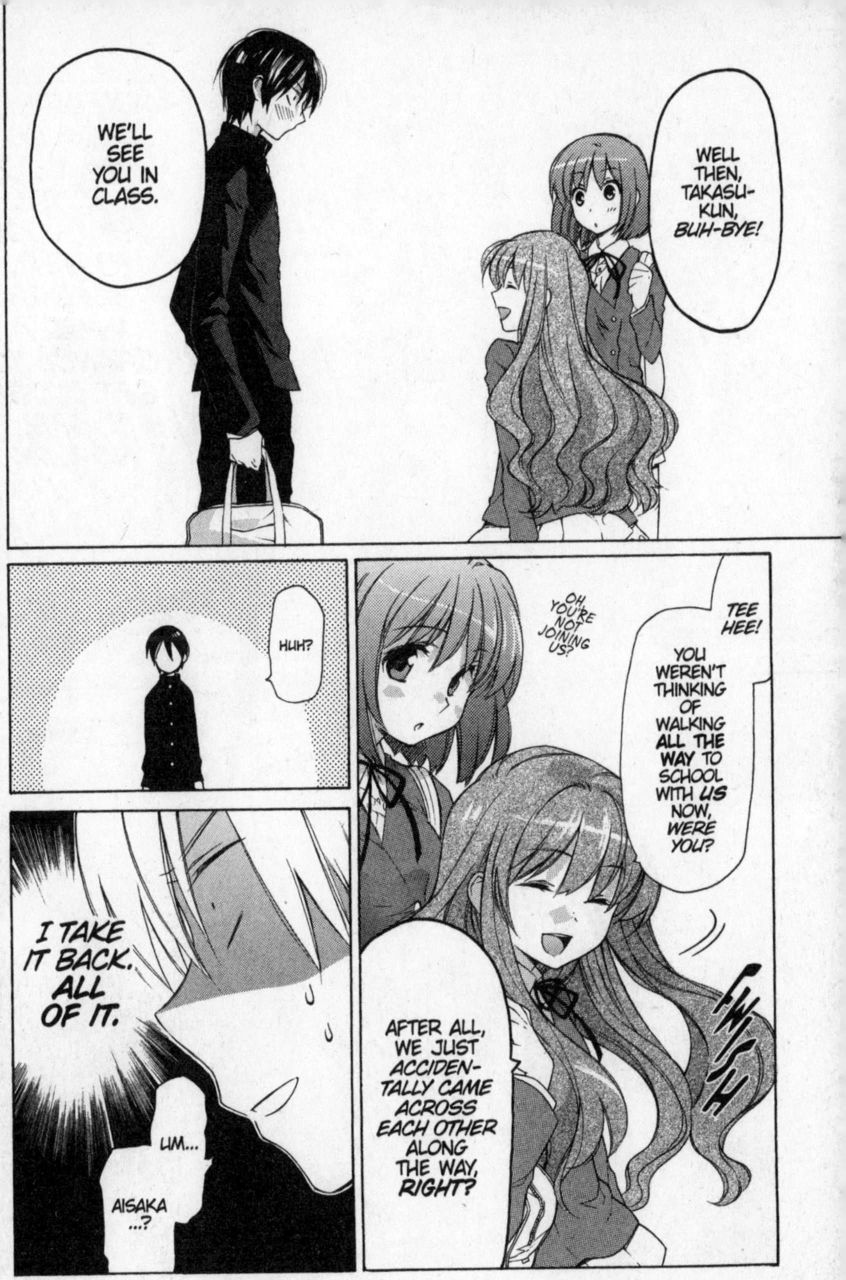
WELL THEN, TAKASU-KUN, BUH-BYE!
WE'LL SEE YOU IN CLASS.
TEE HEE!
YOU WEREN'T THINKING OF WALKING ALL THE WAY TO SCHOOL WITH US NOW, WERE YOU?
OH, YOU'RE NOT JOINING US?
FWISH
AFTER ALL, WE JUST ACCIDENTALLY CAME ACROSS EACH OTHER ALONG THE WAY, RIGHT?
HUH?
I TAKE IT BACK. ALL OF IT.
UM...
AISAKA ...?

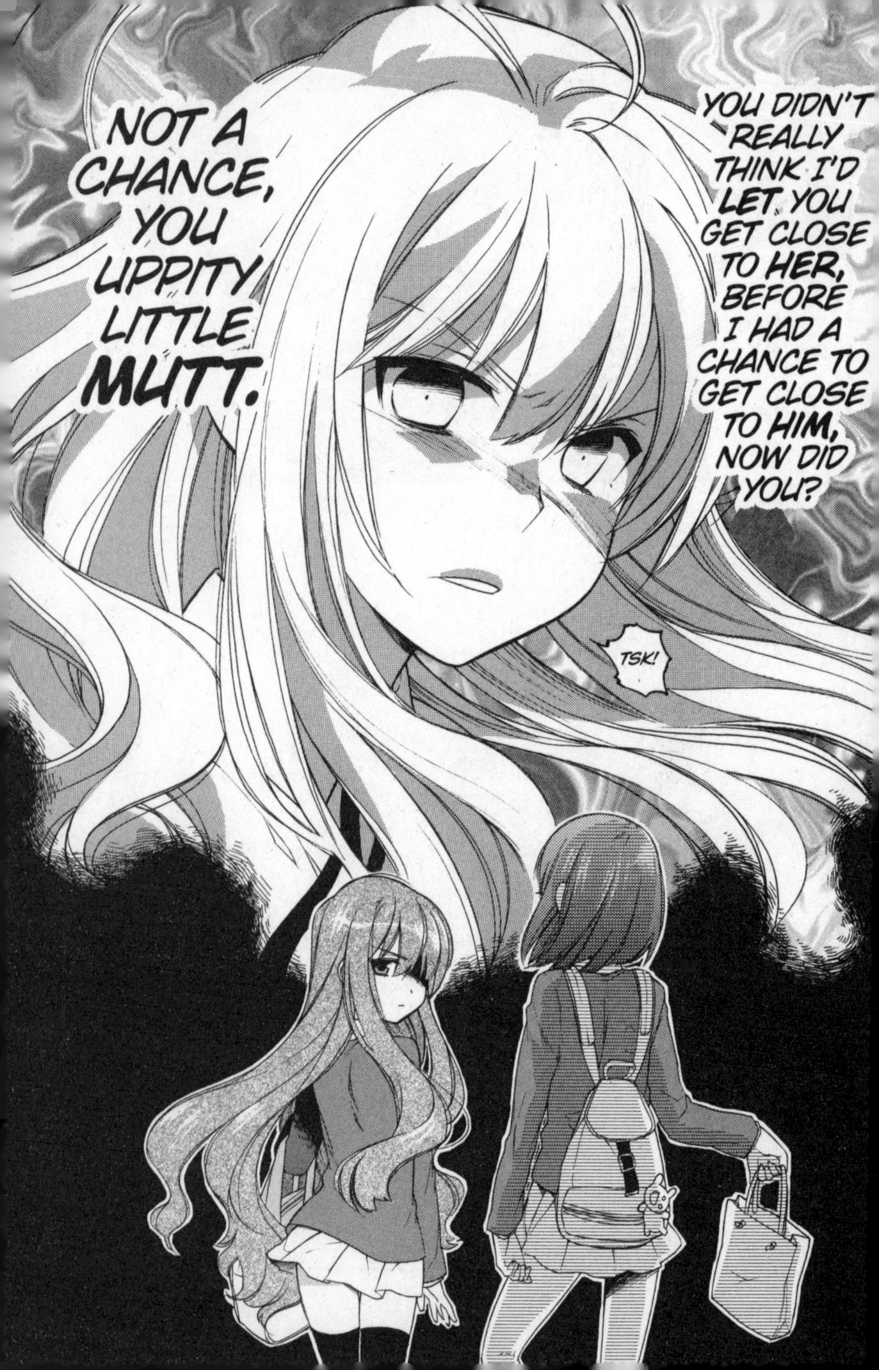
YOU DIDN'T REALLY THINK I'D LET YOU GET CLOSE TO HER, BEFORE I HAD A CHANCE TO GET CLOSE TO HIM, NOW DID YOU?
NOT A CHANCE, YOU UPPITY LITTLE MUTT.
TSK!

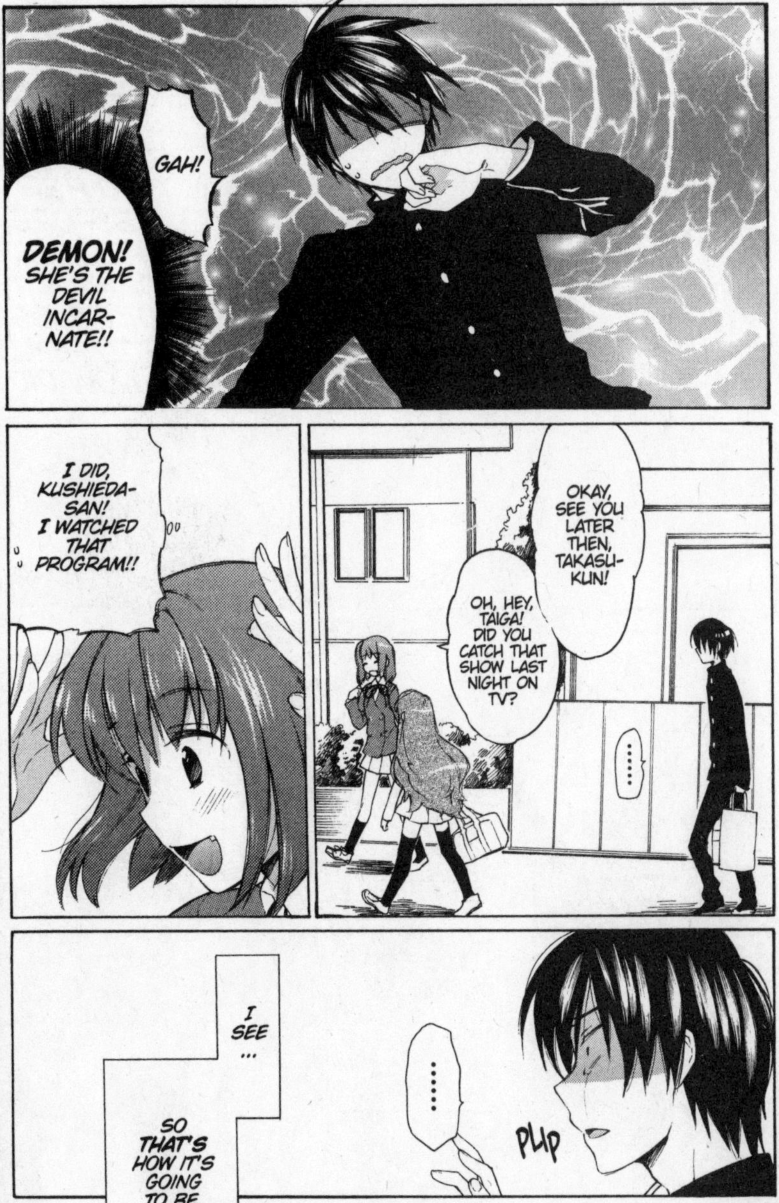
GAH!
DEMON! SHE'S THE DEVIL INCARNATE!!
OKAY, SEE YOU LATER THEN, TAKASU-KUN!
OH, HEY, TAIGA! DID YOU CATCH THAT SHOW LAST NIGHT ON TV?
......
I DID, KUSHIEDA-SAN! I WATCHED THAT PROGRAM!!
......
PLIP
I SEE ...
SO THAT'S HOW IT'S GOING TO BE, HUH?

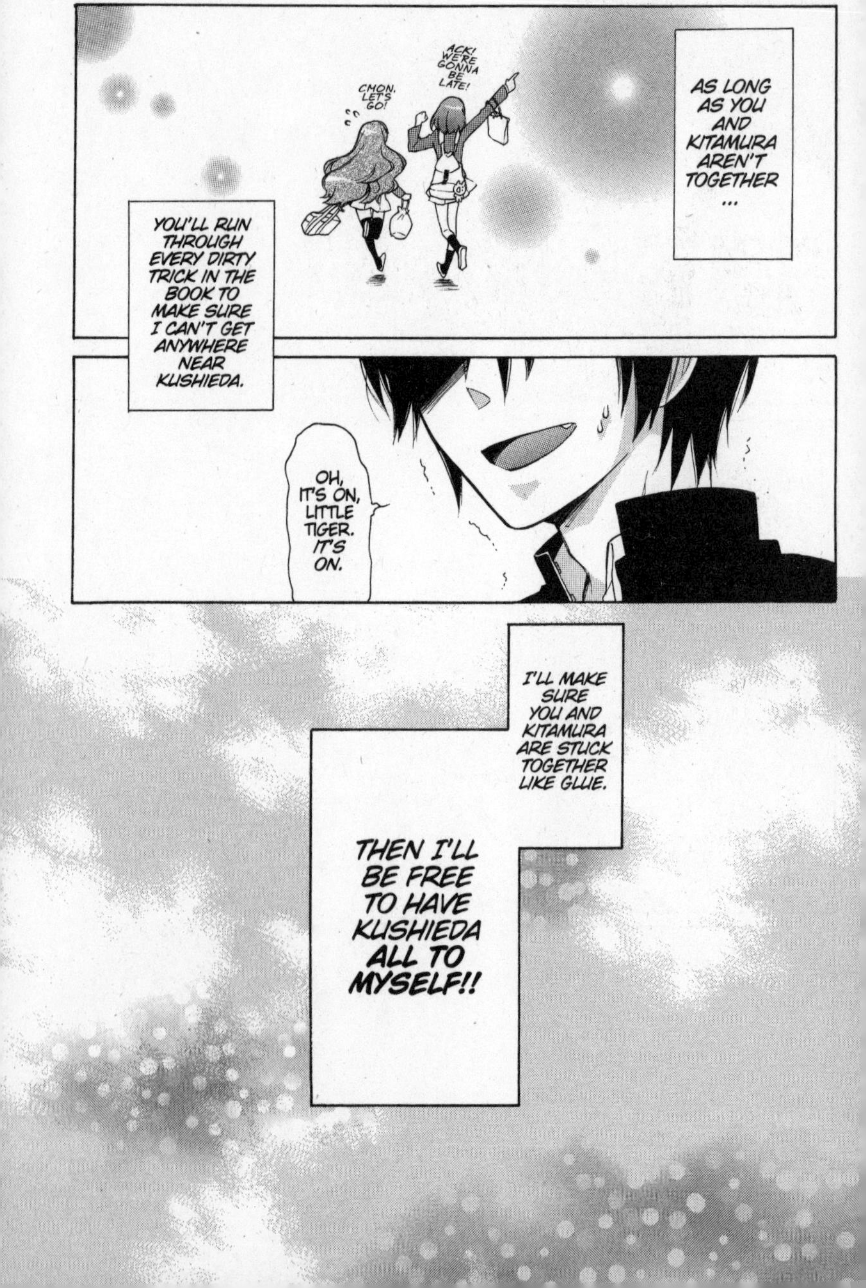
AS LONG AS YOU AND KITAMURA AREN'T TOGETHER...
ACK! WE'RE GONNA BE LATE!
CMON. LET'S GO!
YOU'LL RUN THROUGH EVERY DIRTY TRICK IN THE BOOK TO MAKE SURE I CAN'T GET ANYWHERE NEAR KUSHIEDA.
OH, IT'S ON, LITTLE TIGER. IT'S ON.
I'LL MAKE SURE YOU AND KITAMURA ARE STUCK TOGETHER LIKE GLUE.
THEN I'LL BE FREE TO HAVE KUSHIEDA ALL TO MYSELF!!

Yep,
we don't need this version of Kitamura.

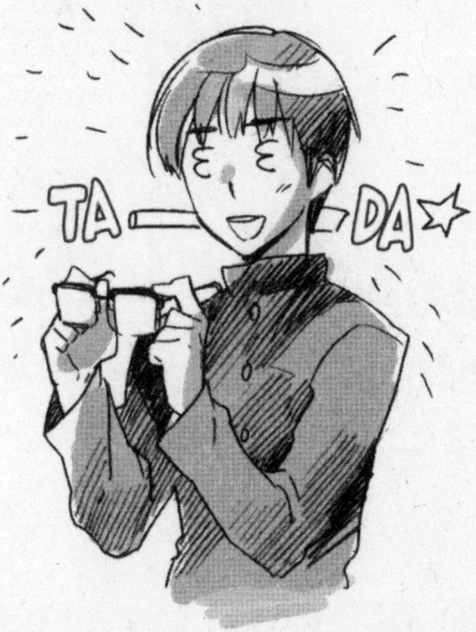
TA—DA☆

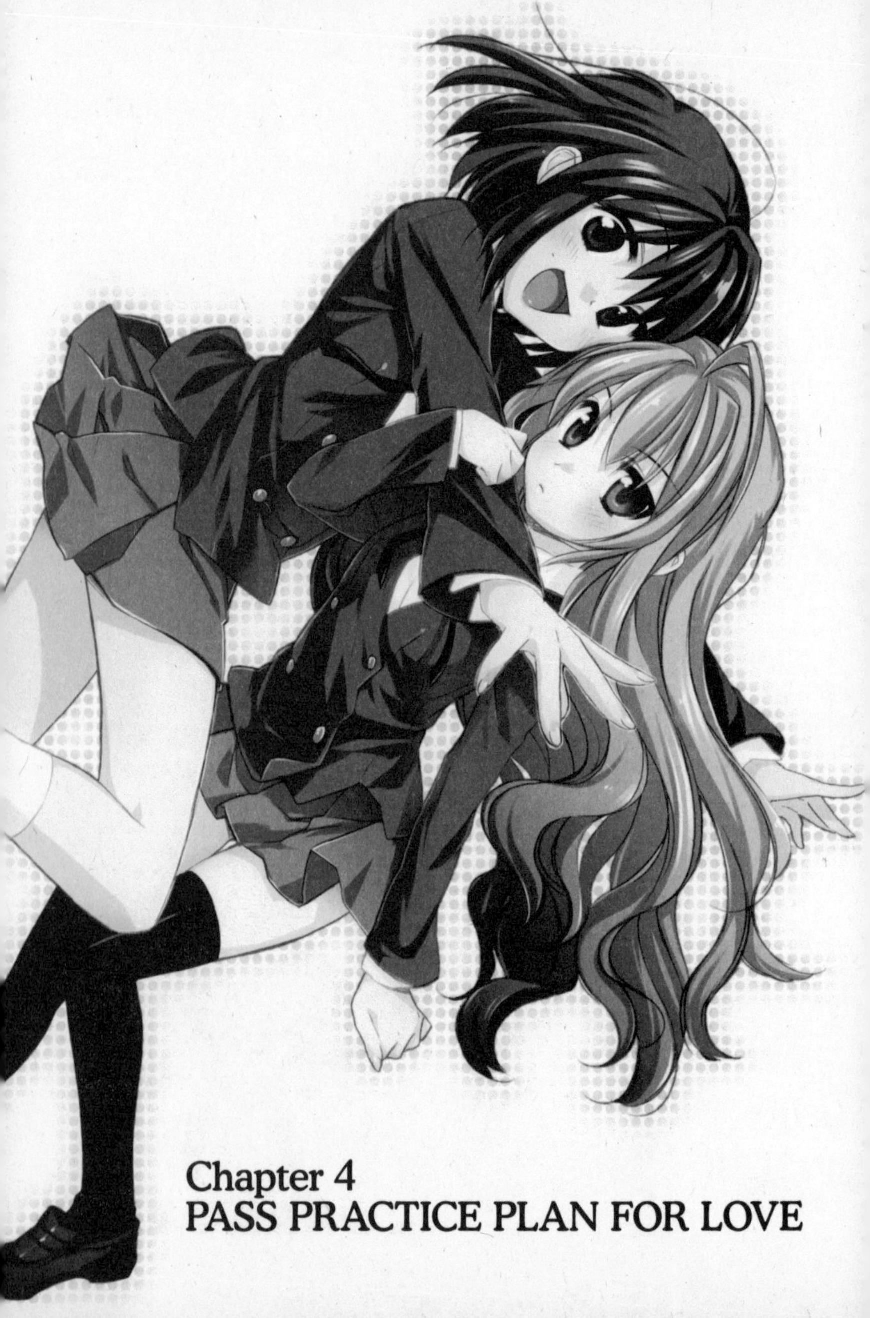

Chapter 4
PASS PRACTICE PLAN FOR LOVE

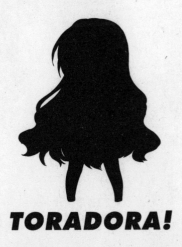

TORADORA!

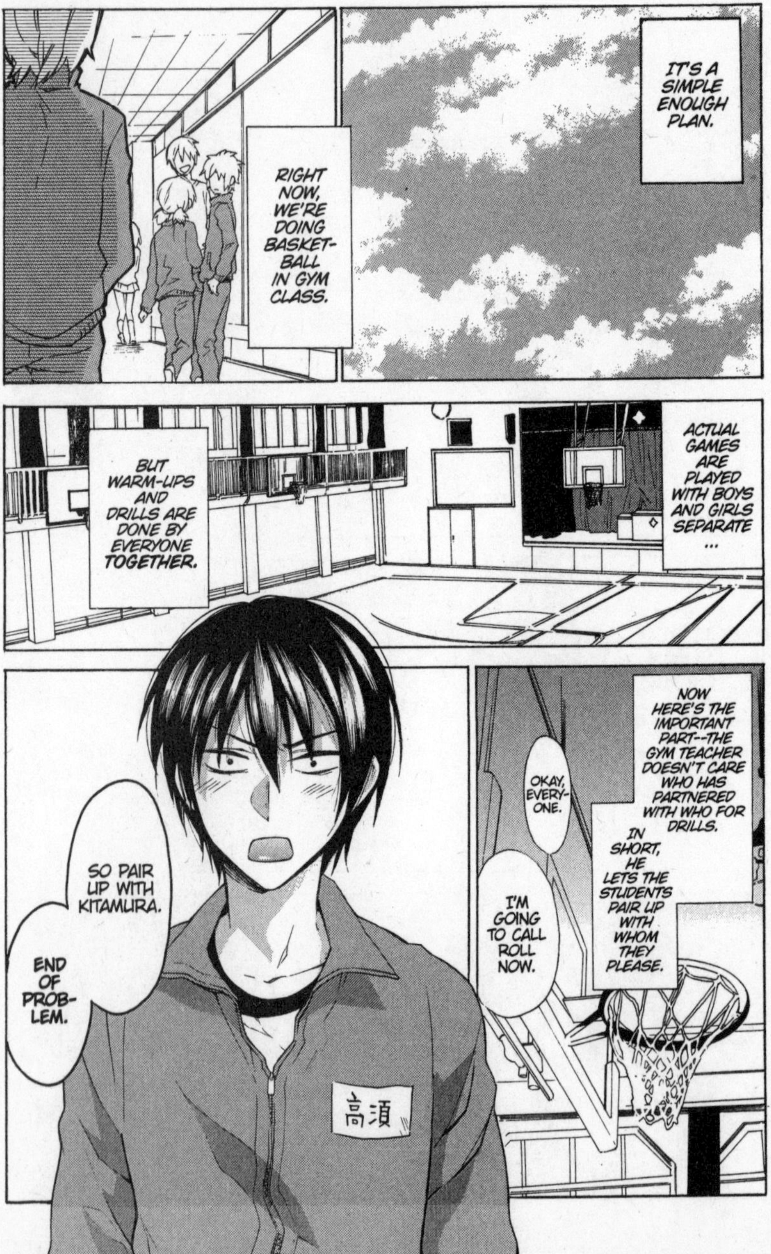
IT'S A SIMPLE ENOUGH PLAN.
RIGHT NOW, WE'RE DOING BASKET-BALL IN GYM CLASS.
ACTUAL GAMES ARE PLAYED WITH BOYS AND GIRLS SEPARATE ...
BUT WARM-UPS AND DRILLS ARE DONE BY EVERYONE TOGETHER.
NOW HERE'S THE IMPORTANT PART--THE GYM TEACHER DOESN'T CARE WHO HAS PARTNERED WITH WHO FOR DRILLS.
OKAY, EVERY-ONE.
IN SHORT, HE LETS THE STUDENTS PAIR UP WITH WHOM THEY PLEASE.
I'M GOING TO CALL ROLL NOW.
SO PAIR UP WITH KITAMURA.
END OF PROB-LEM.
高須

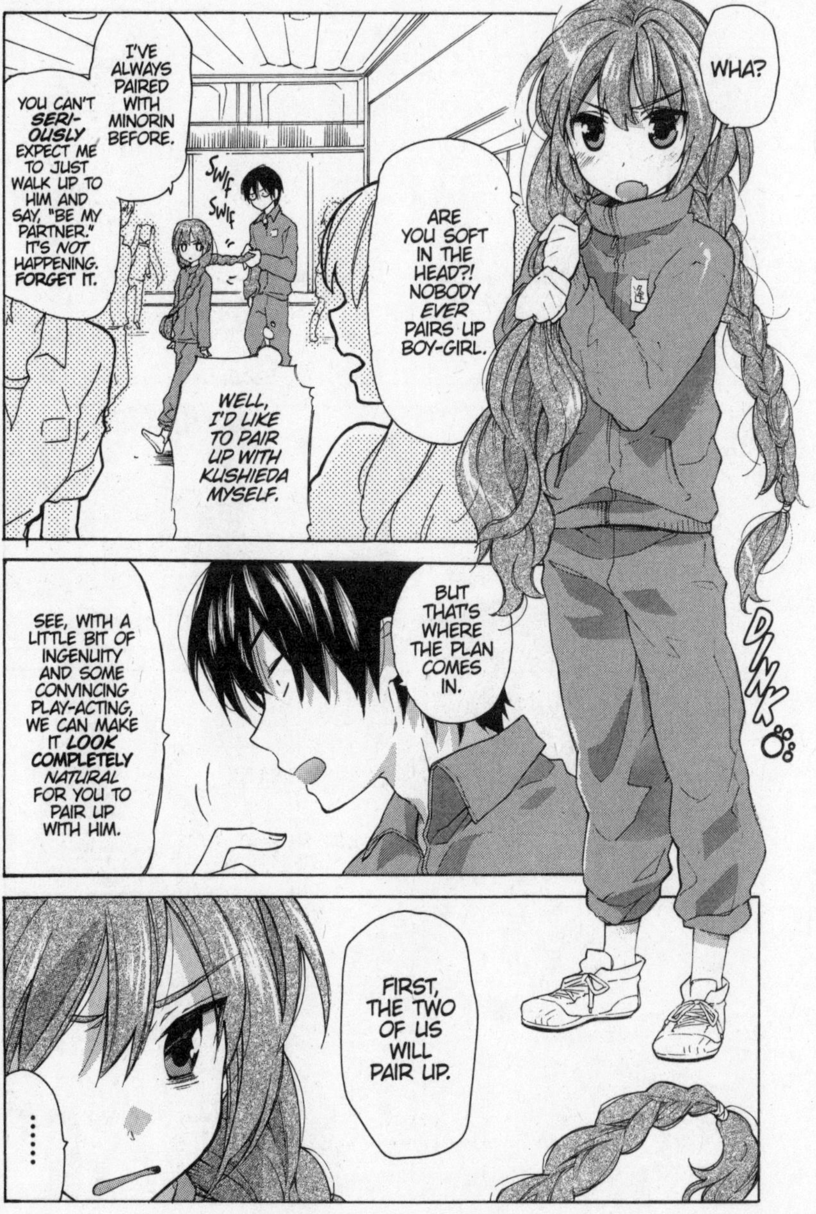
WHA?
ARE YOU SOFT IN THE HEAD?! NOBODY EVER PAIRS UP BOY-GIRL.
I'VE ALWAYS PAIRED WITH MINORIN BEFORE.
YOU CAN'T SERIOUSLY EXPECT ME TO JUST WALK UP TO HIM AND SAY, "BE MY PARTNER." IT'S NOT HAPPENING. FORGET IT.
SWIF SWIF
WELL, I'D LIKE TO PAIR UP WITH KUSHIEDA MYSELF.
DINK
BUT THAT'S WHERE THE PLAN COMES IN.
SEE, WITH A LITTLE BIT OF INGENUITY AND SOME CONVINCING PLAY-ACTING, WE CAN MAKE IT LOOK COMPLETELY NATURAL FOR YOU TO PAIR UP WITH HIM.
FIRST, THE TWO OF US WILL PAIR UP.
......

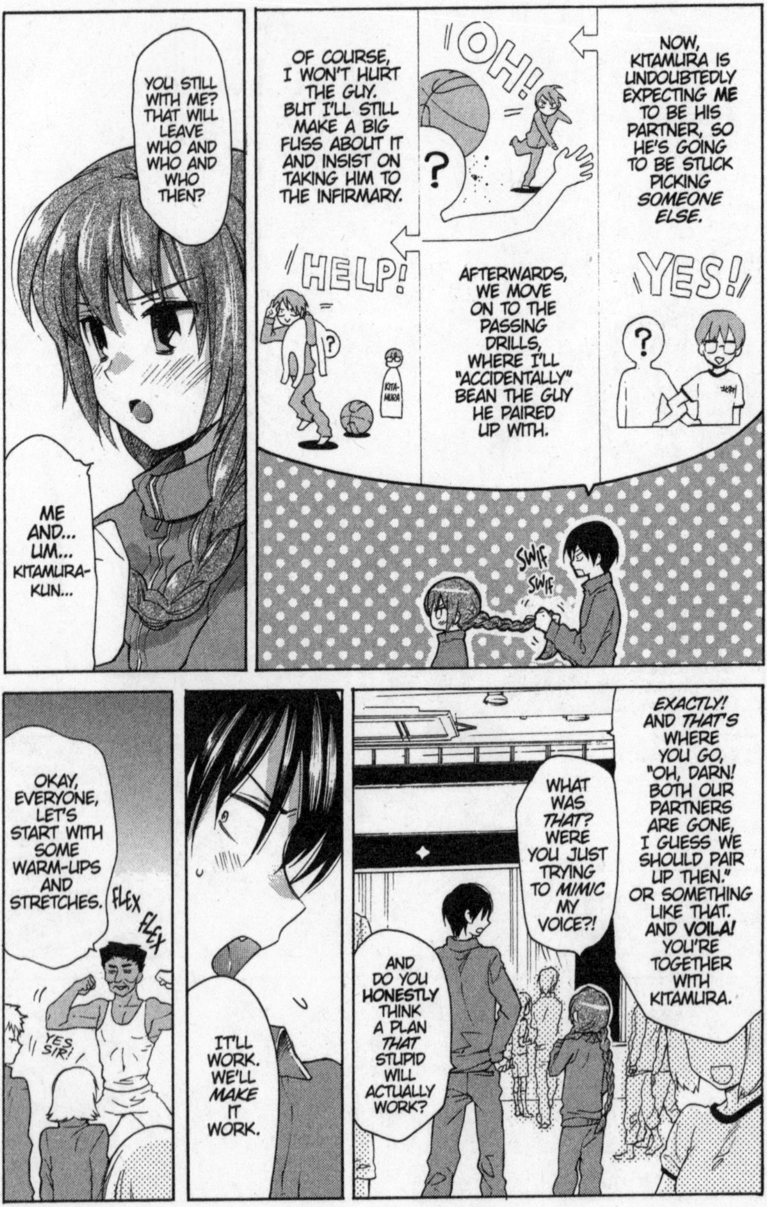
NOW, KITAMURA IS UNDOUBTEDLY EXPECTING ME TO BE HIS PARTNER, SO HE'S GOING TO BE STUCK PICKING SOMEONE ELSE.
YES!
KITAMURA
AFTERWARDS, WE MOVE ON TO THE PASSING DRILLS, WHERE I'LL "ACCIDENTALLY" BEAN THE GUY HE PAIRED UP WITH.
OH!
OF COURSE, I WON'T HURT THE GUY. BUT I'LL STILL MAKE A BIG FUSS ABOUT IT AND INSIST ON TAKING HIM TO THE INFIRMARY.
HELP!
KITA-MURA
SWIF
SWIF
YOU STILL WITH ME? THAT WILL LEAVE WHO AND WHO AND WHO THEN?
ME AND... UM... KITAMURA-KUN...
EXACTLY! AND THAT'S WHERE YOU GO, "OH, DARN! BOTH OUR PARTNERS ARE GONE, I GUESS WE SHOULD PAIR UP THEN." OR SOMETHING LIKE THAT. AND VOILA! YOU'RE TOGETHER WITH KITAMURA.
WHAT WAS THAT? WERE YOU JUST TRYING TO MIMIC MY VOICE?!
AND DO YOU HONESTLY THINK A PLAN THAT STUPID WILL ACTUALLY WORK?
IT'LL WORK. WE'LL MAKE IT WORK.
OKAY, EVERYONE, LET'S START WITH SOME WARM-UPS AND STRETCHES.
FLEX
FLEX
YES SIR!

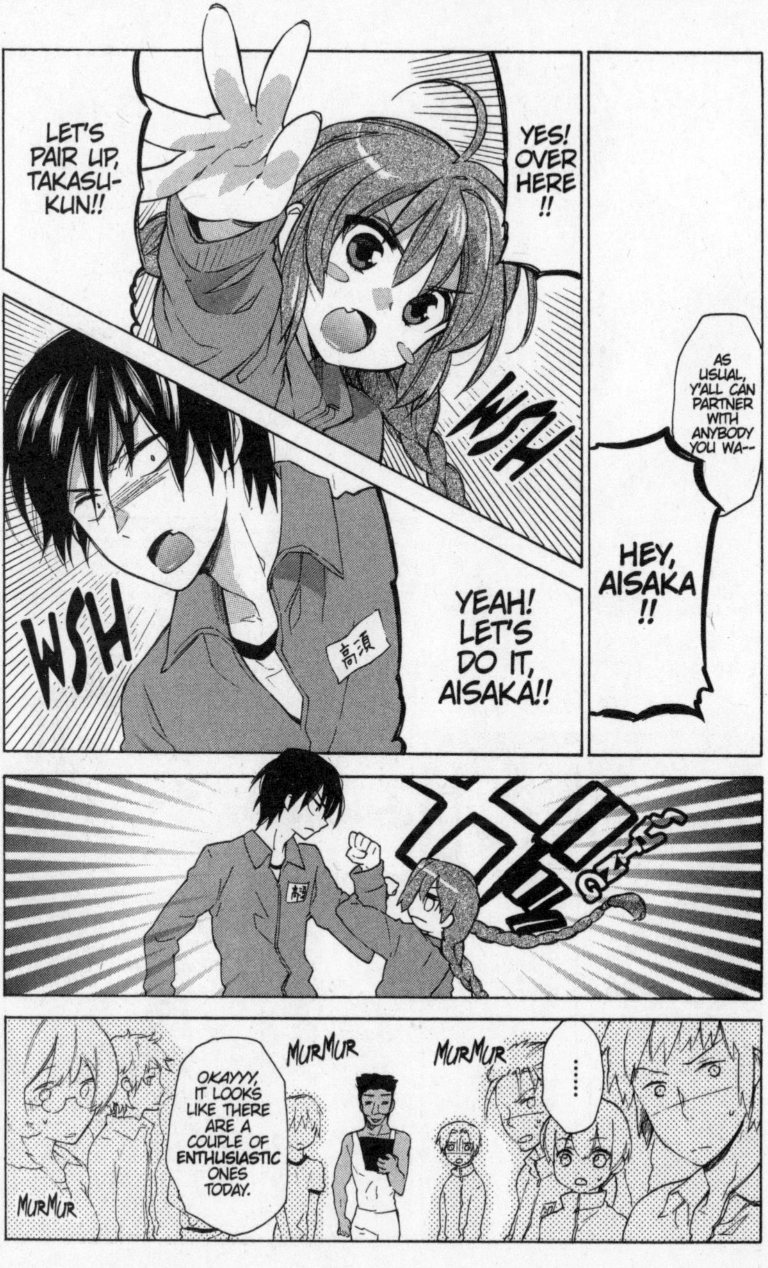
AS USUAL, Y'ALL CAN PARTNER WITH ANYBODY YOU WA--
HEY, AISAKA!!
YES! OVER HERE!!
LET'S PAIR UP, TAKASU-KUN!!
WSH
YEAH! LET'S DO IT, AISAKA!!
高須
WSH
......
MURMUR
OKAYYY, IT LOOKS LIKE THERE ARE A COUPLE OF ENTHUSIASTIC ONES TODAY.
MURMUR
MURMUR

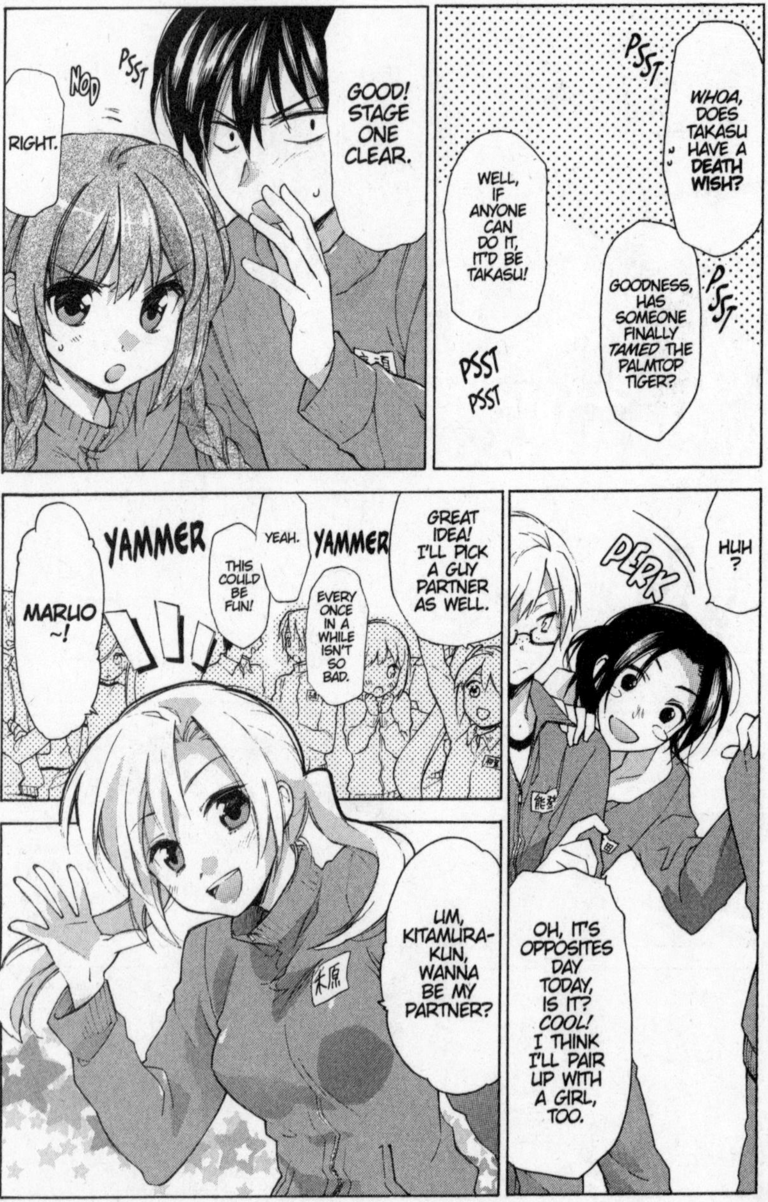

PSSST
WHOA, DOES TAKASU HAVE A DEATH WISH?
GOODNESS, HAS SOMEONE FINALLY *TAMED* THE PALMTOP TIGER?
PSSST
WELL, IF ANYONE CAN DO IT, IT'D BE TAKASU!
PSSST PSSST
GOOD! STAGE ONE CLEAR.
PSSST
NOD
RIGHT.
HUH?
PERK
OH, IT'S OPPOSITES DAY TODAY, IS IT? *COOL!* I THINK I'LL PAIR UP WITH A GIRL, TOO.
GREAT IDEA! I'LL PICK A GUY PARTNER AS WELL.
YAMMER
YEAH.
THIS COULD BE FUN!
EVERY ONCE IN A WHILE ISN'T SO BAD.
YAMMER
MARUO ~!
UM, KITAMURA-KUN, WANNA BE MY PARTNER?

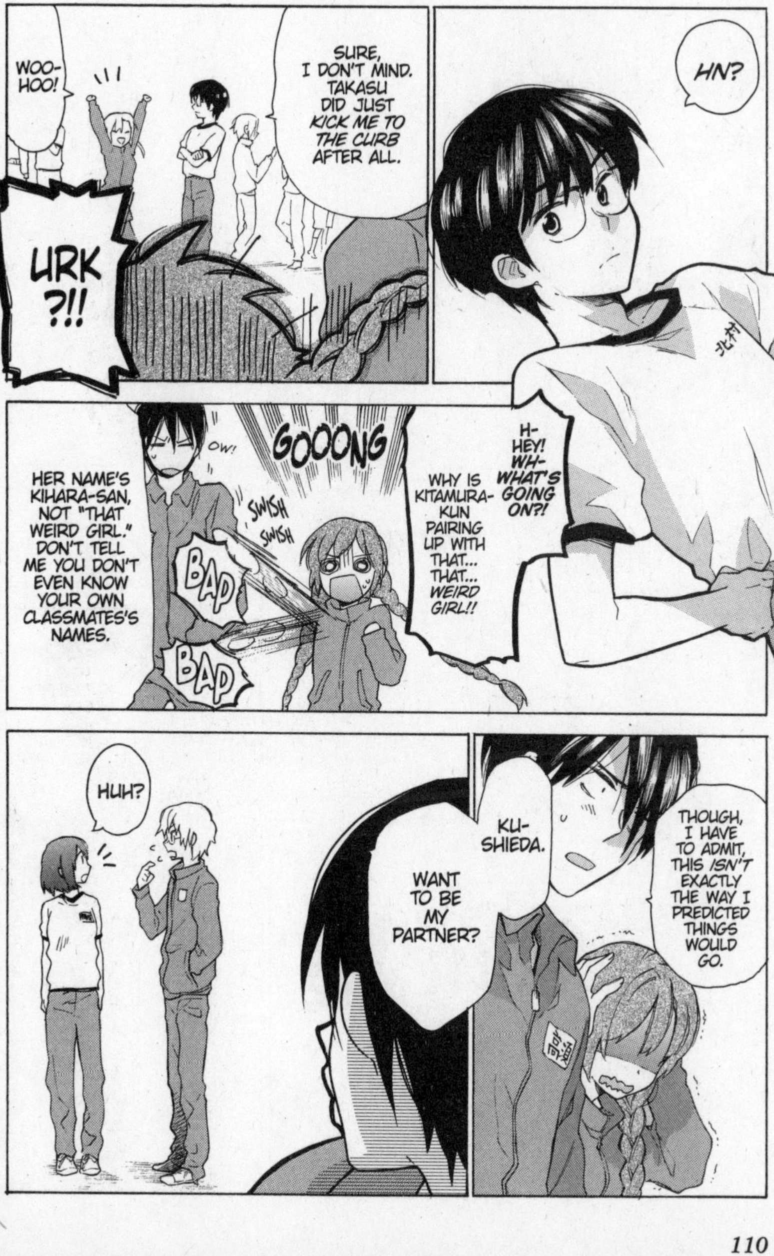
HN?
SURE, I DON'T MIND. TAKASU DID JUST *KICK ME TO THE CURB* AFTER ALL.
WOO-HOO!
URK ?!!
H-HEY! *WH-WHAT'S GOING ON?!*
WHY IS KITAMURA-KUN PAIRING UP WITH THAT... THAT... *WEIRD GIRL!!*
GOOONG
OW!
SWISH SWISH
BAP
BAP
HER NAME'S KIHARA-SAN, NOT "THAT WEIRD GIRL." DON'T TELL ME YOU DON'T EVEN KNOW YOUR OWN CLASSMATES'S NAMES.
THOUGH, I HAVE TO ADMIT, THIS *ISN'T* EXACTLY THE WAY I PREDICTED THINGS WOULD GO.
KU-SHIEDA.
WANT TO BE MY PARTNER?
HUH?

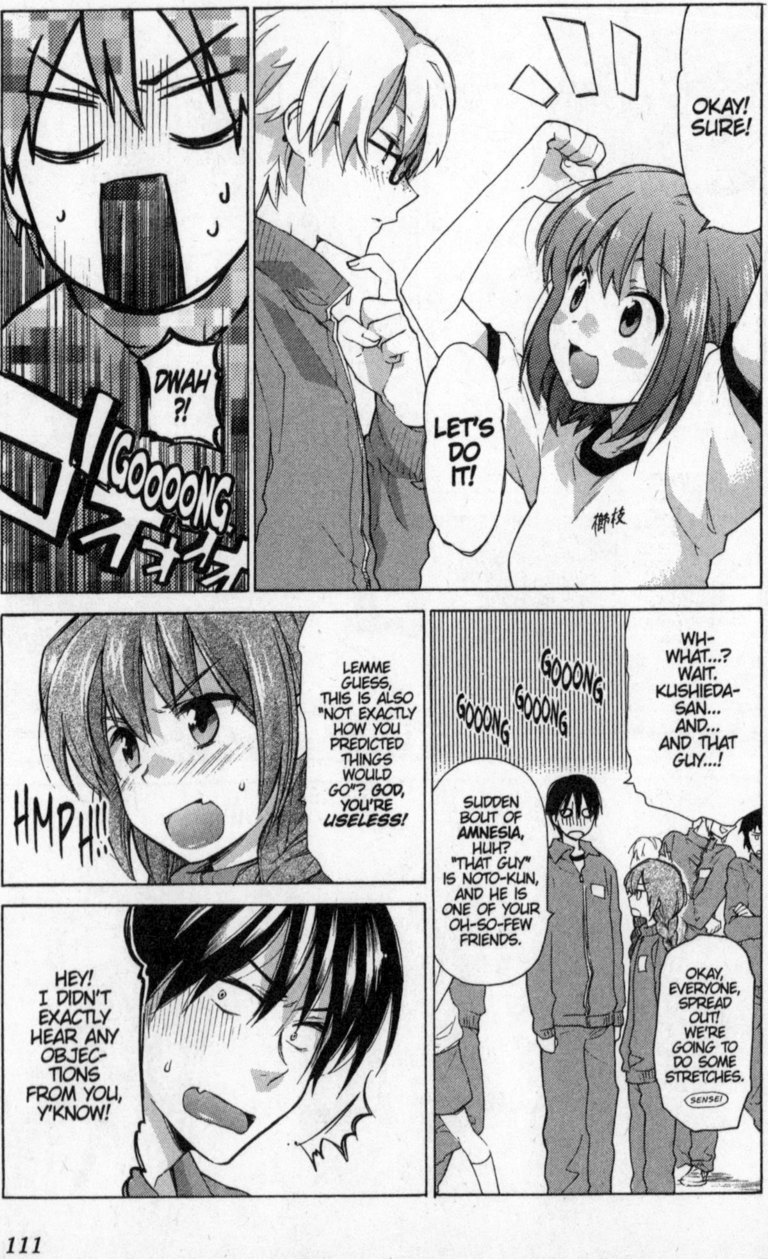

OKAY! SURE!
LET'S DO IT!
DWAH ?!
GOOOONG
WH- WHAT...? WAIT. KUSHIEDA-SAN... AND... AND THAT GUY...!
GOOONG GOOONG GOOONG
SUDDEN BOUT OF AMNESIA, HUH? "THAT GUY" IS NOTO-KUN, AND HE IS ONE OF YOUR OH-SO-FEW FRIENDS.
OKAY, EVERYONE, SPREAD OUT! WE'RE GOING TO DO SOME STRETCHES.
SENSEI
LEMME GUESS, THIS IS ALSO "NOT EXACTLY HOW YOU PREDICTED THINGS WOULD GO"? GOD, YOU'RE USELESS!
HMPH!!
HEY! I DIDN'T EXACTLY HEAR ANY OBJECTIONS FROM YOU, Y'KNOW!

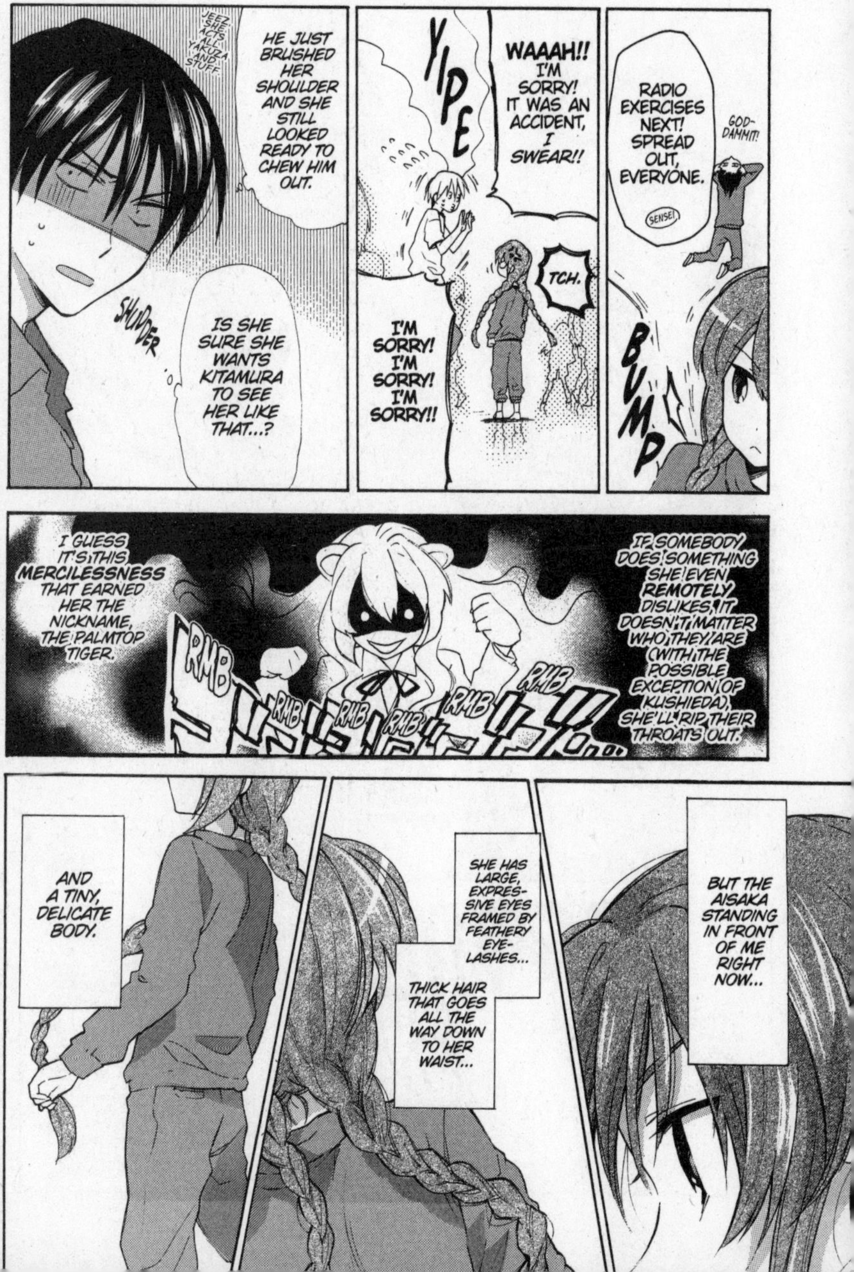
RADIO EXERCISES NEXT! SPREAD OUT, EVERYONE.
GOD-DAMMIT!
SENSEI!
BUMP
YIPE
WAAAH!! I'M SORRY! IT WAS AN ACCIDENT, I SWEAR!!
TCH.
I'M SORRY! I'M SORRY! I'M SORRY!!
HE JUST BRUSHED HER SHOULDER AND SHE STILL LOOKED READY TO CHEW HIM OUT.
JEEZ. SHE ACTS ALL YAKUZA AND STUFF.
SHUDDER
IS SHE SURE SHE WANTS KITAMURA TO SEE HER LIKE THAT...?
IF SOMEBODY DOES SOMETHING SHE EVEN REMOTELY DISLIKES, IT DOESN'T MATTER WHO THEY ARE (WITH THE POSSIBLE EXCEPTION OF KUSHIEDA), SHE'LL RIP THEIR THROATS OUT.
I GUESS IT'S THIS MERCILESSNESS THAT EARNED HER THE NICKNAME, THE PALMTOP TIGER.
RMB RMB RMB RMB RMB RMB RMB
BUT THE AISAKA STANDING IN FRONT OF ME RIGHT NOW...
SHE HAS LARGE, EXPRESSIVE EYES FRAMED BY FEATHERY EYELASHES...
THICK HAIR THAT GOES ALL THE WAY DOWN TO HER WAIST...
AND A TINY, DELICATE BODY.

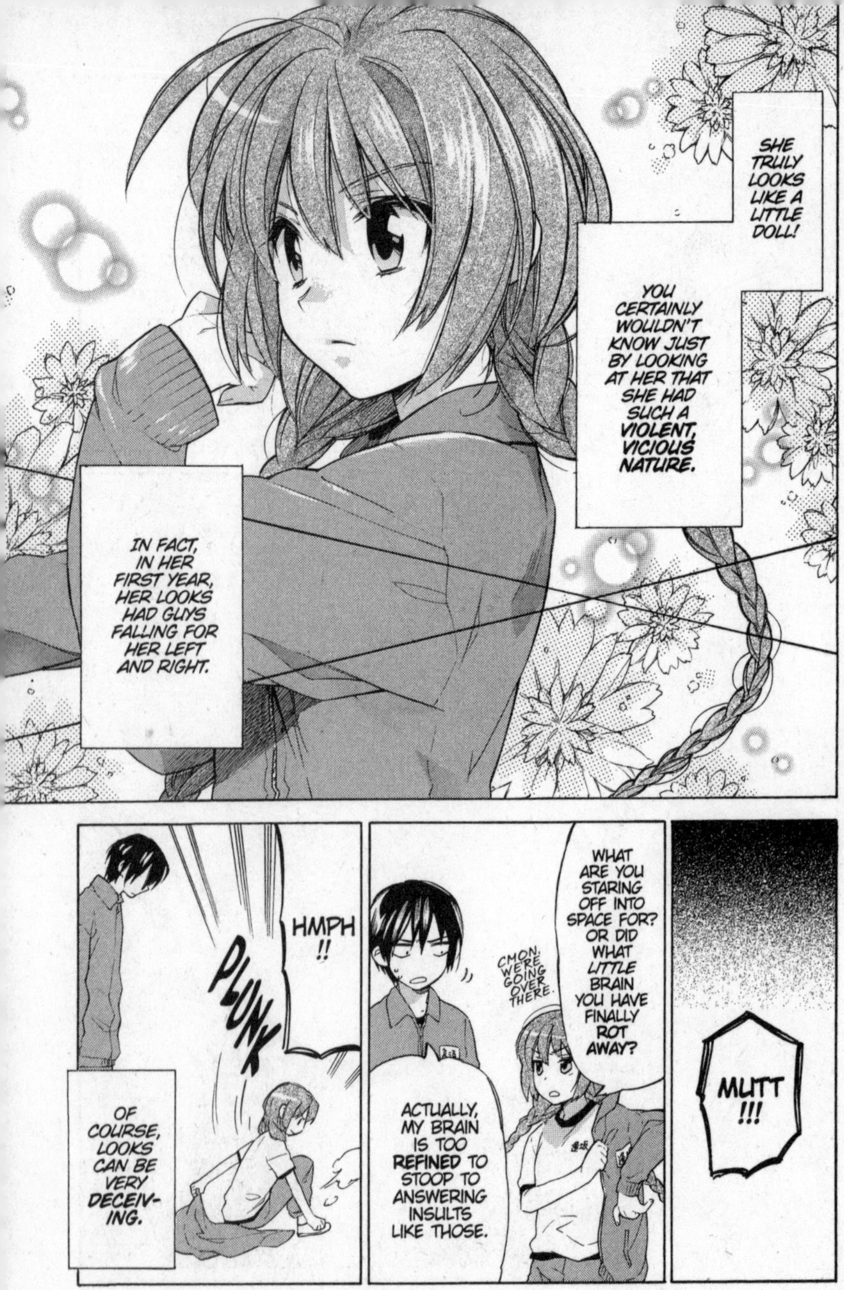
SHE TRULY LOOKS LIKE A LITTLE DOLL!
YOU CERTAINLY WOULDN'T KNOW JUST BY LOOKING AT HER THAT SHE HAD SUCH A **VIOLENT, VICIOUS NATURE.**
IN FACT, IN HER FIRST YEAR, HER LOOKS HAD GUYS FALLING FOR HER LEFT AND RIGHT.
MUTT !!!
WHAT ARE YOU STARING OFF INTO SPACE FOR? OR DID WHAT *LITTLE* BRAIN YOU HAVE FINALLY ROT AWAY?
C'MON, WE'RE GOING OVER THERE.
ACTUALLY, MY BRAIN IS TOO **REFINED** TO STOOP TO ANSWERING INSULTS LIKE THOSE.
HMPH !!
PLUNK
OF COURSE, LOOKS CAN BE VERY **DECEIVING.**

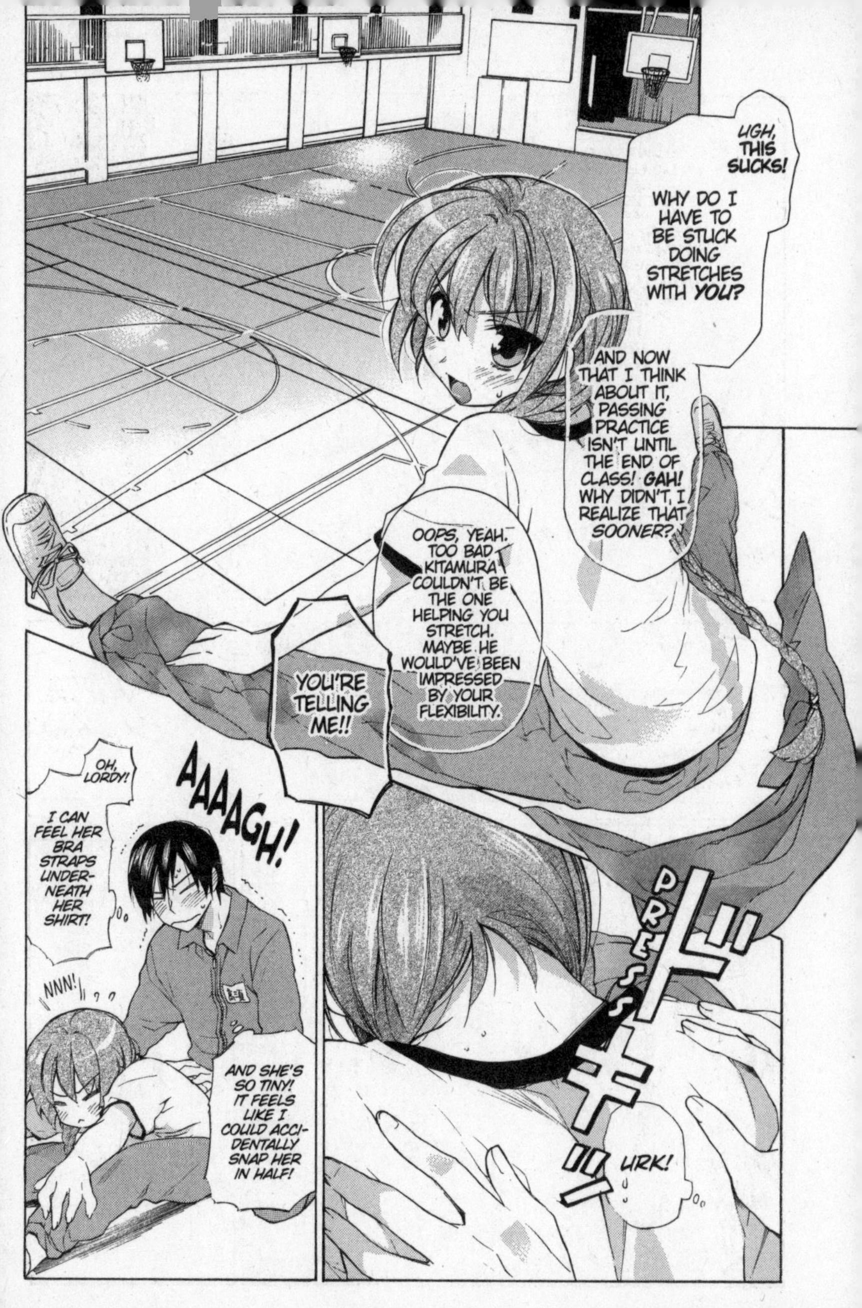
UGH, THIS SUCKS!
WHY DO I HAVE TO BE STUCK DOING STRETCHES WITH *YOU?*
AND NOW THAT I THINK ABOUT IT, PASSING PRACTICE ISN'T UNTIL THE END OF CLASS! GAH! WHY DIDN'T, I REALIZE THAT SOONER?
OOPS, YEAH. TOO BAD KITAMURA COULDN'T BE THE ONE HELPING YOU STRETCH. MAYBE HE WOULD'VE BEEN IMPRESSED BY YOUR FLEXIBILITY.
YOU'RE TELLING ME!!
PRESS
URK!
AAAAGH!
OH, LORDY!
I CAN FEEL HER BRA STRAPS UNDER-NEATH HER SHIRT!
NNN!
AND SHE'S SO TINY! IT FEELS LIKE I COULD ACCI-DENTALLY SNAP HER IN HALF!

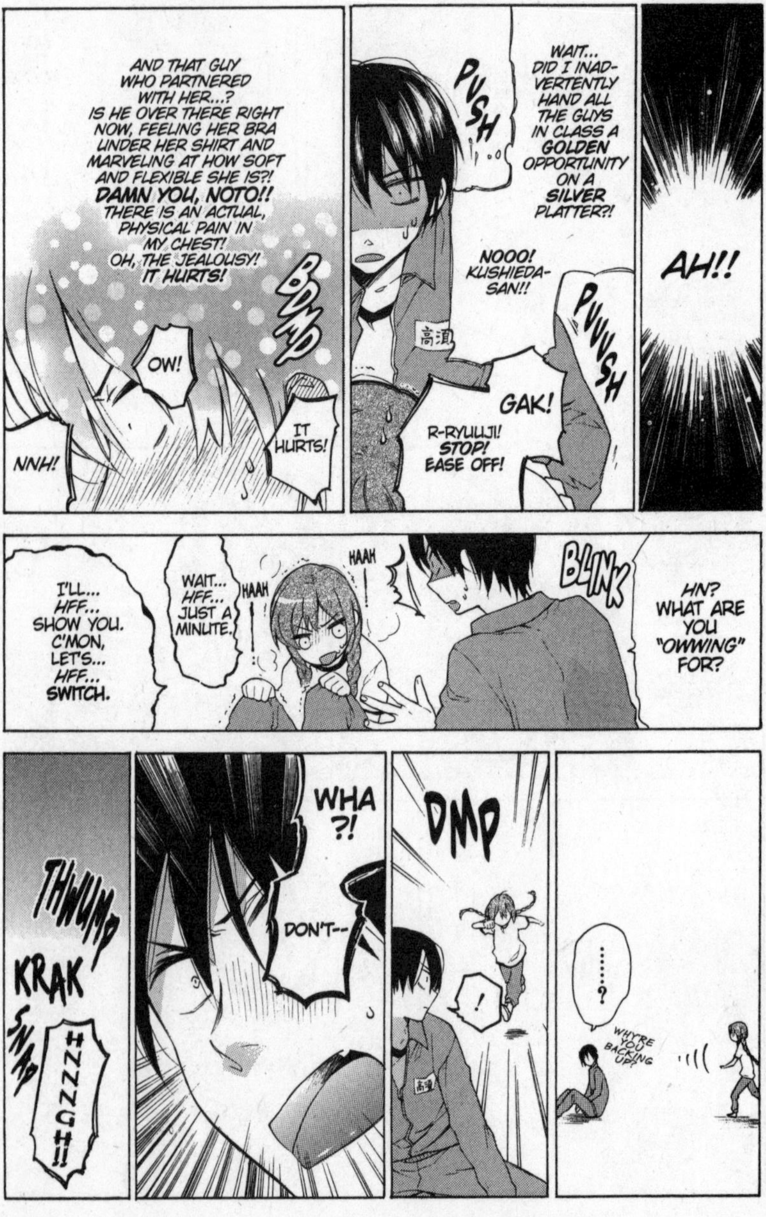
AH!!
WAIT... DID I INADVERTENTLY HAND ALL THE GUYS IN CLASS A GOLDEN OPPORTUNITY ON A SILVER PLATTER?!
PUSH
NOOO! KUSHIEDA-SAN!!
PUUUSH
GAK!
R-RYUUJI! STOP! EASE OFF!
AND THAT GUY WHO PARTNERED WITH HER...? IS HE OVER THERE RIGHT NOW, FEELING HER BRA UNDER HER SHIRT AND MARVELING AT HOW SOFT AND FLEXIBLE SHE IS?! DAMN YOU, NOTO!! THERE IS AN ACTUAL, PHYSICAL PAIN IN MY CHEST! OH, THE JEALOUSY! IT HURTS!
BDMP
OW!
IT HURTS!
NNH!
BLINK
HN? WHAT ARE YOU "OWWING" FOR?
HAAH
HAAH
WAIT... HFF... JUST A MINUTE.
I'LL... HFF... SHOW YOU. C'MON, LET'S... HFF... SWITCH.
......?
WHY'RE YOU BACKING UP?
DMP
!
WHA?!
DON'T--
THWUMP
KRAK
SNAP
HNNNGH!!

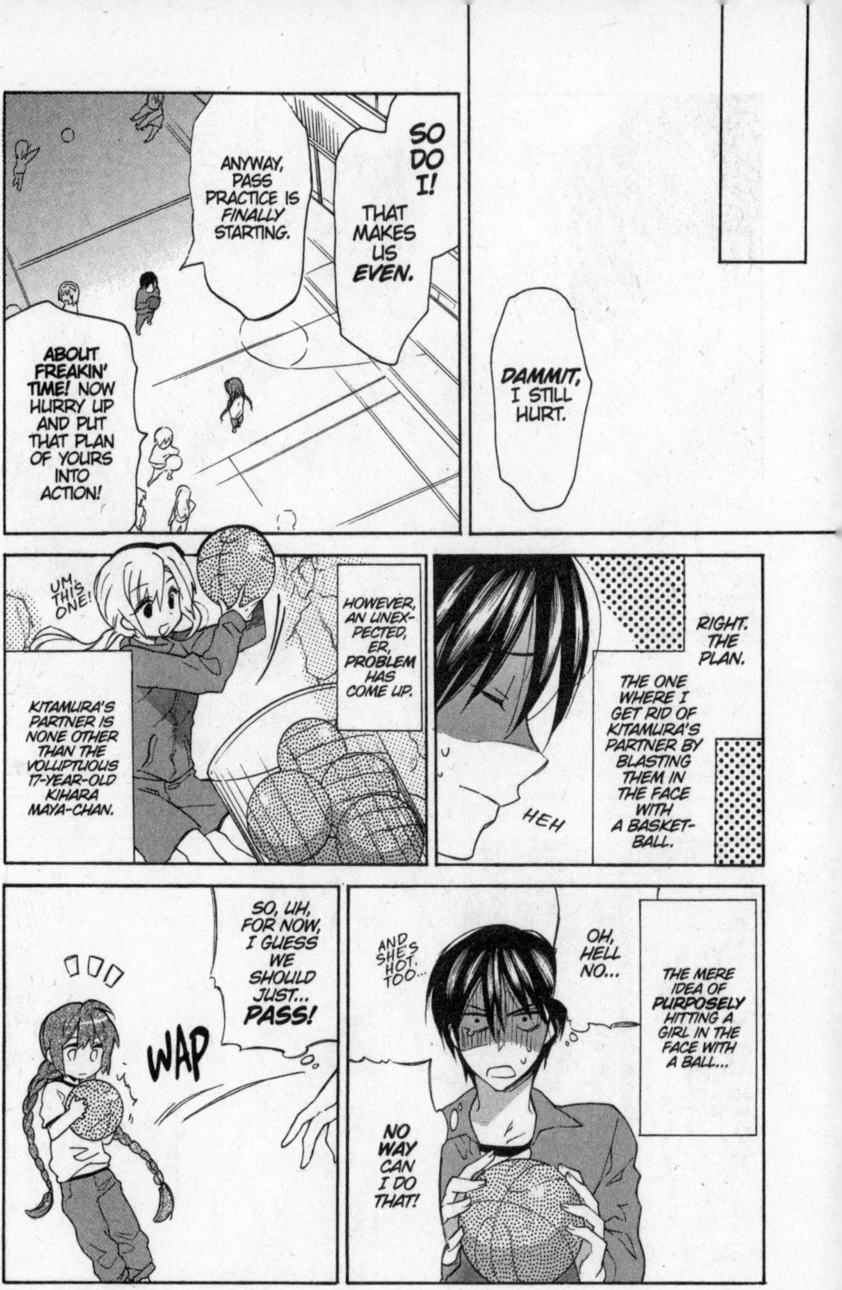
DAMMIT, I STILL HURT.
SO DO I!
THAT MAKES US *EVEN.*
ANYWAY, PASS PRACTICE IS *FINALLY* STARTING.
ABOUT FREAKIN' TIME! NOW HURRY UP AND PUT THAT PLAN OF YOURS INTO ACTION!
RIGHT. THE PLAN.
THE ONE WHERE I GET RID OF KITAMURA'S PARTNER BY BLASTING THEM IN THE FACE WITH A BASKET-BALL.
HEH
HOWEVER, AN UNEXPECTED, ER, PROBLEM HAS COME UP.
UM, THIS ONE!
KITAMURA'S PARTNER IS NONE OTHER THAN THE VOLUPTUOUS 17-YEAR-OLD KIHARA MAYA-CHAN.
THE MERE IDEA OF **PURPOSELY** HITTING A GIRL IN THE FACE WITH A BALL...
OH, HELL NO...
AND SHE'S HOT, TOO...
NO WAY CAN I DO THAT!
SO, UH, FOR NOW, I GUESS WE SHOULD JUST... **PASS!**
WAP

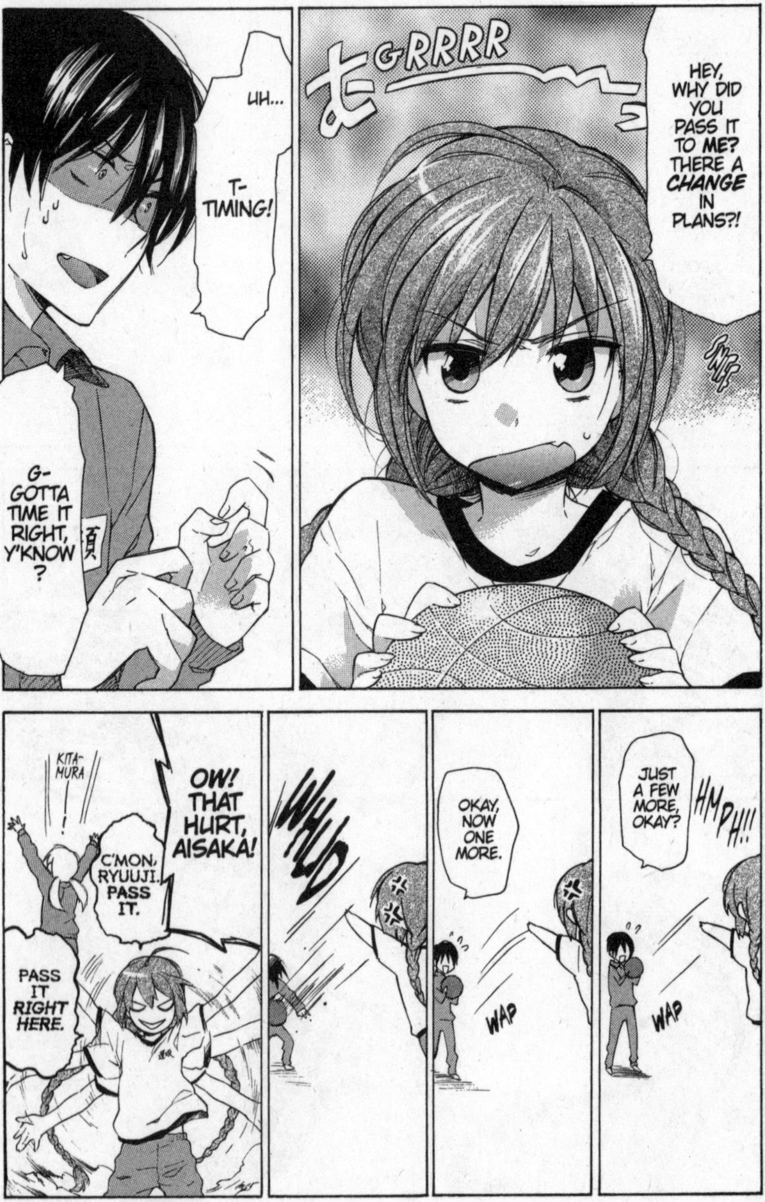
む GRRRR
HEY, WHY DID YOU PASS IT TO ME? THERE A CHANGE IN PLANS?!
UH...
T-TIMING!
G-GOTTA TIME IT RIGHT, Y'KNOW?
JUST A FEW MORE, OKAY?
HMPH!!
WAP
OKAY, NOW ONE MORE.
WAP
WHUD
OW! THAT HURT, AISAKA!
KITA-MURA!
C'MON, RYUUJI. PASS IT.
PASS IT RIGHT HERE.

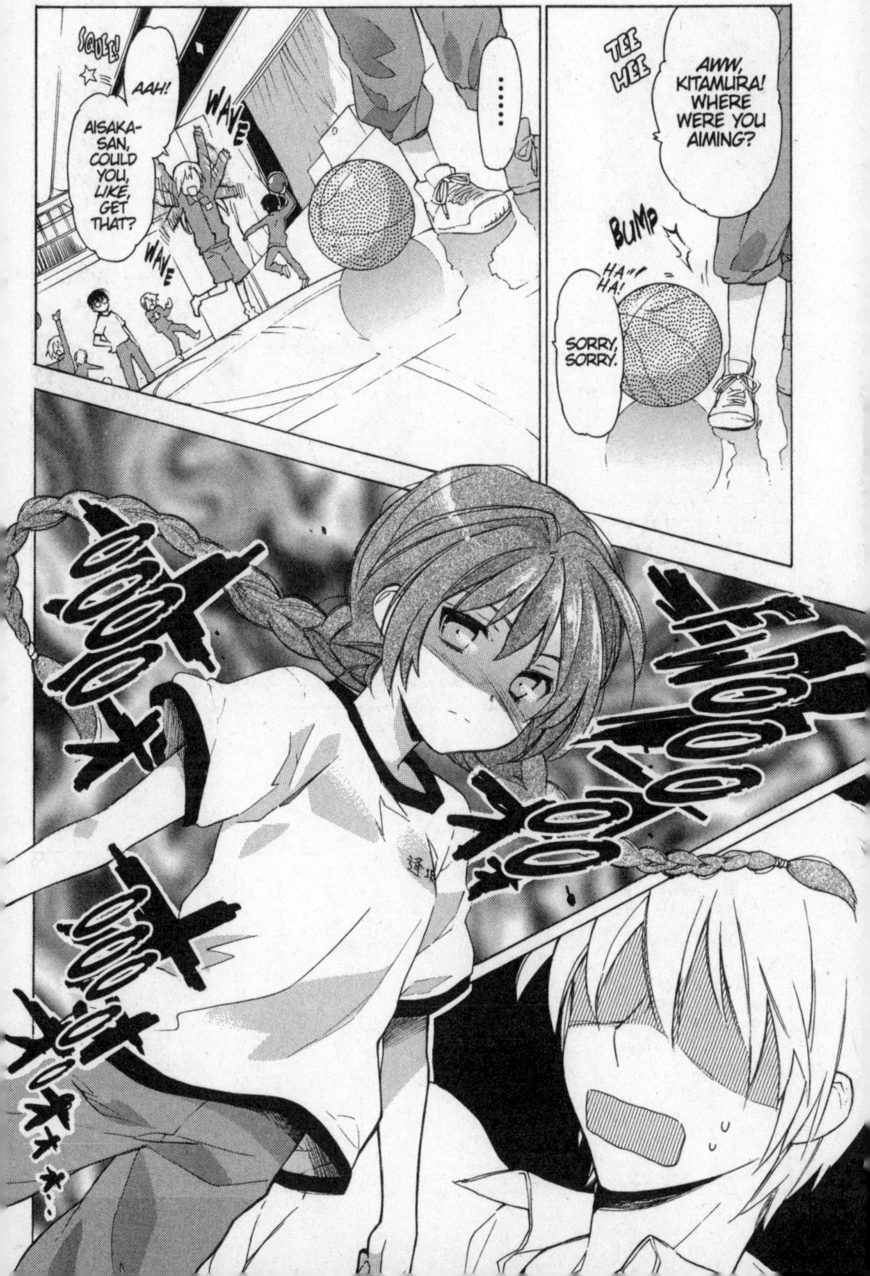
TEE HEE
AWW, KITAMURA! WHERE WERE YOU AIMING?
BUMP
HA HA!
SORRY, SORRY.
......
SQUEE!
AAH!
AISAKA-SAN, COULD YOU, LIKE, GET THAT?
WAVE
WAVE

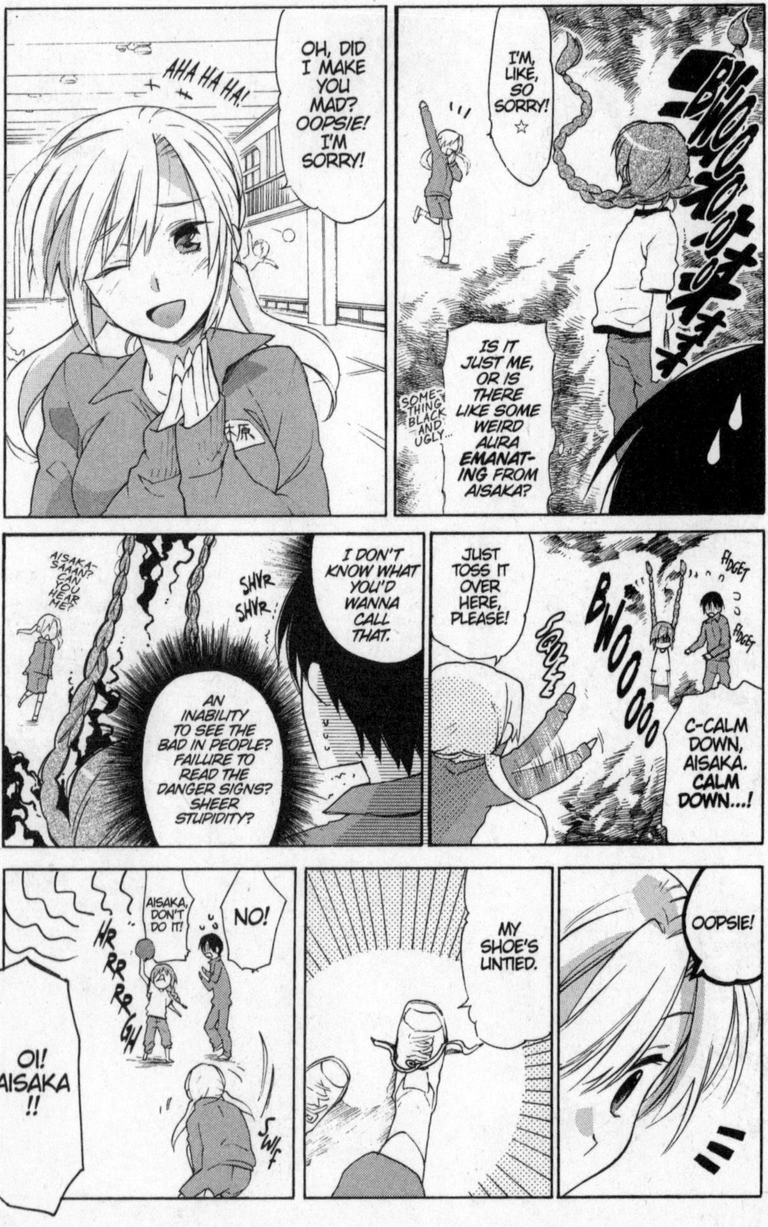
I'M, LIKE, SO SORRY! ☆
IS IT JUST ME, OR IS THERE LIKE SOME WEIRD AURA EMANATING FROM AISAKA?
SOMETHING BLACK AND UGLY...
OH, DID I MAKE YOU MAD? OOPSIE! I'M SORRY!
AHA HA HA!
JUST TOSS IT OVER HERE, PLEASE!
FIDGET
FIDGET
BWOOOOOO
C-CALM DOWN, AISAKA. CALM DOWN...!
I DON'T KNOW WHAT YOU'D WANNA CALL THAT.
SHVR SHVR
AN INABILITY TO SEE THE BAD IN PEOPLE? FAILURE TO READ THE DANGER SIGNS? SHEER STUPIDITY?
AISAKA-SAAAN? CAN YOU HEAR ME?
OOPSIE!
MY SHOE'S UNTIED.
NO!
AISAKA, DON'T DO IT!
HRRRRRGH
OI! AISAKA!!
SWIF

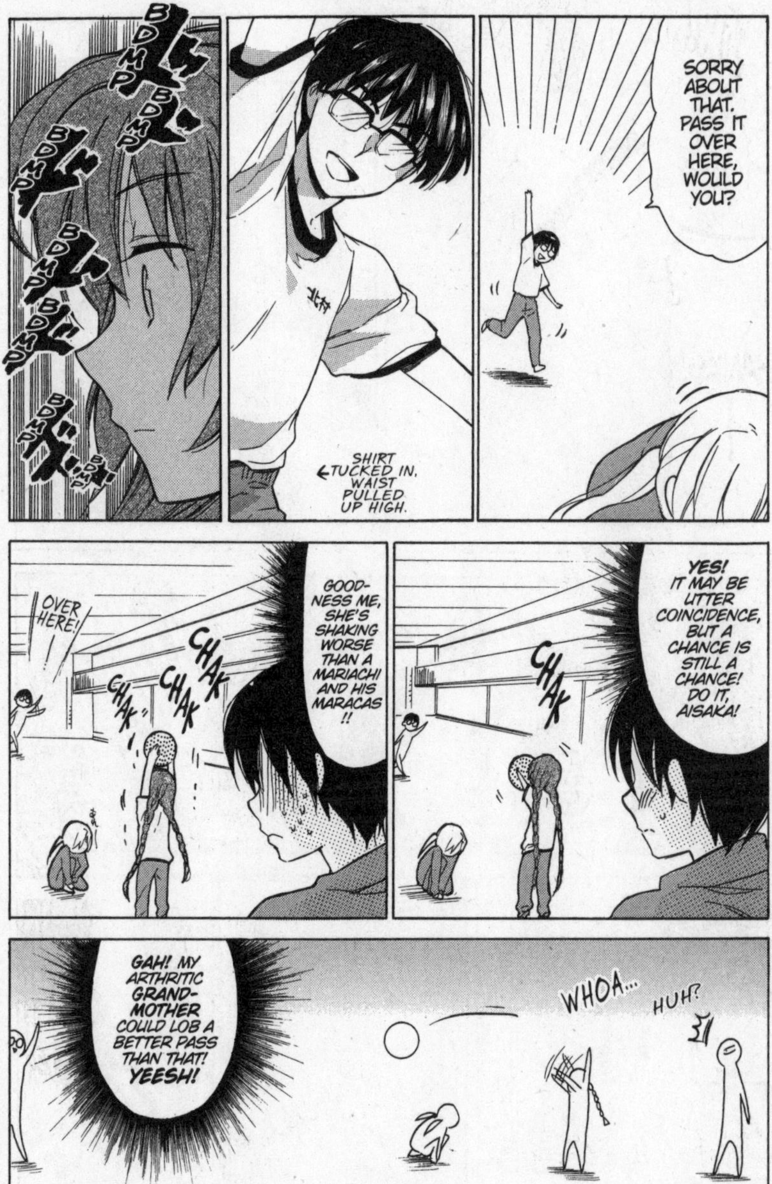
SORRY ABOUT THAT. PASS IT OVER HERE, WOULD YOU?
SHIRT ←TUCKED IN. WAIST PULLED UP HIGH.
BDMP
BDMP
BDMP
BDMP
BDMP
BDMP
BDMP
BDMP
YES! IT MAY BE UTTER COINCIDENCE, BUT A CHANCE IS STILL A CHANCE! DO IT, AISAKA!
CHAK
GOODNESS ME, SHE'S SHAKING WORSE THAN A MARIACHI AND HIS MARACAS!!
CHAK
CHAK
CHAK
OVER HERE!
HUH?
WHOA...
GAH! MY ARTHRITIC GRANDMOTHER COULD LOB A BETTER PASS THAN THAT! YEESH!

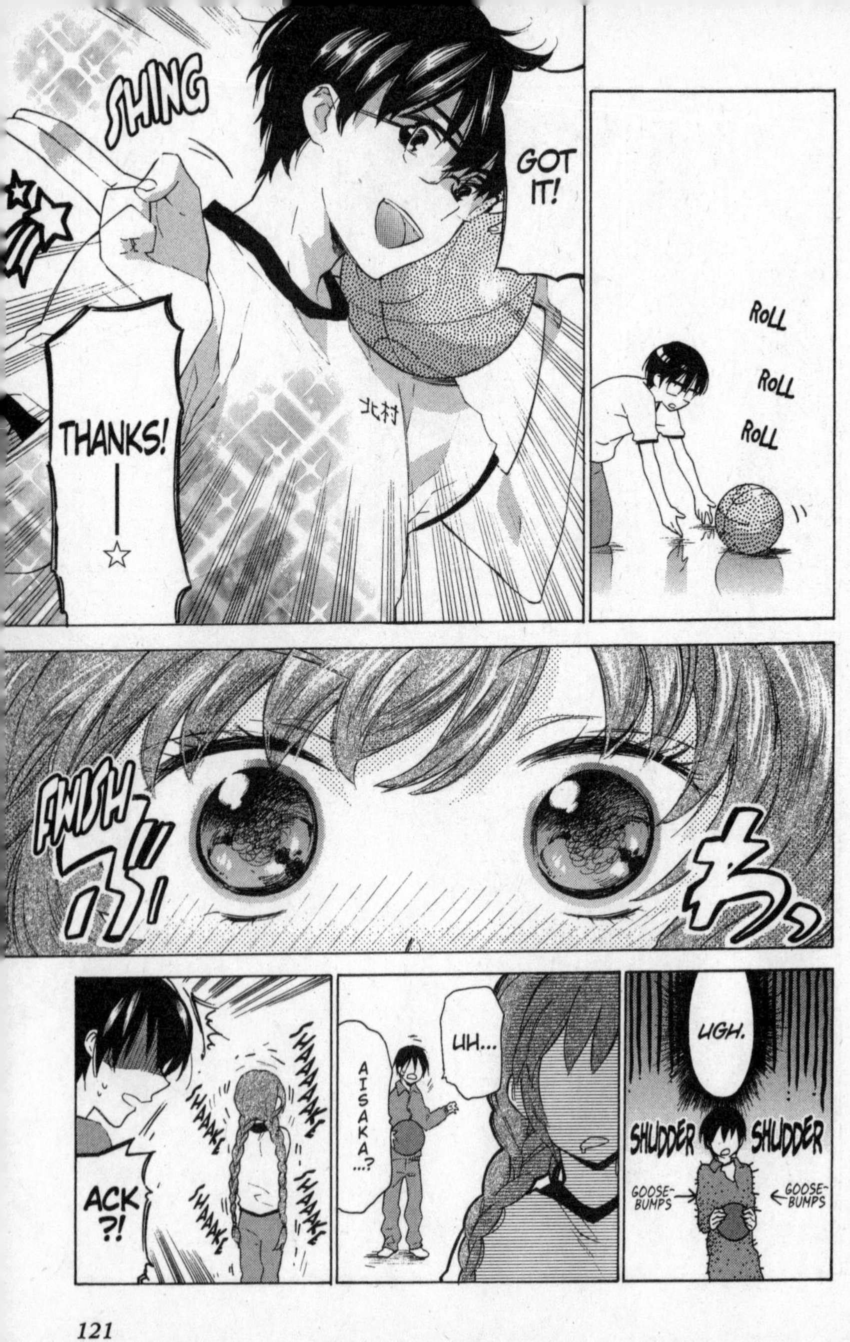
ROLL
ROLL
ROLL
GOT IT!
SHING
北村
THANKS!
わっ
FWISH
ぶ
UGH.
SHUDDER
SHUDDER
GOOSE-BUMPS
GOOSE-BUMPS
UH...
AISAKA...?
SHAAAAAKE
SHAAAKE
SHAAAKE
SHAAAKE
ACK?!

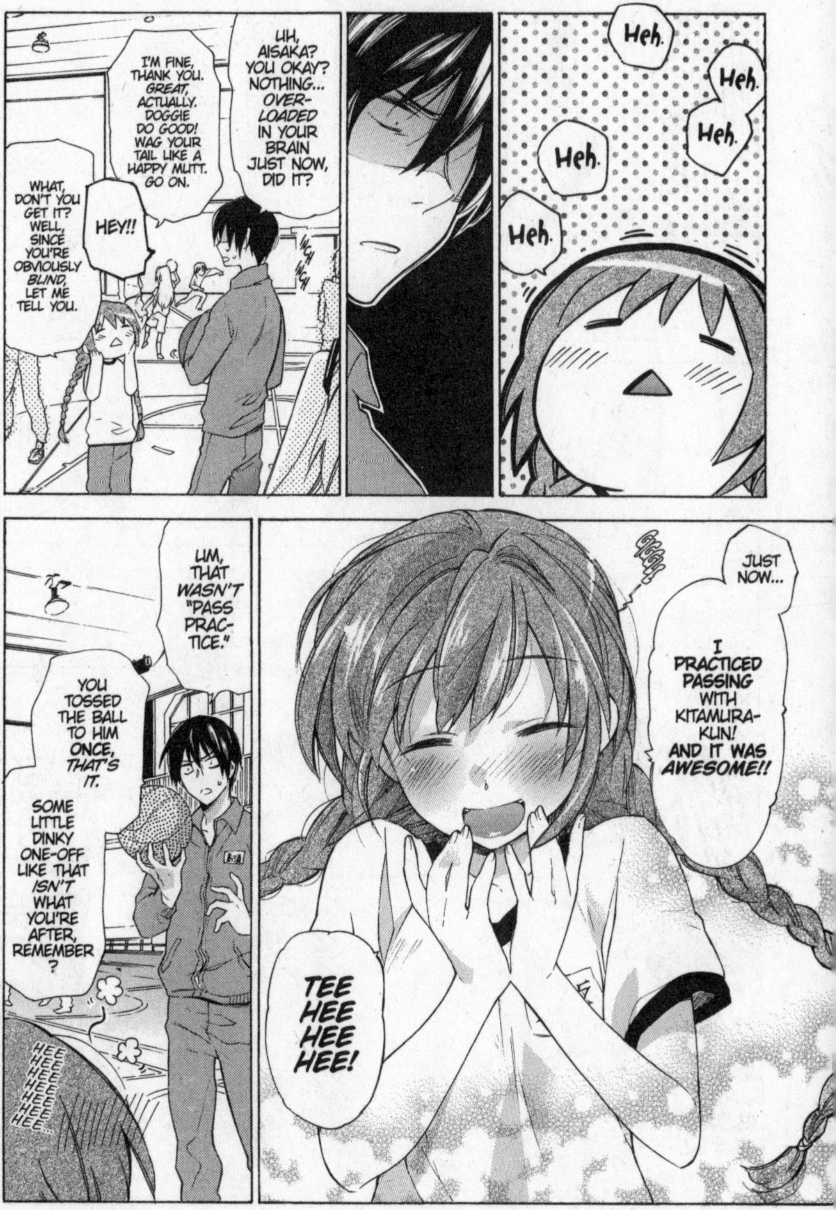
Heh.
Heh.
Heh.
Heh.
Heh.
UH, AISAKA? YOU OKAY? NOTHING... OVER-LOADED IN YOUR BRAIN JUST NOW, DID IT?
I'M FINE, THANK YOU. *GREAT*, ACTUALLY. DOGGIE DO GOOD! WAG YOUR TAIL LIKE A HAPPY MUTT. GO ON.
HEY!!
INCH INCH
WHAT, DON'T YOU GET IT? WELL, SINCE YOU'RE OBVIOUSLY *BLIND*, LET ME TELL YOU.
JUST NOW...
I PRACTICED PASSING WITH KITAMURA-KUN! AND IT WAS *AWESOME!!*
TEE HEE HEE HEE!
UM, THAT *WASN'T* "PASS PRAC-TICE."
YOU TOSSED THE BALL TO HIM ONCE, *THAT'S* IT.
SOME LITTLE DINKY ONE-OFF LIKE THAT *ISN'T* WHAT YOU'RE AFTER, REMEMBER?

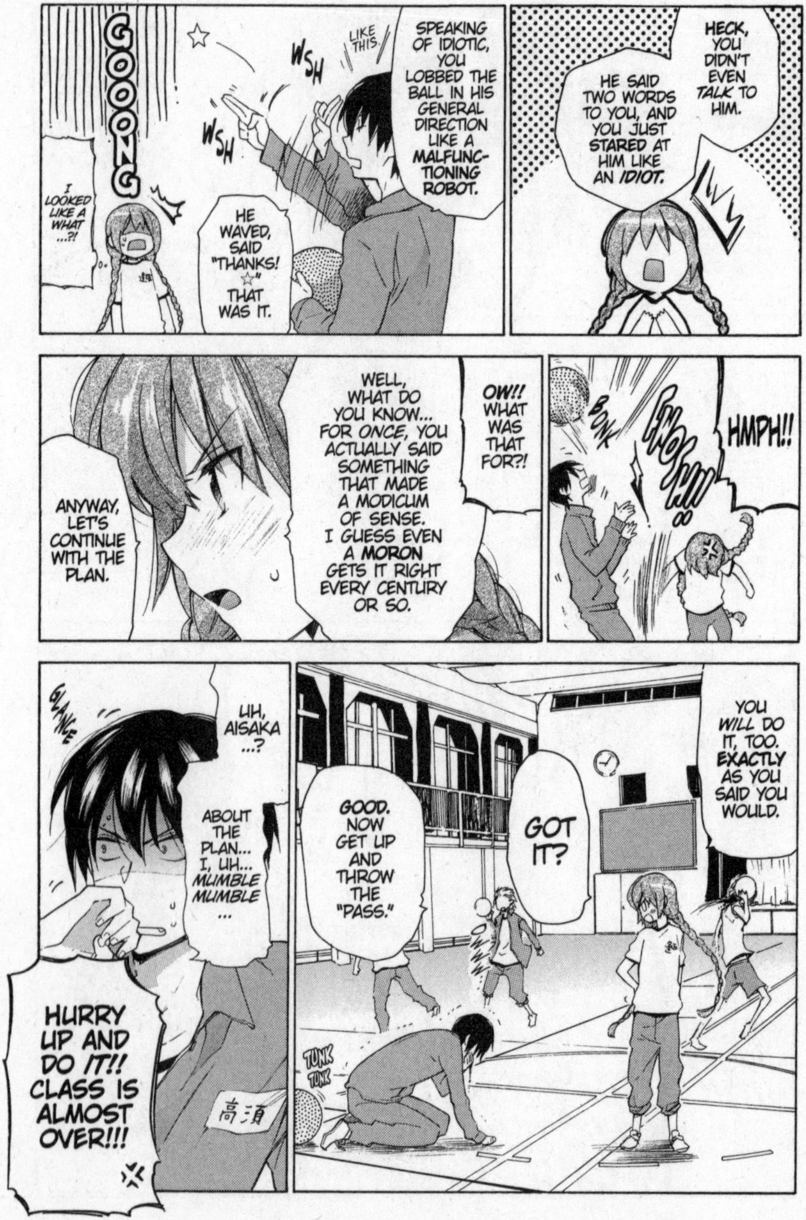
HECK, YOU DIDN'T EVEN TALK TO HIM.
HE SAID TWO WORDS TO YOU, AND YOU JUST STARED AT HIM LIKE AN IDIOT.
SPEAKING OF IDIOTIC, YOU LOBBED THE BALL IN HIS GENERAL DIRECTION LIKE A MALFUNCTIONING ROBOT.
LIKE THIS.
WSH
WSH
HE WAVED, SAID "THANKS! ☆" THAT WAS IT.
GOOOONG
I LOOKED LIKE A WHAT...?!
HMPH!!
BONK
OW!! WHAT WAS THAT FOR?!
WELL, WHAT DO YOU KNOW... FOR ONCE, YOU ACTUALLY SAID SOMETHING THAT MADE A MODICUM OF SENSE. I GUESS EVEN A MORON GETS IT RIGHT EVERY CENTURY OR SO.
ANYWAY, LET'S CONTINUE WITH THE PLAN.
YOU WILL DO IT, TOO. EXACTLY AS YOU SAID YOU WOULD.
GOT IT?
GOOD. NOW GET UP AND THROW THE "PASS."
TUNK
TUNK
UH, AISAKA...?
GLANCE
ABOUT THE PLAN... I, UH... MUMBLE MUMBLE...
高須
HURRY UP AND DO IT!! CLASS IS ALMOST OVER!!!

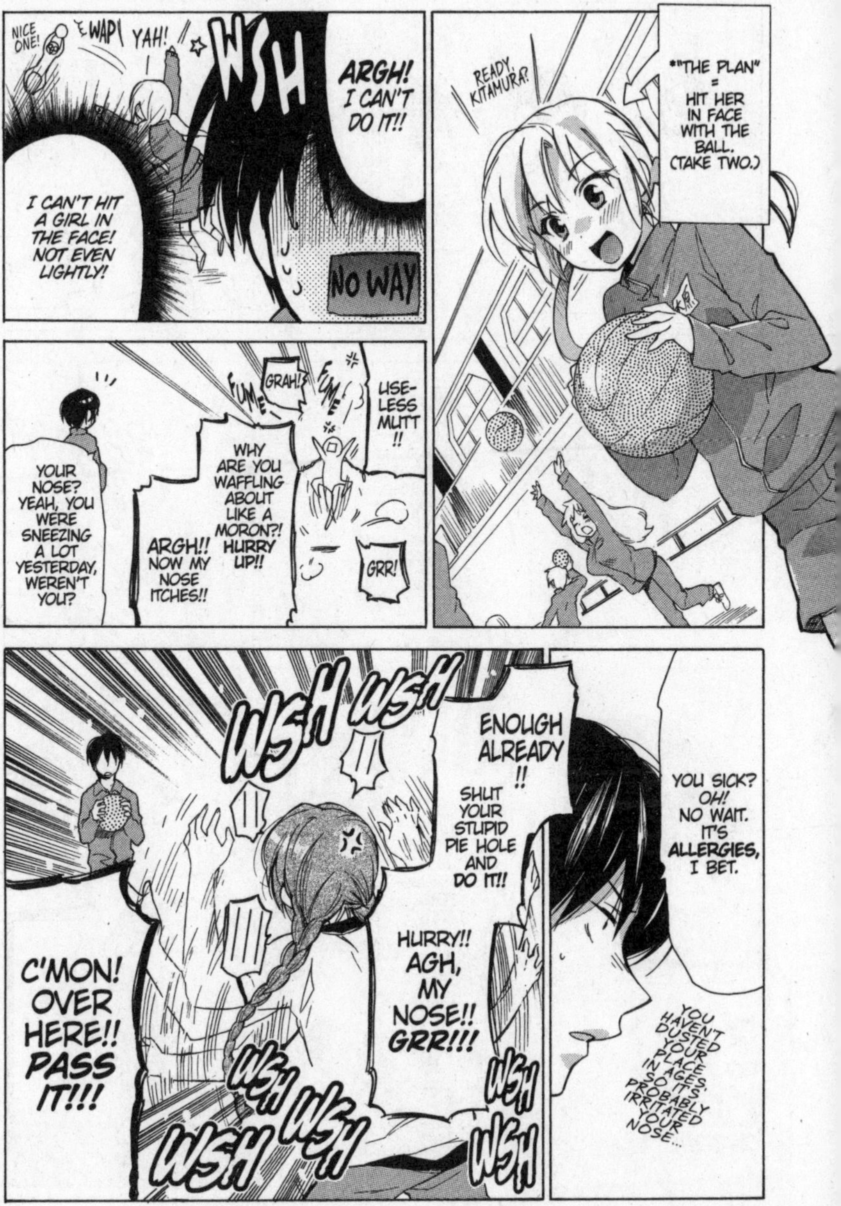
*"THE PLAN" = HIT HER IN FACE WITH THE BALL. (TAKE TWO.)
READY, KITAMURA?
WSH
ARGH! I CAN'T DO IT!!
NO WAY
YAH!
WAP!
NICE ONE!
I CAN'T HIT A GIRL IN THE FACE! NOT EVEN LIGHTLY!
USELESS MUTT!!
FUME
GRAH!
FUME
WHY ARE YOU WAFFLING ABOUT LIKE A MORON?! HURRY UP!!
GRR!
ARGH!! NOW MY NOSE ITCHES!!
YOUR NOSE? YEAH, YOU WERE SNEEZING A LOT YESTERDAY, WEREN'T YOU?
YOU SICK? OH! NO WAIT. IT'S ALLERGIES, I BET.
YOU HAVEN'T DUSTED YOUR PLACE IN AGES, SO IT'S PROBABLY IRRITATED YOUR NOSE...
WSH WSH
ENOUGH ALREADY!!
SHUT YOUR STUPID PIE HOLE AND DO IT!!
WSH WSH
HURRY!! AGH, MY NOSE!! GRR!!!
WSH WSH WSH
C'MON! OVER HERE!! PASS IT!!!

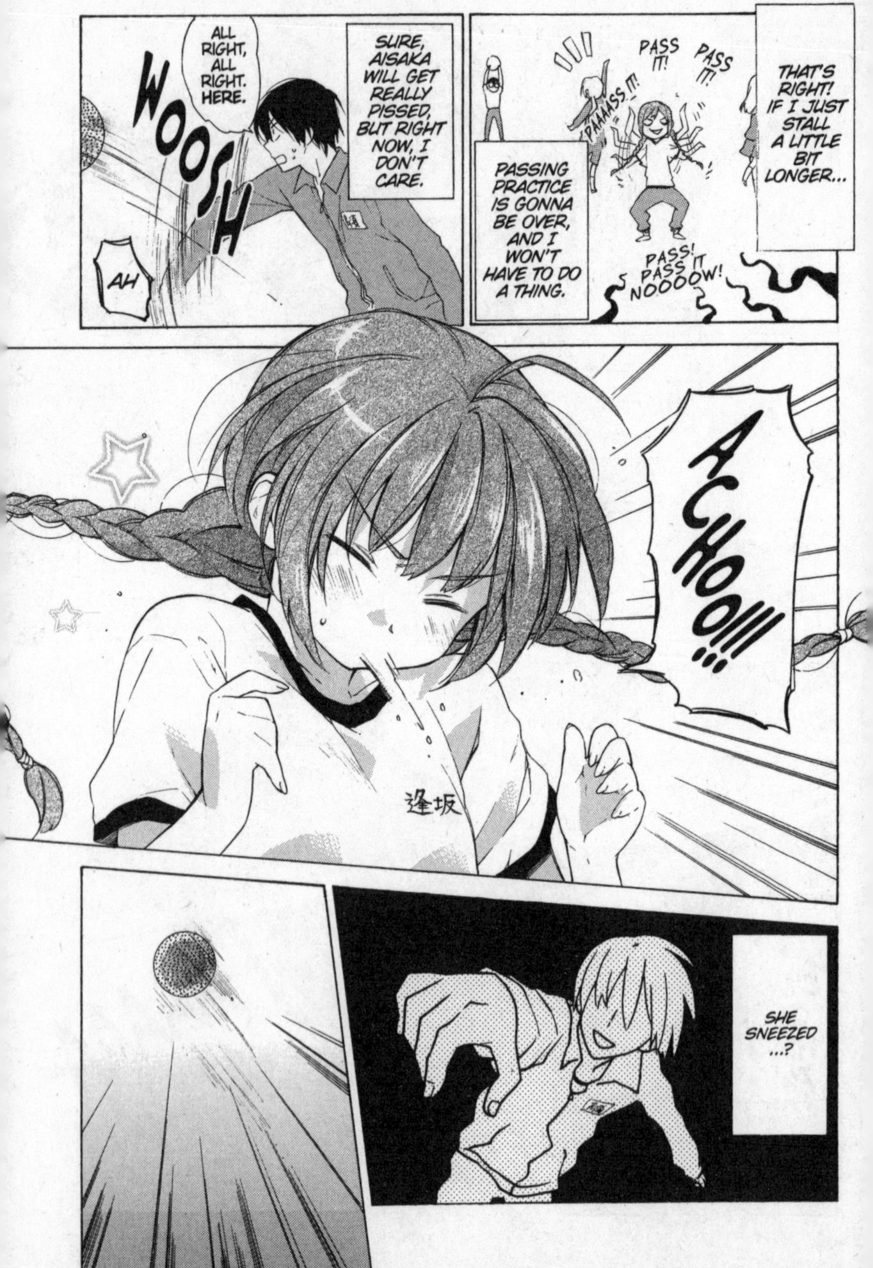
THAT'S RIGHT! IF I JUST STALL A LITTLE BIT LONGER...
PASS IT!
PASS IT!
PAAAASS IT!
PASSING PRACTICE IS GONNA BE OVER, AND I WON'T HAVE TO DO A THING.
PASS! PASS IT NOOOOW!
SURE, AISAKA WILL GET REALLY PISSED, BUT RIGHT NOW, I DON'T CARE.
ALL RIGHT, ALL RIGHT. HERE.
WOOSH
AH
ACHOO!!!!
逢坂
SHE SNEEZED ...?

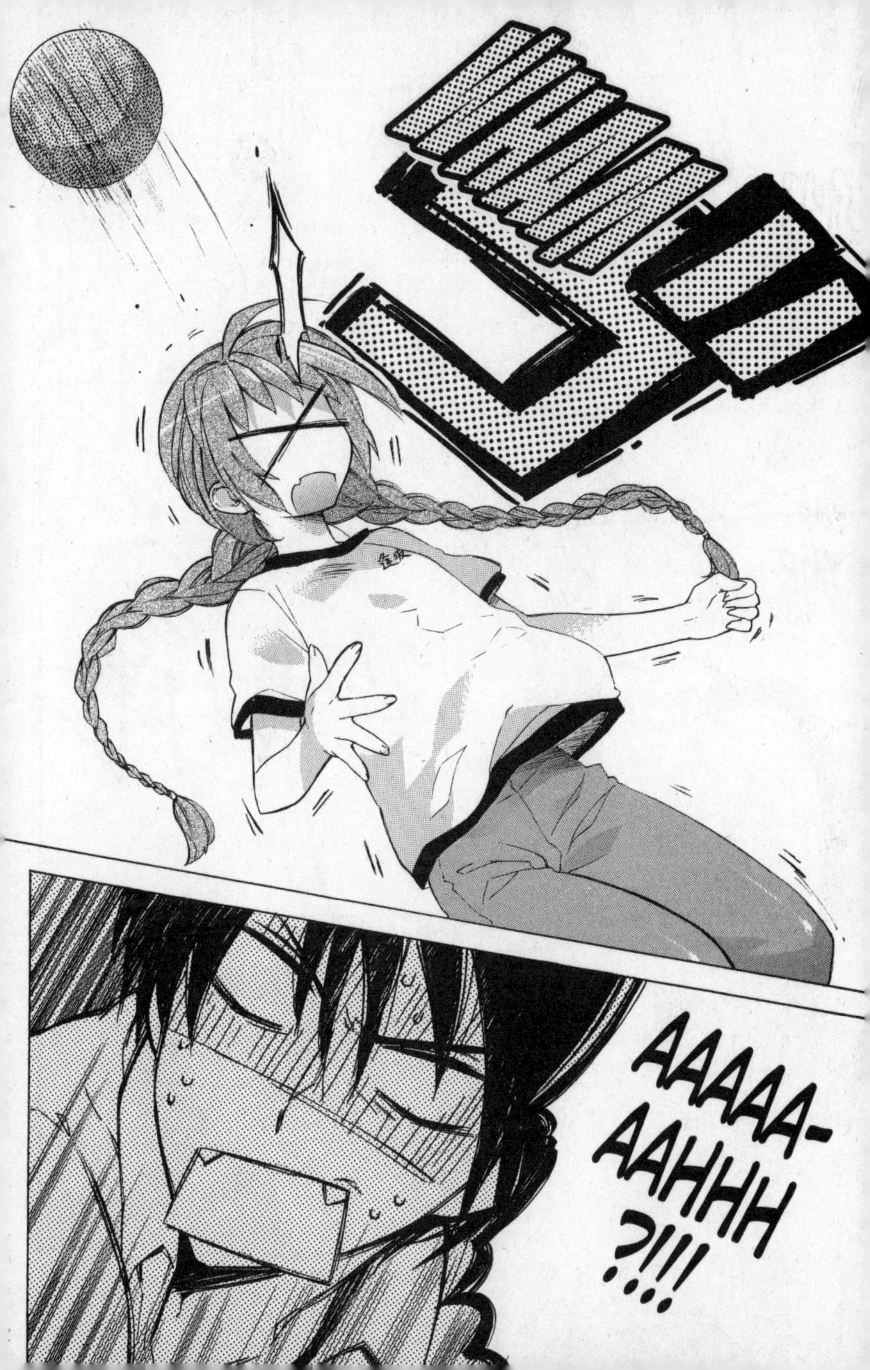
AAAAA-
AAHHH
?!!!

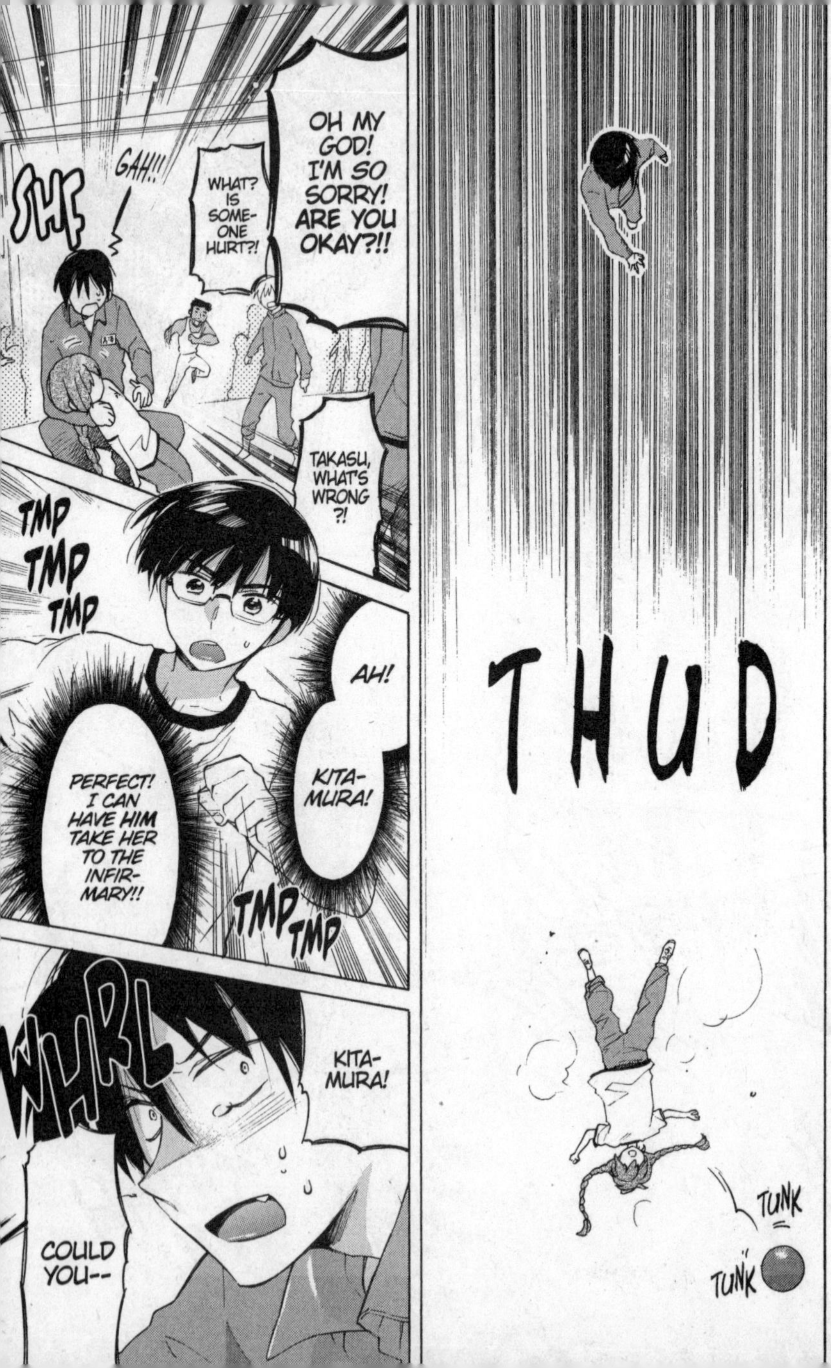
THUD
TUNK
TUNK
OH MY GOD! I'M SO SORRY! ARE YOU OKAY?!!
WHAT? IS SOME-ONE HURT?!
GAH!!
SHF
TAKASU, WHAT'S WRONG ?!
AH! KITA-MURA!
PERFECT! I CAN HAVE HIM TAKE HER TO THE INFIR-MARY!!
TMP TMP TMP
TMP TMP
KITA-MURA!
WHRL
COULD YOU--

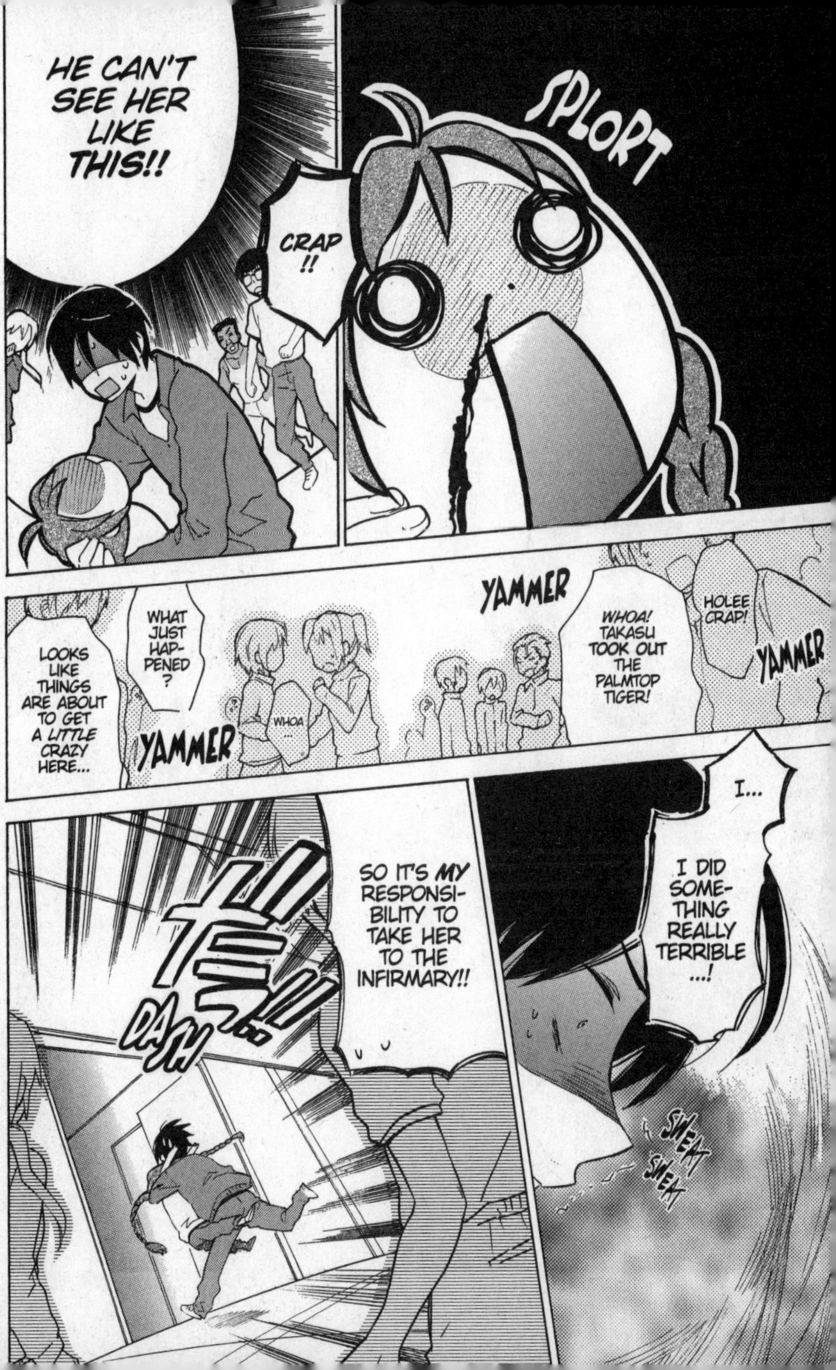
SPLORT
HE CAN'T SEE HER LIKE THIS!!
CRAP!!
HOLEE CRAP!
YAMMER
WHOA! TAKASU TOOK OUT THE PALMTOP TIGER!
YAMMER
WHOA...
WHAT JUST HAP-PENED?
LOOKS LIKE THINGS ARE ABOUT TO GET A LITTLE CRAZY HERE...
YAMMER
I...
I DID SOME-THING REALLY TERRIBLE ...!
SWEAT SWEAT
SO IT'S MY RESPONSI-BILITY TO TAKE HER TO THE INFIRMARY!!
DASH

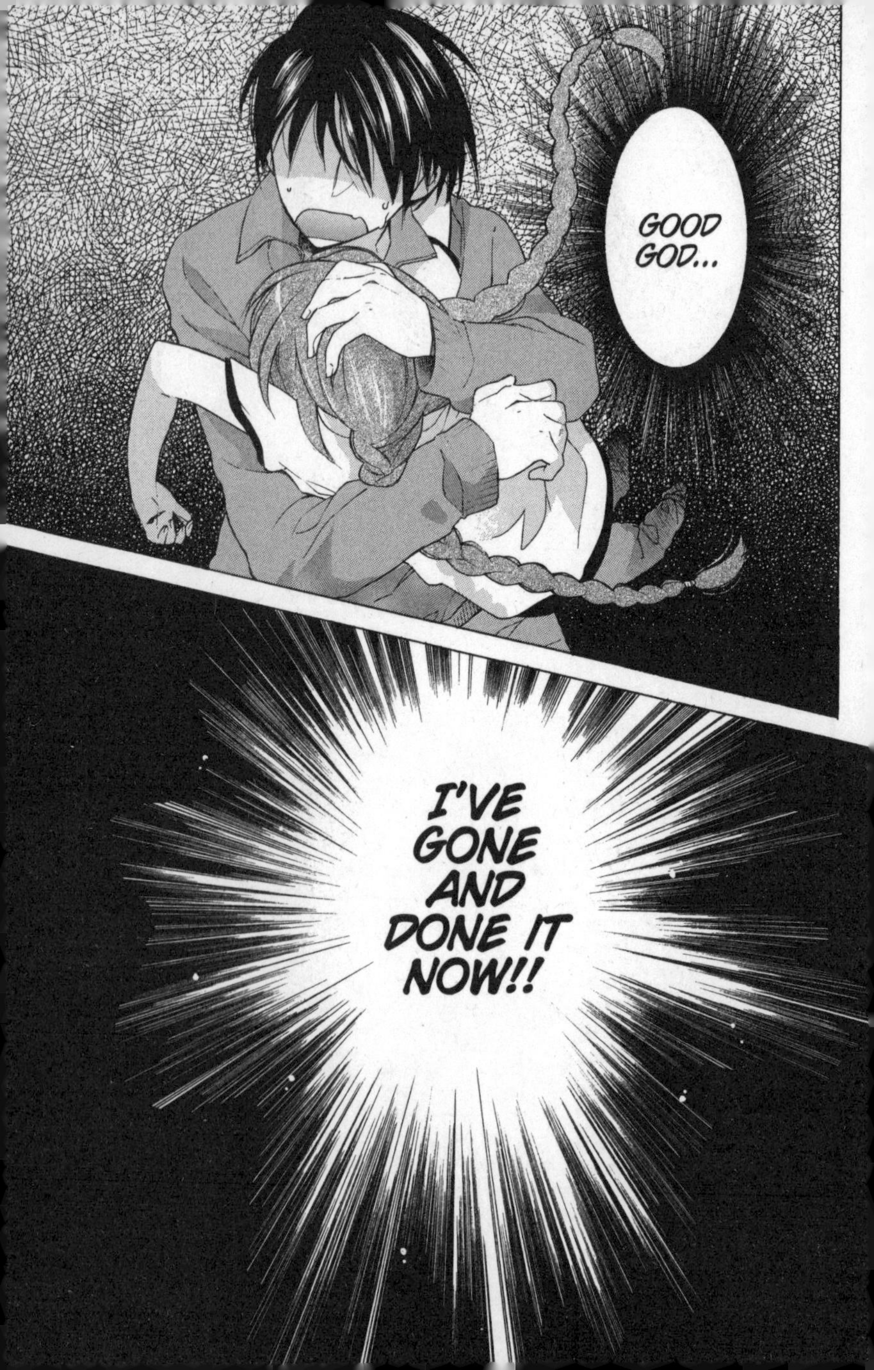
GOOD GOD...
I'VE GONE AND DONE IT NOW!!

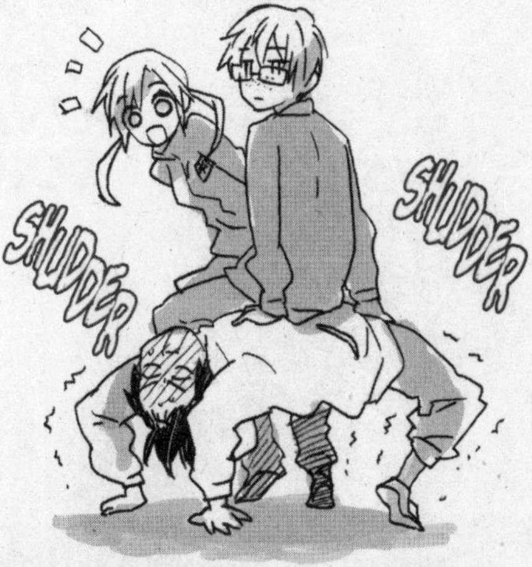
SHUDDER
SHUDDER

Chapter 5
RYUUJI & TAIGA'S FIRST GROUP PROJECT

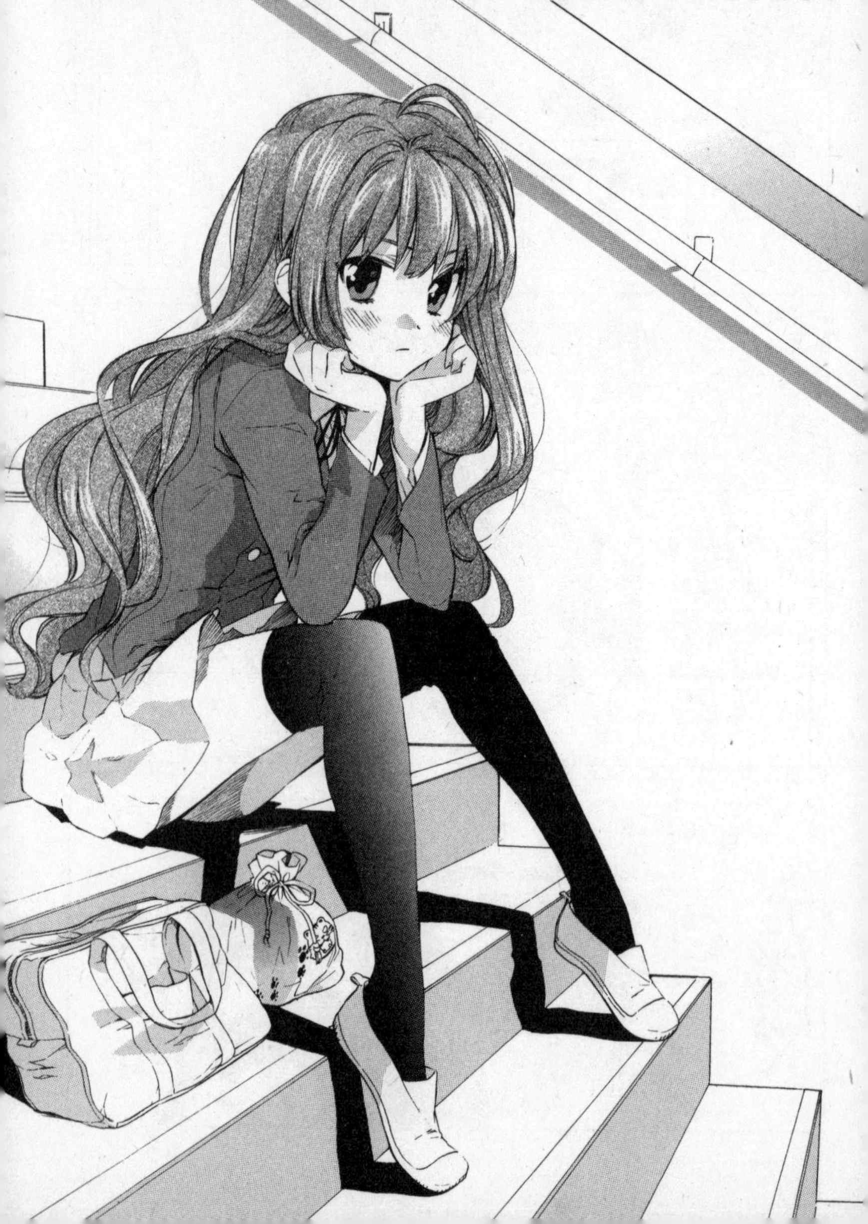

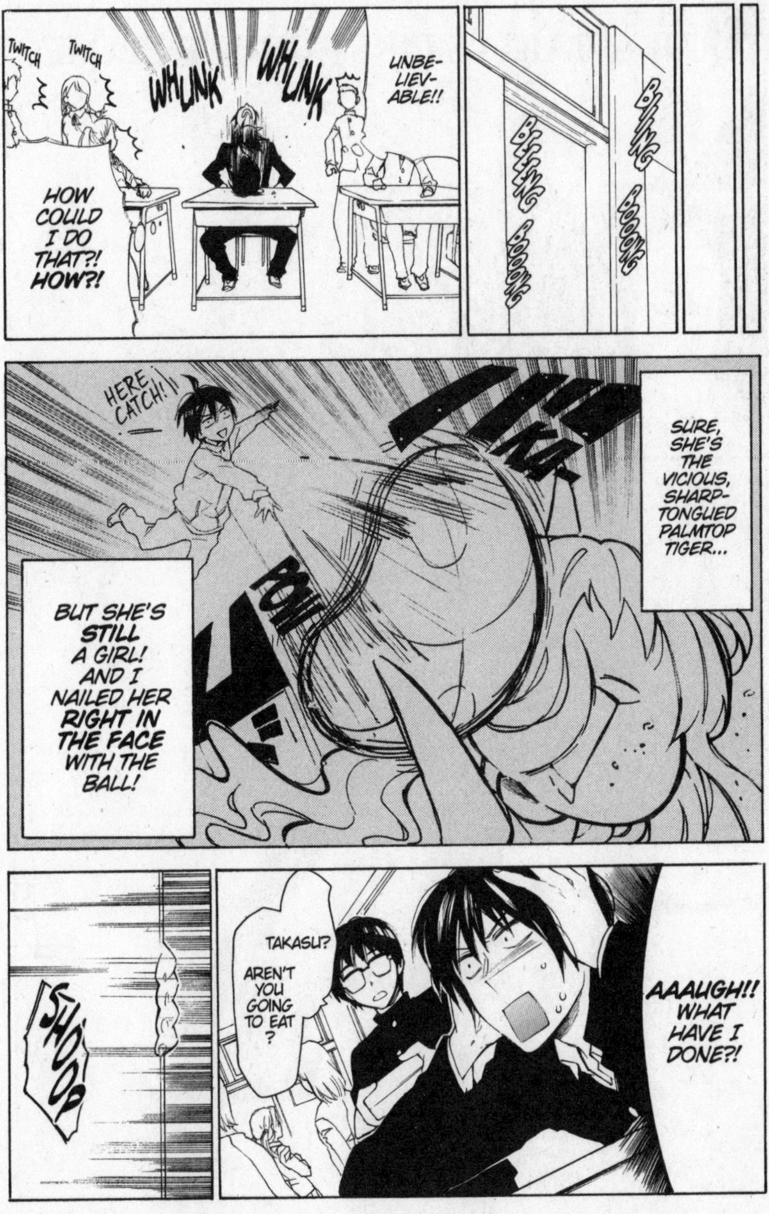
BIIING BOOONG
BIIING BOOONG
UNBE-LIEV-ABLE!!
WHUNK
WHUNK
TWITCH
TWITCH
HOW COULD I DO THAT?! HOW?!
SURE, SHE'S THE VICIOUS, SHARP-TONGUED PALMTOP TIGER...
HERE CATCH!
BUT SHE'S STILL A GIRL! AND I NAILED HER RIGHT IN THE FACE WITH THE BALL!
AAAUGH!! WHAT HAVE I DONE?!
TAKASU?
AREN'T YOU GOING TO EAT?
SHOOP

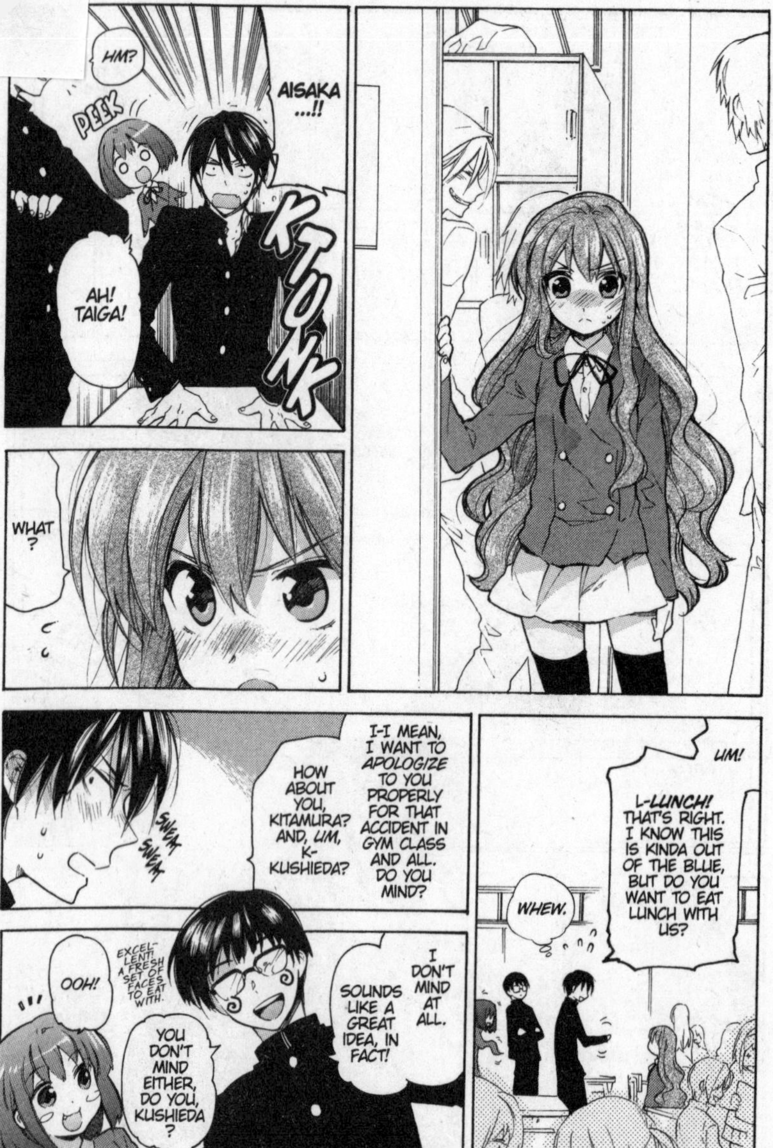

AISAKA ...!!
HM?
PEEK
KTUNK
AH! TAIGA!
WHAT ?
UM!
L-LUNCH! THAT'S RIGHT. I KNOW THIS IS KINDA OUT OF THE BLUE, BUT DO YOU WANT TO EAT LUNCH WITH US?
WHEW.
I-I MEAN, I WANT TO APOLOGIZE TO YOU PROPERLY FOR THAT ACCIDENT IN GYM CLASS AND ALL. DO YOU MIND?
HOW ABOUT YOU, KITAMURA? AND, UM, K-KUSHIEDA?
SWEAT SWEAT
I DON'T MIND AT ALL.
SOUNDS LIKE A GREAT IDEA, IN FACT!
YOU DON'T MIND EITHER, DO YOU, KUSHIEDA?
EXCEL-LENT! A FRESH SET OF FACES TO EAT WITH.
OOH!

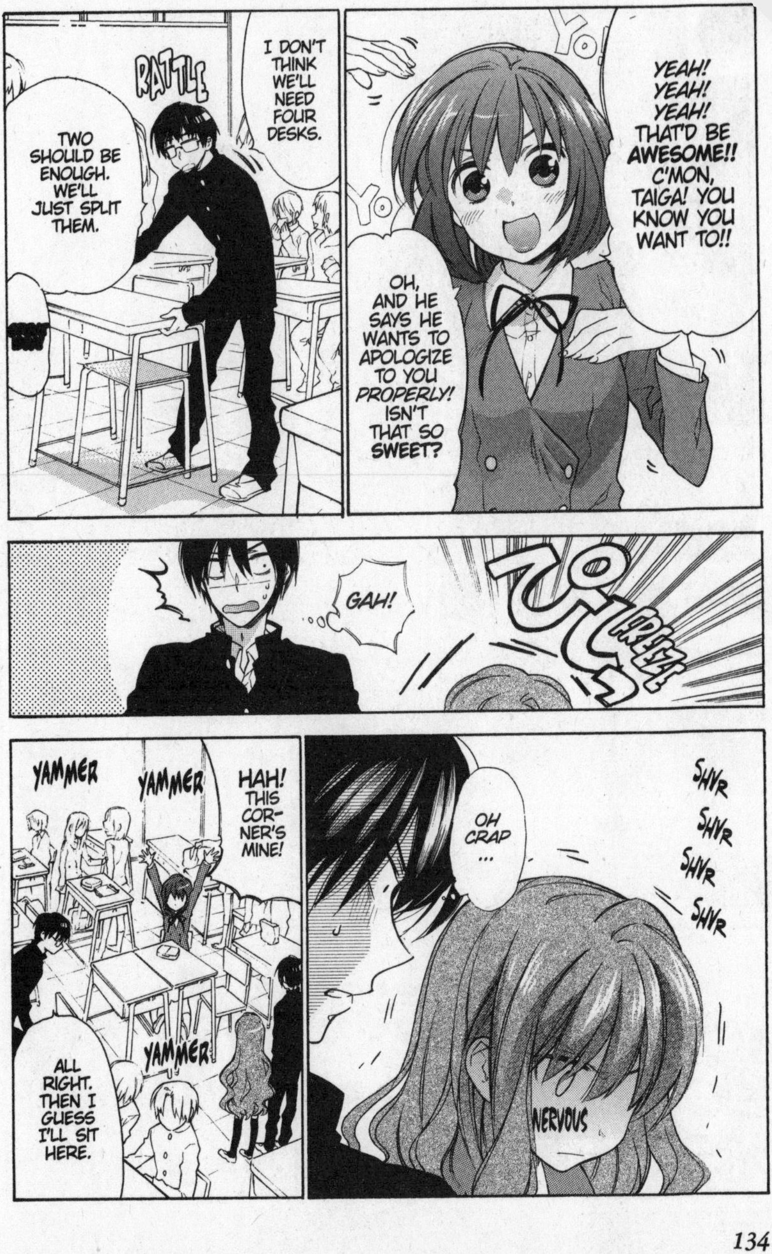
YO!
YO!
YEAH! YEAH! YEAH! THAT'D BE AWESOME!! C'MON, TAIGA! YOU KNOW YOU WANT TO!!
OH, AND HE SAYS HE WANTS TO APOLOGIZE TO YOU PROPERLY! ISN'T THAT SO SWEET?
I DON'T THINK WE'LL NEED FOUR DESKS.
RATTLE
TWO SHOULD BE ENOUGH. WE'LL JUST SPLIT THEM.
FREEZE
GAH!
SHVR
SHVR
SHVR
SHVR
OH CRAP ...
NERVOUS
HAH! THIS COR-NER'S MINE!
YAMMER
YAMMER
YAMMER
ALL RIGHT. THEN I GUESS I'LL SIT HERE.

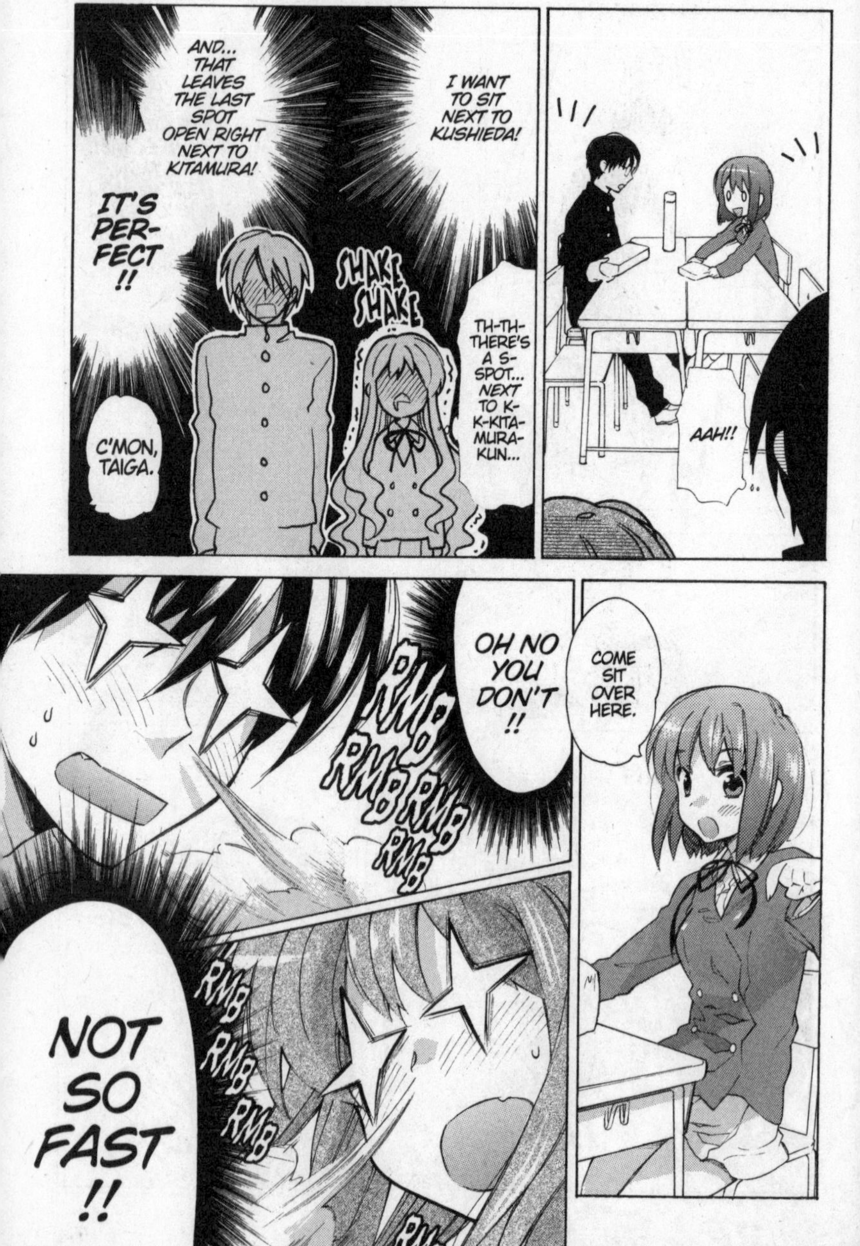
AAH!!
I WANT TO SIT NEXT TO KUSHIEDA!
AND... THAT LEAVES THE LAST SPOT OPEN RIGHT NEXT TO KITAMURA!
IT'S PER-FECT!!
SHAKE SHAKE
TH-TH-THERE'S A S-SPOT... NEXT TO K-K-KITA-MURA-KUN...
C'MON, TAIGA.
COME SIT OVER HERE.
OH NO YOU DON'T!!
RMB RMB RMB RMB RMB RMB RMB
NOT SO FAST!!
RMB RMB RMB RMB RMB

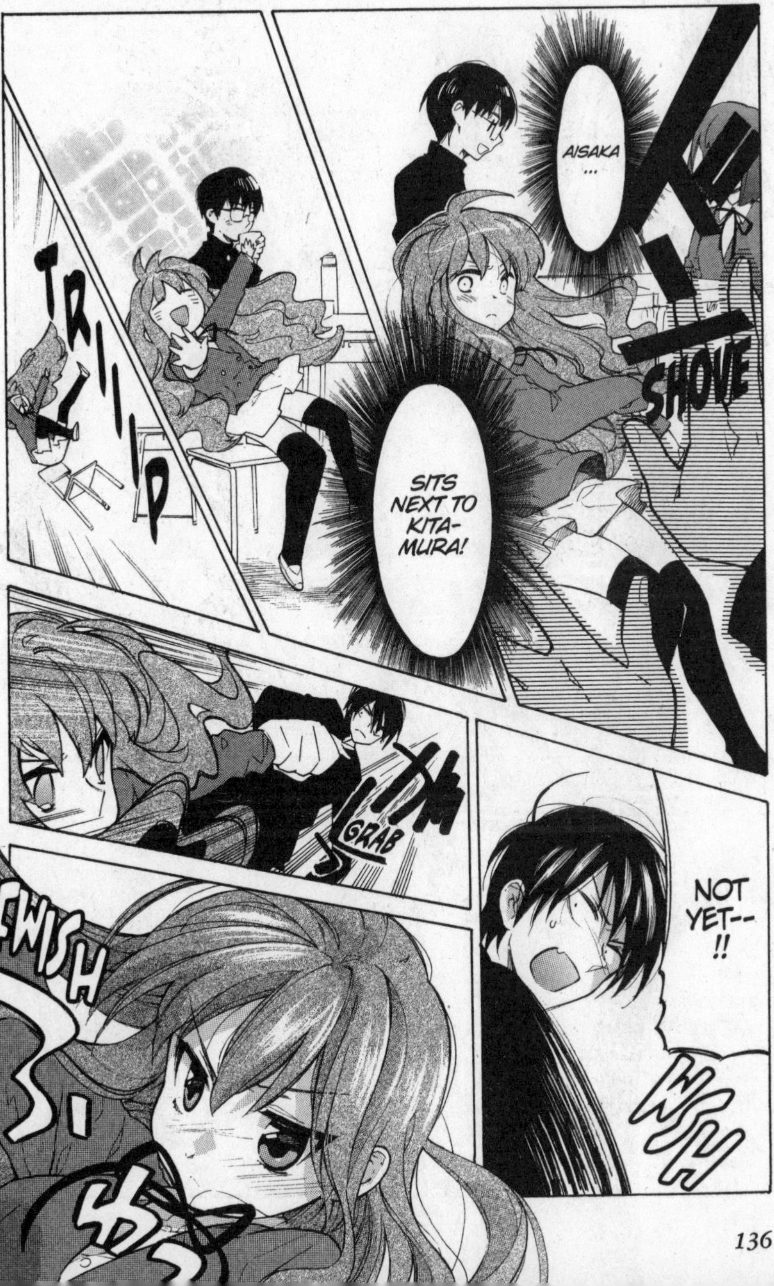
AISAKA ...
SHOVE
SITS NEXT TO KITA-MURA!
TRIIIP
NOT YET-- !!
WSSH
GRAB
FWISH

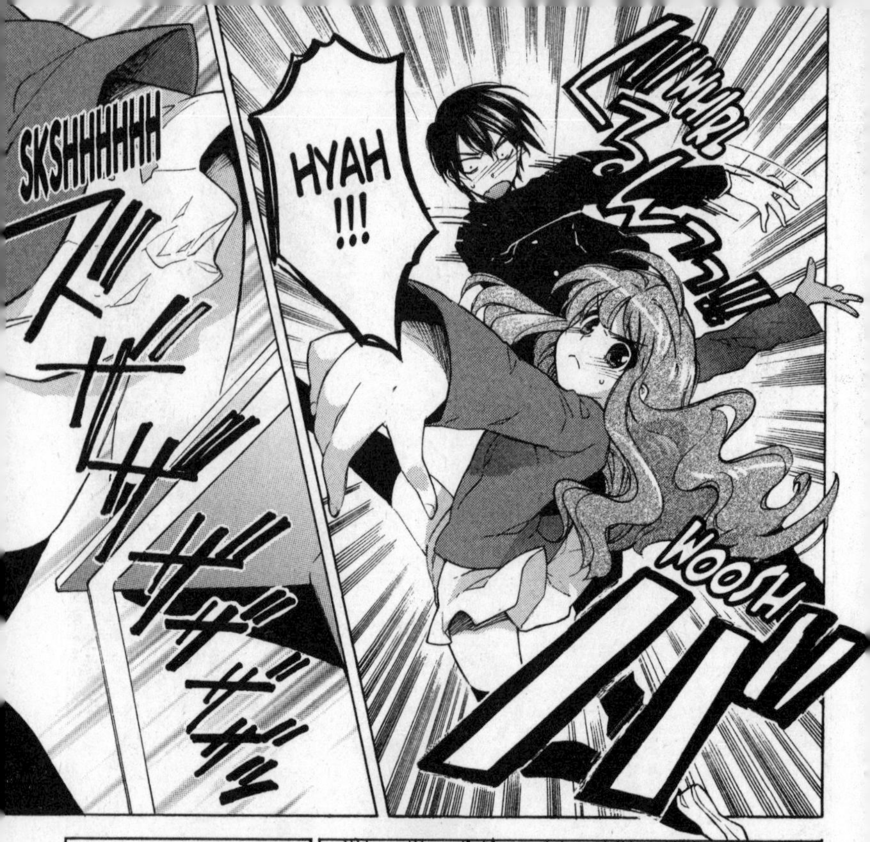
WHIRL
HYAH !!!
SKSHHHHHH
WOOSH
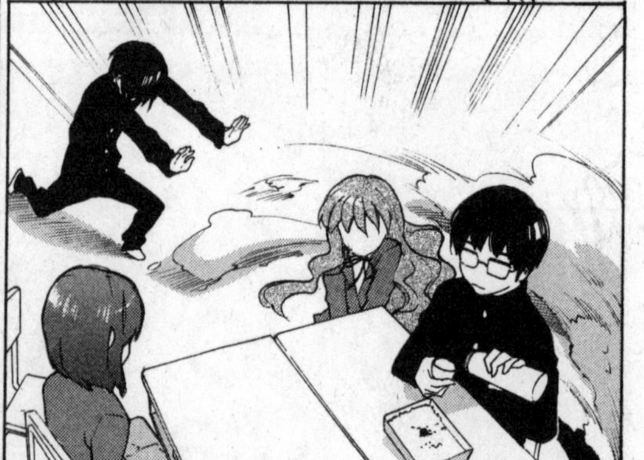
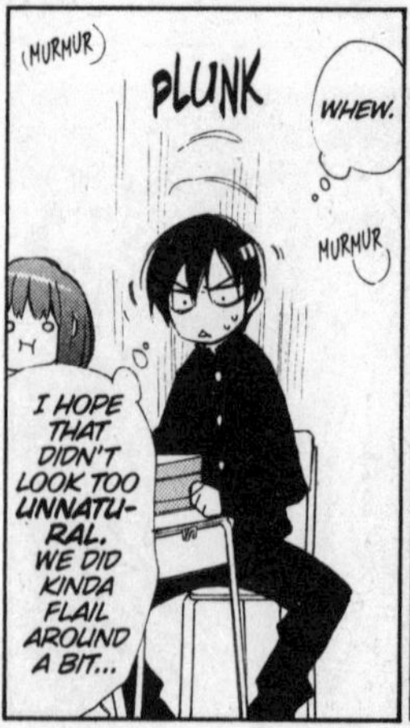
(MURMUR)
PLUNK
WHEW.
MURMUR
I HOPE THAT DIDN'T LOOK TOO UNNATURAL. WE DID KINDA FLAIL AROUND A BIT...

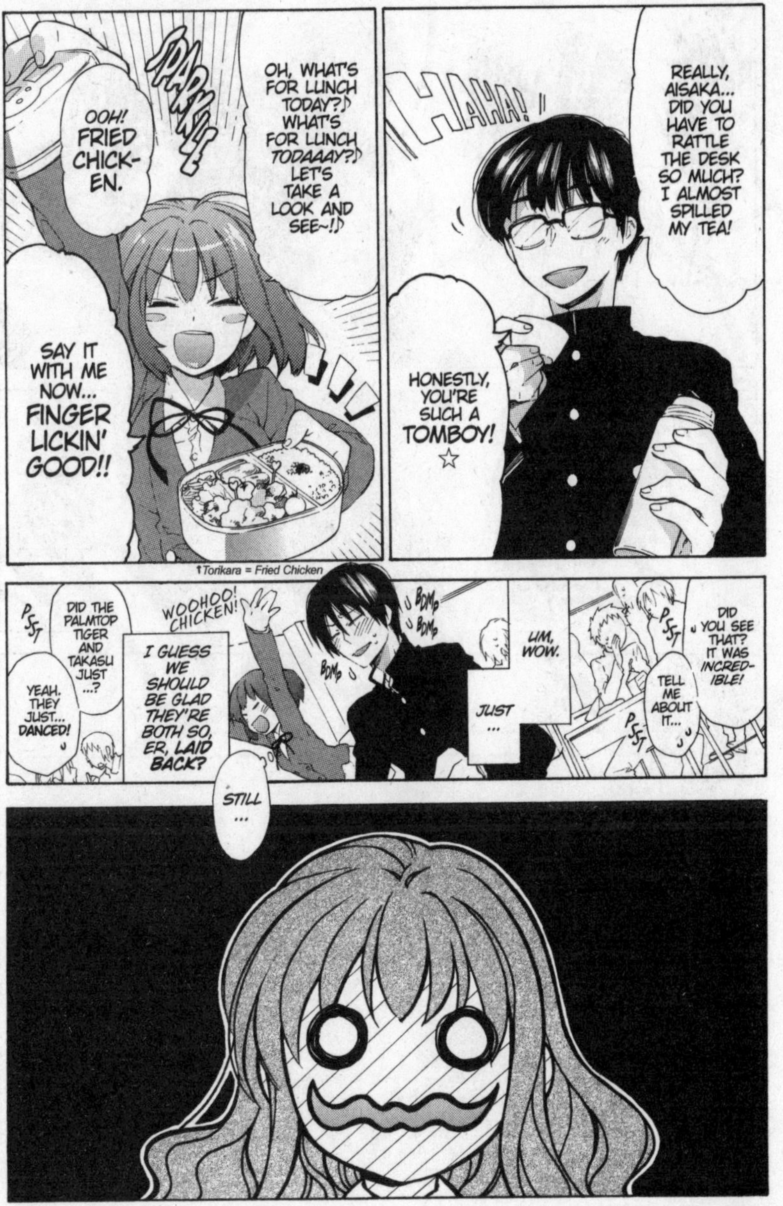
REALLY, AISAKA... DID YOU HAVE TO RATTLE THE DESK SO MUCH? I ALMOST SPILLED MY TEA!
HAHA!
HONESTLY, YOU'RE SUCH A TOMBOY! ☆
OH, WHAT'S FOR LUNCH TODAY?♪ WHAT'S FOR LUNCH TODAAAY?♪ LET'S TAKE A LOOK AND SEE~!♪
SPARKLE
OOH! FRIED CHICK-EN.
SAY IT WITH ME NOW... FINGER LICKIN' GOOD!!
↑Torikara = Fried Chicken
DID YOU SEE THAT? IT WAS INCREDIBLE!
PSST
TELL ME ABOUT IT...
PSST
UM, WOW.
JUST...
BDMP
BDMP
BDMP
WOOHOO! CHICKEN!
I GUESS WE SHOULD BE GLAD THEY'RE BOTH SO, ER, LAID BACK?
DID THE PALMTOP TIGER AND TAKASU JUST ...?
PSST
YEAH. THEY JUST... DANCED!
STILL ...

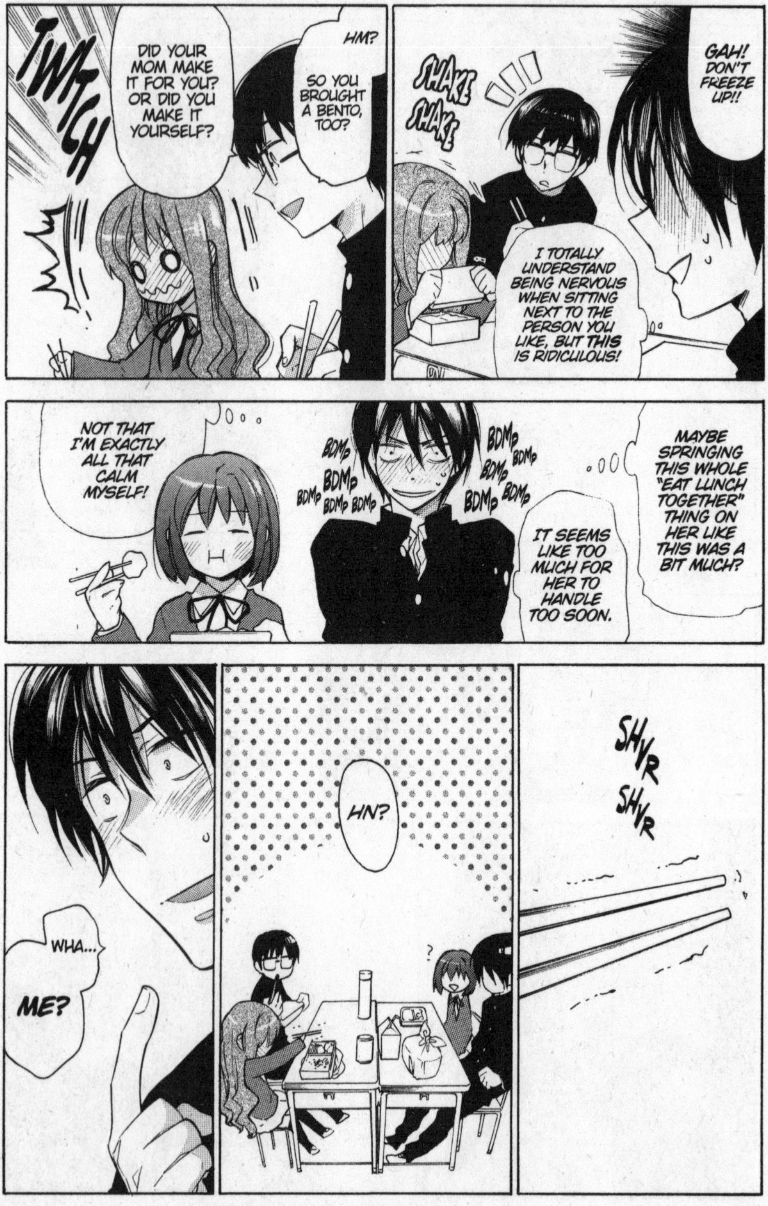
GAH! DON'T FREEZE UP!!
SHAKE SHAKE
I TOTALLY UNDERSTAND BEING NERVOUS WHEN SITTING NEXT TO THE PERSON YOU LIKE, BUT THIS IS RIDICULOUS!
HM?
SO YOU BROUGHT A BENTO, TOO?
DID YOUR MOM MAKE IT FOR YOU? OR DID YOU MAKE IT YOURSELF?
TWITCH
MAYBE SPRINGING THIS WHOLE "EAT LUNCH TOGETHER" THING ON HER LIKE THIS WAS A BIT MUCH?
IT SEEMS LIKE TOO MUCH FOR HER TO HANDLE TOO SOON.
BDMP BDMP BDMP BDMP BDMP BDMP BDMP BDMP BDMP BDMP
NOT THAT I'M EXACTLY ALL THAT CALM MYSELF!
SHVR SHVR
HN?
WHA...
ME?

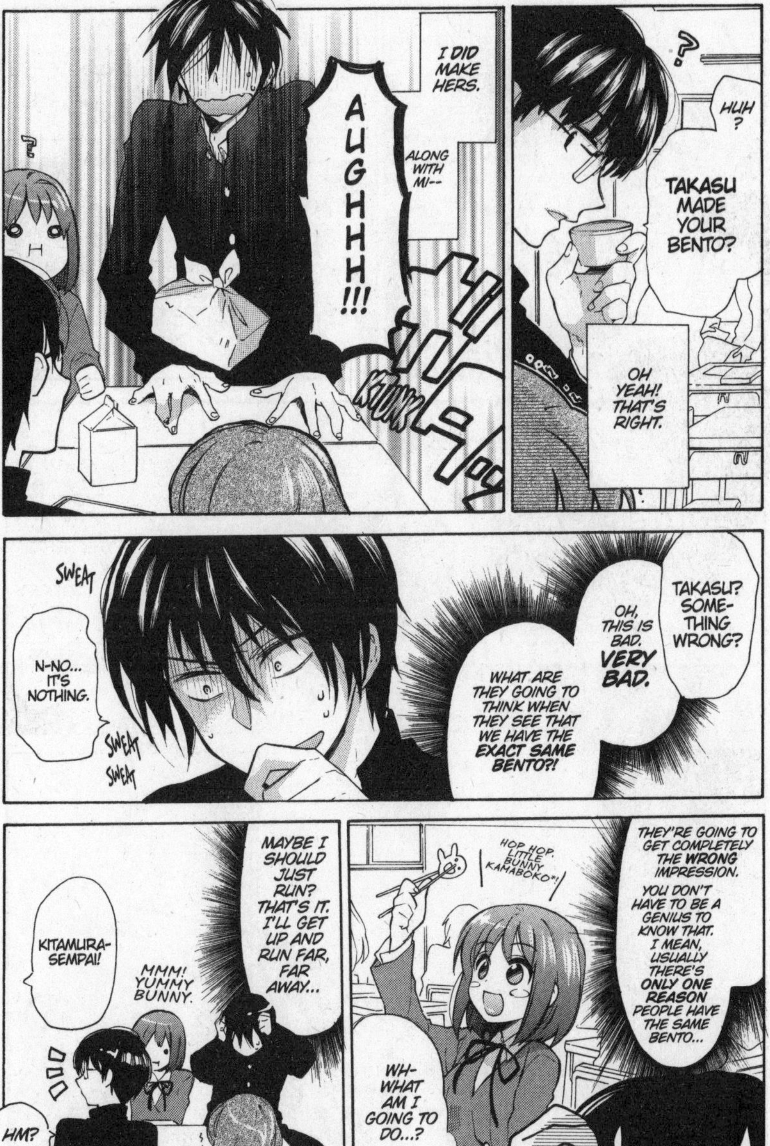
HUH?
TAKASU MADE YOUR BENTO?
OH YEAH! THAT'S RIGHT.
I DID MAKE HERS.
ALONG WITH MI--
AUGHHH!!!
KLUNK
TAKASU? SOME-THING WRONG?
OH, THIS IS BAD. VERY BAD.
WHAT ARE THEY GOING TO THINK WHEN THEY SEE THAT WE HAVE THE EXACT SAME BENTO?!
SWEAT
N-NO... IT'S NOTHING.
SWEAT SWEAT
THEY'RE GOING TO GET COMPLETELY THE WRONG IMPRESSION. YOU DON'T HAVE TO BE A GENIUS TO KNOW THAT. I MEAN, USUALLY THERE'S ONLY ONE REASON PEOPLE HAVE THE SAME BENTO...
HOP HOP, LITTLE BUNNY KAMABOKO*!
WH-WHAT AM I GOING TO DO...?
MAYBE I SHOULD JUST RUN? THAT'S IT. I'LL GET UP AND RUN FAR, FAR AWAY...
KITAMURA-SEMPAI!
MMM! YUMMY BUNNY.
HM?

*Kamaboko is processed fish, or fish sausage.

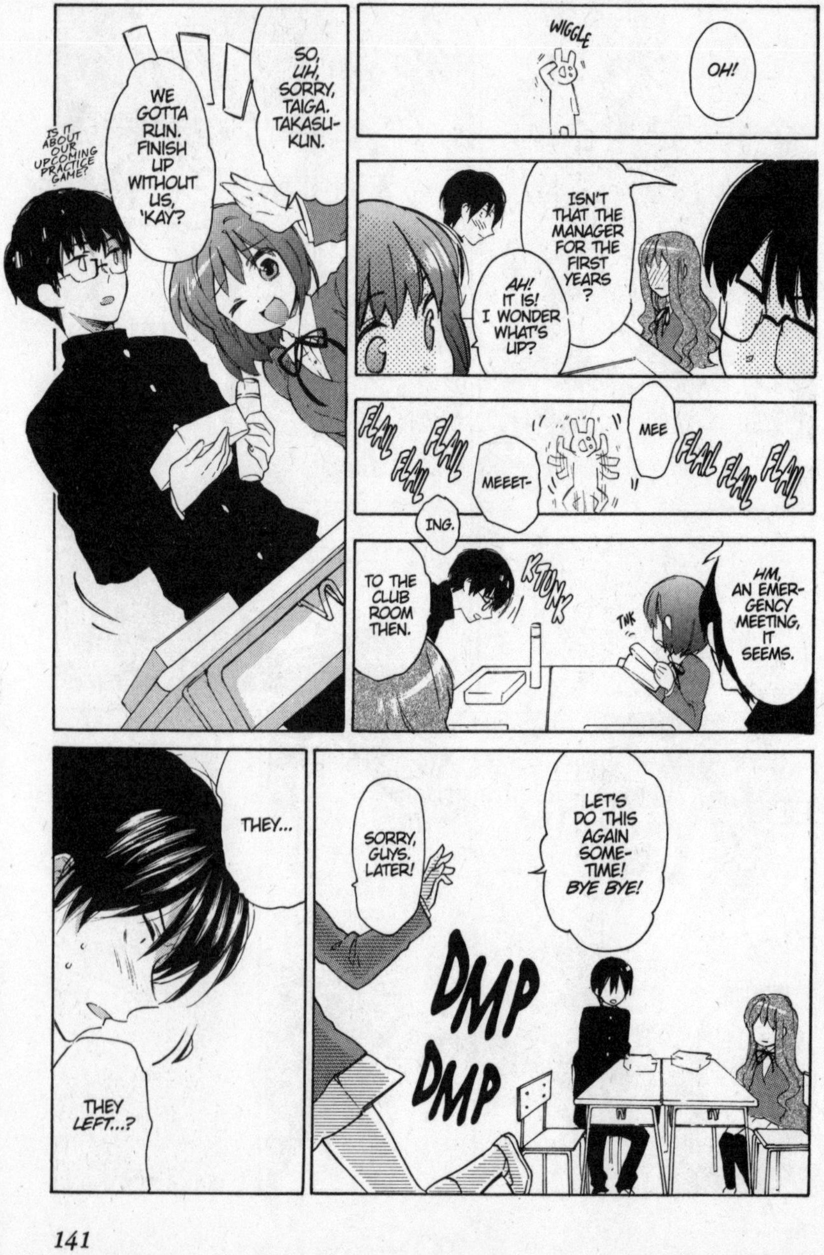
OH!
WIGGLE
ISN'T THAT THE MANAGER FOR THE FIRST YEARS?
AH! IT IS! I WONDER WHAT'S UP?
FLAIL FLAIL FLAIL
MEE
MEEET-
ING.
FLAIL FLAIL FLAIL
HM, AN EMER-GENCY MEETING, IT SEEMS.
TNK
KTUNK
TO THE CLUB ROOM THEN.
SO, UH, SORRY, TAIGA. TAKASU-KUN.
WE GOTTA RUN. FINISH UP WITHOUT US, 'KAY?
IS IT ABOUT OUR UPCOMING PRACTICE GAME?
LET'S DO THIS AGAIN SOME-TIME! BYE BYE!
SORRY, GUYS. LATER!
DMP
DMP
THEY...
THEY LEFT...?

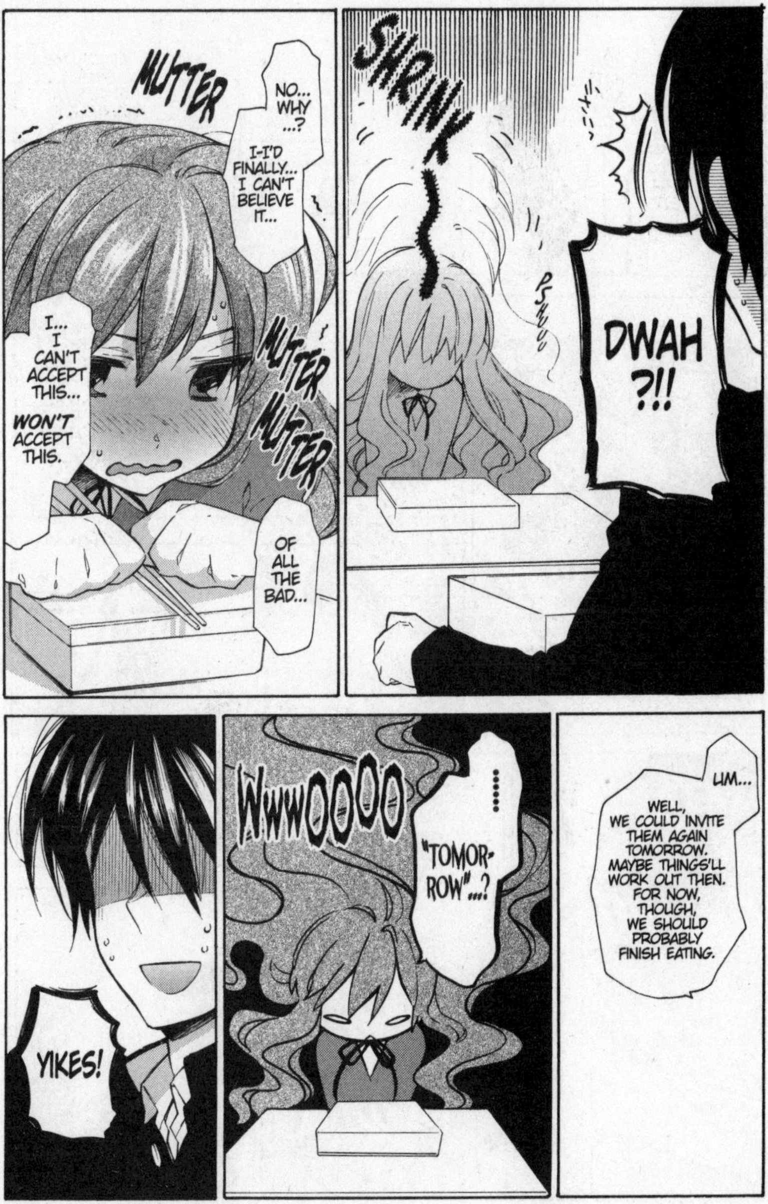
SHRINK
PSHUUU
DWAH ?!!
NO... WHY ...?
I-I'D FINALLY... I CAN'T BELIEVE IT...
MUTTER
MUTTER MUTTER
I... I CAN'T ACCEPT THIS... *WON'T* ACCEPT THIS.
OF ALL THE BAD...
UM...
WELL, WE COULD INVITE THEM AGAIN TOMORROW. MAYBE THINGS'LL WORK OUT THEN. FOR NOW, THOUGH, WE SHOULD PROBABLY FINISH EATING.
......
"TOMOR-ROW"...?
WwwOOOO
YIKES!

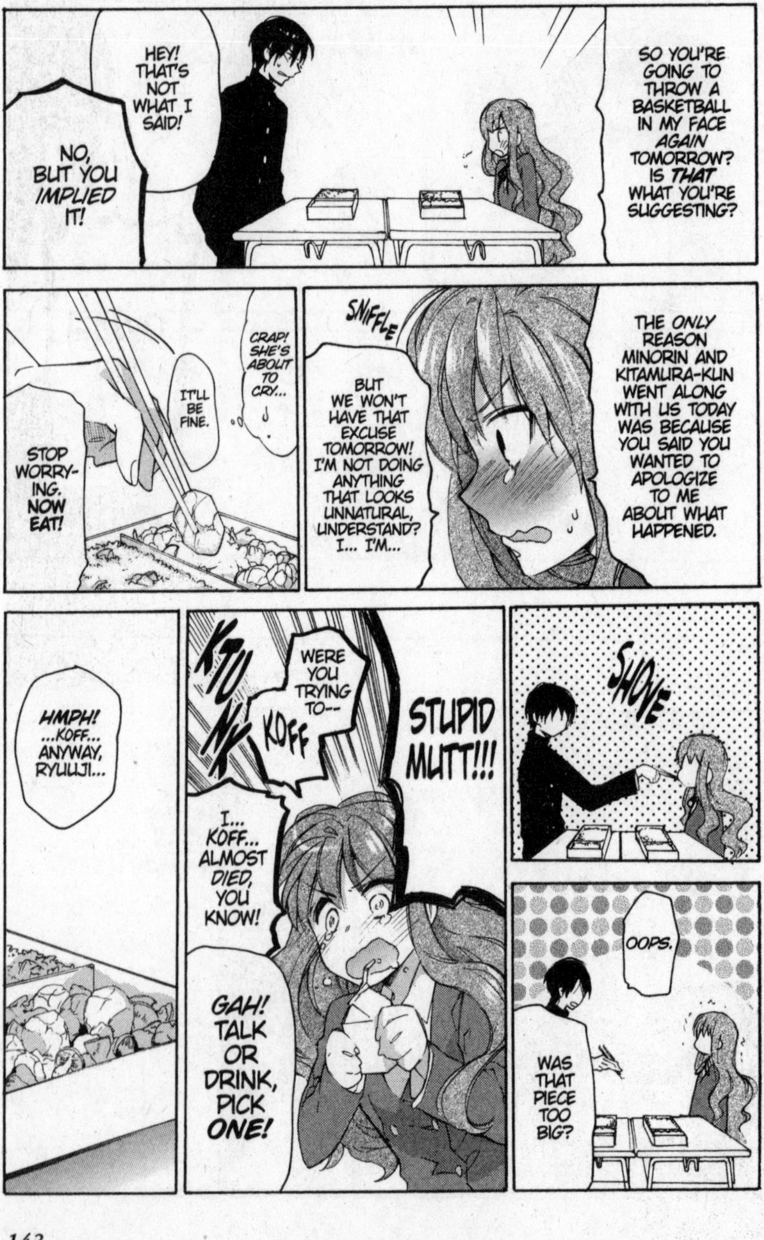
SO YOU'RE GOING TO THROW A BASKETBALL IN MY FACE AGAIN TOMORROW? IS THAT WHAT YOU'RE SUGGESTING?
HEY! THAT'S NOT WHAT I SAID!
NO, BUT YOU IMPLIED IT!
SNIFFLE
THE ONLY REASON MINORIN AND KITAMURA-KUN WENT ALONG WITH US TODAY WAS BECAUSE YOU SAID YOU WANTED TO APOLOGIZE TO ME ABOUT WHAT HAPPENED.
BUT WE WON'T HAVE THAT EXCUSE TOMORROW! I'M NOT DOING ANYTHING THAT LOOKS UNNATURAL, UNDERSTAND? I... I'M...
CRAP! SHE'S ABOUT TO CRY...
IT'LL BE FINE.
STOP WORRYING. NOW EAT!
SHOVE
OOPS.
WAS THAT PIECE TOO BIG?
KTUNK
WERE YOU TRYING TO-- KOFF
STUPID MUTT!!!
I... KOFF... ALMOST DIED, YOU KNOW!
GAH! TALK OR DRINK, PICK ONE!
HMPH! ...KOFF... ANYWAY, RYUUJI...

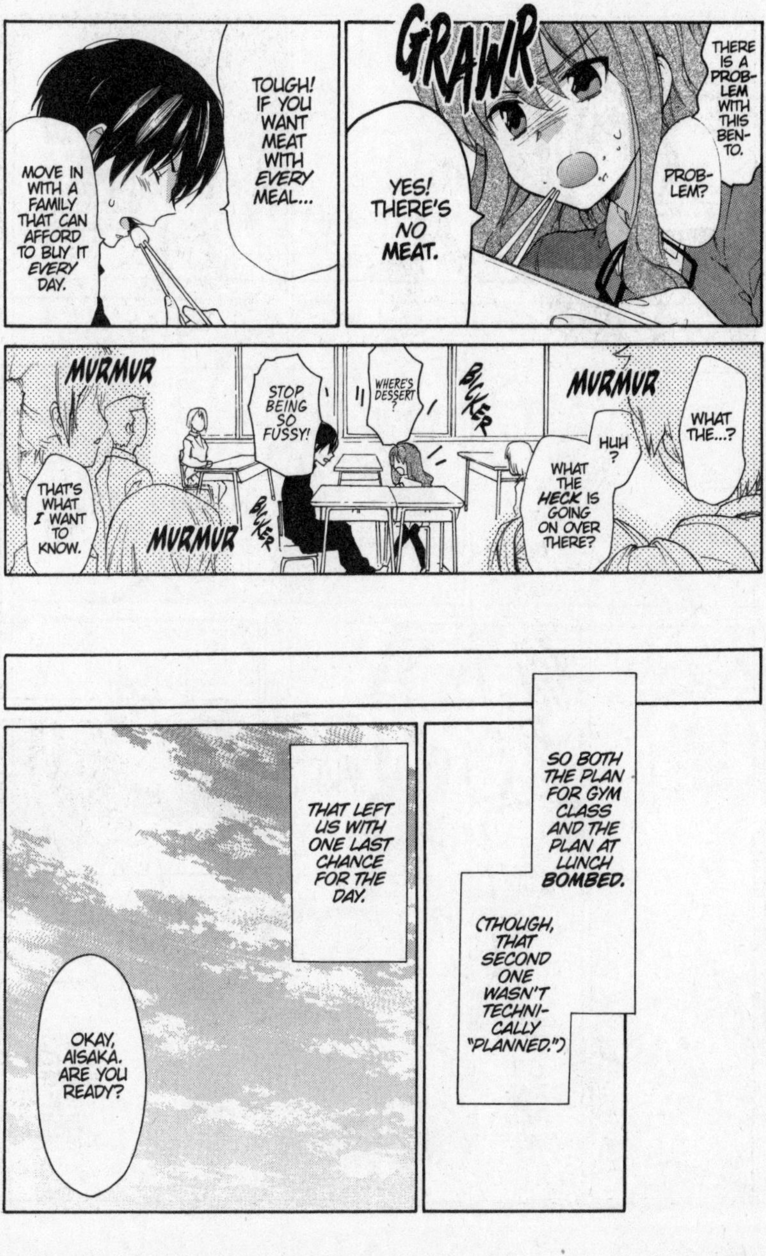
THERE IS A PROBLEM WITH THIS BENTO.
PROBLEM?
GRAWR
YES! THERE'S NO MEAT.
TOUGH! IF YOU WANT MEAT WITH EVERY MEAL...
MOVE IN WITH A FAMILY THAT CAN AFFORD TO BUY IT EVERY DAY.
WHAT THE...?
MURMUR
HUH?
WHAT THE HECK IS GOING ON OVER THERE?
BICKER
WHERE'S DESSERT?
STOP BEING SO FUSSY!
BICKER
MURMUR
THAT'S WHAT I WANT TO KNOW.
MURMUR
SO BOTH THE PLAN FOR GYM CLASS AND THE PLAN AT LUNCH BOMBED.
(THOUGH, THAT SECOND ONE WASN'T TECHNICALLY "PLANNED.")
THAT LEFT US WITH ONE LAST CHANCE FOR THE DAY.
OKAY, AISAKA. ARE YOU READY?

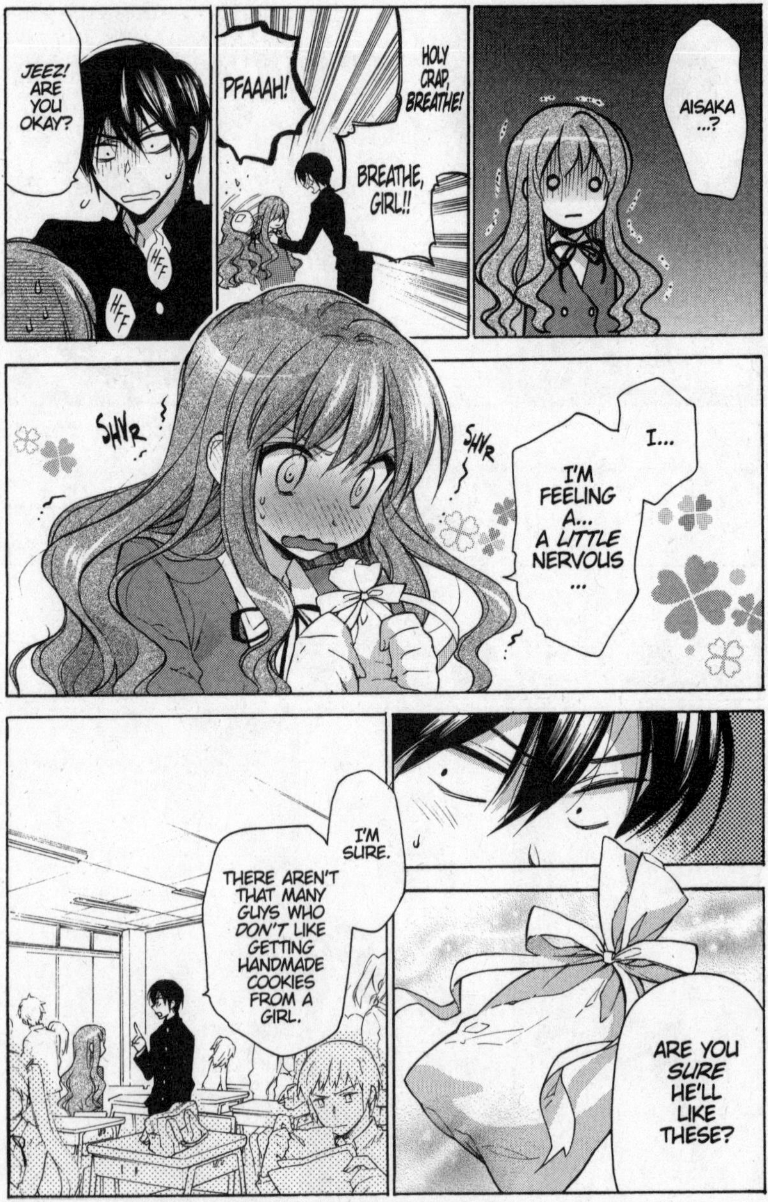
AISAKA ...?
HOLY CRAP, BREATHE!
PFAAAH!
BREATHE, GIRL!!
JEEZ! ARE YOU OKAY?
HFF
HFF
SHVR
I...
I'M FEELING A... A LITTLE NERVOUS ...
SHVR
ARE YOU SURE HE'LL LIKE THESE?
I'M SURE.
THERE AREN'T THAT MANY GUYS WHO DON'T LIKE GETTING HANDMADE COOKIES FROM A GIRL.

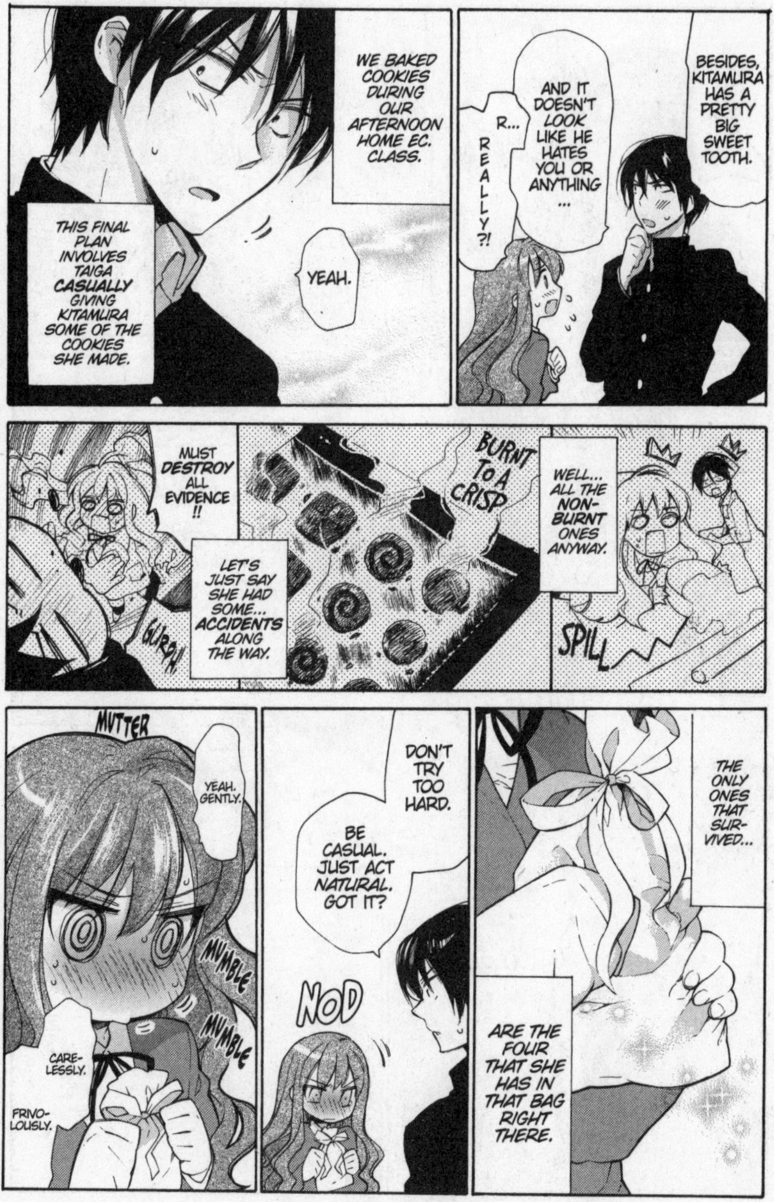
BESIDES, KITAMURA HAS A PRETTY BIG SWEET TOOTH.
AND IT DOESN'T LOOK LIKE HE HATES YOU OR ANYTHING...
R... REALLY?!
WE BAKED COOKIES DURING OUR AFTERNOON HOME EC. CLASS.
YEAH.
THIS FINAL PLAN INVOLVES TAIGA CASUALLY GIVING KITAMURA SOME OF THE COOKIES SHE MADE.
WELL... ALL THE NON-BURNT ONES ANYWAY.
SPILL
BURNT TO A CRISP
LET'S JUST SAY SHE HAD SOME... ACCIDENTS ALONG THE WAY.
MUST DESTROY ALL EVIDENCE!!
GURGH!
THE ONLY ONES THAT SUR-VIVED...
ARE THE FOUR THAT SHE HAS IN THAT BAG RIGHT THERE.
DON'T TRY TOO HARD.
BE CASUAL. JUST ACT NATURAL. GOT IT?
NOD
MUTTER
YEAH. GENTLY.
MUMBLE
MUMBLE
CARE-LESSLY.
FRIVO-LOUSLY.

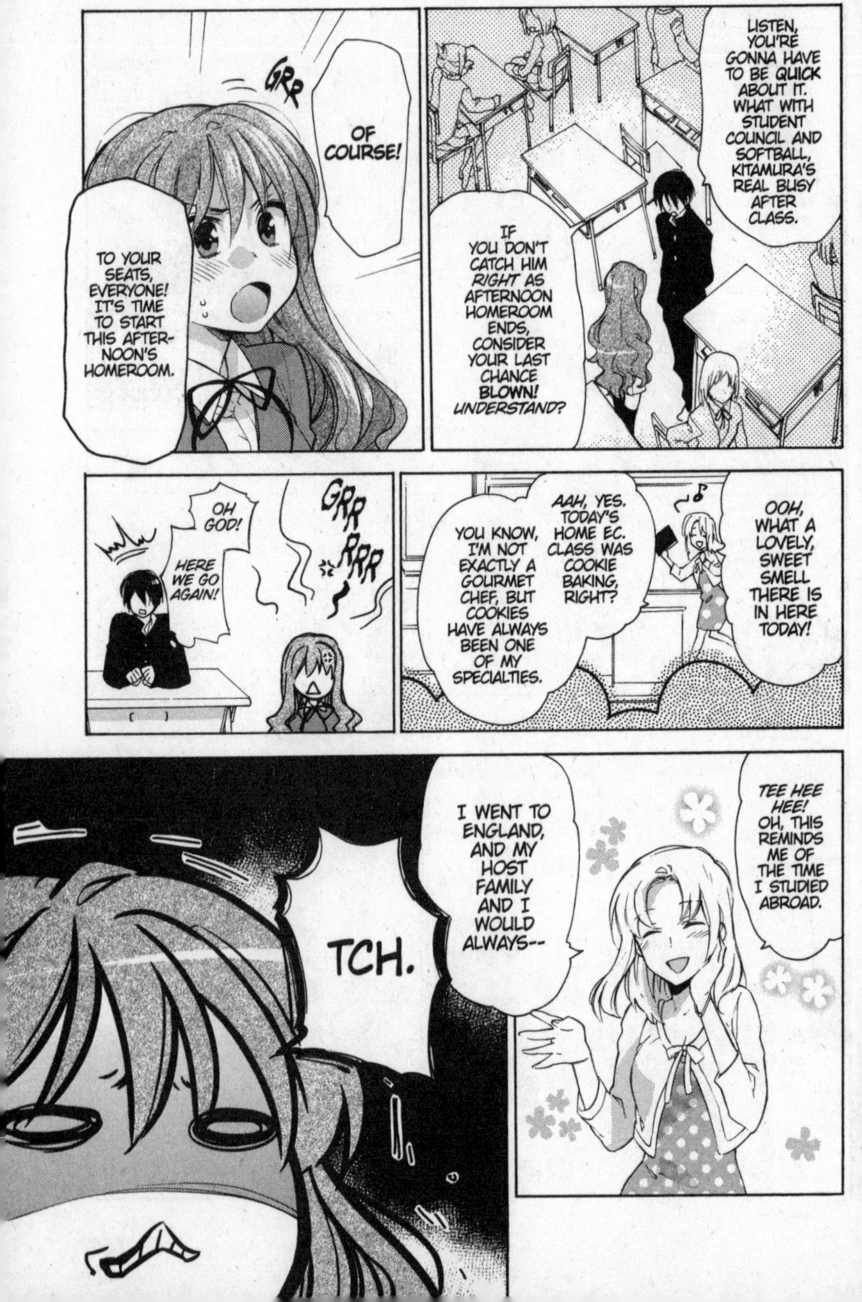
LISTEN, YOU'RE GONNA HAVE TO BE QUICK ABOUT IT. WHAT WITH STUDENT COUNCIL AND SOFTBALL, KITAMURA'S REAL BUSY AFTER CLASS.
IF YOU DON'T CATCH HIM *RIGHT* AS AFTERNOON HOMEROOM ENDS, CONSIDER YOUR LAST CHANCE **BLOWN!** *UNDERSTAND?*
GRR
OF COURSE!
TO YOUR SEATS, EVERYONE! IT'S TIME TO START THIS AFTER-NOON'S HOMEROOM.
OOH, WHAT A LOVELY, SWEET SMELL THERE IS IN HERE TODAY!
AAH, YES. TODAY'S HOME EC. CLASS WAS COOKIE BAKING, RIGHT?
YOU KNOW, I'M NOT EXACTLY A GOURMET CHEF, BUT COOKIES HAVE ALWAYS BEEN ONE OF MY SPECIALTIES.
GRR RRR
OH GOD!
HERE WE GO AGAIN!
TEE HEE HEE! OH, THIS REMINDS ME OF THE TIME I STUDIED ABROAD.
I WENT TO ENGLAND, AND MY HOST FAMILY AND I WOULD ALWAYS--
TCH.

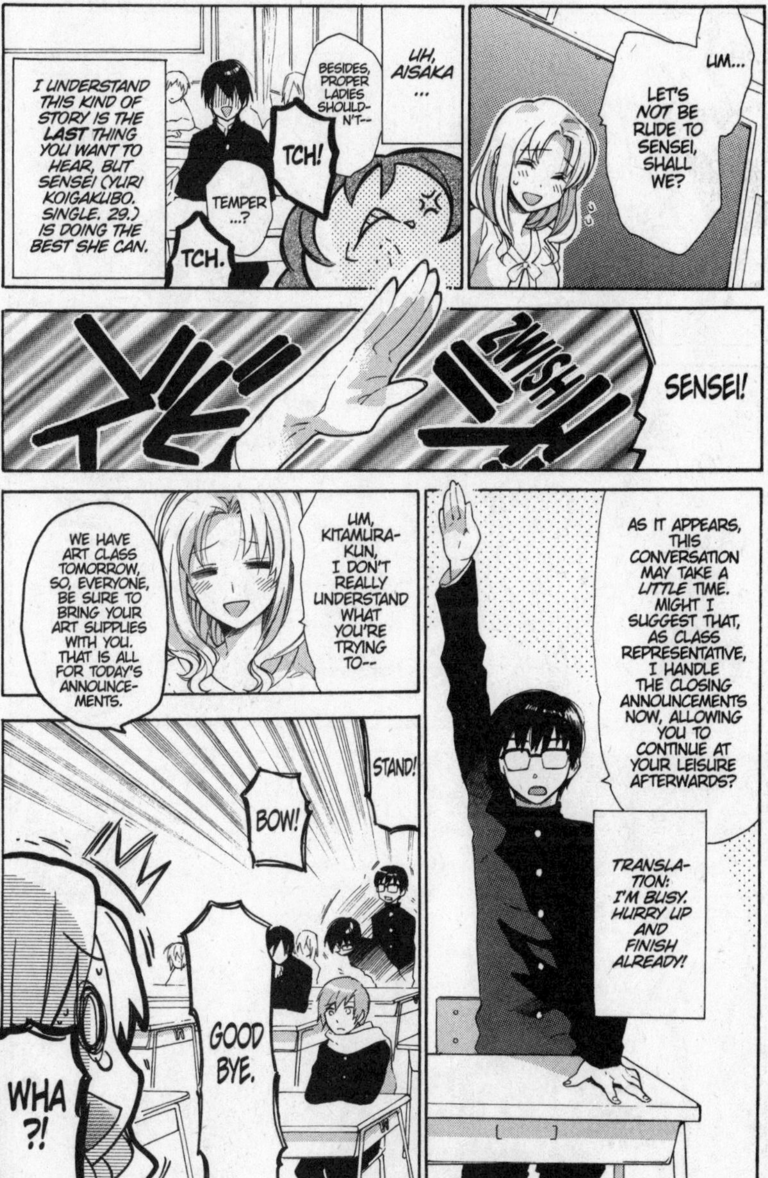
UM...
LET'S NOT BE RUDE TO SENSEI, SHALL WE?
UH, AISAKA ...
BESIDES, PROPER LADIES SHOULDN'T--
TCH!
TEMPER ...?
TCH.
I UNDERSTAND THIS KIND OF STORY IS THE LAST THING YOU WANT TO HEAR, BUT SENSEI (YURI KOIGAKUBO. SINGLE. 29.) IS DOING THE BEST SHE CAN.
SENSEI!
ZWISH
AS IT APPEARS, THIS CONVERSATION MAY TAKE A LITTLE TIME. MIGHT I SUGGEST THAT, AS CLASS REPRESENTATIVE, I HANDLE THE CLOSING ANNOUNCEMENTS NOW, ALLOWING YOU TO CONTINUE AT YOUR LEISURE AFTERWARDS?
TRANSLATION: I'M BUSY. HURRY UP AND FINISH ALREADY!
UM, KITAMURA-KUN, I DON'T REALLY UNDERSTAND WHAT YOU'RE TRYING TO--
WE HAVE ART CLASS TOMORROW, SO, EVERYONE, BE SURE TO BRING YOUR ART SUPPLIES WITH YOU. THAT IS ALL FOR TODAY'S ANNOUNCEMENTS.
STAND!
BOW!
GOOD BYE.
WHA ?!

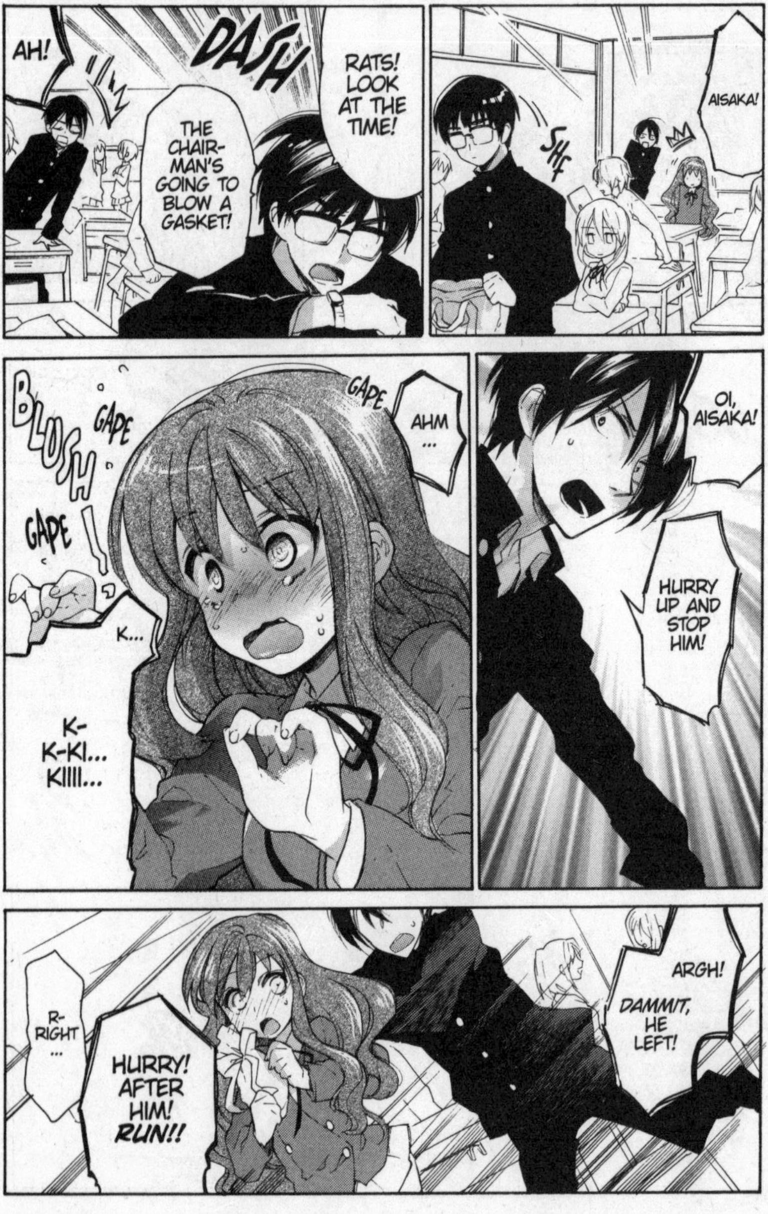
AISAKA!
SHF
RATS! LOOK AT THE TIME!
DASH
THE CHAIRMAN'S GOING TO BLOW A GASKET!
AH!
OI, AISAKA!
HURRY UP AND STOP HIM!
GAPE
AHM ...
BLUSH
GAPE
GAPE
K...
K-K-KI... KIIII...
ARGH!
DAMMIT, HE LEFT!
HURRY! AFTER HIM! RUN!!
R-RIGHT ...

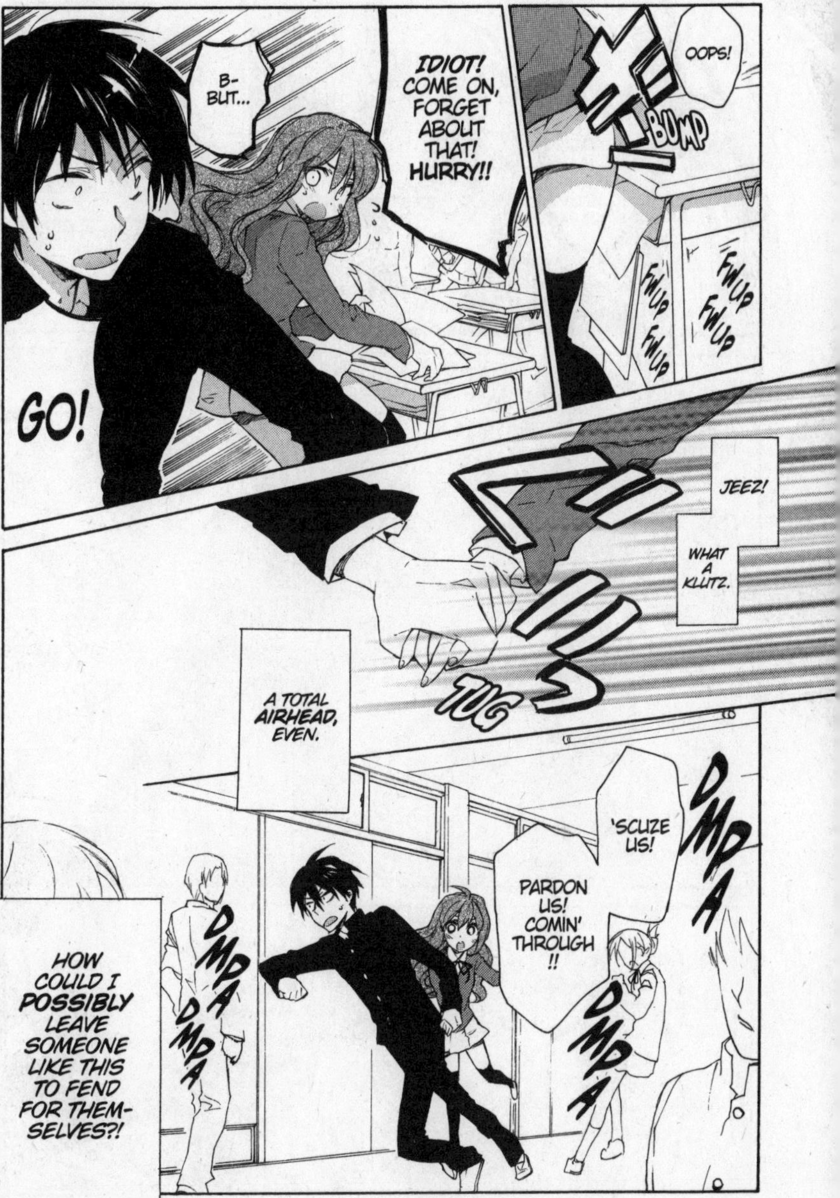
OOPS!
BUMP
FWUP FWUP
FWUP FWUP
IDIOT! COME ON, FORGET ABOUT THAT! HURRY!!
B-BUT...
GO!
JEEZ!
WHAT A KLUTZ.
TUG
A TOTAL AIRHEAD, EVEN.
'SCUZE US!
DMPA
PARDON US! COMIN' THROUGH!!
DMPA
DMPA DMPA
HOW COULD I POSSIBLY LEAVE SOMEONE LIKE THIS TO FEND FOR THEM-SELVES?!

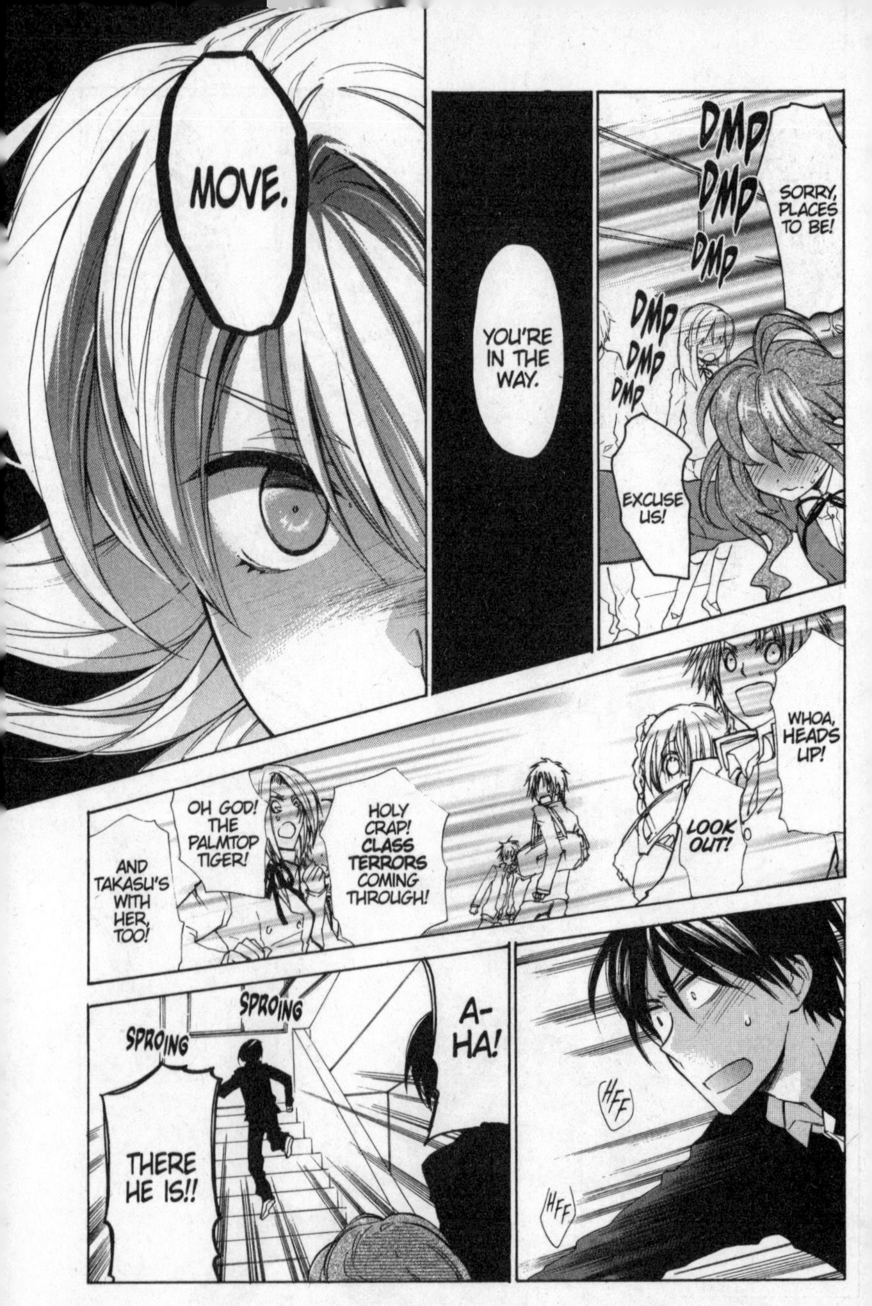
DMP
DMP
DMP
DMP
SORRY, PLACES TO BE!
DMP
DMP
DMP
EXCUSE US!
YOU'RE IN THE WAY.
MOVE.
WHOA, HEADS UP!
LOOK OUT!
HOLY CRAP! CLASS TERRORS COMING THROUGH!
OH GOD! THE PALMTOP TIGER!
AND TAKASU'S WITH HER, TOO!
HFF
HFF
A-HA!
SPROING
SPROING
THERE HE IS!!

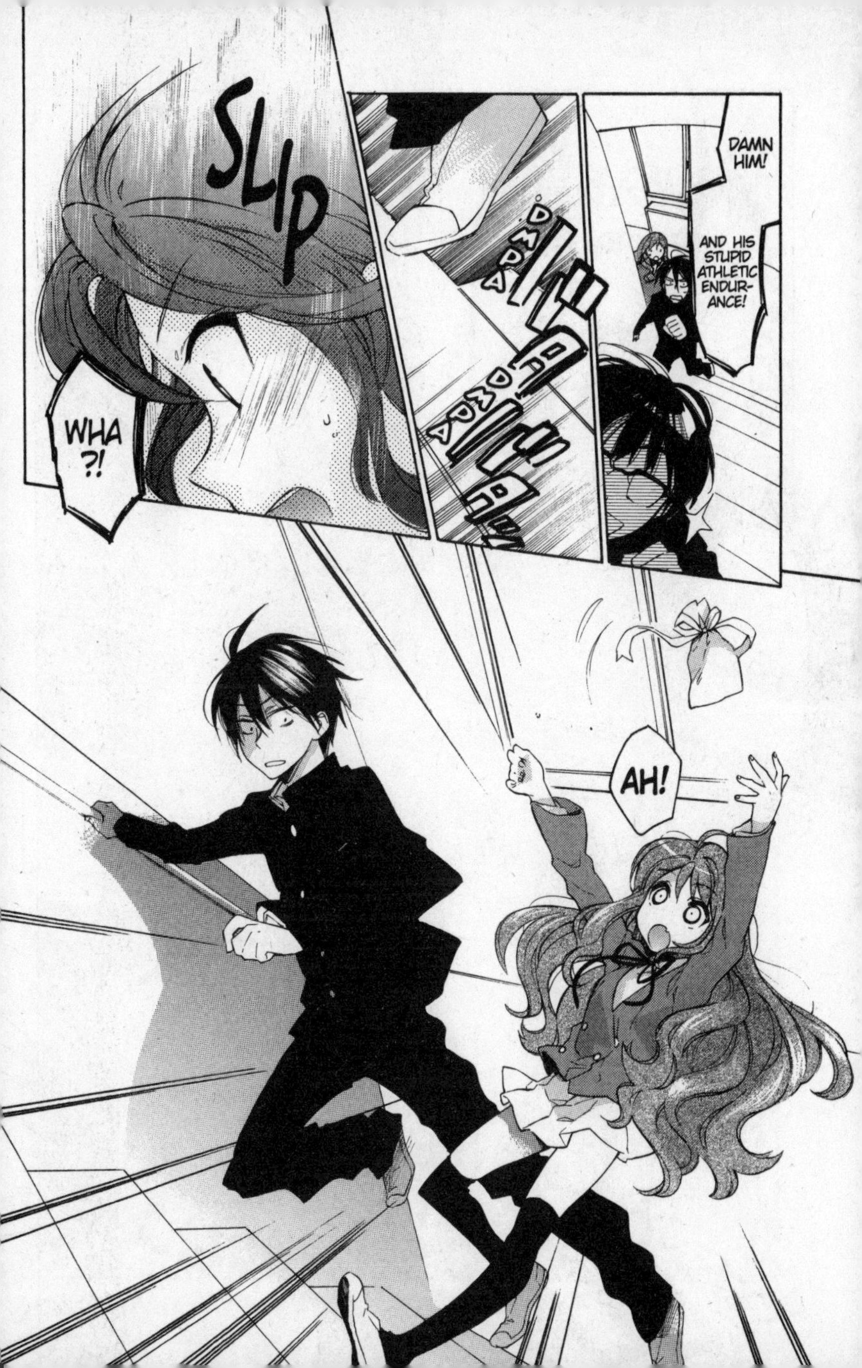
DAMN HIM!
AND HIS STUPID ATHLETIC ENDUR-ANCE!
SLIP
WHA ?!
AH!

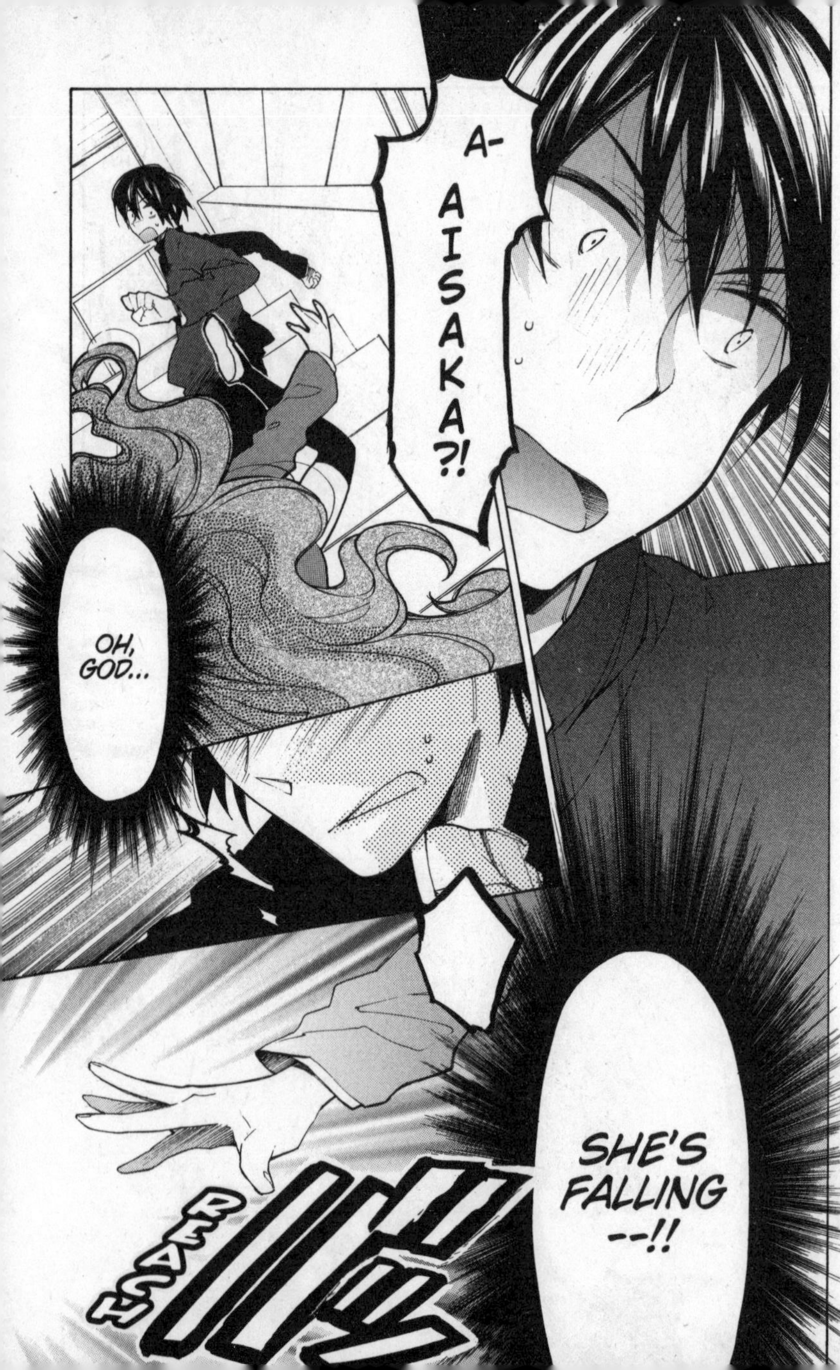
A- AISAKA?!
OH, GOD...
SHE'S FALLING --!!
REACH

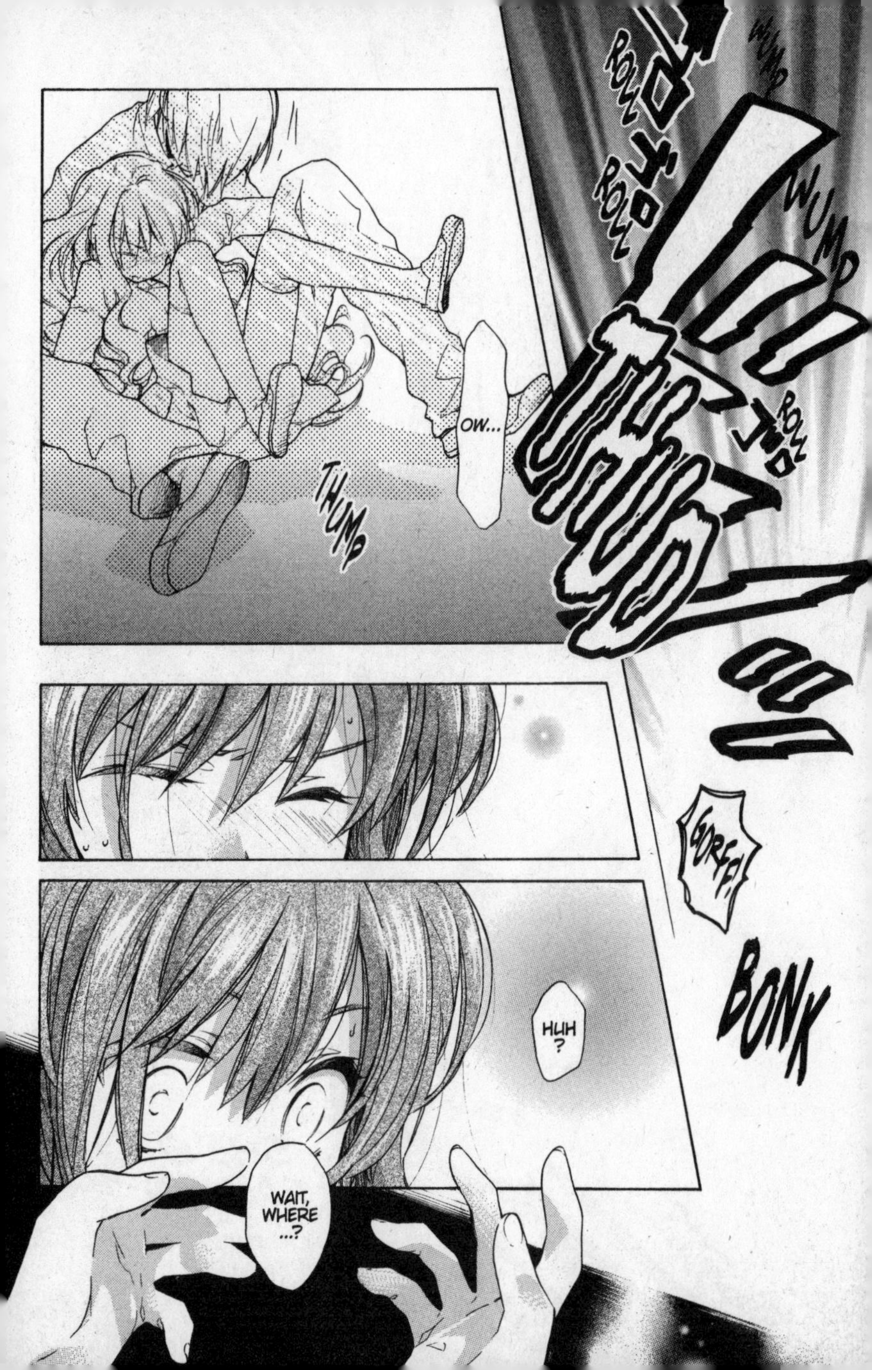
WUMP
ROLL ROLL
WUMP
ROLL ROLL
GORF!
BONK
OW...
THUMP
HUH?
WAIT, WHERE ...?

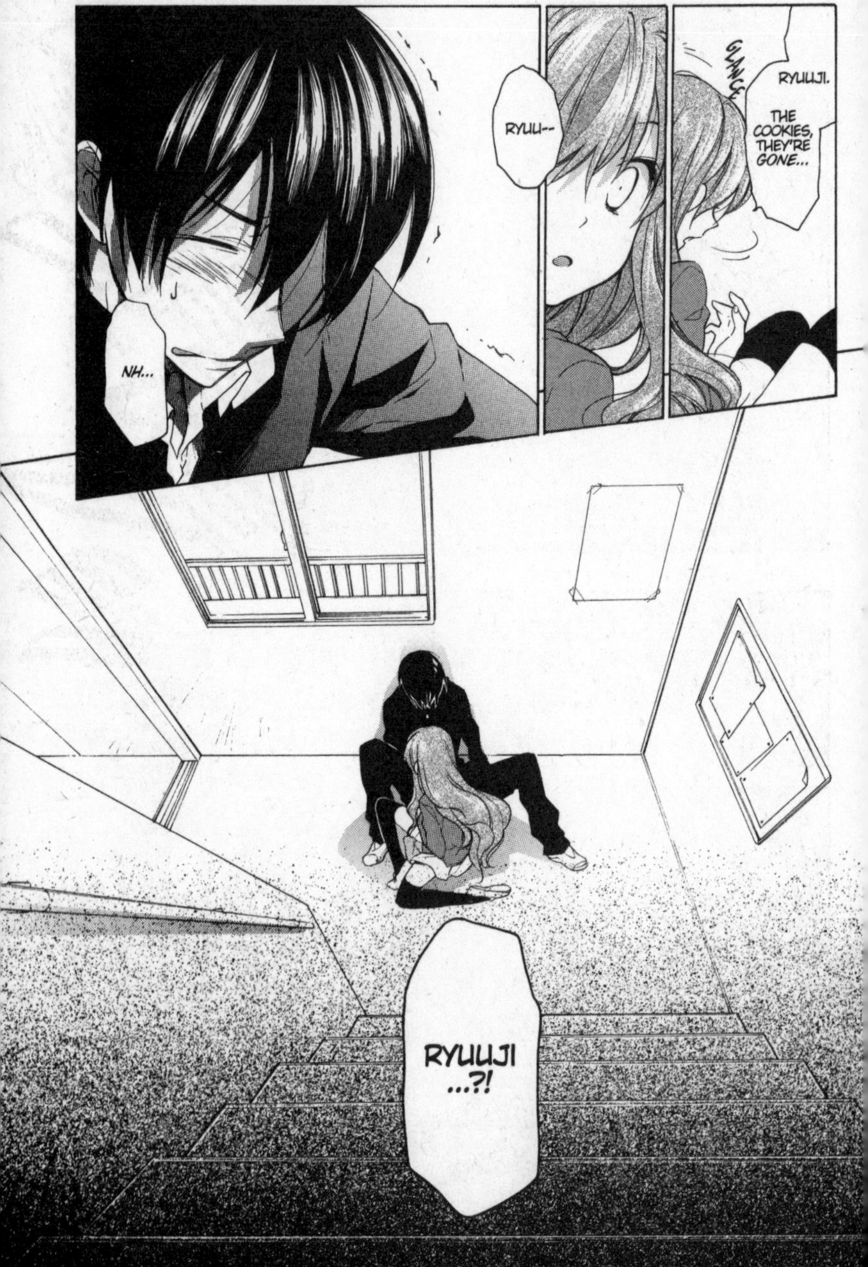
GLANCE
RYUUJI.
THE COOKIES, THEY'RE GONE...
RYUU--
NH...
RYUUJI ...?!

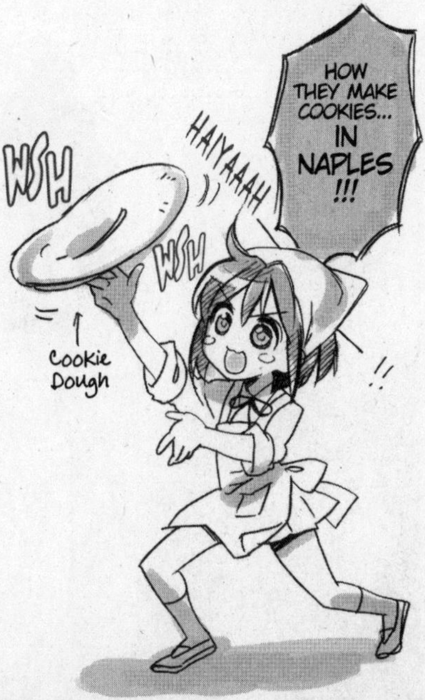
HOW THEY MAKE COOKIES... IN NAPLES !!!
HAIYAAAH
WSH
WSH
Cookie Dough
!!

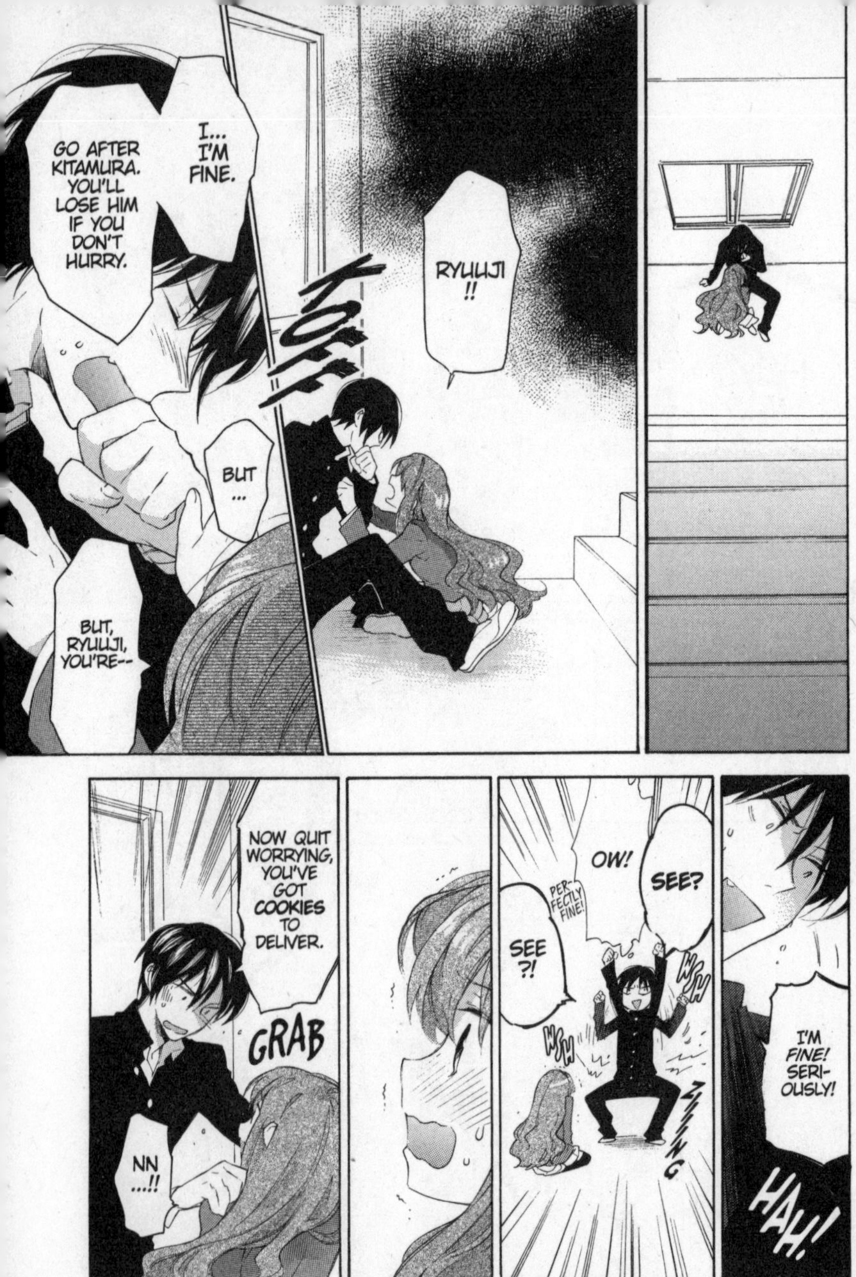
RYUUJI !!
KOFF
I... I'M FINE.
GO AFTER KITAMURA. YOU'LL LOSE HIM IF YOU DON'T HURRY.
BUT ...
BUT, RYUUJI, YOU'RE--
I'M FINE! SERI-OUSLY!
HAH!
SEE?
OW!
PER-FECTLY FINE!
SEE ?!
WSH
WSH
ZIIIING
NOW QUIT WORRYING, YOU'VE GOT COOKIES TO DELIVER.
GRAB
NN ...!!

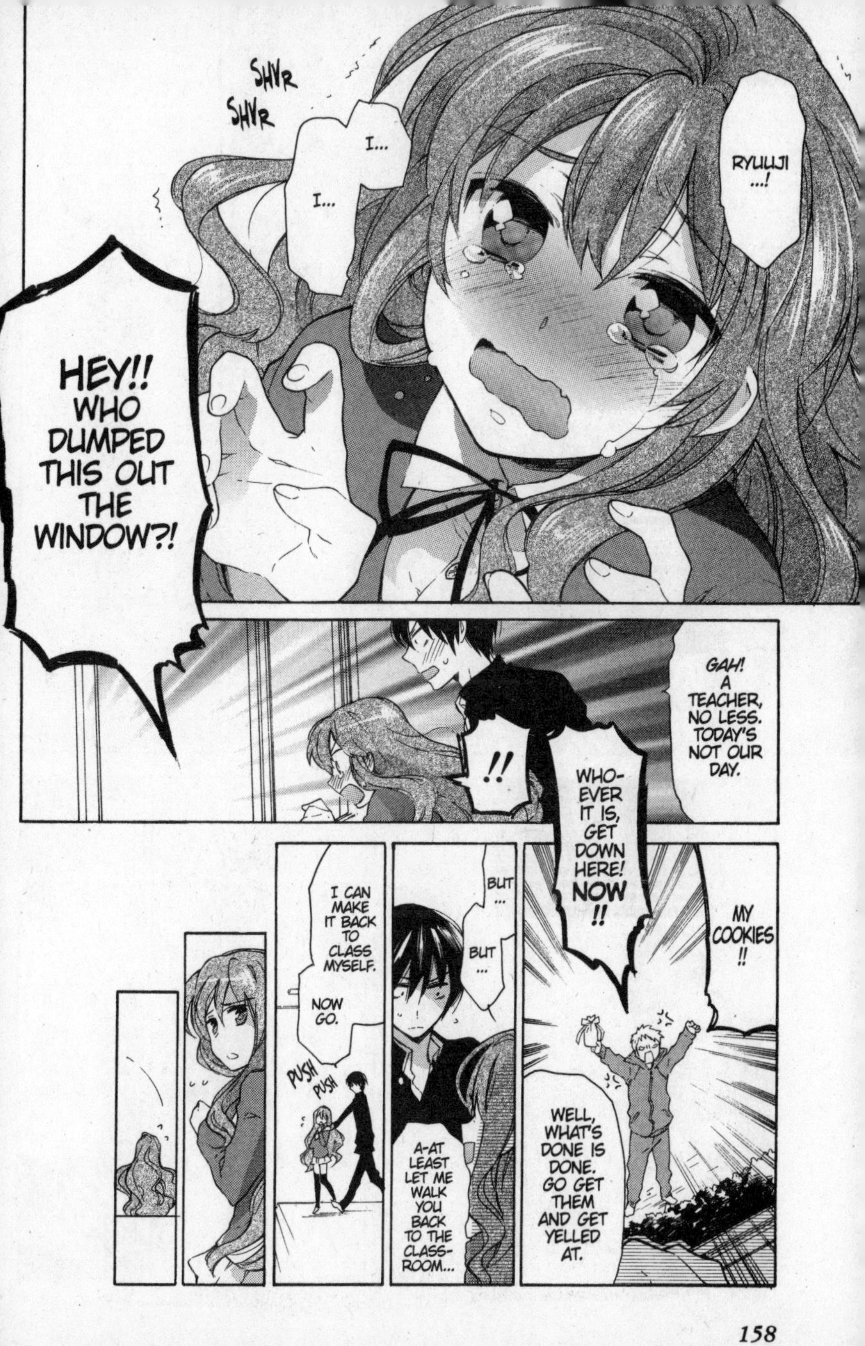
RYUUJI...!
SHVR
SHVR
I... I...
HEY!! WHO DUMPED THIS OUT THE WINDOW?!
GAH! A TEACHER, NO LESS. TODAY'S NOT OUR DAY.
!!
WHOEVER IT IS, GET DOWN HERE! NOW!!
MY COOKIES!!
WELL, WHAT'S DONE IS DONE. GO GET THEM AND GET YELLED AT.
BUT... BUT...
A-AT LEAST LET ME WALK YOU BACK TO THE CLASSROOM...
I CAN MAKE IT BACK TO CLASS MYSELF.
NOW GO.
PUSH PUSH

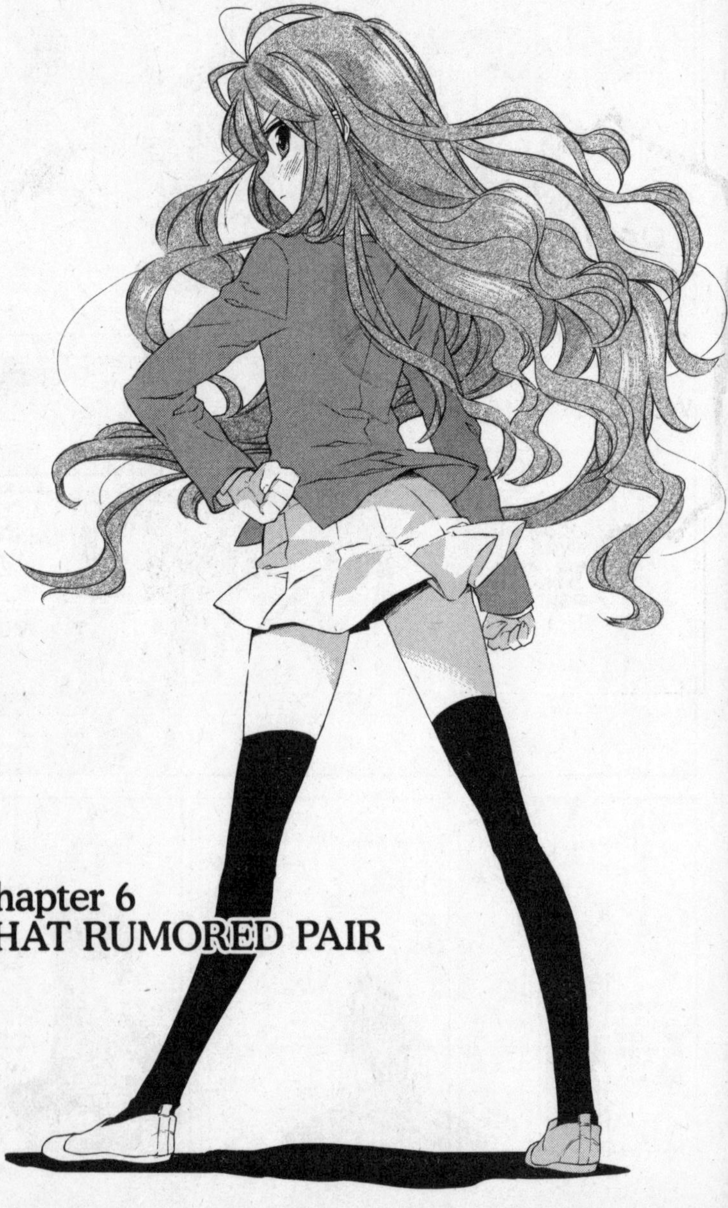

Chapter 6
THAT RUMORED PAIR

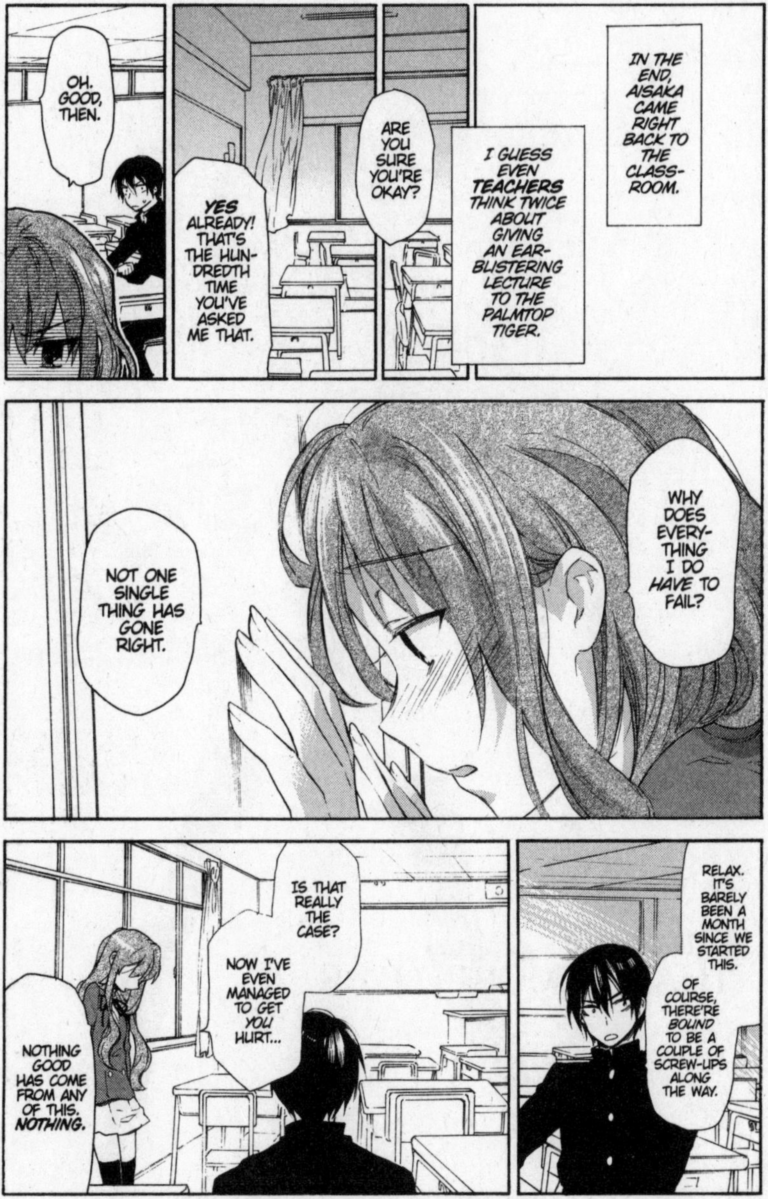
IN THE END, AISAKA CAME RIGHT BACK TO THE CLASSROOM.
I GUESS EVEN TEACHERS THINK TWICE ABOUT GIVING AN EAR-BLISTERING LECTURE TO THE PALMTOP TIGER.
ARE YOU SURE YOU'RE OKAY?
YES ALREADY! THAT'S THE HUNDREDTH TIME YOU'VE ASKED ME THAT.
OH. GOOD, THEN.
WHY DOES EVERYTHING I DO HAVE TO FAIL?
NOT ONE SINGLE THING HAS GONE RIGHT.
RELAX. IT'S BARELY BEEN A MONTH SINCE WE STARTED THIS.
OF COURSE, THERE'RE BOUND TO BE A COUPLE OF SCREW-UPS ALONG THE WAY.
IS THAT REALLY THE CASE?
NOW I'VE EVEN MANAGED TO GET YOU HURT...
NOTHING GOOD HAS COME FROM ANY OF THIS. NOTHING.

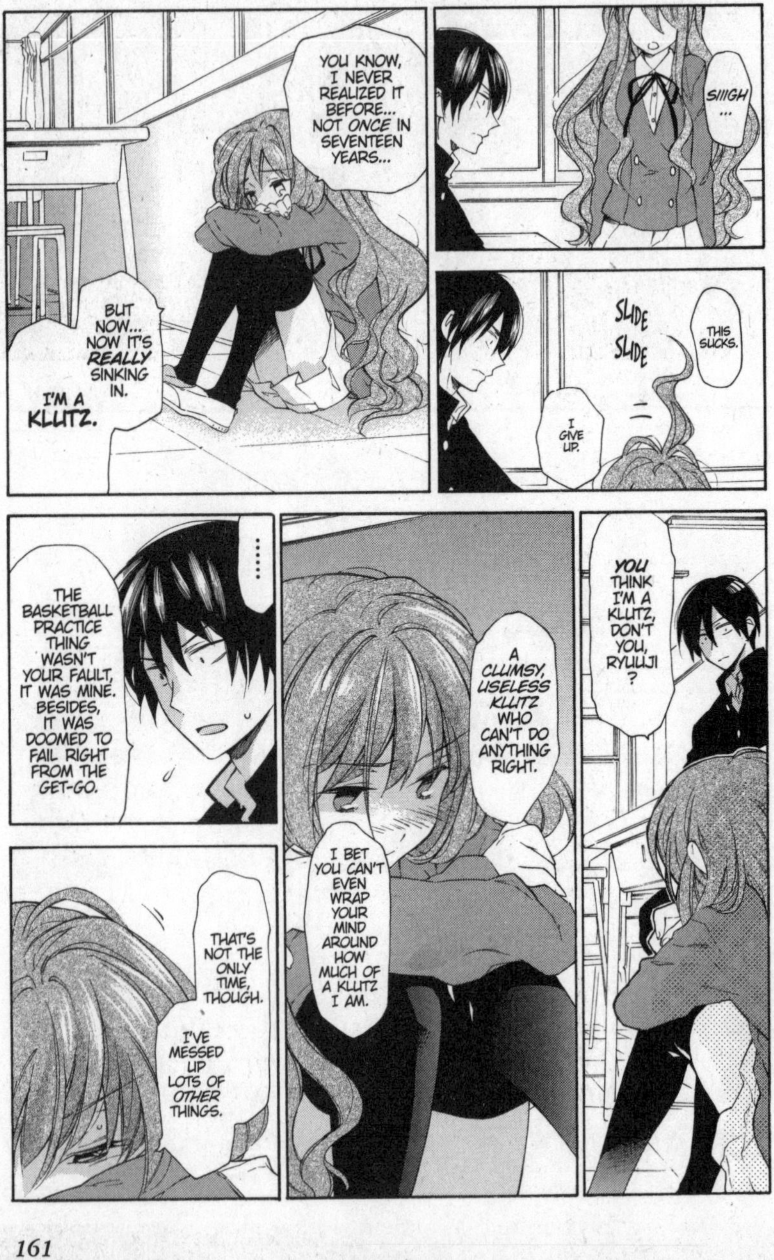
SIIGH ...
THIS SUCKS.
SLIDE SLIDE
I GIVE UP.
YOU KNOW, I NEVER REALIZED IT BEFORE... NOT *ONCE* IN SEVENTEEN YEARS...
BUT NOW... NOW IT'S ***REALLY*** SINKING IN.
I'M A **KLUTZ.**
YOU THINK I'M A KLUTZ, DON'T YOU, RYUUJI ?
A *CLUMSY, USELESS KLUTZ* WHO CAN'T DO ANYTHING RIGHT.
I BET YOU CAN'T EVEN WRAP YOUR MIND AROUND HOW MUCH OF A KLUTZ I AM.
......
THE BASKETBALL PRACTICE THING WASN'T YOUR FAULT, IT WAS MINE. BESIDES, IT WAS DOOMED TO FAIL RIGHT FROM THE GET-GO.
THAT'S NOT THE ONLY TIME, THOUGH.
I'VE MESSED UP LOTS OF *OTHER* THINGS.

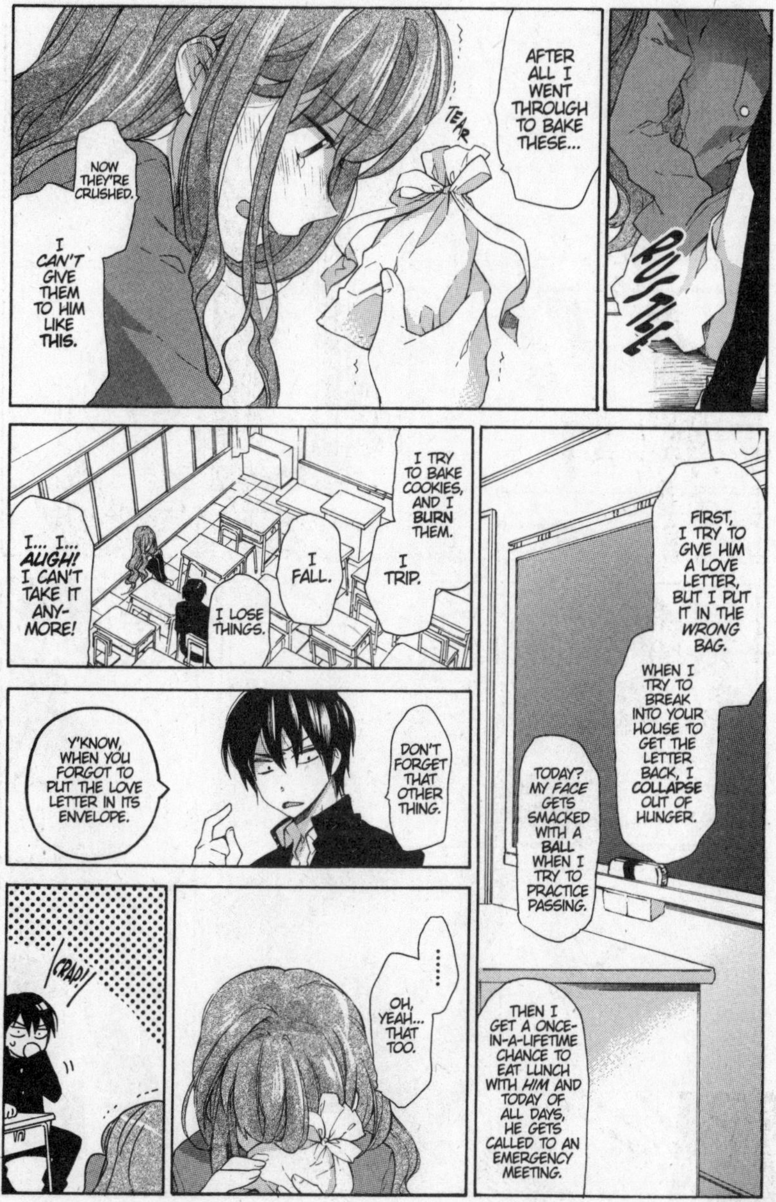
RUSTLE!
AFTER ALL I WENT THROUGH TO BAKE THESE...
TEAR
NOW THEY'RE CRUSHED.
I CAN'T GIVE THEM TO HIM LIKE THIS.
FIRST, I TRY TO GIVE HIM A LOVE LETTER, BUT I PUT IT IN THE *WRONG* BAG.
WHEN I TRY TO BREAK INTO YOUR HOUSE TO GET THE LETTER BACK, I COLLAPSE OUT OF HUNGER.
TODAY? MY *FACE* GETS SMACKED WITH A BALL WHEN I TRY TO PRACTICE PASSING.
THEN I GET A ONCE-IN-A-LIFETIME CHANCE TO EAT LUNCH WITH *HIM* AND TODAY OF ALL DAYS, HE GETS CALLED TO AN EMERGENCY MEETING.
I TRY TO BAKE COOKIES, AND I BURN THEM.
I TRIP.
I FALL.
I LOSE THINGS.
I... I... ***ALIGH!*** I CAN'T TAKE IT ANYMORE!
DON'T FORGET THAT OTHER THING.
Y'KNOW, WHEN YOU FORGOT TO PUT THE LOVE LETTER IN ITS ENVELOPE.
......
OH, YEAH... THAT TOO.
CRAP!!

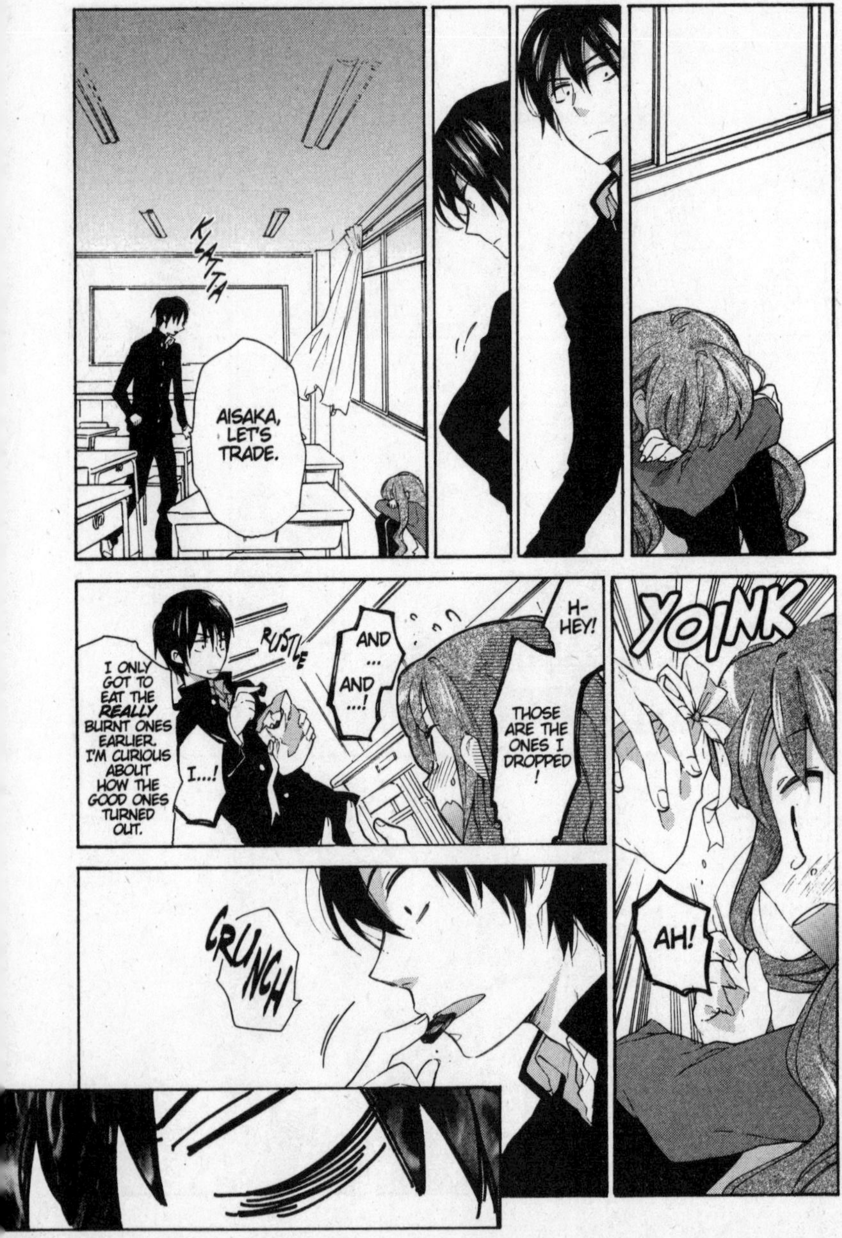

KLATTA
AISAKA, LET'S TRADE.
YOINK
AH!
H-HEY!
THOSE ARE THE ONES I DROPPED!
AND... AND...!
RUSTLE
I...!
I ONLY GOT TO EAT THE *REALLY* BURNT ONES EARLIER. I'M CURIOUS ABOUT HOW THE GOOD ONES TURNED OUT.
CRUNCH

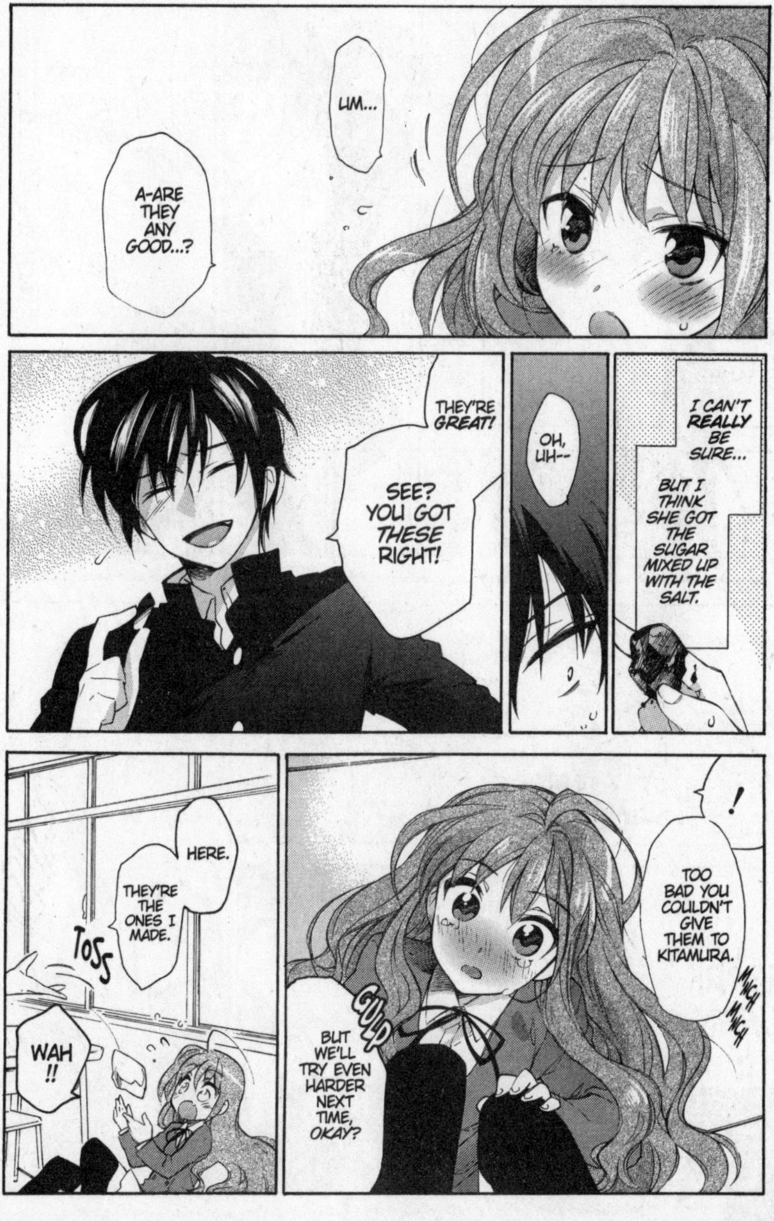
UM...
A-ARE THEY ANY GOOD...?
I CAN'T REALLY BE SURE...
BUT I THINK SHE GOT THE SUGAR MIXED UP WITH THE SALT.
OH, UH--
THEY'RE GREAT!
SEE? YOU GOT THESE RIGHT!
!
TOO BAD YOU COULDN'T GIVE THEM TO KITAMURA.
MNCH MNCH
GULP
BUT WE'LL TRY EVEN HARDER NEXT TIME, OKAY?
HERE.
THEY'RE THE ONES I MADE.
TOSS
WAH !!

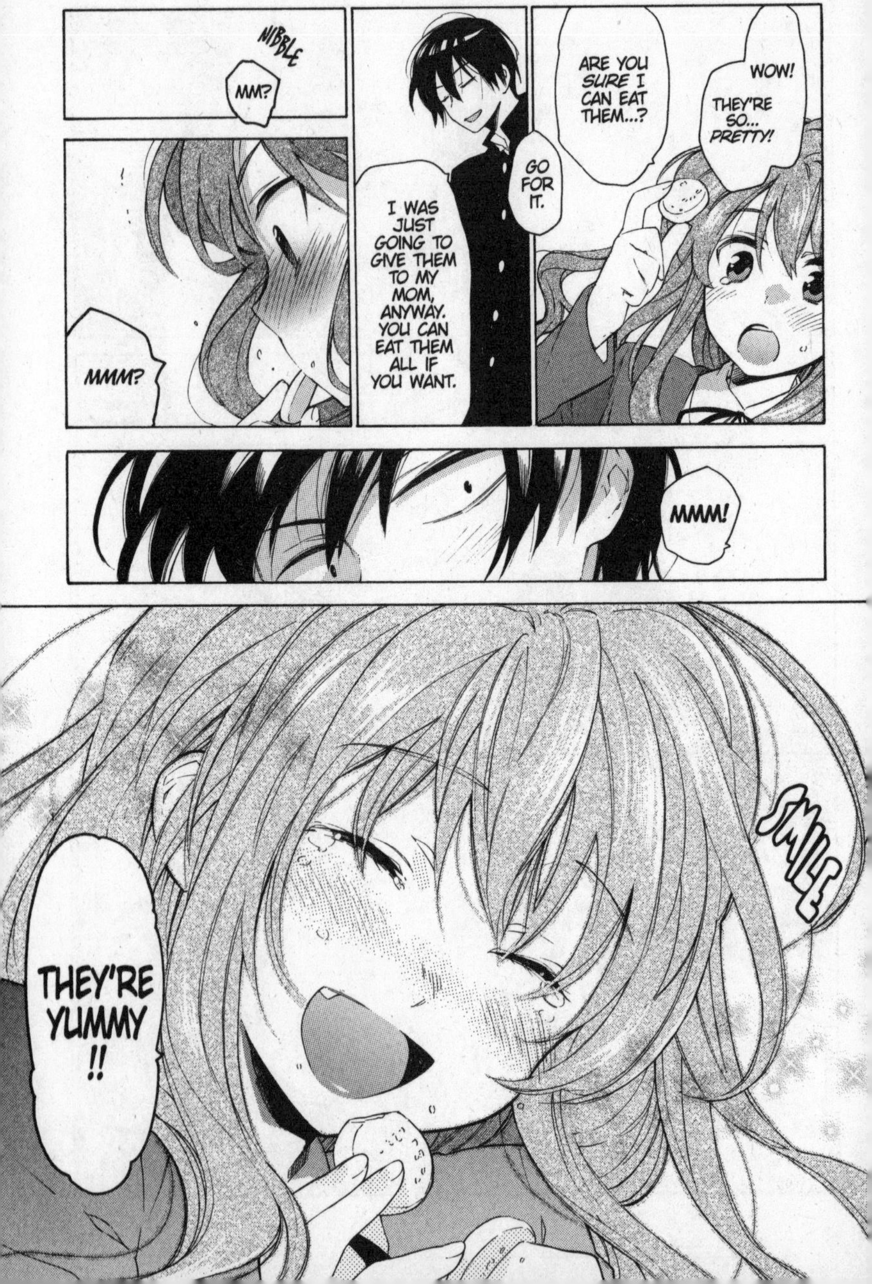
WOW!
THEY'RE SO... PRETTY!
ARE YOU SURE I CAN EAT THEM...?
GO FOR IT.
I WAS JUST GOING TO GIVE THEM TO MY MOM, ANYWAY. YOU CAN EAT THEM ALL IF YOU WANT.
NIBBLE
MM?
MMM?
MMM!
SMILE
THEY'RE YUMMY!!

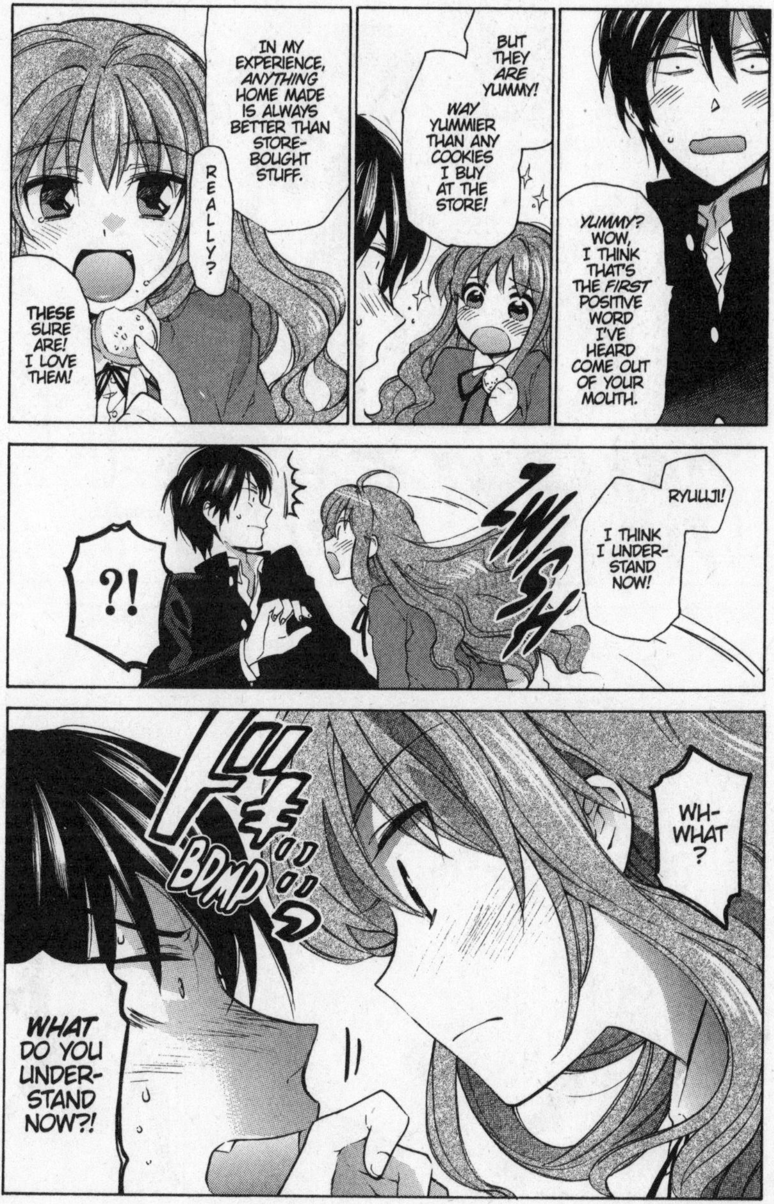
YUMMY? WOW, I THINK THAT'S THE FIRST POSITIVE WORD I'VE HEARD COME OUT OF YOUR MOUTH.
BUT THEY ARE YUMMY!
WAY YUMMIER THAN ANY COOKIES I BUY AT THE STORE!
IN MY EXPERIENCE, ANYTHING HOME MADE IS ALWAYS BETTER THAN STORE-BOUGHT STUFF.
REALLY?
THESE SURE ARE! I LOVE THEM!
RYUUJI!
I THINK I UNDERSTAND NOW!
?!
WH-WHAT?
BDMP
WHAT DO YOU UNDERSTAND NOW?!

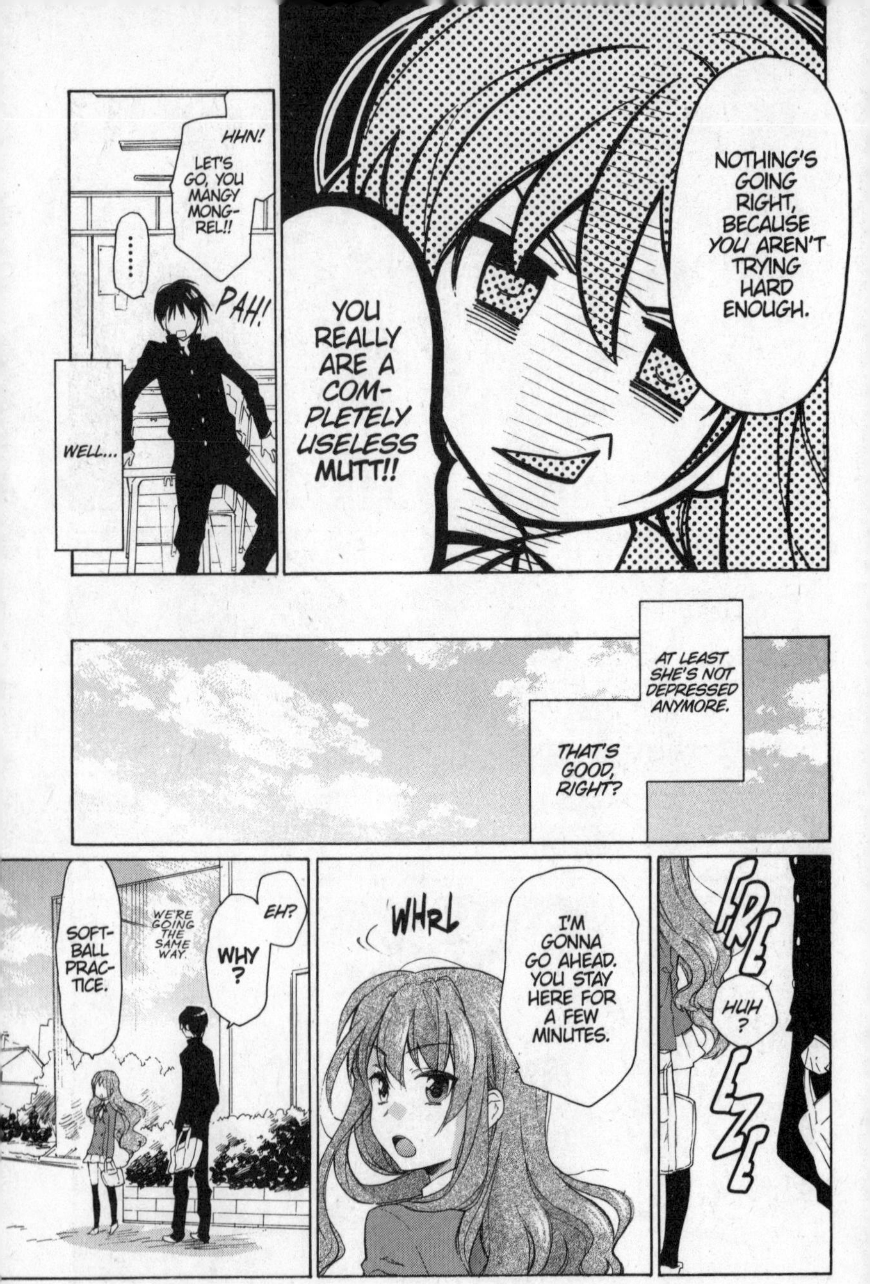
NOTHING'S GOING RIGHT, BECAUSE YOU AREN'T TRYING HARD ENOUGH.
YOU REALLY ARE A COM-PLETELY USELESS MUTT!!
HHN!
LET'S GO, YOU MANGY MONG-REL!!
......
PAH!
WELL...
AT LEAST SHE'S NOT DEPRESSED ANYMORE.
THAT'S GOOD, RIGHT?
FREEZE
HUH?
WHRL
I'M GONNA GO AHEAD. YOU STAY HERE FOR A FEW MINUTES.
EH?
WHY?
WE'RE GOING THE SAME WAY.
SOFT-BALL PRAC-TICE.

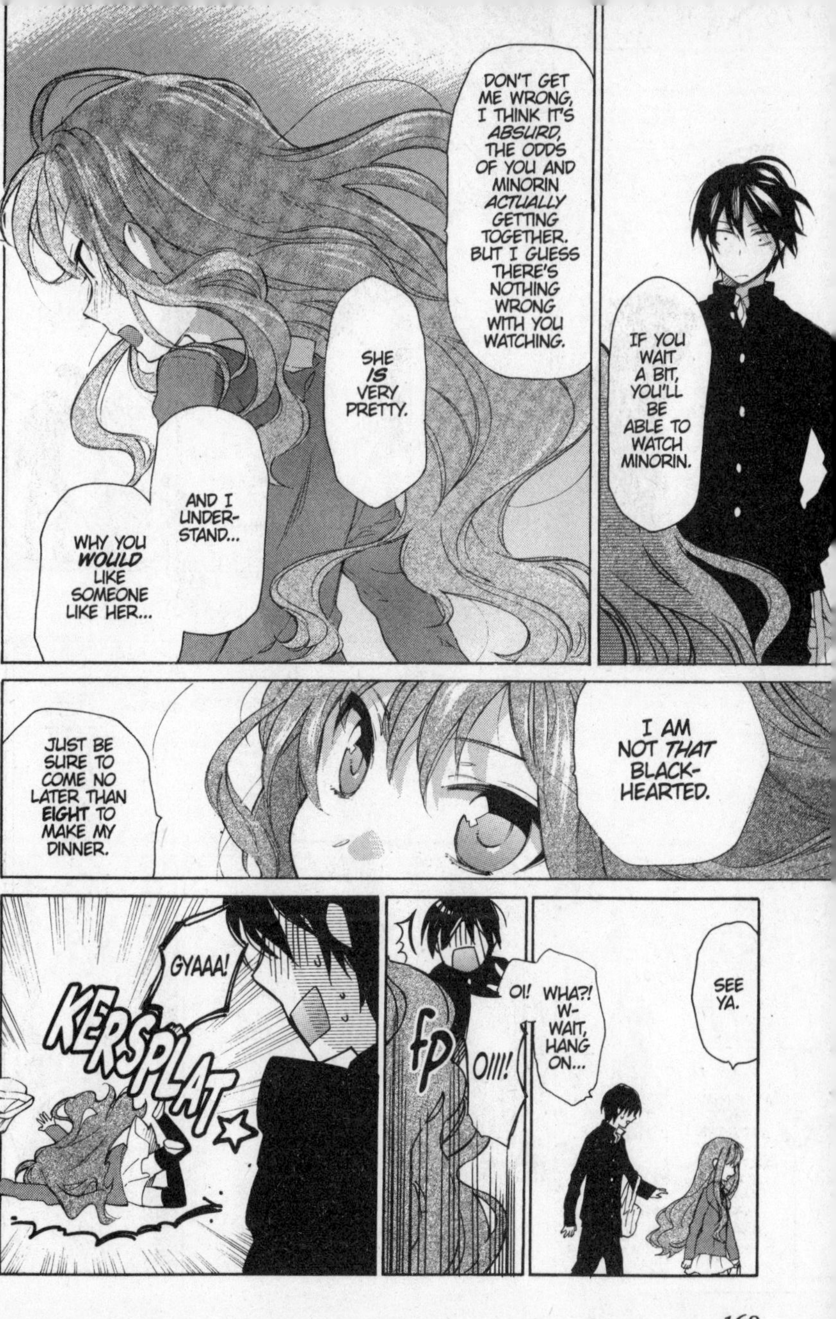
IF YOU WAIT A BIT, YOU'LL BE ABLE TO WATCH MINORIN.
DON'T GET ME WRONG, I THINK IT'S *ABSURD*, THE ODDS OF YOU AND MINORIN *ACTUALLY* GETTING TOGETHER. BUT I GUESS THERE'S NOTHING WRONG WITH YOU WATCHING.
SHE ***IS*** VERY PRETTY.
AND I UNDER-STAND...
WHY YOU ***WOULD*** LIKE SOMEONE LIKE HER...
I AM NOT *THAT* BLACK-HEARTED.
JUST BE SURE TO COME NO LATER THAN **EIGHT** TO MAKE MY DINNER.
SEE YA.
WHA?! W-WAIT, HANG ON...
OI!
fp
OIII!
GYAAA!
KERSPLAT

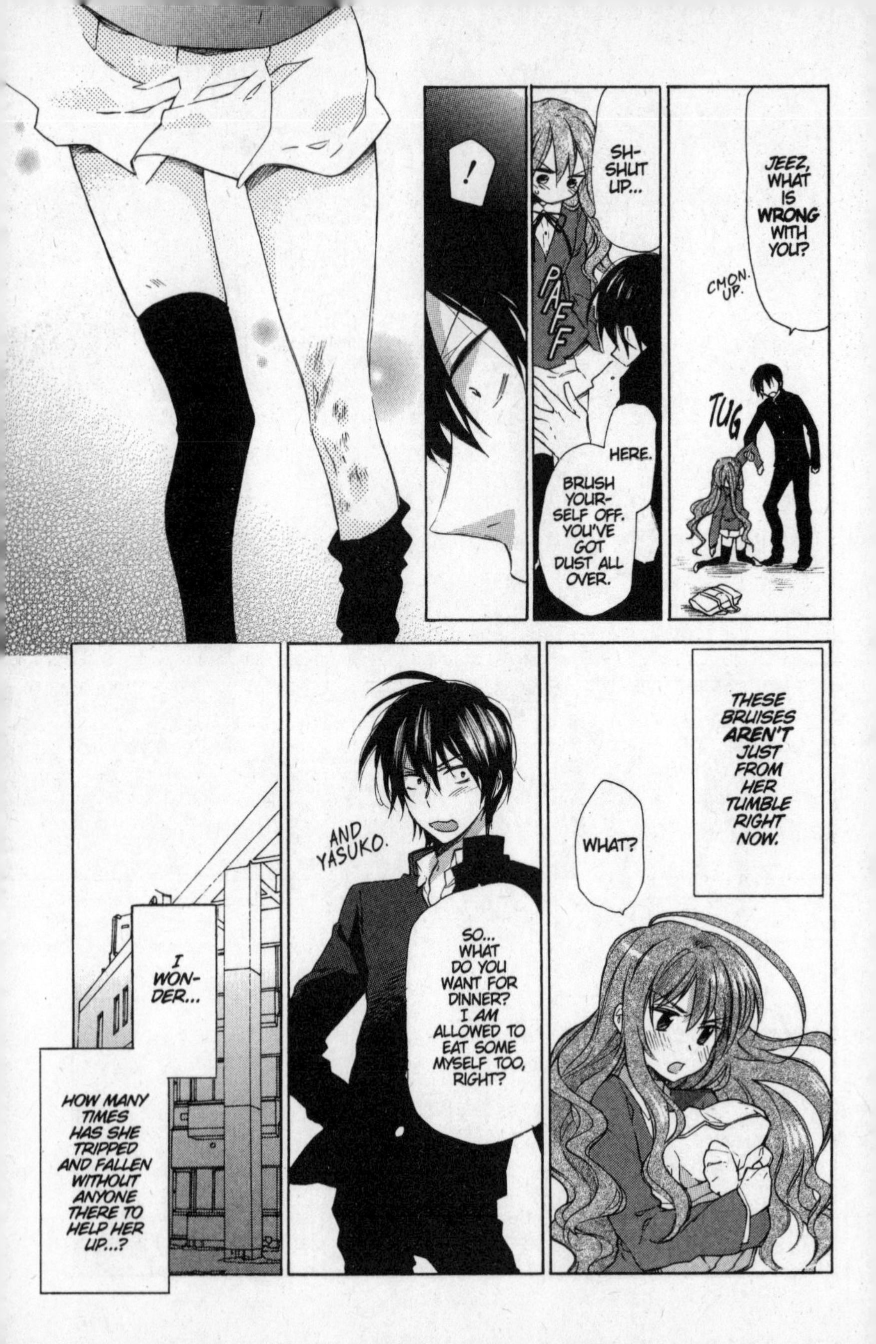
JEEZ, WHAT IS WRONG WITH YOU?
CMON. UP.
TUG
SH-SHUT UP...
PAFF
HERE.
BRUSH YOURSELF OFF. YOU'VE GOT DUST ALL OVER.
!
THESE BRUISES AREN'T JUST FROM HER TUMBLE RIGHT NOW.
WHAT?
SO... WHAT DO YOU WANT FOR DINNER? I AM ALLOWED TO EAT SOME MYSELF TOO, RIGHT?
AND YASUKO.
I WONDER...
HOW MANY TIMES HAS SHE TRIPPED AND FALLEN WITHOUT ANYONE THERE TO HELP HER UP...?

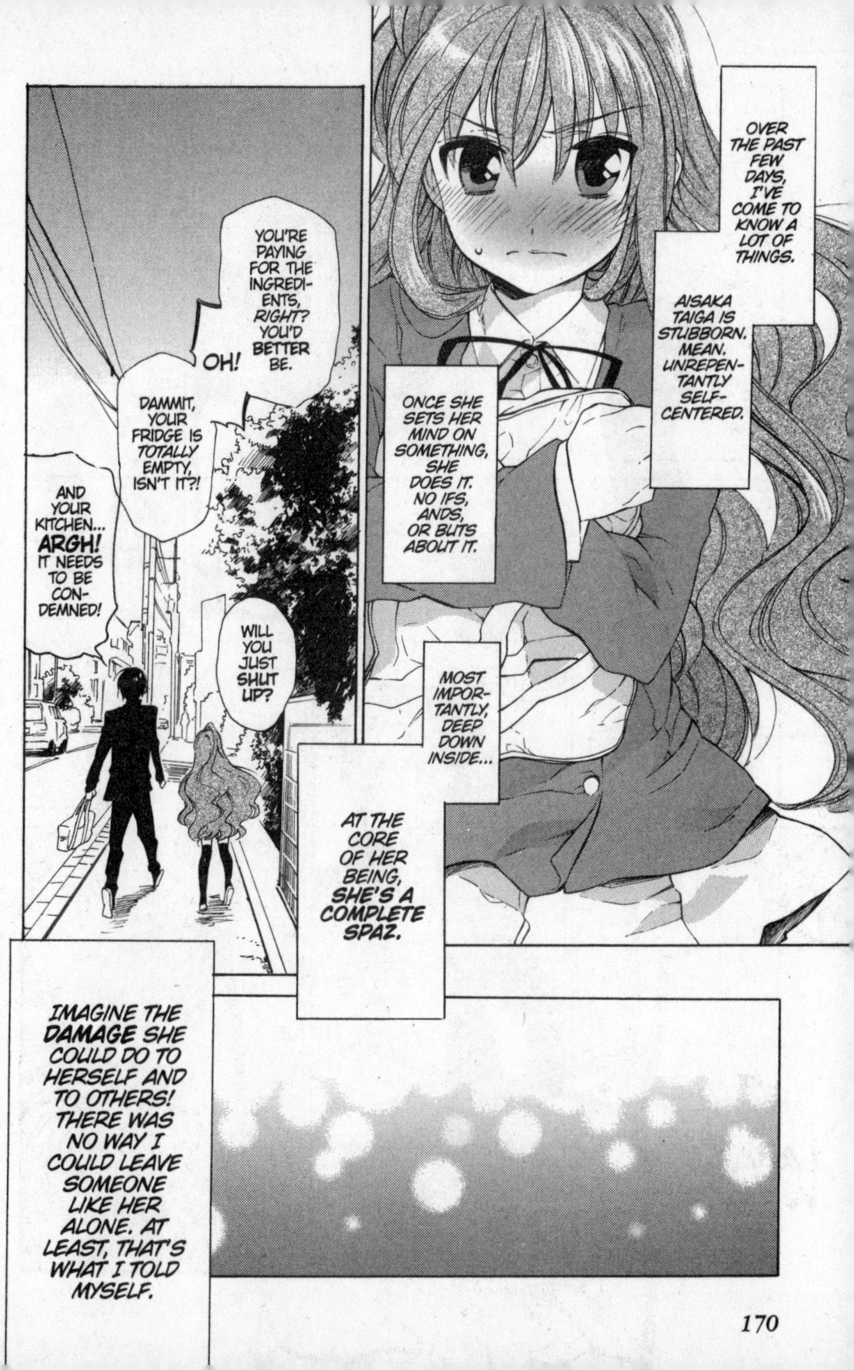
OVER THE PAST FEW DAYS, I'VE COME TO KNOW A LOT OF THINGS.
AISAKA TAIGA IS STUBBORN. MEAN. UNREPENTANTLY SELF-CENTERED.
ONCE SHE SETS HER MIND ON SOMETHING, SHE DOES IT. NO IFS, ANDS, OR BUTS ABOUT IT.
MOST IMPORTANTLY, DEEP DOWN INSIDE...
AT THE CORE OF HER BEING, SHE'S A COMPLETE SPAZ.
YOU'RE PAYING FOR THE INGREDIENTS, RIGHT? YOU'D BETTER BE.
OH!
DAMMIT, YOUR FRIDGE IS TOTALLY EMPTY, ISN'T IT?!
AND YOUR KITCHEN... ARGH! IT NEEDS TO BE CONDEMNED!
WILL YOU JUST SHUT UP?
IMAGINE THE DAMAGE SHE COULD DO TO HERSELF AND TO OTHERS! THERE WAS NO WAY I COULD LEAVE SOMEONE LIKE HER ALONE. AT LEAST, THAT'S WHAT I TOLD MYSELF.

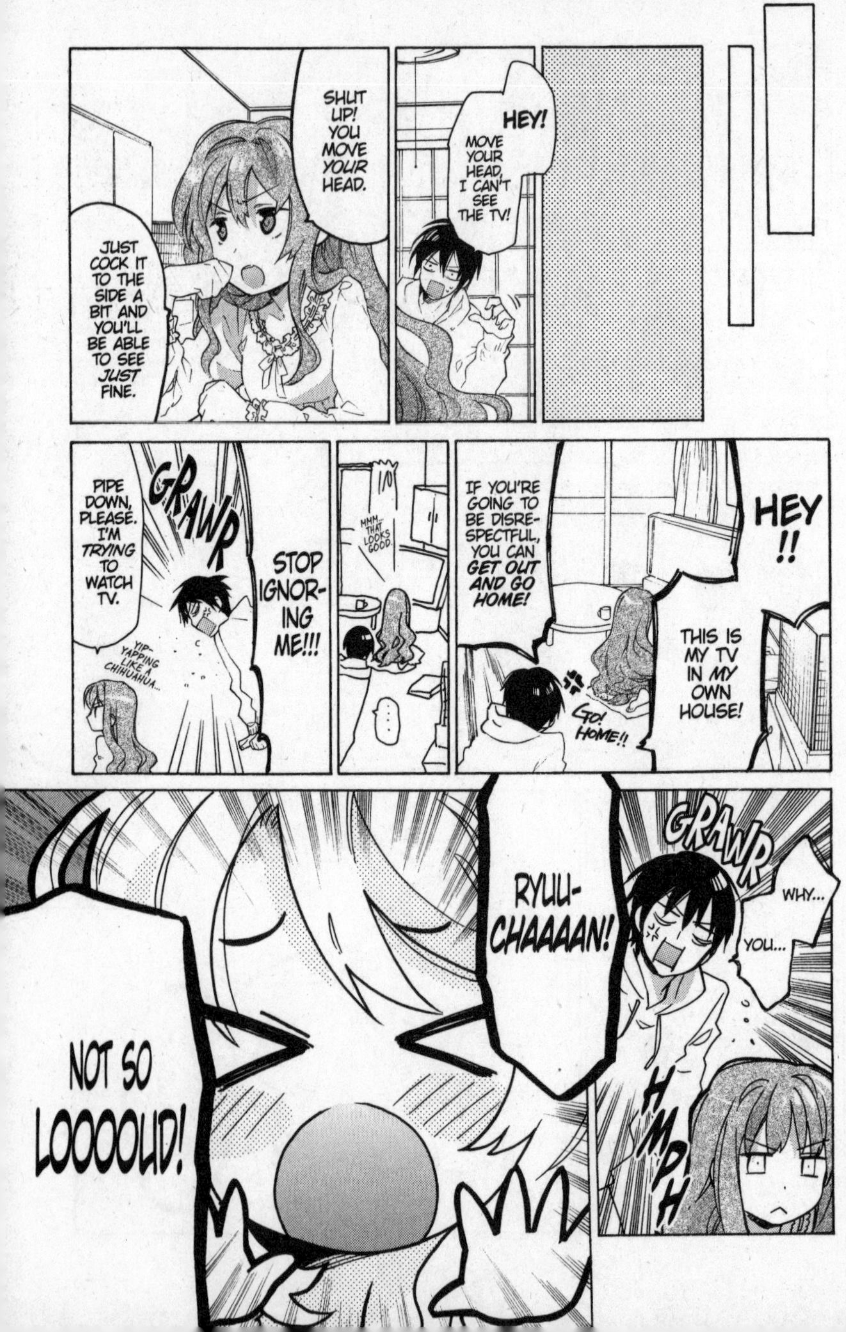
HEY!
MOVE YOUR HEAD, I CAN'T SEE THE TV!
SHUT UP! YOU MOVE YOUR HEAD.
JUST COCK IT TO THE SIDE A BIT AND YOU'LL BE ABLE TO SEE JUST FINE.
HEY !!
THIS IS MY TV IN MY OWN HOUSE!
IF YOU'RE GOING TO BE DISRE-SPECTFUL, YOU CAN GET OUT AND GO HOME!
GO! HOME!!
MMM... THAT LOOKS GOOD.
...
STOP IGNOR-ING ME!!!
GRAWR
PIPE DOWN, PLEASE. I'M TRYING TO WATCH TV.
YIP-YAPPING LIKE A CHIHUAHUA...
GRAWR
WHY...
YOU...
HMPH
RYUU-CHAAAAN!
NOT SO LOOOOUD!

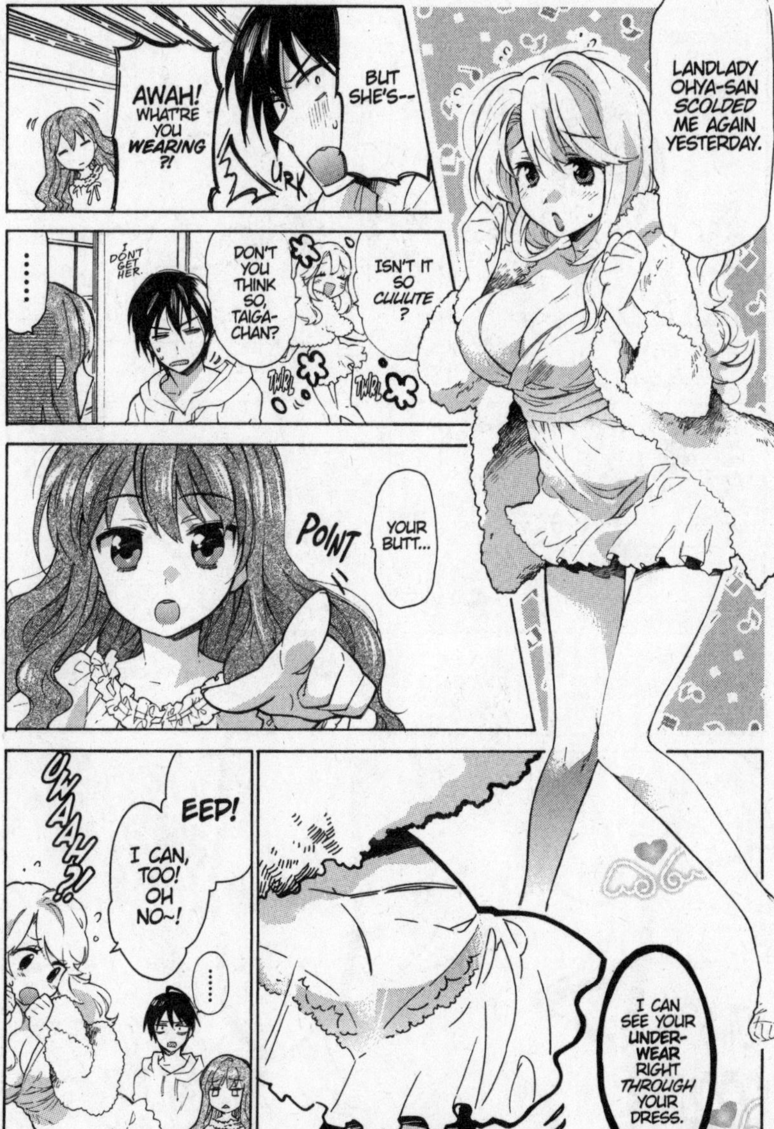
LANDLADY OHYA-SAN SCOLDED ME AGAIN YESTERDAY.
BUT SHE'S--
URK
AWAH! WHAT'RE YOU WEARING ?!
ISN'T IT SO CUUUTE ?
DON'T YOU THINK SO, TAIGA-CHAN?
TWIRL
TWIRL
I DON'T GET HER.
......
YOUR BUTT...
POINT
I CAN SEE YOUR UNDER-WEAR RIGHT THROUGH YOUR DRESS.
UWAAH ?!
EEP!
I CAN, TOO! OH NO~!
......

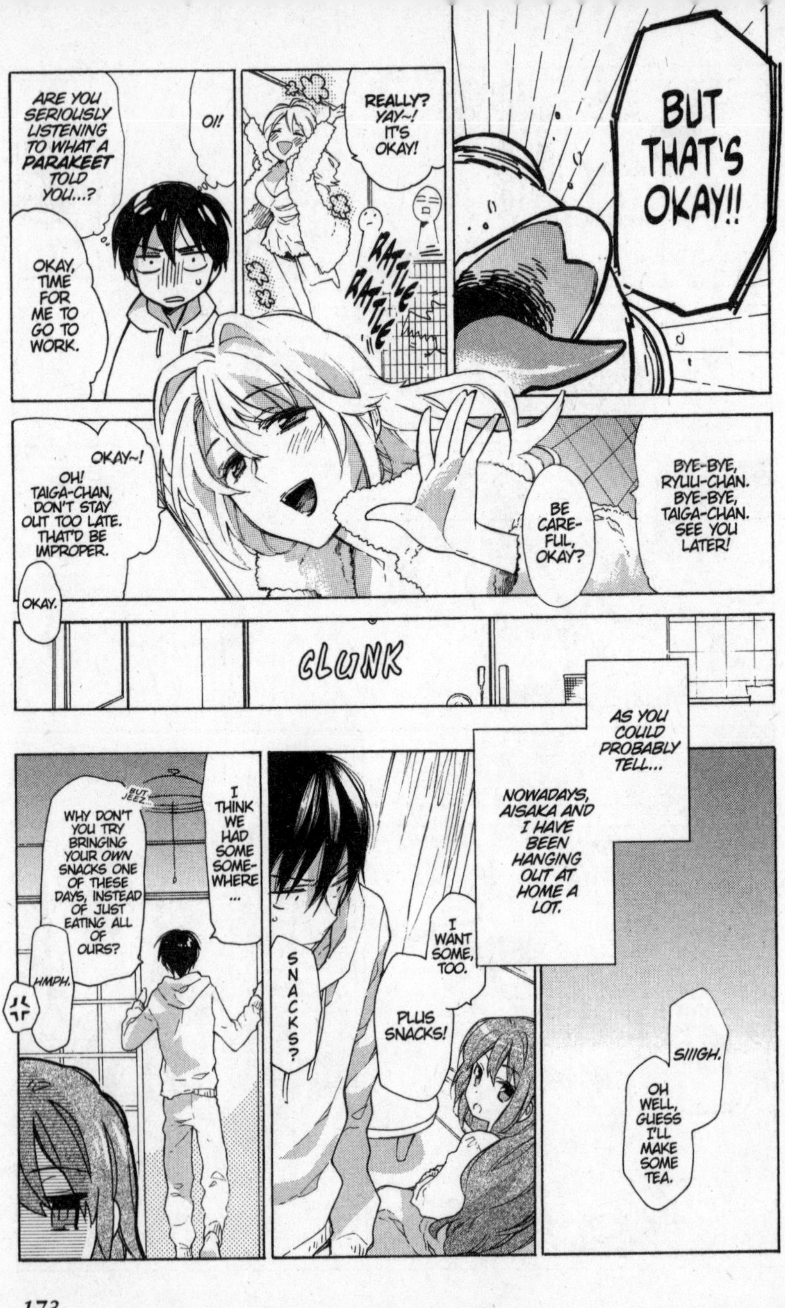
BUT THAT'S OKAY!!
REALLY? YAY~! IT'S OKAY!
RATTLE RATTLE
OI!
ARE YOU SERIOUSLY LISTENING TO WHAT A PARAKEET TOLD YOU...?
OKAY, TIME FOR ME TO GO TO WORK.
BYE-BYE, RYUU-CHAN. BYE-BYE, TAIGA-CHAN. SEE YOU LATER!
BE CAREFUL, OKAY?
OKAY~! OH! TAIGA-CHAN, DON'T STAY OUT TOO LATE. THAT'D BE IMPROPER.
OKAY.
CLUNK
AS YOU COULD PROBABLY TELL...
NOWADAYS, AISAKA AND I HAVE BEEN HANGING OUT AT HOME A LOT.
SIIIGH.
OH WELL, GUESS I'LL MAKE SOME TEA.
I WANT SOME, TOO.
PLUS SNACKS!
SNACKS?
I THINK WE HAD SOME SOMEWHERE...
BUT JEEZ...
WHY DON'T YOU TRY BRINGING YOUR OWN SNACKS ONE OF THESE DAYS, INSTEAD OF JUST EATING ALL OF OURS?
HMPH.

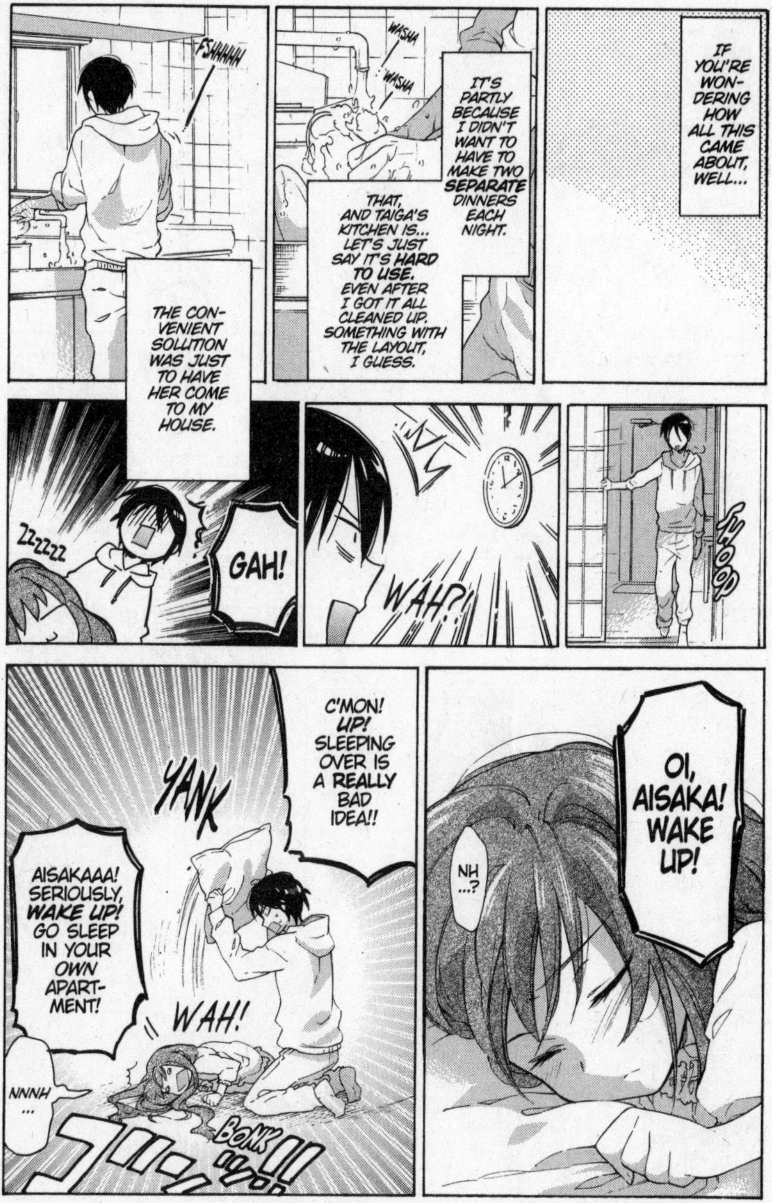
IF YOU'RE WON-DERING HOW ALL THIS CAME ABOUT, WELL...
WASHA
WASHA
IT'S PARTLY BECAUSE I DIDN'T WANT TO HAVE TO MAKE TWO SEPARATE DINNERS EACH NIGHT.
THAT, AND TAIGA'S KITCHEN IS... LET'S JUST SAY IT'S HARD TO USE. EVEN AFTER I GOT IT ALL CLEANED UP. SOMETHING WITH THE LAYOUT, I GUESS.
FSHHHHH
THE CON-VENIENT SOLUTION WAS JUST TO HAVE HER COME TO MY HOUSE.
WHOOP
WAH?!
ZZZZZZ
GAH!
OI, AISAKA! WAKE UP!
NH ...?
C'MON! UP! SLEEPING OVER IS A REALLY BAD IDEA!!
YANK
AISAKAAA! SERIOUSLY, WAKE UP! GO SLEEP IN YOUR OWN APART-MENT!
WAH!
NNNH ...
BONK!!

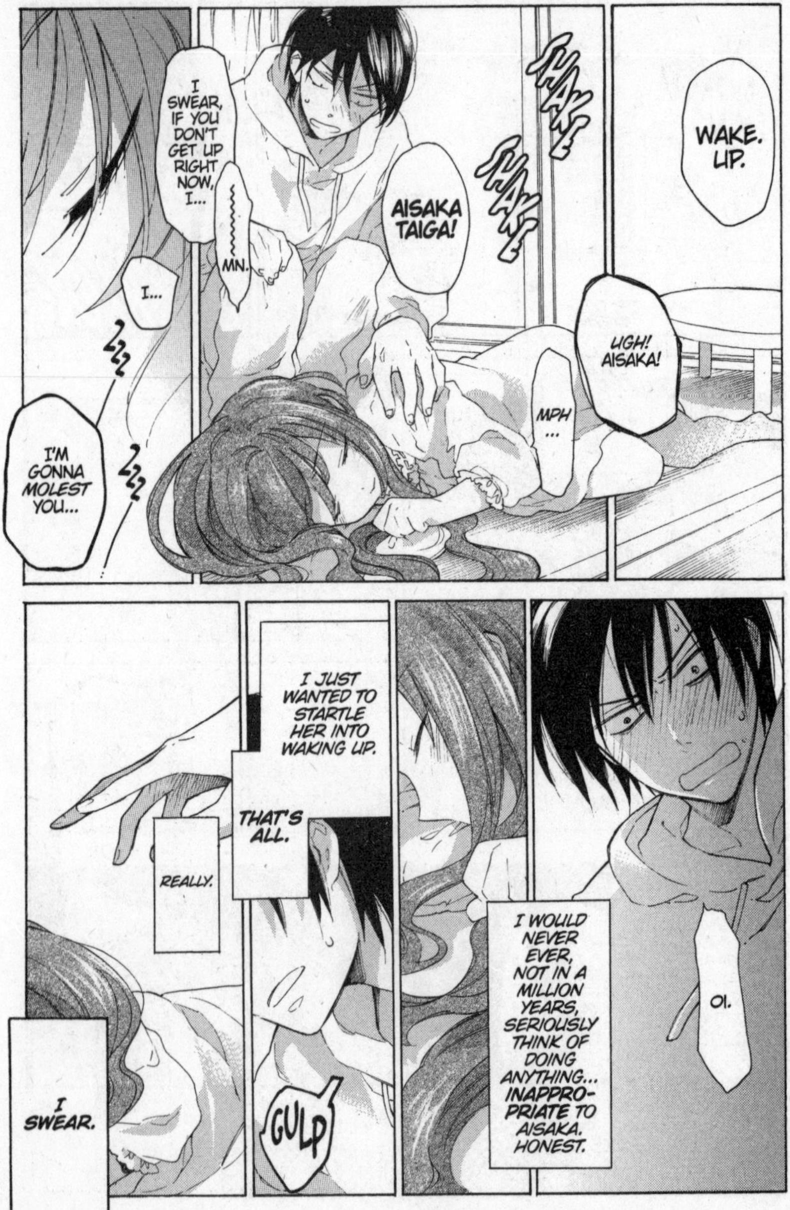
WAKE. UP.
UGH! AISAKA!
MPH...
SHAKE!
SHAKE!
AISAKA TAIGA!
I SWEAR, IF YOU DON'T GET UP RIGHT NOW, I...
MN.
I...
ZZZ
I'M GONNA MOLEST YOU...
ZZZ
OI.
I WOULD NEVER EVER, NOT IN A MILLION YEARS, SERIOUSLY THINK OF DOING ANYTHING... INAPPROPRIATE TO AISAKA. HONEST.
I JUST WANTED TO STARTLE HER INTO WAKING UP.
THAT'S ALL.
GULP
REALLY.
I SWEAR.

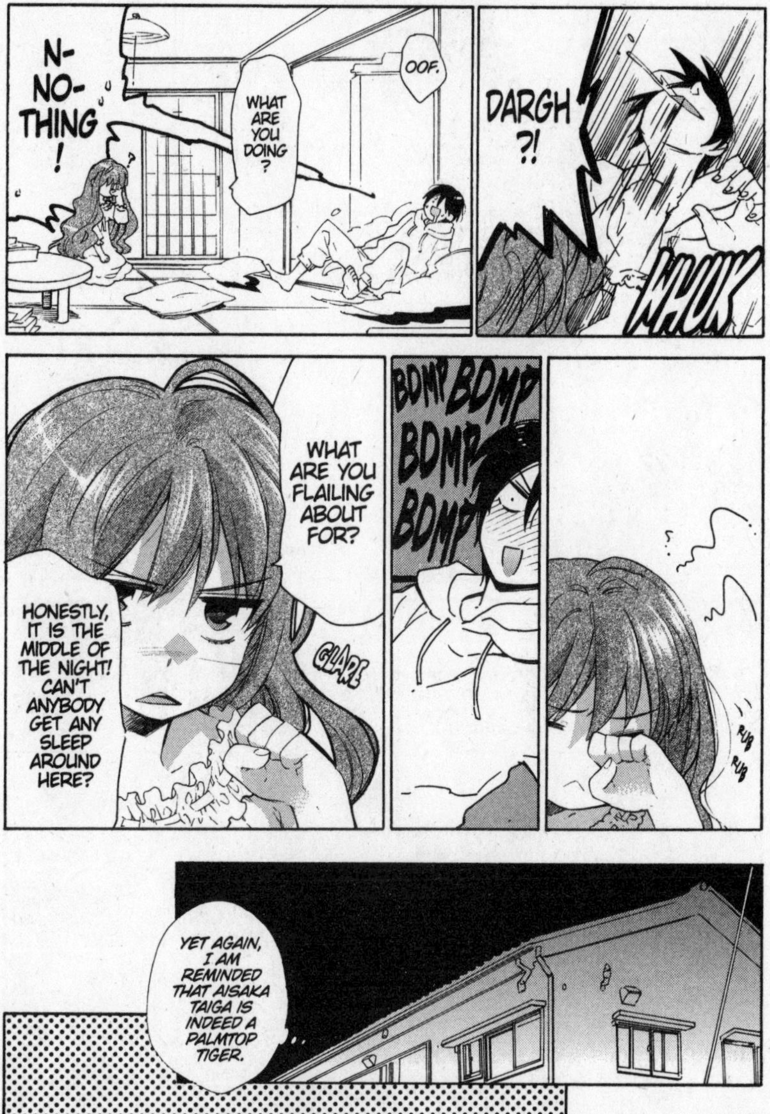
DARGH ?!
WHUK
OOF.
WHAT ARE YOU DOING?
N-NO-THING!
RUB RUB
BDMP BDMP
BDMP
BDMP
WHAT ARE YOU FLAILING ABOUT FOR?
GLARE
HONESTLY, IT IS THE MIDDLE OF THE NIGHT! CAN'T ANYBODY GET ANY SLEEP AROUND HERE?
YET AGAIN, I AM REMINDED THAT AISAKA TAIGA IS INDEED A PALMTOP TIGER...

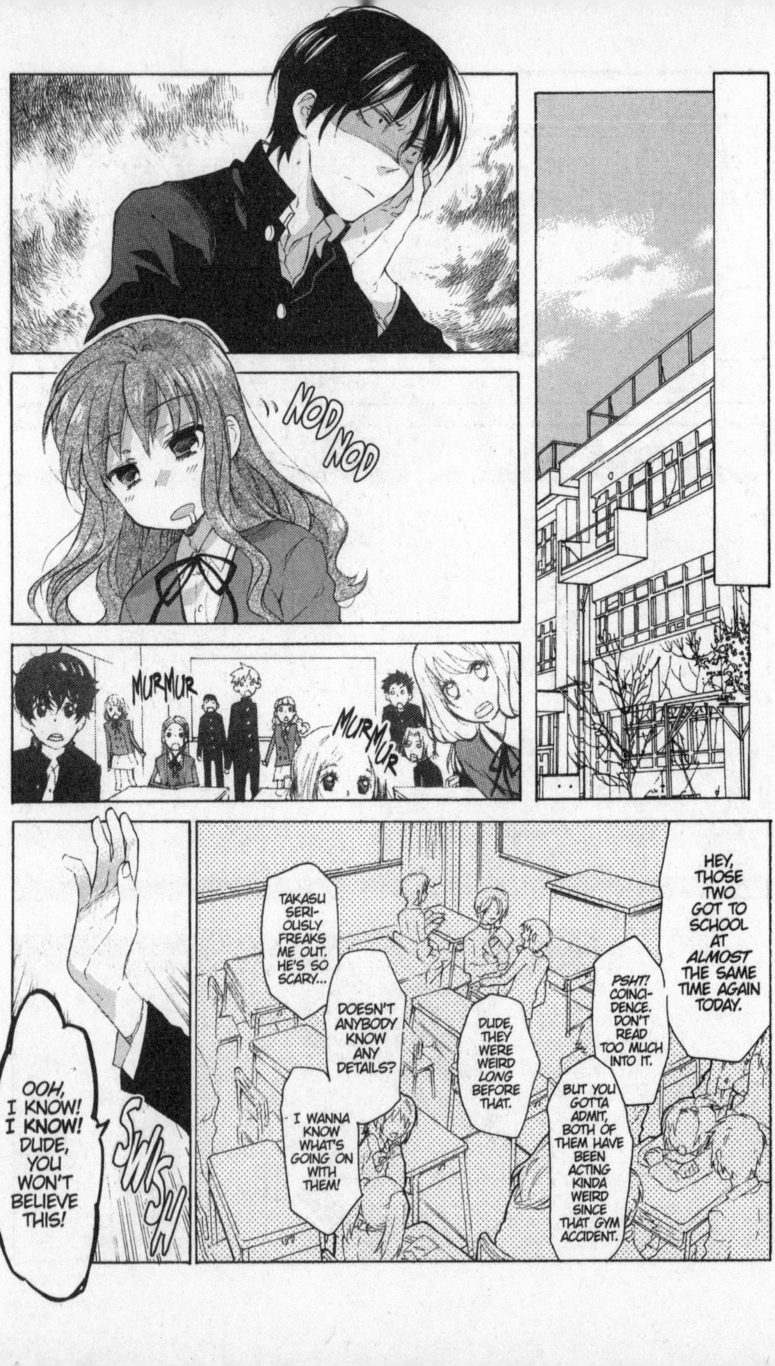
NOD NOD
MURMUR
MURMUR
HEY, THOSE TWO GOT TO SCHOOL AT ALMOST THE SAME TIME AGAIN TODAY.
PSHT! COINCIDENCE. DON'T READ TOO MUCH INTO IT.
BUT YOU GOTTA ADMIT, BOTH OF THEM HAVE BEEN ACTING KINDA WEIRD SINCE THAT GYM ACCIDENT.
DUDE, THEY WERE WEIRD LONG BEFORE THAT.
TAKASU SERIOUSLY FREAKS ME OUT. HE'S SO SCARY...
DOESN'T ANYBODY KNOW ANY DETAILS?
I WANNA KNOW WHAT'S GOING ON WITH THEM!
SWISH
OOH, I KNOW! I KNOW! DUDE, YOU WON'T BELIEVE THIS!

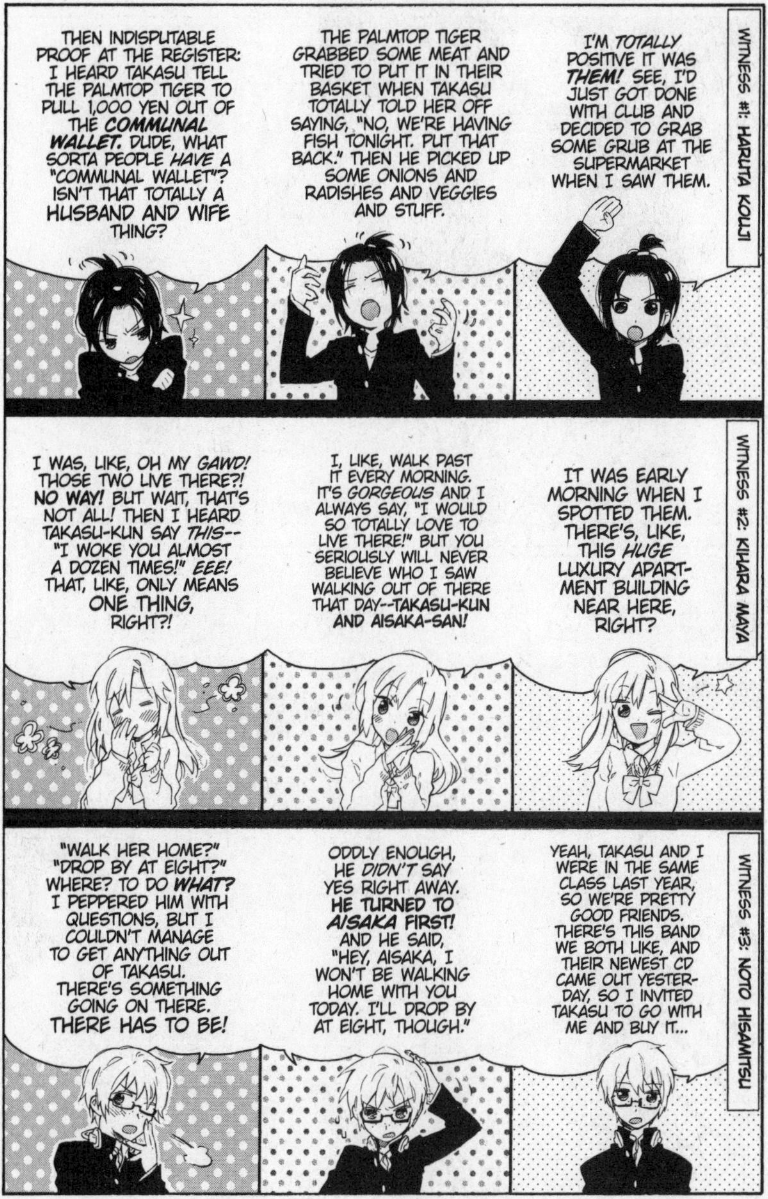
WITNESS #1: HARUTA KOUJI
I'M TOTALLY POSITIVE IT WAS THEM! SEE, I'D JUST GOT DONE WITH CLUB AND DECIDED TO GRAB SOME GRUB AT THE SUPERMARKET WHEN I SAW THEM.
THE PALMTOP TIGER GRABBED SOME MEAT AND TRIED TO PUT IT IN THEIR BASKET WHEN TAKASU TOTALLY TOLD HER OFF SAYING, "NO, WE'RE HAVING FISH TONIGHT. PUT THAT BACK." THEN HE PICKED UP SOME ONIONS AND RADISHES AND VEGGIES AND STUFF.
THEN INDISPUTABLE PROOF AT THE REGISTER: I HEARD TAKASU TELL THE PALMTOP TIGER TO PULL 1,000 YEN OUT OF THE COMMUNAL WALLET. DUDE, WHAT SORTA PEOPLE HAVE A "COMMUNAL WALLET"? ISN'T THAT TOTALLY A HUSBAND AND WIFE THING?
WITNESS #2: KIHARA MAYA
IT WAS EARLY MORNING WHEN I SPOTTED THEM. THERE'S, LIKE, THIS HUGE LUXURY APARTMENT BUILDING NEAR HERE, RIGHT?
I, LIKE, WALK PAST IT EVERY MORNING. IT'S GORGEOUS AND I ALWAYS SAY, "I WOULD SO TOTALLY LOVE TO LIVE THERE!" BUT YOU SERIOUSLY WILL NEVER BELIEVE WHO I SAW WALKING OUT OF THERE THAT DAY--TAKASU-KUN AND AISAKA-SAN!
I WAS, LIKE, OH MY GAWD! THOSE TWO LIVE THERE?! NO WAY! BUT WAIT, THAT'S NOT ALL! THEN I HEARD TAKASU-KUN SAY THIS--"I WOKE YOU ALMOST A DOZEN TIMES!" EEE! THAT, LIKE, ONLY MEANS ONE THING, RIGHT?!
WITNESS #3: NOTO HISAMITSU
YEAH, TAKASU AND I WERE IN THE SAME CLASS LAST YEAR, SO WE'RE PRETTY GOOD FRIENDS. THERE'S THIS BAND WE BOTH LIKE, AND THEIR NEWEST CD CAME OUT YESTERDAY, SO I INVITED TAKASU TO GO WITH ME AND BUY IT...
ODDLY ENOUGH, HE DIDN'T SAY YES RIGHT AWAY. HE TURNED TO AISAKA FIRST! AND HE SAID, "HEY, AISAKA, I WON'T BE WALKING HOME WITH YOU TODAY. I'LL DROP BY AT EIGHT, THOUGH."
"WALK HER HOME?" "DROP BY AT EIGHT?" WHERE? TO DO WHAT? I PEPPERED HIM WITH QUESTIONS, BUT I COULDN'T MANAGE TO GET ANYTHING OUT OF TAKASU. THERE'S SOMETHING GOING ON THERE. THERE HAS TO BE!

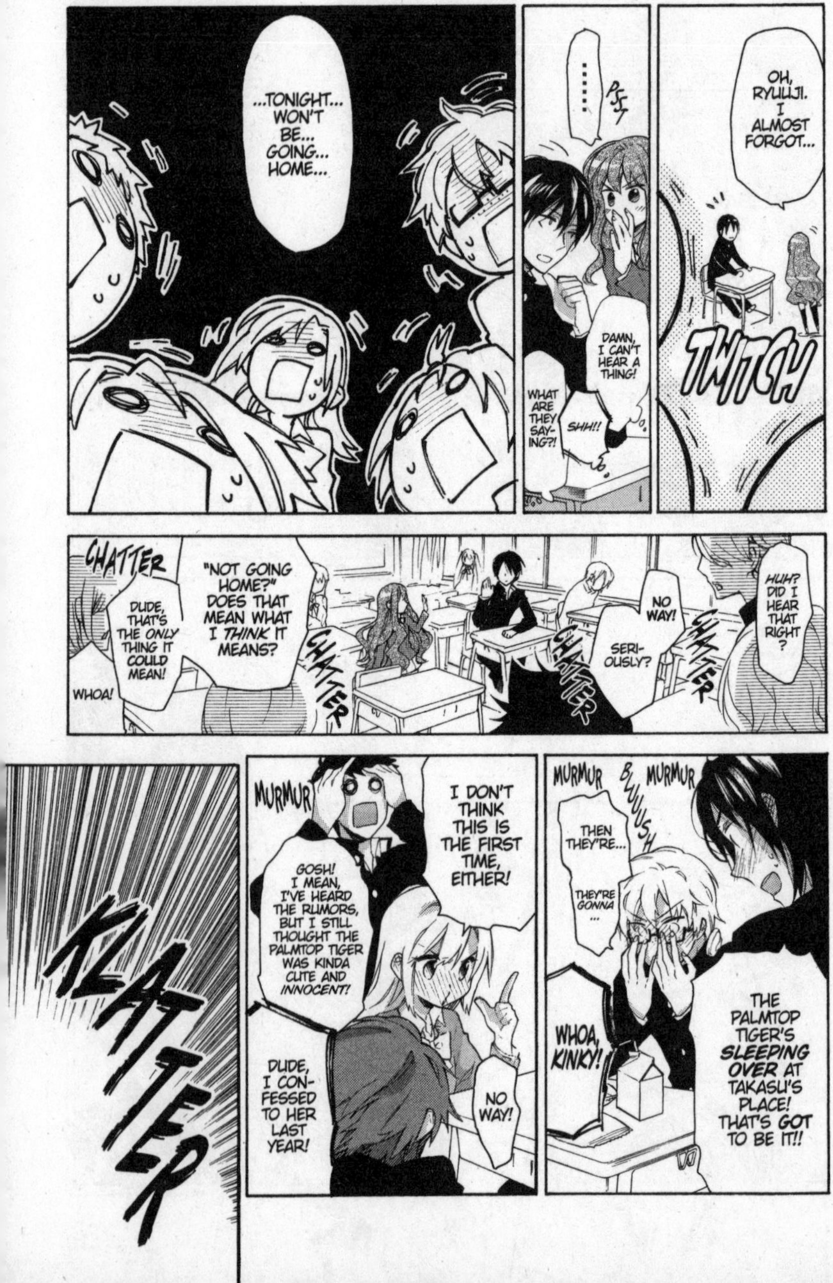

OH, RYUUJI. I ALMOST FORGOT...
TWITCH
......
PSST
DAMN, I CAN'T HEAR A THING!
SHH!!
WHAT ARE THEY SAYING?!
...TONIGHT... WON'T BE... GOING... HOME...
HUH? DID I HEAR THAT RIGHT?
CHATTER
NO WAY!
SERIOUSLY?
CHATTER
"NOT GOING HOME?" DOES THAT MEAN WHAT I *THINK* IT MEANS?
CHATTER
CHATTER
DUDE, THAT'S THE *ONLY* THING IT COULD MEAN!
WHOA!
MURMUR
BLUUUSH
MURMUR
THEN THEY'RE...
THEY'RE GONNA ...
THE PALMTOP TIGER'S **SLEEPING OVER** AT TAKASU'S PLACE! THAT'S **GOT** TO BE IT!!
WHOA, KINKY!
I DON'T THINK THIS IS THE FIRST TIME, EITHER!
MURMUR
GOSH! I MEAN, I'VE HEARD THE RUMORS, BUT I STILL THOUGHT THE PALMTOP TIGER WAS KINDA CUTE AND *INNOCENT!*
NO WAY!
DUDE, I CONFESSED TO HER LAST YEAR!
KLATTER

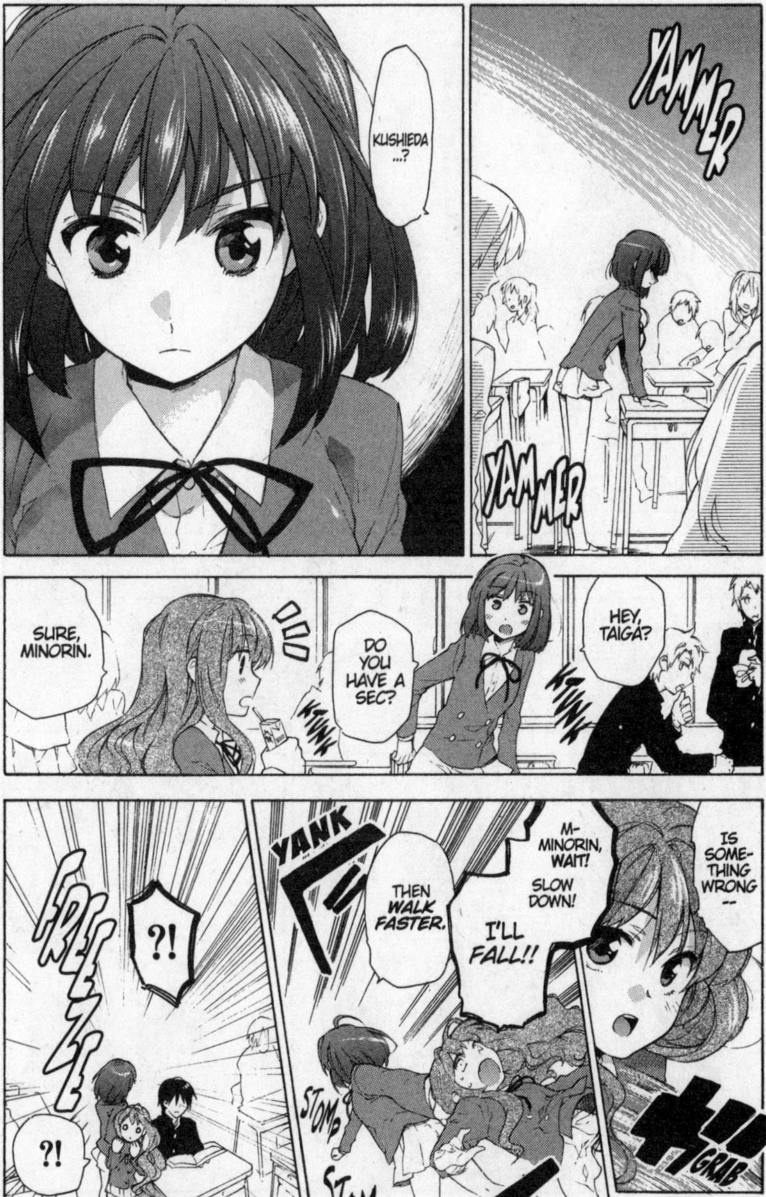
YAMMER
YAMMER
KUSHIEDA ...?
HEY, TAIGA?
KLUNK
DO YOU HAVE A SEC?
KLUNK
SURE, MINORIN.
IS SOME-THING WRONG --
M-MINORIN, WAIT!
SLOW DOWN!
I'LL FALL!!
THEN *WALK FASTER.*
YANK
GRAB
STOMP
STOMP
FREEZE
?!
?!

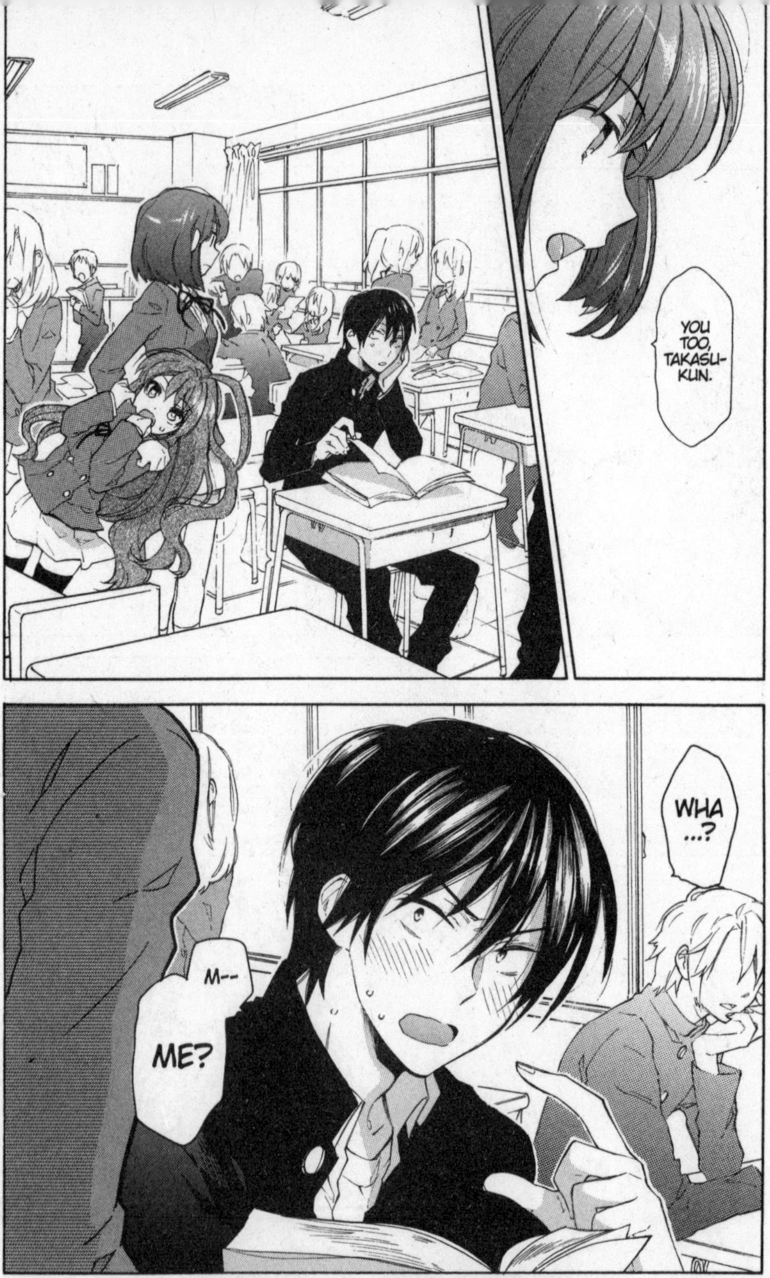
YOU TOO, TAKASU-KUN.
WHA ...?
M--
ME?

TO BE CONTINUED!!

Ya-chan sent a message.
She said, TONIGHT she
WON'T BE early.
She's GOING to listen to
customer complaints, so
she'll be HOME late.

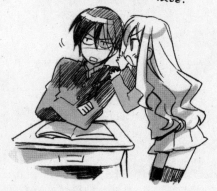

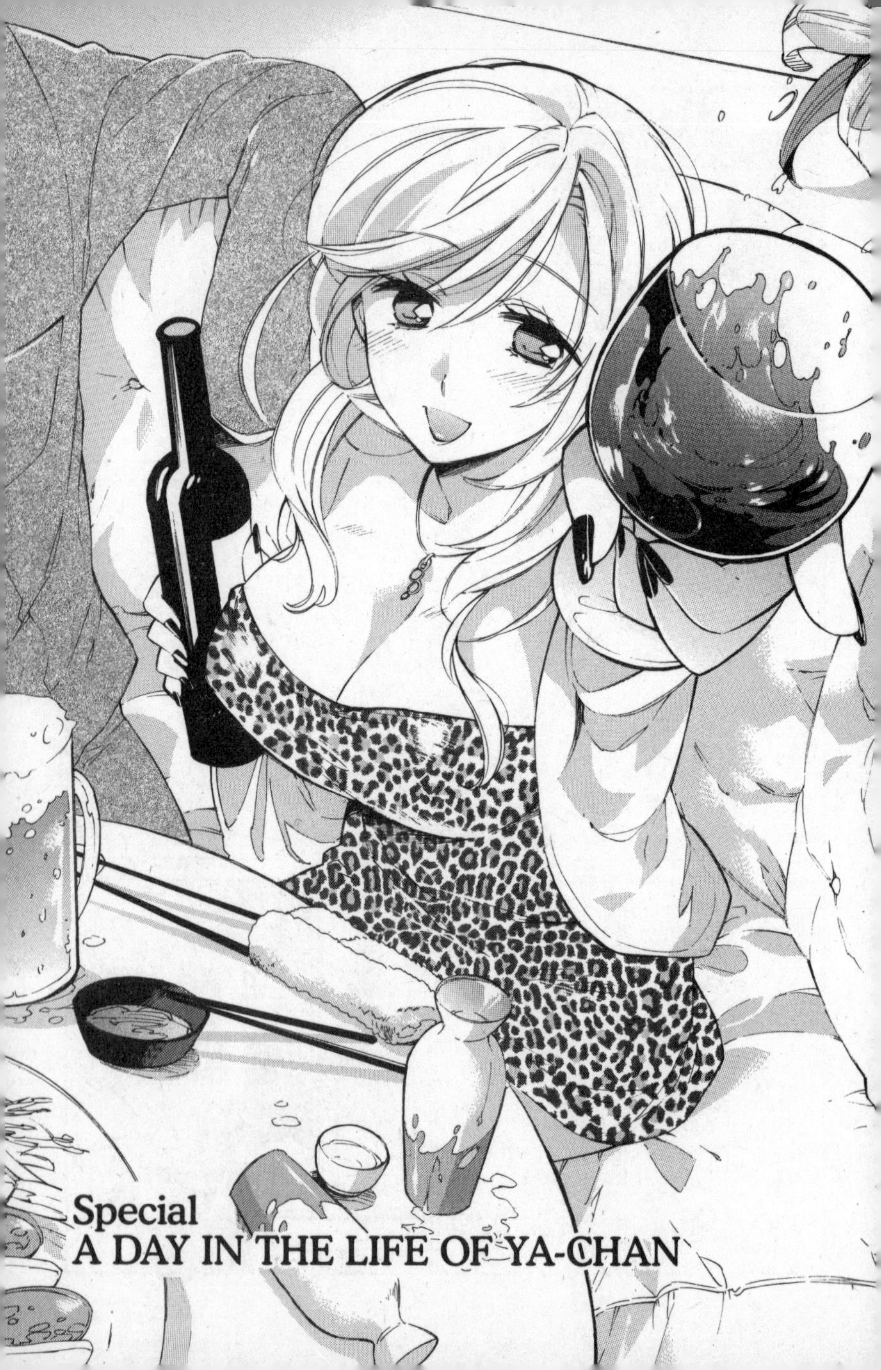

Special
A DAY IN THE LIFE OF YA-CHAN

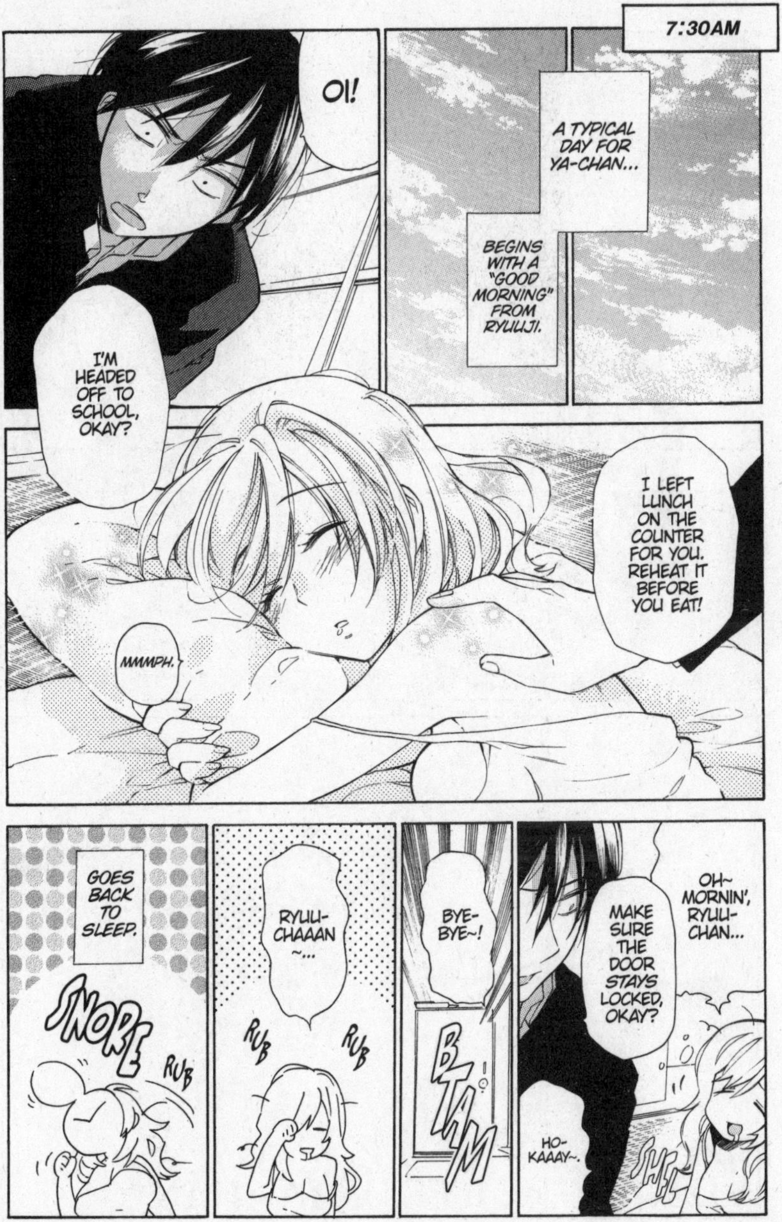
7:30AM
A TYPICAL DAY FOR YA-CHAN...
BEGINS WITH A "GOOD MORNING" FROM RYUUJI.
OI!
I'M HEADED OFF TO SCHOOL, OKAY?
I LEFT LUNCH ON THE COUNTER FOR YOU. REHEAT IT BEFORE YOU EAT!
MMMPH.
OH~ MORNIN', RYUU-CHAN...
MAKE SURE THE DOOR STAYS LOCKED, OKAY?
SHFL
HO-KAAAY~.
BYE-BYE~!
BTAM
RYUU-CHAAAN ~...
RUB
RUB
GOES BACK TO SLEEP.
SNORE
RUB

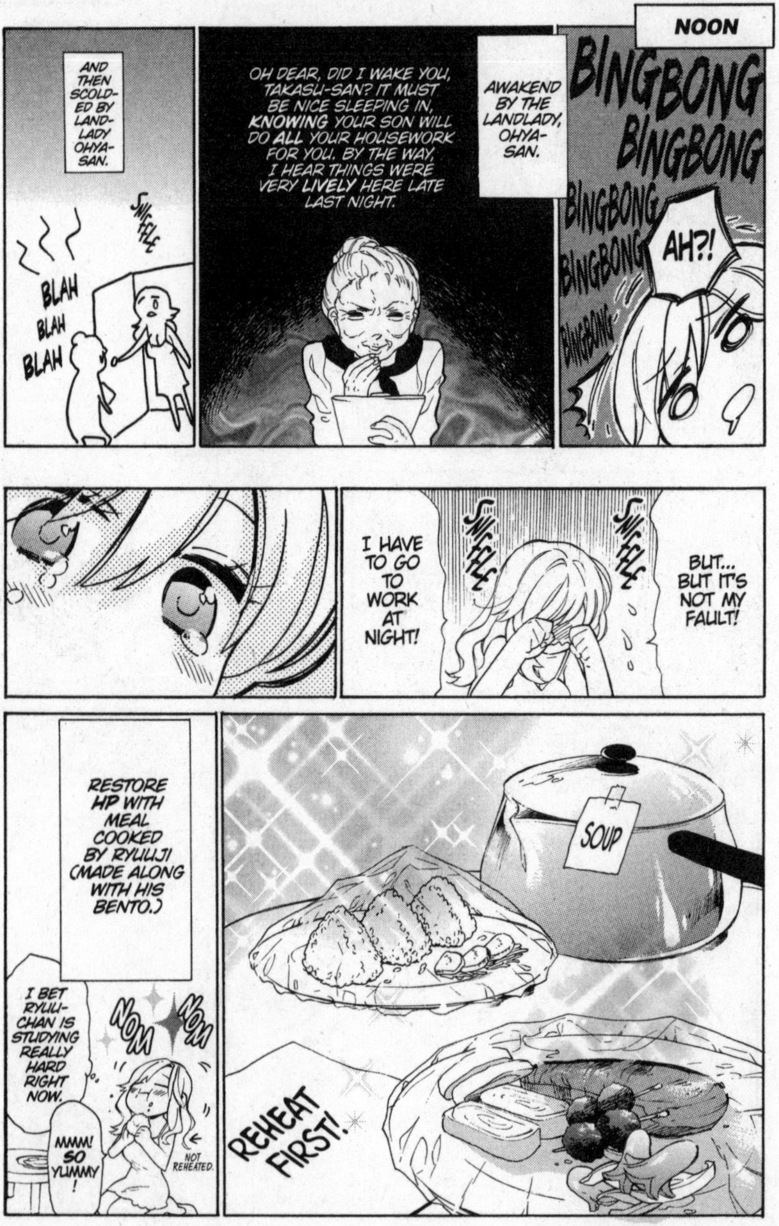
NOON
BINGBONG BINGBONG BINGBONG BINGBONG BINGBONG
AWAKEND BY THE LANDLADY, OHYA-SAN.
AH?!
OH DEAR, DID I WAKE YOU, TAKASU-SAN? IT MUST BE NICE SLEEPING IN, **KNOWING** YOUR SON WILL DO **ALL** YOUR HOUSEWORK FOR YOU. BY THE WAY, I HEAR THINGS WERE VERY **LIVELY** HERE LATE LAST NIGHT.
AND THEN SCOLDED BY LANDLADY OHYA-SAN.
SNIFFLE
BLAH BLAH BLAH
BUT... BUT IT'S NOT MY FAULT!
SNIFFLE
SNIFFLE
I HAVE TO GO TO WORK AT NIGHT!
SOUP
REHEAT FIRST!
RESTORE **HP** WITH MEAL COOKED BY RYUUJI (MADE ALONG WITH HIS BENTO.)
NOM NOM
I BET RYUU-CHAN IS STUDYING REALLY HARD RIGHT NOW.
MMM! SO YUMMY!
NOT REHEATED.

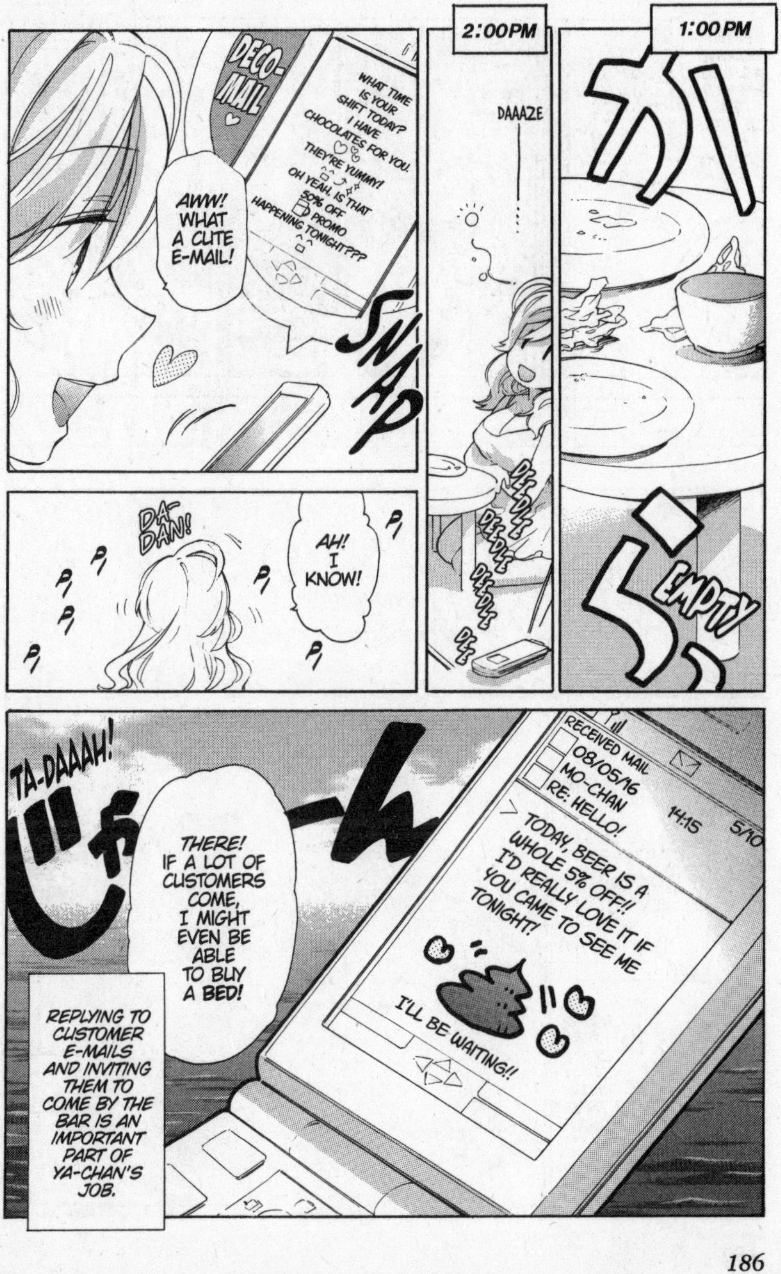
1:00 PM
EMPTY
2:00 PM
DAAAZE
DEDLE DEDLE DEDLE DE
DECO-MAIL
WHAT TIME IS YOUR SHIFT TODAY? I HAVE CHOCOLATES FOR YOU. THEY'RE YUMMY! OH YEAH, IS THAT 50% OFF PROMO HAPPENING TONIGHT???
AWW! WHAT A CUTE E-MAIL!
SNAP
DA-DAN!
AH! I KNOW!
PI PI PI PI PI PI PI
TA-DAAAH!
THERE! IF A LOT OF CUSTOMERS COME, I MIGHT EVEN BE ABLE TO BUY A BED!
RECEIVED MAIL
08/05/16
MO-CHAN
RE: HELLO!
14:15
5/10
TODAY, BEER IS A WHOLE 5% OFF!! I'D REALLY LOVE IT IF YOU CAME TO SEE ME TONIGHT!
I'LL BE WAITING!!
REPLYING TO CUSTOMER E-MAILS AND INVITING THEM TO COME BY THE BAR IS AN IMPORTANT PART OF YA-CHAN'S JOB.

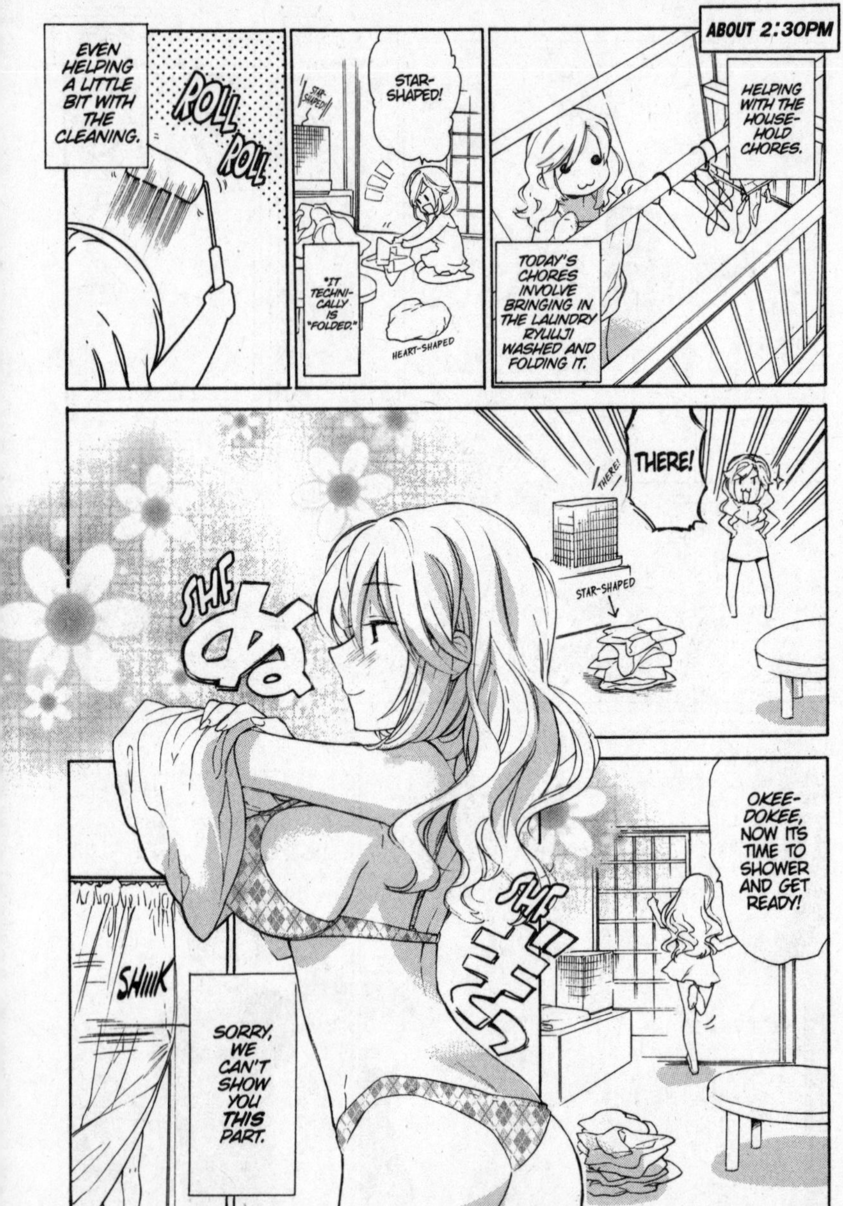
ABOUT 2:30PM
HELPING WITH THE HOUSE-HOLD CHORES.
TODAY'S CHORES INVOLVE BRINGING IN THE LAUNDRY RYUUJI WASHED AND FOLDING IT.
STAR-SHAPED!
STAR-SHAPED!
*IT TECHNICALLY IS "FOLDED."
HEART-SHAPED
EVEN HELPING A LITTLE BIT WITH THE CLEANING.
ROLL
ROLL
THERE!
THERE!
STAR-SHAPED
SHF
OKEE-DOKEE, NOW ITS TIME TO SHOWER AND GET READY!
SHF
SHIIIK
SORRY, WE CAN'T SHOW YOU THIS PART.

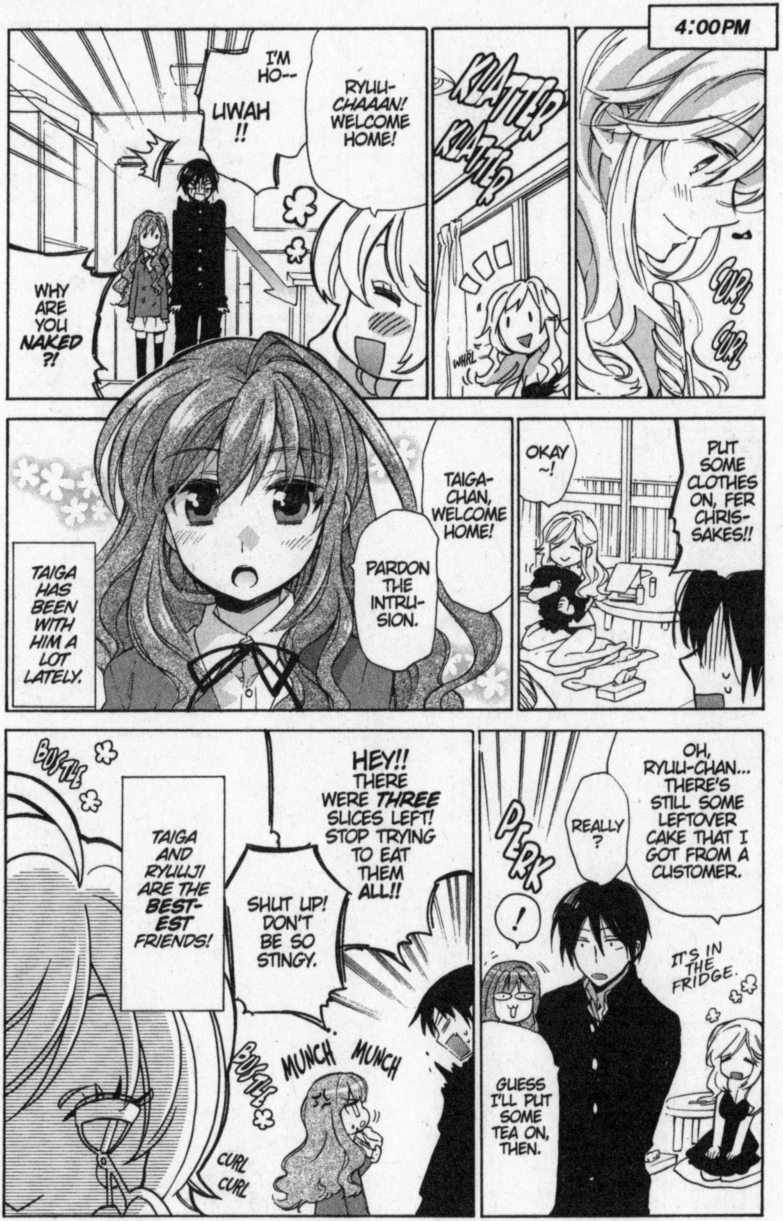
4:00PM
CURL CURL
KLATTER KLATTER
WHRL
RYUU-CHAAAN! WELCOME HOME!
I'M HO--
UWAH !!
WHY ARE YOU NAKED ?!
PUT SOME CLOTHES ON, FER CHRIS-SAKES!!
OKAY ~!
TAIGA-CHAN, WELCOME HOME!
PARDON THE INTRU-SION.
TAIGA HAS BEEN WITH HIM A LOT LATELY.
OH, RYUU-CHAN... THERE'S STILL SOME LEFTOVER CAKE THAT I GOT FROM A CUSTOMER.
REALLY ?
PERK
!
IT'S IN THE FRIDGE.
GUESS I'LL PUT SOME TEA ON, THEN.
HEY!! THERE WERE THREE SLICES LEFT! STOP TRYING TO EAT THEM ALL!!
SHUT UP! DON'T BE SO STINGY.
BUSTLE
TAIGA AND RYUUJI ARE THE BEST-EST FRIENDS!
MUNCH MUNCH
BUSTLE
CURL CURL

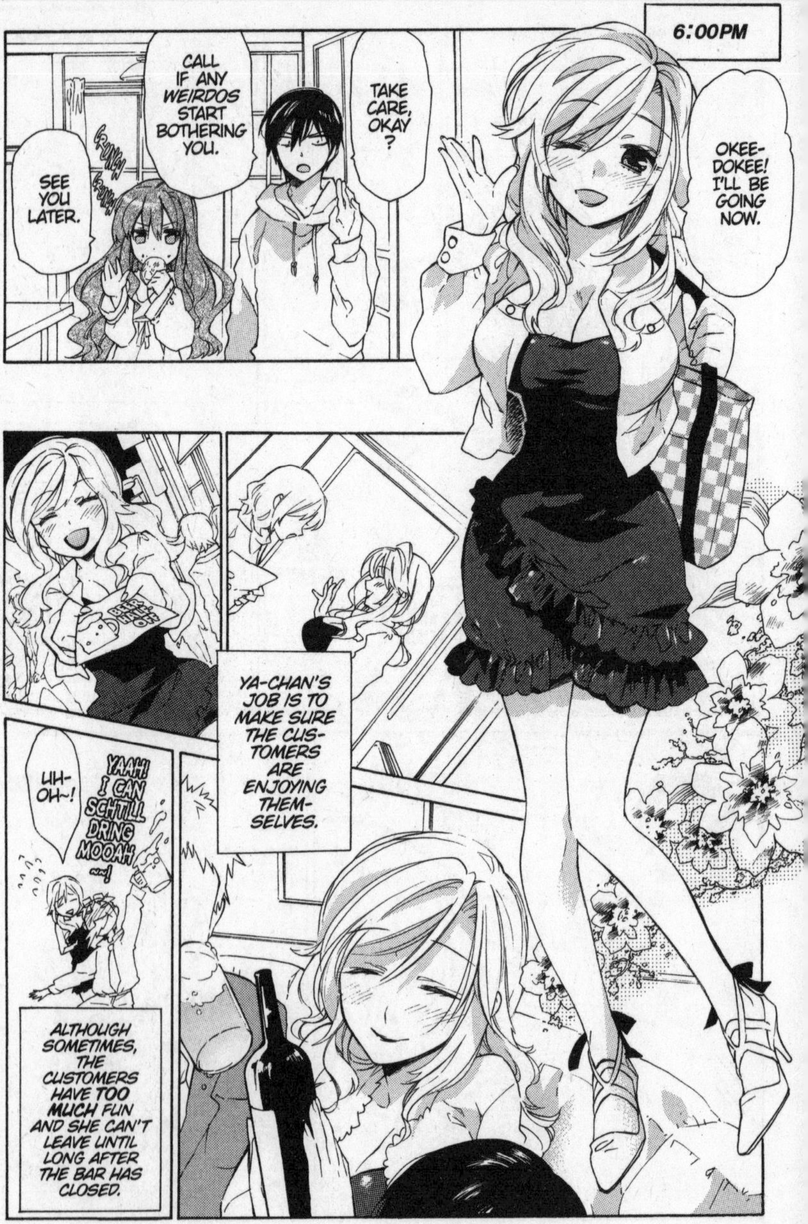
6:00PM
OKEE-DOKEE! I'LL BE GOING NOW.
TAKE CARE, OKAY?
CALL IF ANY WEIRDOS START BOTHERING YOU.
CRUNCH CRUNCH
SEE YOU LATER.
YA-CHAN'S JOB IS TO MAKE SURE THE CUS-TOMERS ARE ENJOYING THEM-SELVES.
YAAH! I CAN SCHTILL DRING MOOAH ~~!
UH-OH~!
ALTHOUGH SOMETIMES, THE CUSTOMERS HAVE TOO MUCH FUN AND SHE CAN'T LEAVE UNTIL LONG AFTER THE BAR HAS CLOSED.

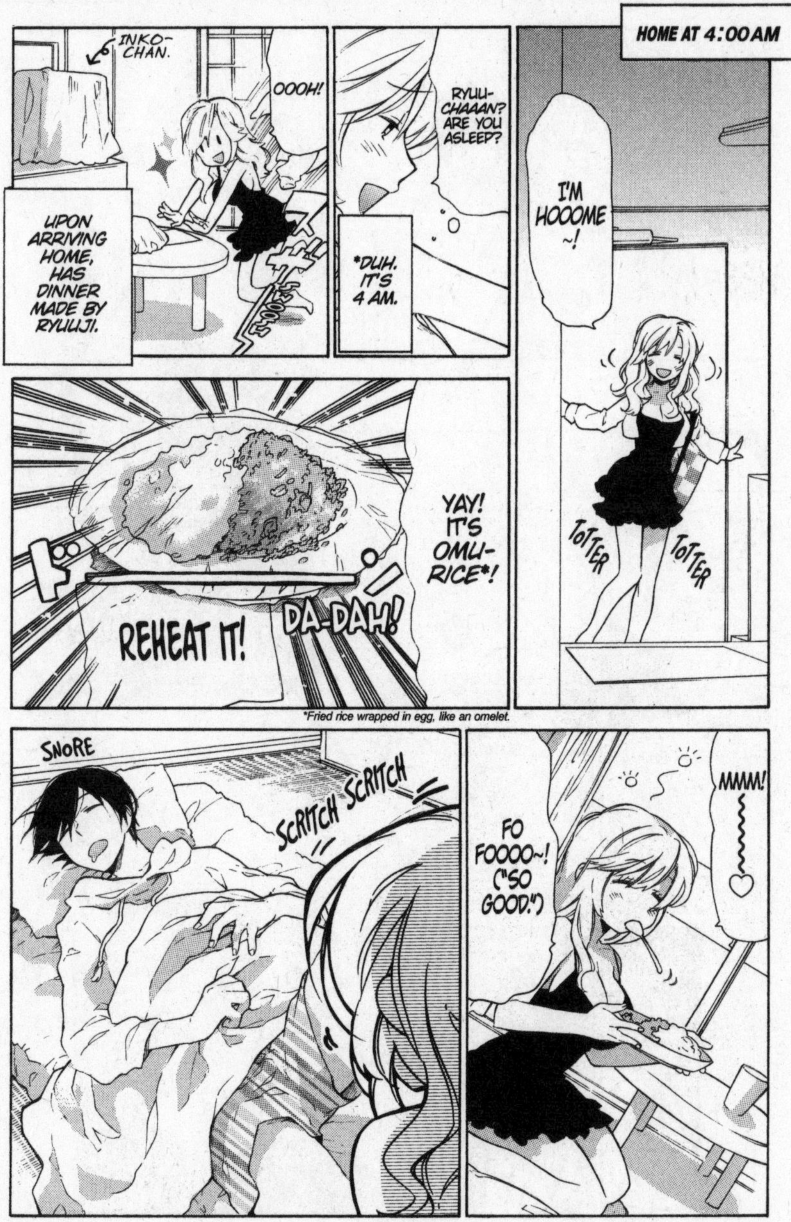
HOME AT 4:00 AM
I'M HOOOME ~!
TOTTER
TOTTER
RYUU-CHAAAN? ARE YOU ASLEEP?
*DUH. IT'S 4 AM.
OOOH!
INKO-CHAN.
UPON ARRIVING HOME, HAS DINNER MADE BY RYUUJI.
YAY! IT'S OMU-RICE*!
DA-DAH!
REHEAT IT!
MMM!
FO FOOOO~! ("SO GOOD!")
SCRITCH SCRITCH
SNORE

*Fried rice wrapped in egg, like an omelet.

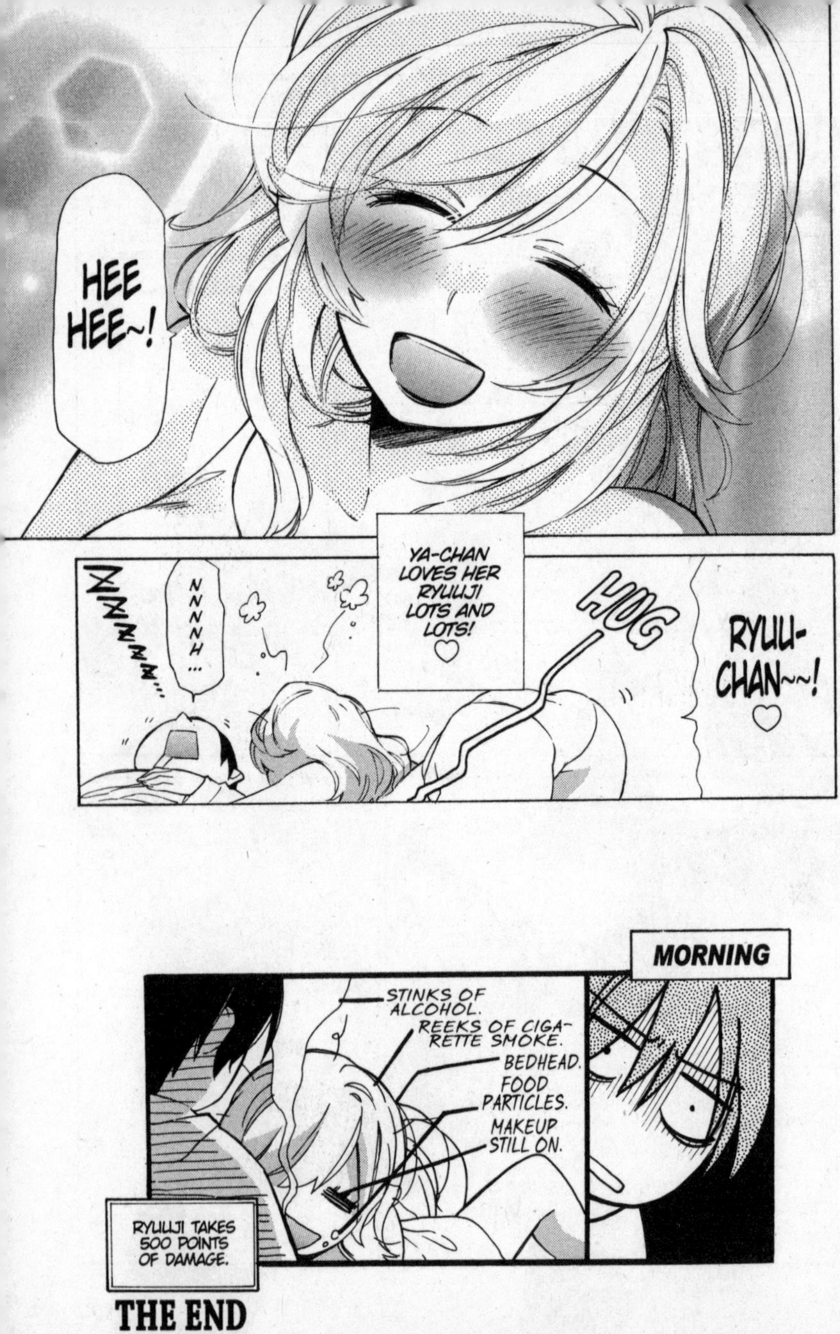
HEE HEE~!
RYUU-CHAN~~! ♡
HUG
YA-CHAN LOVES HER RYUUJI LOTS AND LOTS! ♡
NNNNH...
ZZZZZZ...
MORNING
STINKS OF ALCOHOL.
REEKS OF CIGARETTE SMOKE.
BEDHEAD.
FOOD PARTICLES.
MAKEUP STILL ON.
RYUUJI TAKES 500 POINTS OF DAMAGE.
THE END

GUEST PAGE

Hello, everyone. Thank you for picking up *Toradora! Volume 1.* I am very grateful! I hope you enjoyed reading Ryuuji's & Taiga's romance and comedy hijinks. Right now (2/2008), the original light novel series, as published by Dengeki Bunko, has reached six volumes and one gaiden side story, and is still going strong. If you have some time, I highly suggest you check those out, too! Zekkyo-sensei, thank you very much for all your hard work. However, our journey has just begun.
I look forward to working with you next volume!

Text by Yuyuko Takemiya

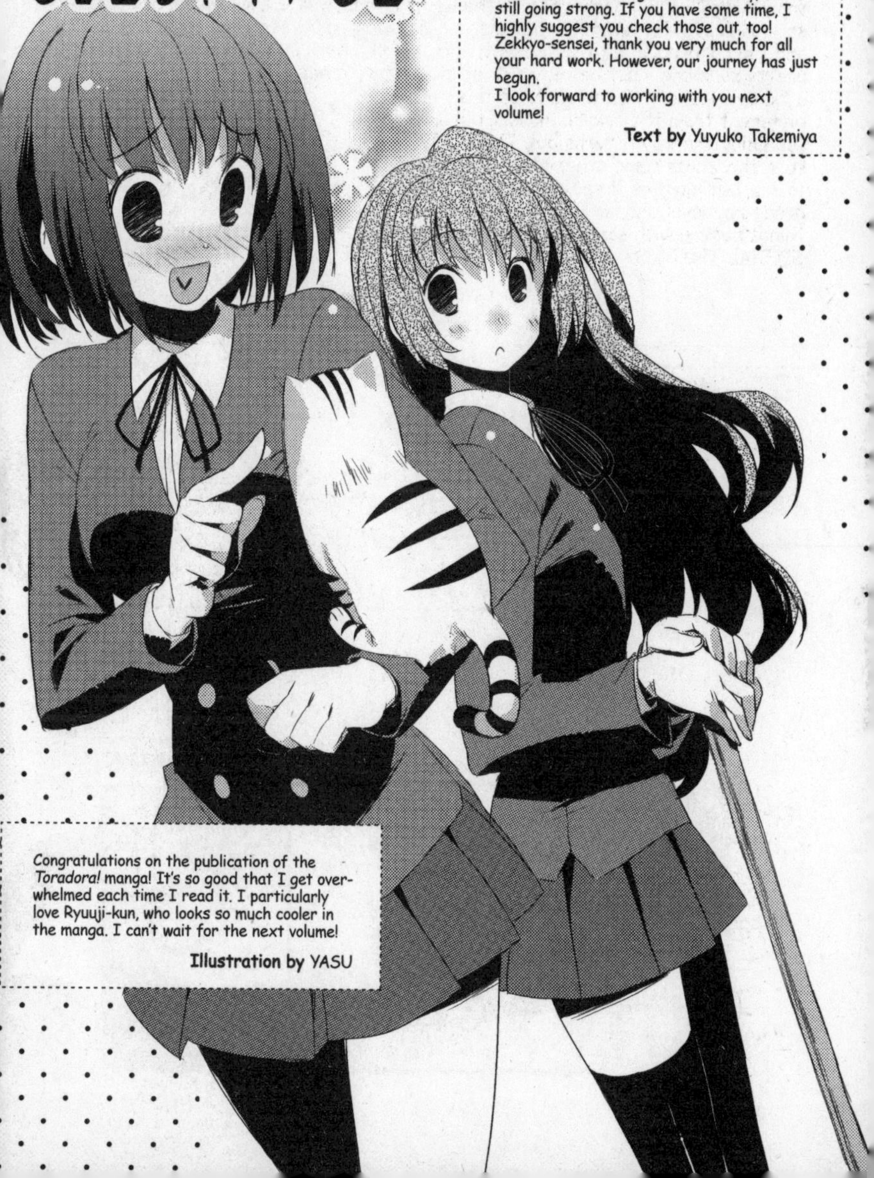

Congratulations on the publication of the *Toradora!* manga! It's so good that I get overwhelmed each time I read it. I particularly love Ryuuji-kun, who looks so much cooler in the manga. I can't wait for the next volume!

Illustration by YASU

So yeah, sometime back in spring(?) I got asked "Hey, d'ya wanna give that whole manga thing a shot?" To which I immediately said, "Sure!" Never in my wildest dreams did I think it would be something as huge as this. See, I don't read light novels that much, so when I ducked into a bookstore to check it out, I was totally unprepared for the size of Yuyuko-sensei's corner. "Oh crap," I thought to myself, breaking out in a cold sweat, "I'm in it now." (I'm still sweating, by the way.) Now, *Toradora!* is an awesome series, and I love it. But if it had been something I could barely read all the way through, well, I would have been in a serious pickle. Fortunately, that didn't happen. I'm a big Yuyuko-sensei fan now, and I'm honored to be trusted with adapting her work into a manga—though I'm pretty sure she must be very sick of me pestering her with a zillion questions. Some parts of this will be different from the original novels, but I hope you enjoy the way it turns out. I'm pretty sure there was some other stuff I wanted to say, but most of it seems to be second grade boy level bad, so I'll just close things up now with some SPECIAL THANKS.

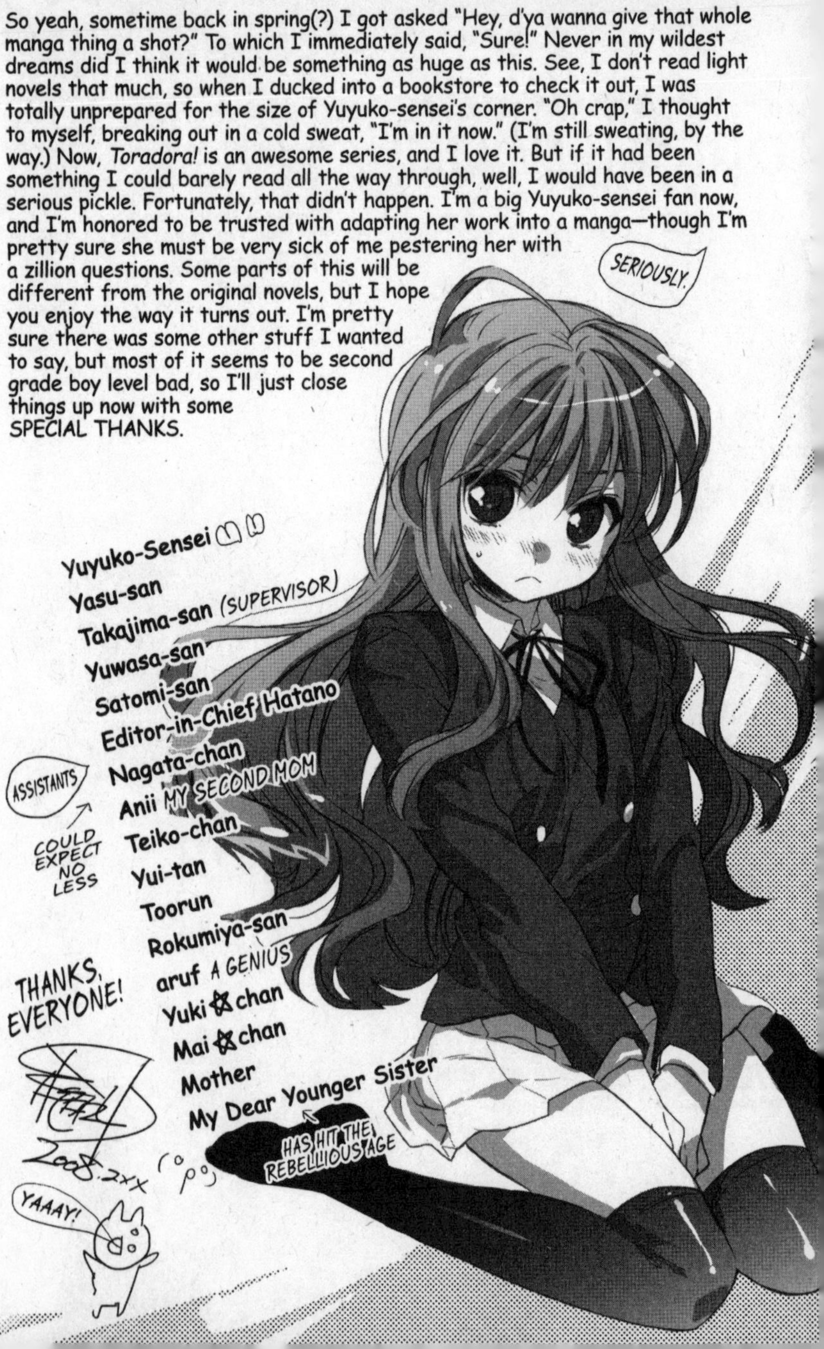
SERIOUSLY.

Yuyuko-Sensei
Yasu-san
Takajima-san (SUPERVISOR)
Yuwasa-san
Satomi-san
Editor-in-Chief Hatano
Nagata-chan
Anii MY SECOND MOM
Teiko-chan
Yui-tan
Toorun
Rokumiya-san
aruf A GENIUS
Yuki☆chan
Mai☆chan
Mother
My Dear Younger Sister

ASSISTANTS
COULD EXPECT NO LESS
HAS HIT THE REBELLIOUS AGE

THANKS, EVERYONE!

2008.2XX

YAAAY!

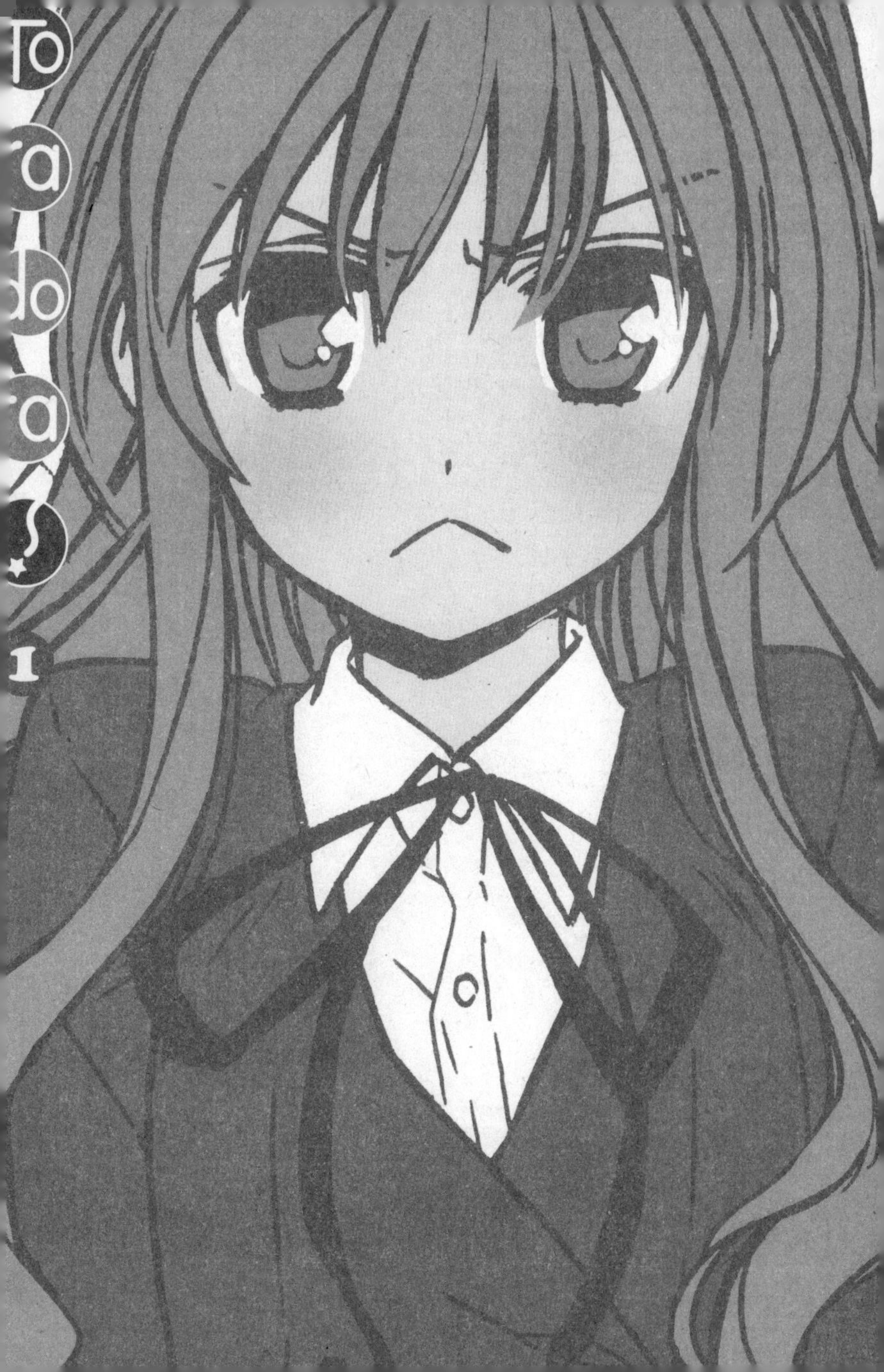
Toradora!
1

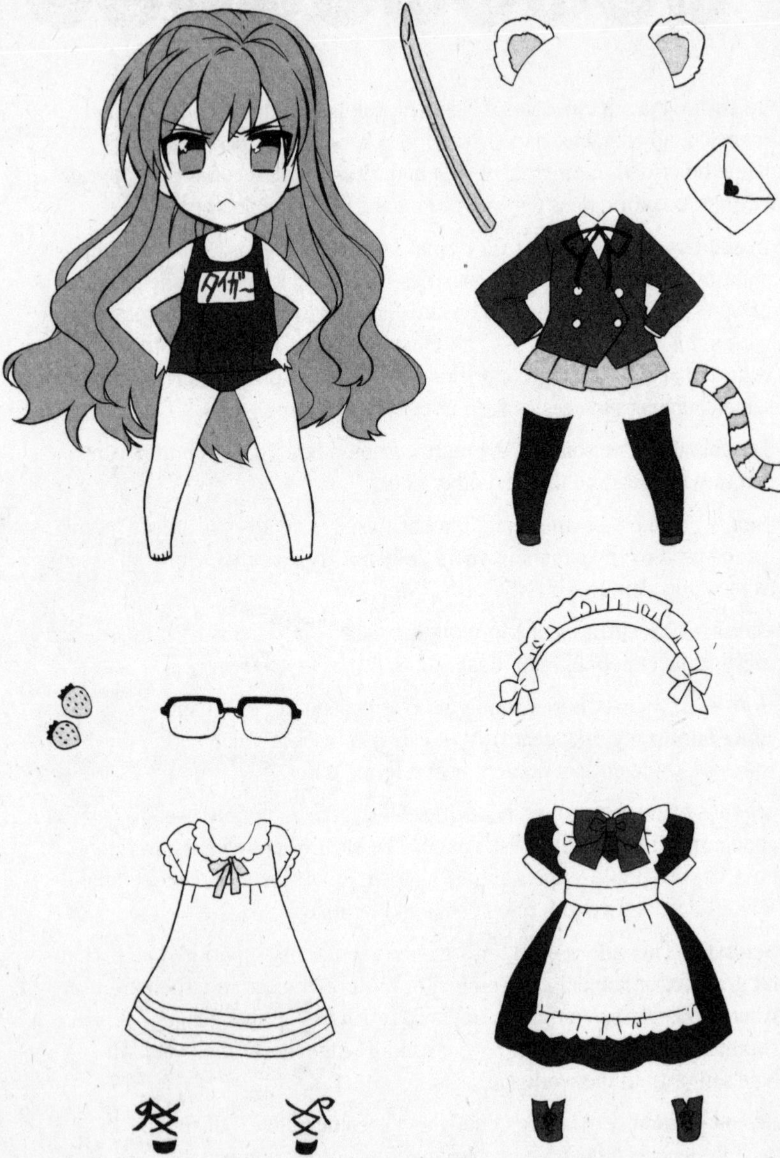
タイガ～

HONORIFICS

To ensure that all character relationships appear as they were originally intended, all character names have been kept in their original Japanese name order with family name first and given name second. For copyright reasons, creator names appear in standard English name order.

In addition to preserving the original Japanese name order, Seven Seas is committed to ensuring that honorifics—polite speech that indicates a person's status or relationship towards another individual—are retained within this book. Politeness is an integral facet of Japanese culture and we believe that maintaining honorifics in our translations helps bring out the same character nuances as seen in the original work.

The following are some of the more common honorifics you may come across while reading this and other books:

-san – The most common of all honorifics, it is an all-purpose suffix that can be used in any situation where politeness is expected. Generally seen as the equivalent to Mr., Miss, Ms., Mrs., etc.

-sama – This suffix is one level higher than "-san" and is used to confer great respect upon an individual.

-kun – This suffix is commonly used at the end of boys' names to express either familiarity or endearment. It can also be used when addressing someone younger than oneself or of a lower status.

-chan – Another common honorific. This suffix is mainly used to express endearment towards girls, but can also be used when referring to little boys or even pets. Couples are also known to use the term between themselves to convey a sense of cuteness and intimacy.

Sempai – This title is used towards one's senior or "superior" in a particular group or organization. "Sempai" is most often used in a school setting, where underclassmen refer to upperclassmen as "sempai," though it is also commonly said by employees when addressing fellow employees who hold seniority in the workplace.

Sensei – Literally meaning "one who has come before," this title is used for teachers, doctors, or masters of any profession or art.

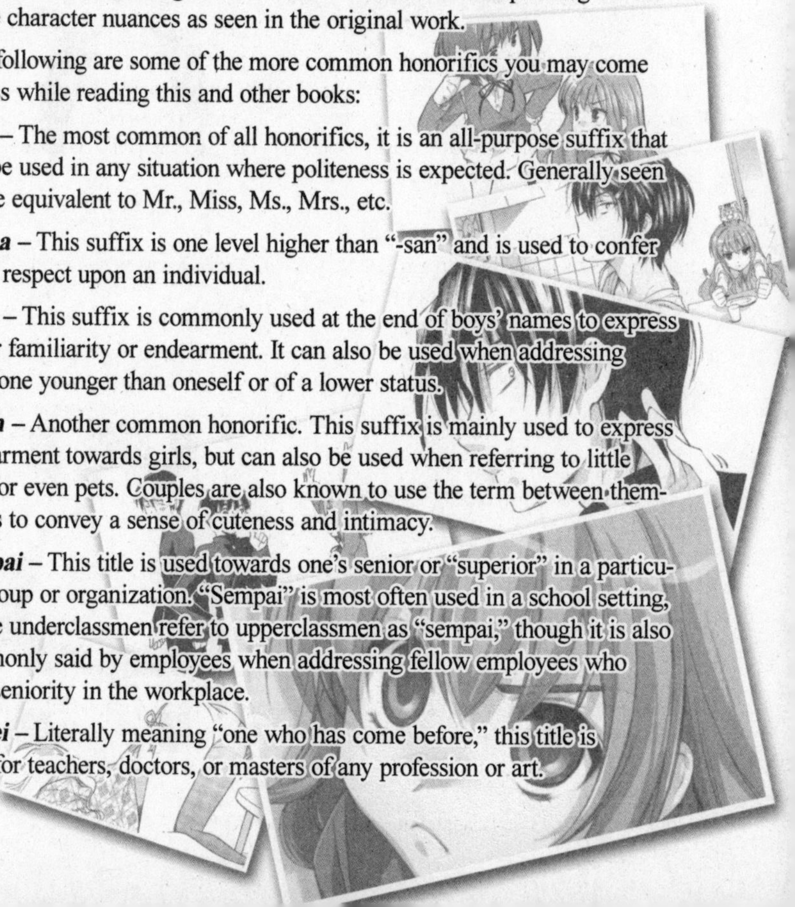

TRANSLATION NOTES

Series Title

The title of the series, *Toradora!*, refers to the two main characters. *Taiga,* which sounds like the English "tiger," and *tora* are both Japanese terms for tiger. While the *"ryuu"* in Ryuuji's name means dragon, a transliteration of dragon into Japanese is *"doragon."*

Chapter 1

Inko is the Japanese word for parakeet. So Ryuuji's name for his pet parakeet is, essentially, "Parakeet-chan."

Maruo-kun is a character in the popular shojo manga series *Chibi Maruko-chan.* A slice-of-life comedy series set in 1970's Japan, Maruo-kun is a classmate of the main character Maruko-chan. Maruo-kun, known for his thick, coke-bottle glasses, is a very serious student. He is also class president and always wants his classmates to look up to him and respect him.

Chapter 2

Ina Bauer is the name of both a figure skater from West Germany and of the move she was the first to perform back in 1957.

When Taiga said that she had fast food for three meals in a row, she actually meant *"konbini-ben,"* which is short for "convenience store bento." Most Japanese convenience stores have an extensive selection of pre-prepared bento and meals available.

Chapter 3

Takikomi rice is a dish where rice is steamed together with meat or vegetables in a broth.

Chapter 5

Kamaboko is processed fish, or fish sausage.

Epilogue

DECO-mail is a special mail-service by the Japanese phone company NTT, which allows the use of cHTML (a.k.a. i-mode HTML). This is currently exclusive to Japan.

Omu-rice is fried rice wrapped in egg, like an omelet.

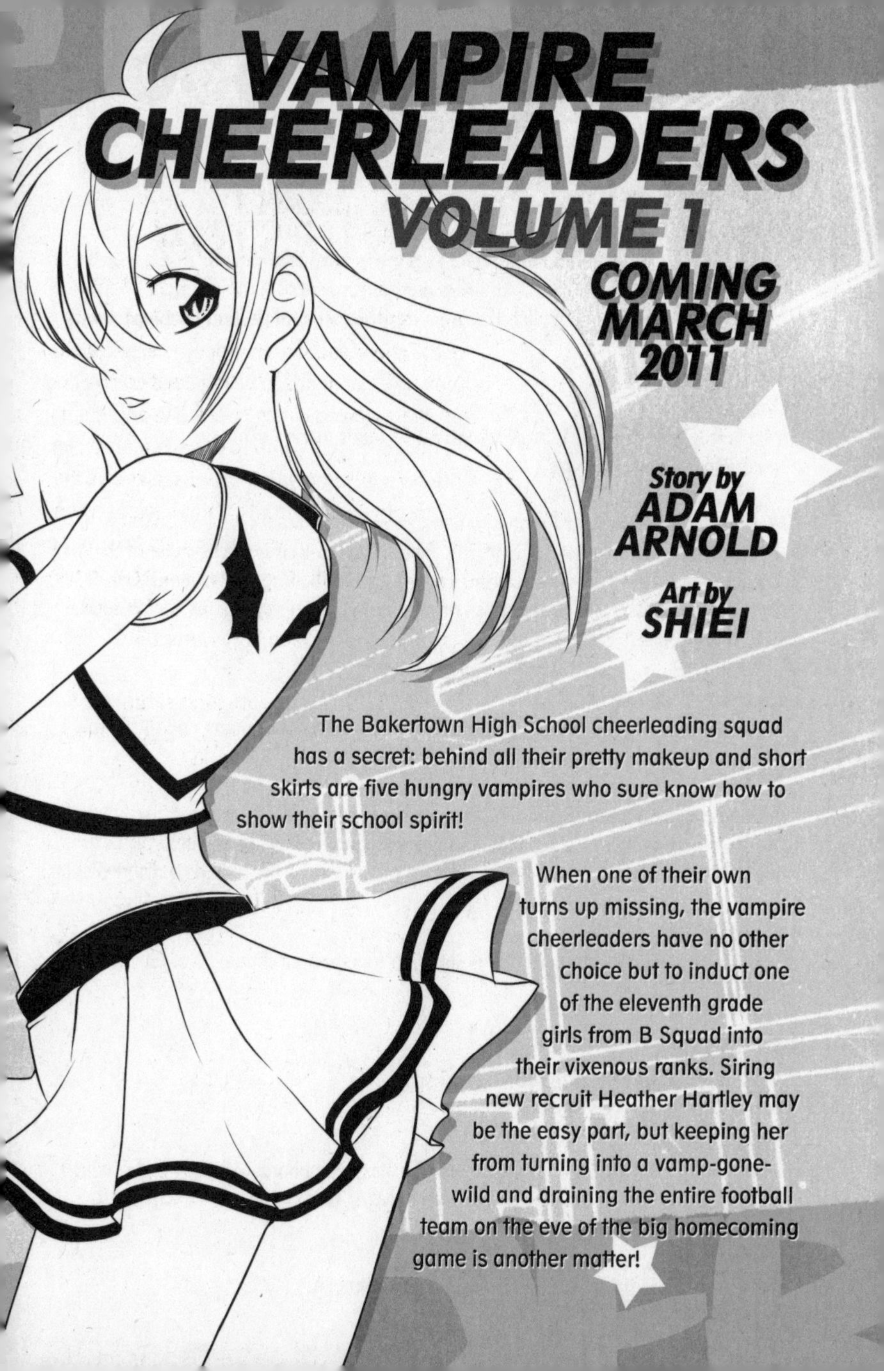

VAMPIRE CHEERLEADERS

VOLUME 1

COMING MARCH 2011

Story by **ADAM ARNOLD**

Art by **SHIEI**

The Bakertown High School cheerleading squad has a secret: behind all their pretty makeup and short skirts are five hungry vampires who sure know how to show their school spirit!

When one of their own turns up missing, the vampire cheerleaders have no other choice but to induct one of the eleventh grade girls from B Squad into their vixenous ranks. Siring new recruit Heather Hartley may be the easy part, but keeping her from turning into a vamp-gone-wild and draining the entire football team on the eve of the big homecoming game is another matter!

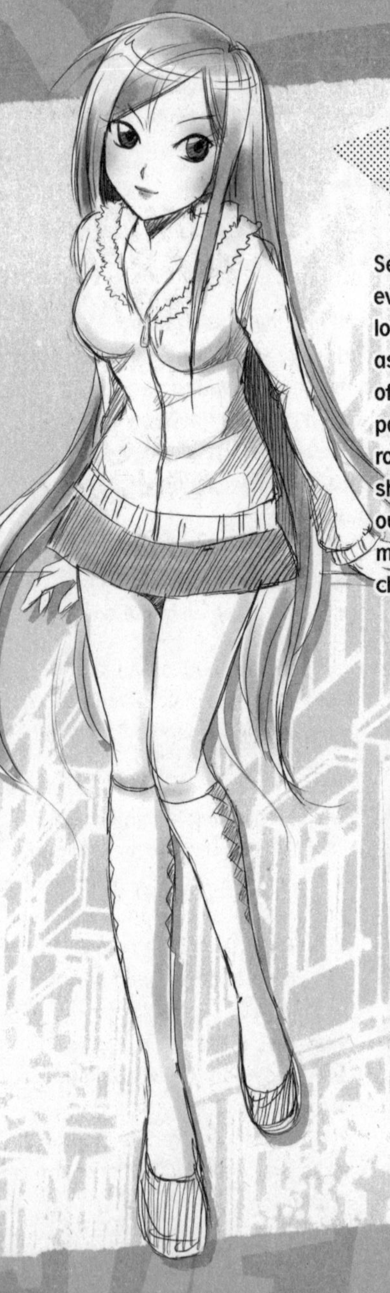

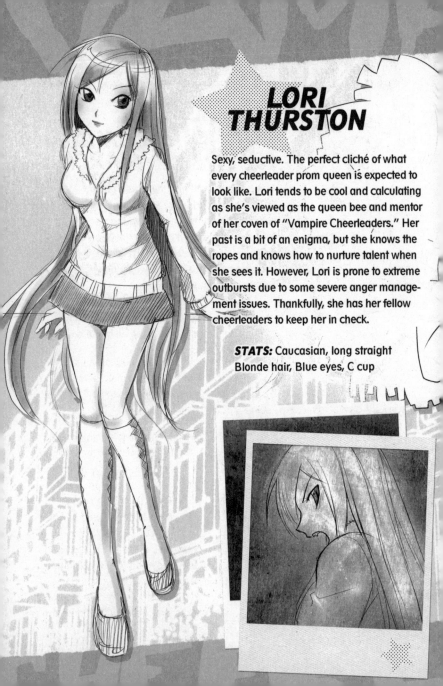

LORI THURSTON

Sexy, seductive. The perfect cliché of what every cheerleader prom queen is expected to look like. Lori tends to be cool and calculating as she's viewed as the queen bee and mentor of her coven of "Vampire Cheerleaders." Her past is a bit of an enigma, but she knows the ropes and knows how to nurture talent when she sees it. However, Lori is prone to extreme outbursts due to some severe anger management issues. Thankfully, she has her fellow cheerleaders to keep her in check.

STATS: Caucasian, long straight Blonde hair, Blue eyes, C cup

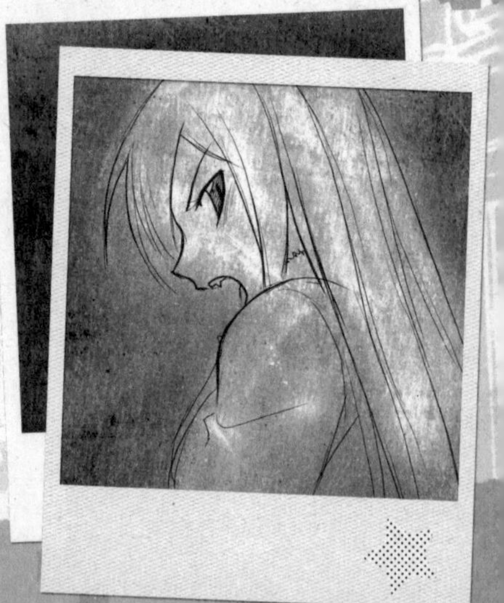

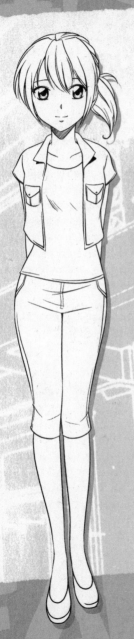

HEATHER HARTLEY

An eleventh grader on the B Squad who is seen as a goodie-two-shoes. Indeed, Heather's parents are overbearing and avid churchgoers, so Heather has lived a sheltered life. Once Heather gets turned into a vampire, however, a whole new world opens up for her.

STATS: Caucasian, Short (Petite), Brown hair done in a single pony tail in the back, Green eyes, B cup

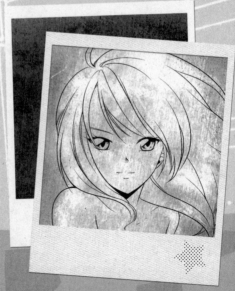

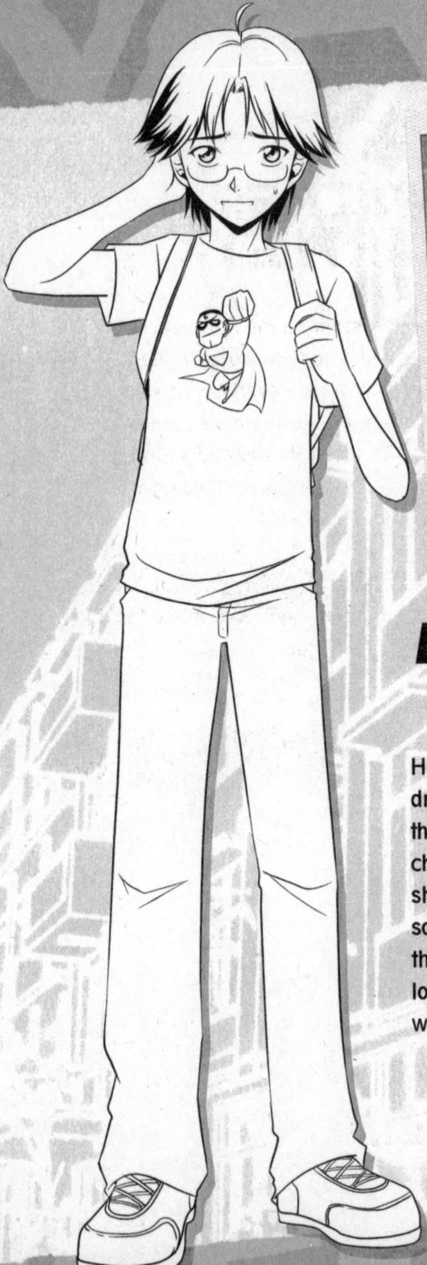

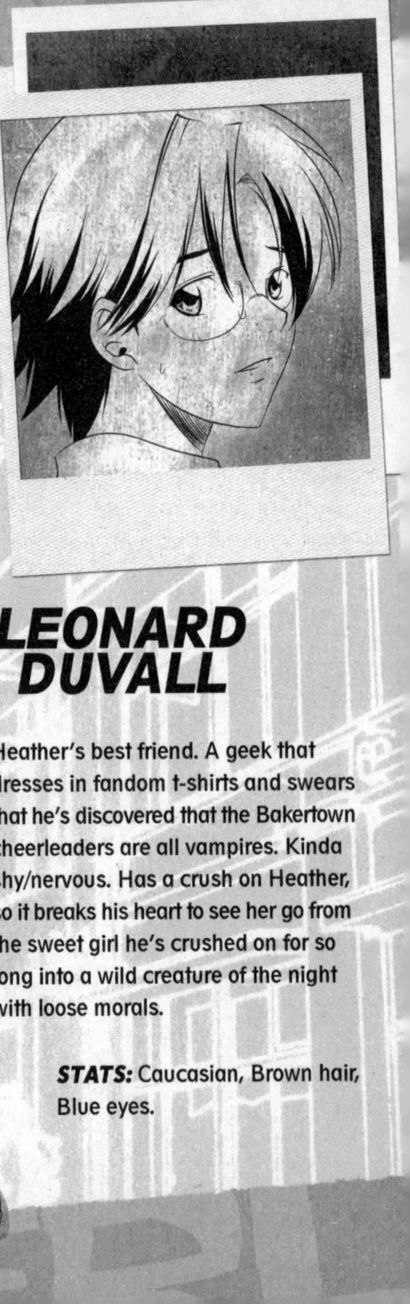

LEONARD DUVALL

Heather's best friend. A geek that dresses in fandom t-shirts and swears that he's discovered that the Bakertown cheerleaders are all vampires. Kinda shy/nervous. Has a crush on Heather, so it breaks his heart to see her go from the sweet girl he's crushed on for so long into a wild creature of the night with loose morals.

STATS: Caucasian, Brown hair, Blue eyes.

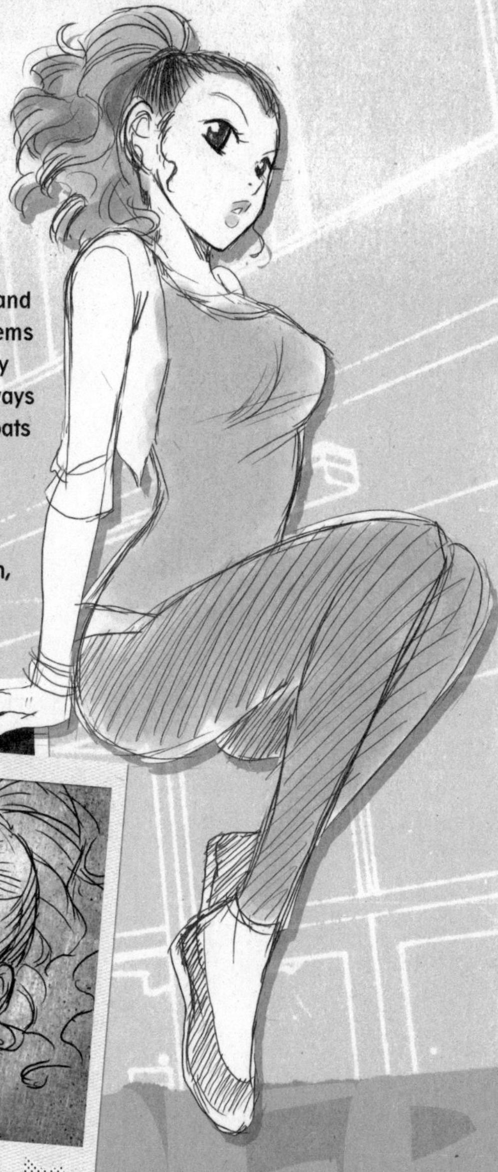

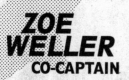

ZOE WELLER

CO-CAPTAIN

Zoe has a good head on her shoulders and is Lori's right-hand woman. Unfortunately, Zoe seems to get rubbed the wrong way by Suki at every turn. The two always seem to be at each other's throats over the most trivial things. Playful rivalry? Or something else...?

STATS: African American, Brown/Black hair, Brown eyes, C cup

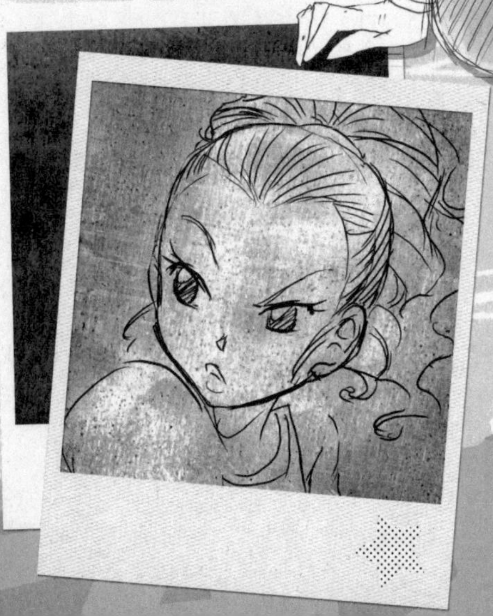

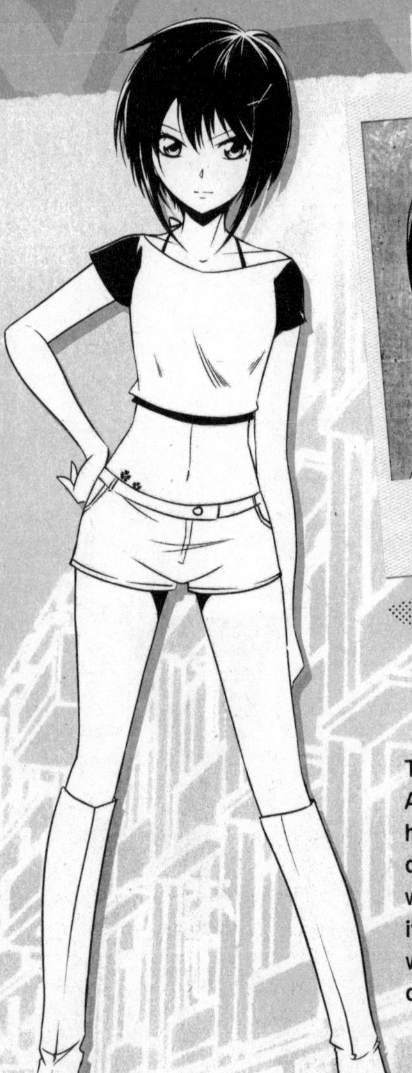

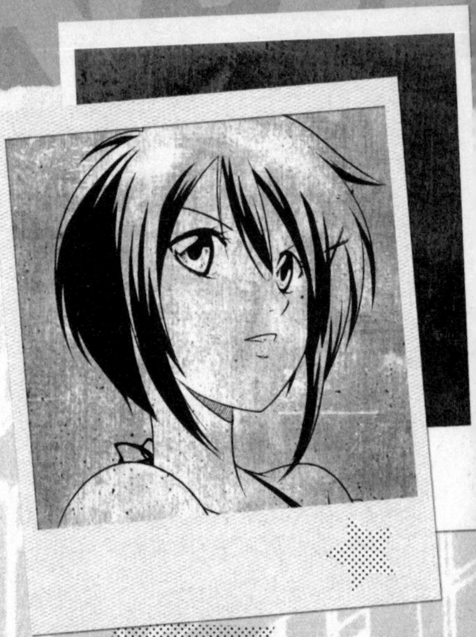

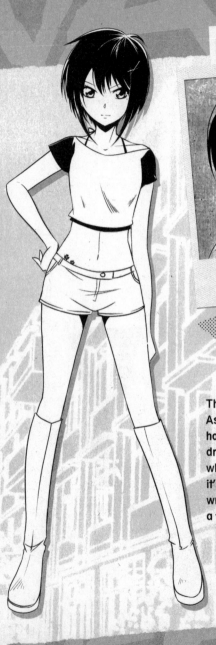

SUKI TAFT

CO-CAPTAIN

The bad seed. She knows guys dig Asian chicks and she knows just how to use her talents to bleed 'em dry (pun intended). Always saying whatever's on her mind...even when it's totally inappropriate and the wrong thing at the wrong time. Has a friendly(?) rivalry with Zoe.

STATS: **Asian American, Black hair with highlights, Brown eyes but sometimes wears colored contacts, A cup**

LESLEY CHANDRA
TEAM TREASURER

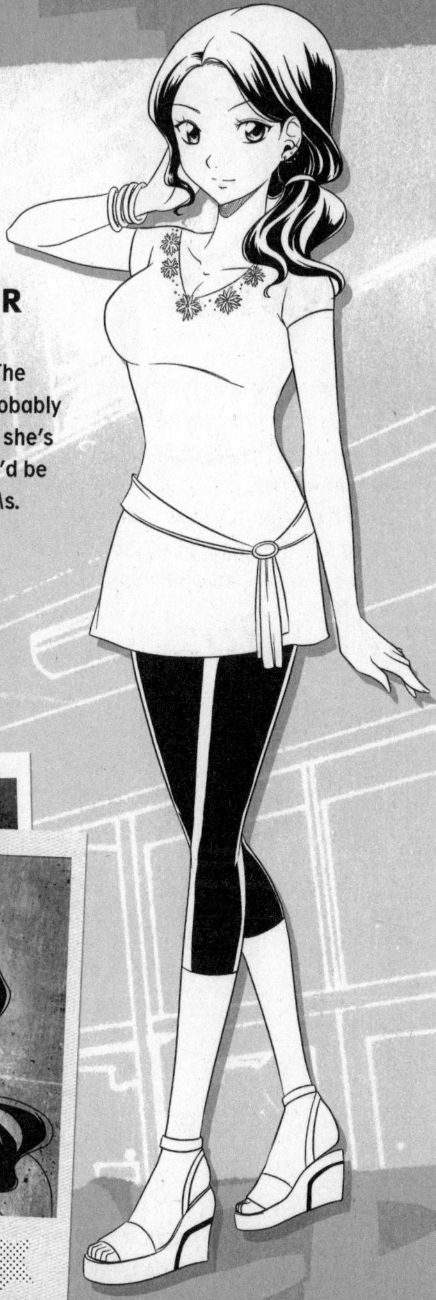

Pleasant personality, friendly. The voice of reason in the group. Probably the smartest of all the girls. But she's also got a wild side. In fact, you'd be surprised to know that she's "Ms. Kama Sutra" in a cheerleading costume.

STATS: East Indian American, Black/Brown hair, Brown eyes, D cup

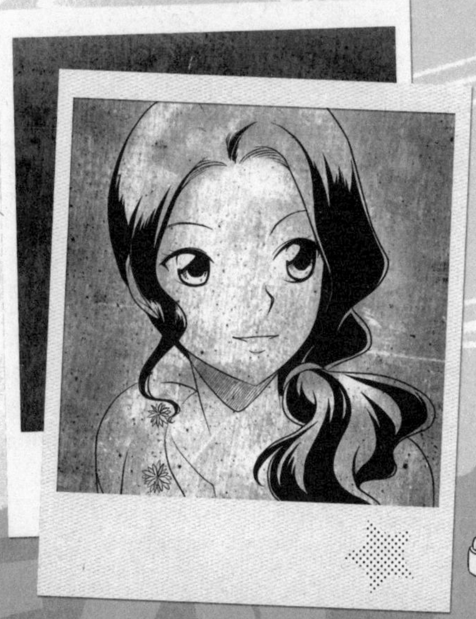

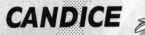

CANDICE

The team's former fifth member. She's up and disappeared without a trace. One of the rumors floating around school is that she got pregnant and her parents freaked and had her sent to a monastery. But the Vampire Cheerleaders know otherwise.

STATS: Caucasian, semi-curly/wavy hair, Brown eyes, C cup, Braces on her teeth.

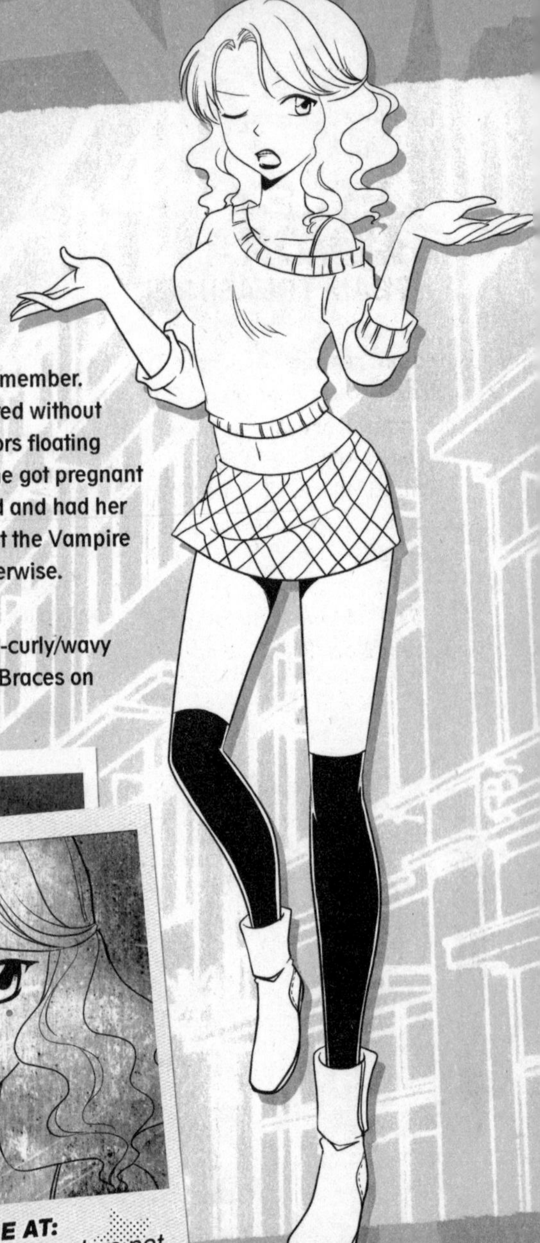

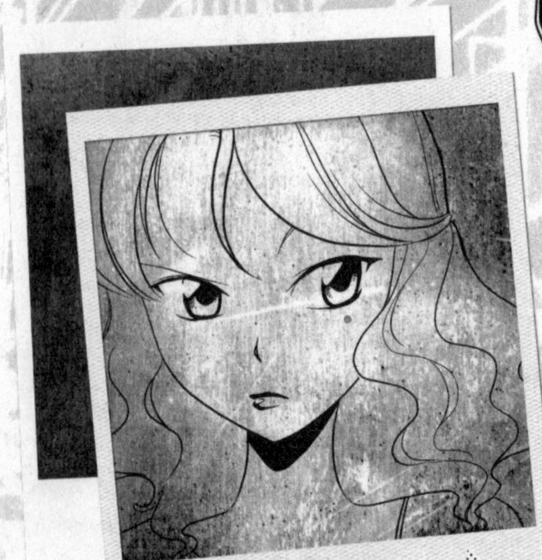

FIND OUT MORE AT:
www.vampirecheerleaders.net

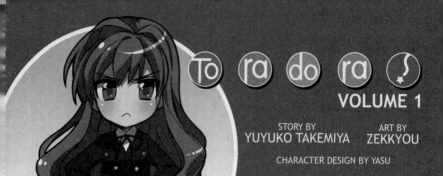

To ra do ra ♪

VOLUME 1

STORY BY
YUYUKO TAKEMIYA

ART BY
ZEKKYOU

CHARACTER DESIGN BY YASU

STAFF CREDITS

translation	**Adrienne Beck**
adaptation	**Janet Houck**
retouch & lettering	**Roland Amago**
cover design	**Nicky Lim**
layout	**Bambi Eloriaga-Amago**
copy editor	**Shanti Whitesides**
editor	**Adam Arnold**

publisher	**Jason DeAngelis** **Seven Seas Entertainment**

TORADORA! VOL. 1
Copyright © 2008 Yuyuko Takemiya / Zekkyou
First published in 2008 by Media Works Inc., Tokyo, Japan.
English translation rights arranged with ASCII MEDIA WORKS.

Visit us online at www.gomanga.com

ISBN: 978-1-934876-94-7

Printed in Canada

First Printing: March 2011

10 9 8 7 6 5 4

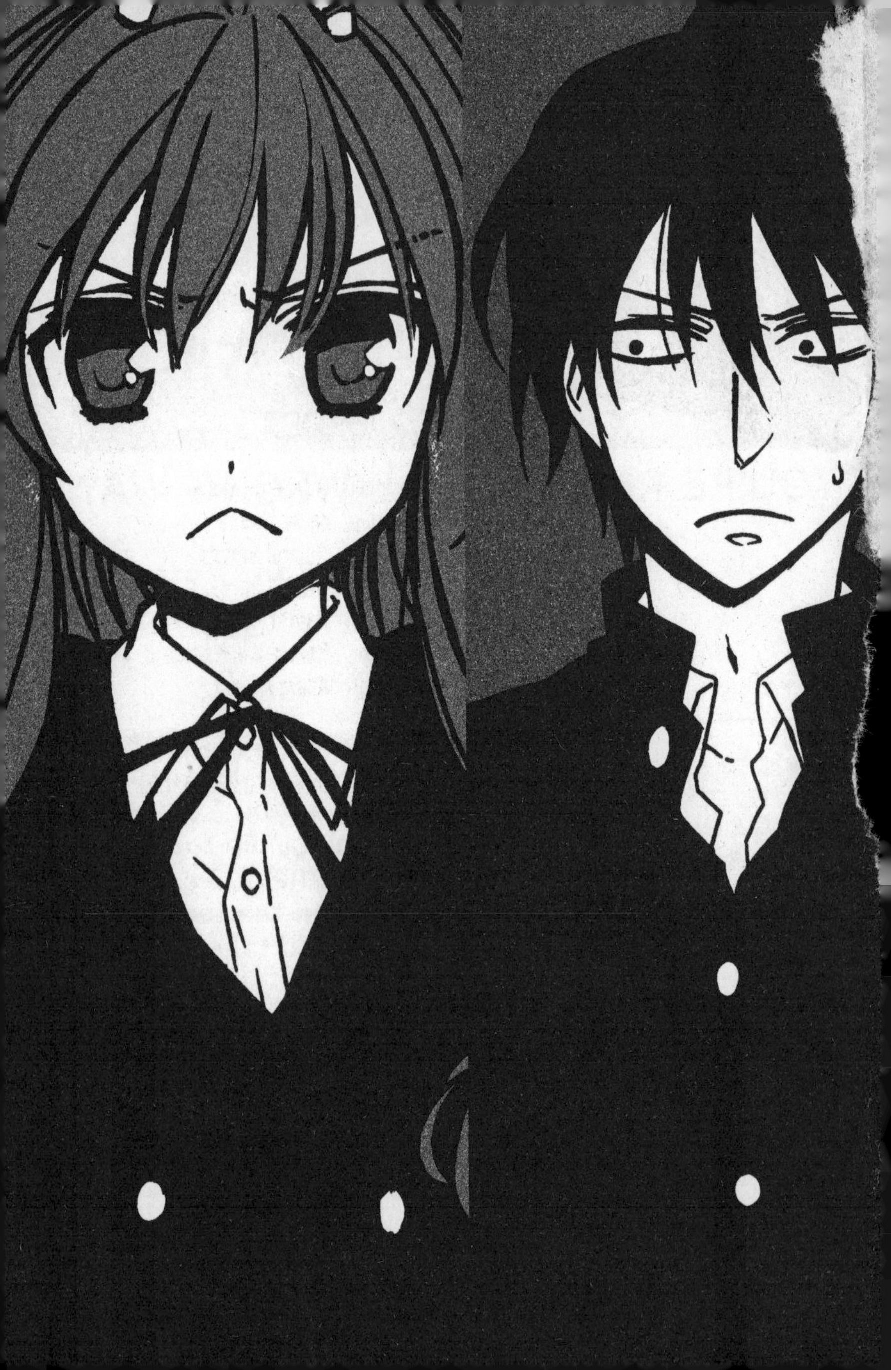

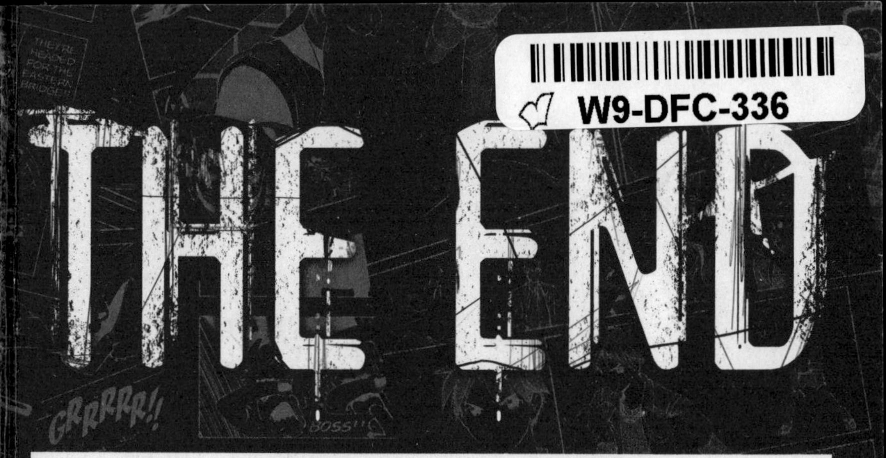
THE END

YOU'RE READING THE WRONG WAY

This is the last page of
Toradora!
Volume 1

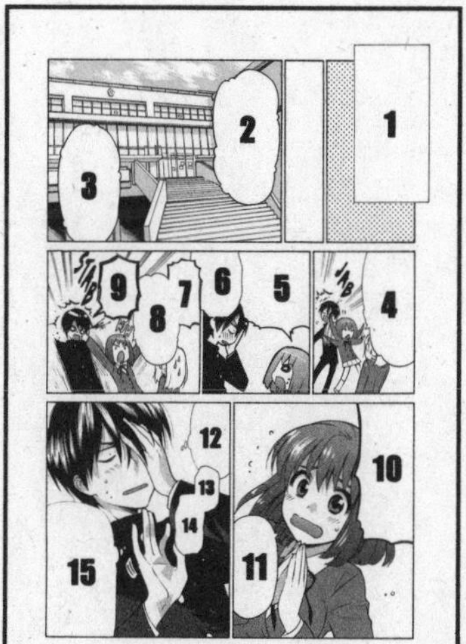
1
2
3
4
5
6
7
8
9
10
11
12
13
14
15

This book reads from right to left, Japanese style. To read from the beginning, flip the book over to the other side, start with the top right panel, and take it from there.

If this is your first time reading manga, just follow the diagram. It may seem backwards at first, but you'll get used to it! Have fun!